The Essential Guide to
The Best (and Worst) Legal Sites
on the Web

by
Robert J. Ambrogi, Esq.

Second Edition

2004

ALM Publishing
New York

VISIT OUR WEB SITE AT
www.lawcatalog.com

Library of Congress Cataloging-in-Publication Data
Ambrogi, Robert J.
I. Title The Essential Guide to the Best (and Worst) Legal Sites on the Web / Robert J.
Ambrogi—2nd ed.
p. cm.—
Includes Indexes
ISBN 1-58852-117-6 (pbk.)
1. Legal Research—United States—Computer network resources. 2. Internet—United States.
3. Information storage and retrieval systems—Law—United States. I. Title
  KF242.A1 A45 2001
  025.06'34—dc21
                                                     2004010526

Praise for the First Edition:

"A highly-useful and well-organized reference tool that should be kept beside every lawyer's computer. Forget about fumbling around with search engines—I do not know of a better way to locate the best Internet resources for legal subject matter areas than using this excellent book." *Dennis M. Kennedy, attorney, Thompson Coburn LLP (Intellectual Property and Information Technology Department)*

"The challenge in Internet research is not finding sites, but culling out the most useful sites. This is where this book excels. Ambrogi's insights and writing skill make this book a must-have for any lawyer serious about using the Internet productively." *Jerry Lawson, author, "The Complete Internet Handbook for Lawyers"*

"Ambrogi takes the reader on a beautifully organized and readable tour of virtually everything the practitioner needs to know about locating essential legal information in the vast cyber superstore. The lawyer's (and law student's and judge's) library of the 21st century need include only two items: a computer and Ambrogi's Essential Guide." *William T.G. Litant, Communications and Publications Director, Massachusetts Bar Association (1986 – 2001)*

"Ambrogi has skillfully selected, evaluated and organized the most valuable legal Web sites . . . . Indeed, your browser's Bookmarks or Favorites file will likely be in for quite a jolt upon your reading about, and then clicking on and preserving any of the abundant sites smartly presented in this volume." *Alan J. Rothman, Esq., Computer Law Lab Coordinator, New York County Lawyers' Association*

"Only someone with Robert Ambrogi's familiarity with the Internet could identify, catalog and organize the wealth of quality web sites that he's found for us. The comprehensive coverage and practice area organization ensures that there's something here for everyone." *Cindy Chick, Co-Editor, LLRX.com*

"Since the spring of 1995, attorney Bob Ambrogi has been scouting out legal Web destinations for lawyers in his syndicated column, legal.online, essential reading for solo and small-firm attorneys looking to keep pace with their large-firm counterparts. In low-tech, straight talk, this book provides a current and comprehensive view of the ever-changing landscape of legal stops in cyberspace." *Susan J. Ferrer, Director of Communications, Indiana State Bar Association*

"I thought I was a pretty fair hand at finding legal resources on the Internet. Bob Ambrogi's book surprised me with how much I don't know is out there. The depth of his research, in field after field of the law, is really impressive, as is the quality of his analysis of site quality. Even in the constantly changing world of the Web, this book is a benchmark guide to law in cyberspace." *Lindsay T. Thompson, attorney (corporate and Internet law, civil litigation)*

"More than merely a list of Web sites, this book has sifted through the good, the bad, and the ugly on the Web, and presented the information with a clarity that fans of Siskel and Ebert's 'thumbs-up or down' evaluation system would appreciate. Mr. Ambrogi's authority is unquestioned — he has written and ranked legal Web sites for years in his newsletter, legal.online. This book is an extension of his expertise. It will be particularly useful for practitioners who are interested in sites devoted to a specific area of practice, such as bankruptcy, estate planning, intellectual property and environmental law." *Wendy Leibowitz, Legal Technology Columnist*

"There are only a handful of Internet lawyers who understand and can convey the usefulness of the Internet like Ambrogi. This book incorporates the best of Ambrogi's work in an easy to follow, easy to read reference. A must for every legal professional using the Net." *Andrew Z. Adkins III, Director, Legal Technology Institute, University of Florida Levin College of Law*

"Nobody knows law-related Web sites and resources better than Bob Ambrogi, the legal profession's online guru and guide since the early days of the Web. Keep a copy of this Guide handy and use Bob's smart, capsule reviews and ratings to make the most out of your precious online time, do smarter research, and locate legal gems across webspace. Don't log-on without it." *Jesse Londin, Esq., legal Web producer, author of "Law Buzz" (on lawyers.com)*

"I have followed Bob's superb syndicated column about the Web, legal.online, in newspapers for years. Now this book collects his choices for the most valuable web resources into one plan — organized by areas of law practice. Bob cuts through the clutter and has created an invaluable resource for practicing lawyers. The chapter on marketing is worth getting all by itself." *Larry Bodine, LawMarketing Portal Operator, www.LawMarketing.com*

Acknowledgements

This book grew out of the newsletter I edited starting in 1995, "legal.online," which, in turn, was an offspring of the syndicated column I started writing in 1995. I owe a debt of gratitude to everyone who supported these projects over the years.

I am particularly beholden to Jane Seagrave, who, as president of Legal Communications Ltd. (now part of American Lawyer Media), encouraged me to create the legal.online newsletter and then served as its publisher. Thanks, as well, to all the staff at the former LCL who helped edit, design, produce, print and fulfill the newsletter, and to Malee Nuesse for her marketing skill.

To the editors who published my column over the years, I thank you. Special thanks to the three editors who signed on for the first installment back in 1994 and never signed off: Susan Ferrer, director of communications for the Indiana State Bar Association, Judson Haverkamp, director of communications for the Minnesota State Bar Association, and William Litant, former director of communications for the Massachusetts Bar Association.

This book would never have come about without Sara Diamond, vice president in charge of American Lawyer Media's book publishing division, who urged me to write it. I am indebted to Caroline Sorokoff, director of ALM Publishing, for the ideas that helped shape the book and the prodding that kept me at it. Sincere thanks to ALM Senior Editor Mike Tenner for his precise and patient editing.

My deepest gratitude goes to my wife Kathy Gregg and my sons Ben and Matt for their encouragement, support and, above all, patience, as I devoted far too many nights and weekends to this project.

Second Edition Acknowledgements

In addition to the individuals acknowledged in the first edition, I would like to add a note of thanks to Monica Bay, editor-in-chief of Law Technology News, who has published my monthly Web Watch column since her earliest days as editor. Her support over the years would have been enough in itself, but her energy and creativity helped keep the column vital and drove it in new directions. Her continued encouragement helped make possible the second edition of this book.

About the Author

Robert J. Ambrogi, Esq. is vice president for editorial services of Jaffe Associates, a business-development consulting firm. He formerly was editorial director of American Lawyer Media's Litigation Services Division and editor-in-chief of the National Law Journal. He writes a monthly column titled "Web Watch" in *Law Technology News*, a national magazine with the largest circulation of any legal technology publication. Since 1995, he has authored a column syndicated to various bar association and legal periodicals titled "legal.online." From 1995-1999, he edited a newsletter, also titled "legal.online," the first Internet periodical for lawyers that covered and reviewed legal resources on the Web. A graduate of Boston College Law School, Ambrogi is the author of the Internet research guide: *The Internet Guide for Massachusetts Lawyers*.

Table of Contents

Chapter 1

Introduction: How We Picked and Why

Time, as the saying goes, is a lawyer's stock in trade. On the Internet, every second spent searching for the right resource is time away from critical legal work.

The Internet has become an indispensable resource for the practicing lawyer. It is the gateway to court opinions, laws, regulations, treatises, legal forms, practice guides, and a host of business and personal research tools. Many of these resources are free or cost far less than traditional electronic research tools.

However, for all but the most experienced Internet researchers, finding the right resource can be a project in itself. There can be hundreds, even thousands, of sites devoted to a single topic. With time ever in short supply, how is one to sort through them all to find the sites that are on point and trustworthy?

For almost as long as lawyers have been using the Internet, my ratings and reviews have been helping them home in on the most valuable resources and tools. In 1995, when I introduced the syndicated column, "legal.online," fewer than ten law firms and only a handful of courts had Web sites. The newsletter I edited, also called legal.online, was the first periodical for lawyers to cover and review legal resources on the Web.

Through the newsletter, we introduced our five-star rating system and the annual "Best of the Web for Lawyers" awards, both helping lawyers zero in on the most valuable Web sites for their practices.

This book carries on that tradition. Each chapter highlights the best Web sites for lawyers in the practice area it covers. Each site is given a complete review and assigned a rating of up to five stars. Only the best of the Web achieve the five-star rating.

The book is an invaluable guide for lawyers, law librarians, paralegals, and anyone interested in legal resources on the Web. It zeroes in on the best Web sites through more than two dozen chapters devoted to law and legal practice, from alternative dispute resolution to international trade, legal ethics to law office management.

Permeating it all is the perspective of a practicing lawyer. In fact, it was my search for affordable, reliable access to legal research for my own law practice that first drew me to explore the then nascent Internet. When I discovered the wealth of what was available, even in those early days, I could not help but want to share it with other legal professionals.

How We Rate

This book does not just list Web sites by topic—it analyzes and evaluates them, so you do not have to waste your valuable time. Only the best sites earn the five-star rating.

For every site I visit, I evaluate it in each of five categories and then award a star for excellence in any one. The best sites, the five-star sites, excel in each of these ways:

- Overall usefulness to legal professionals.
- Content.
- Design and presentation.
- Accessibility and ease of use.
- Innovation.

Within each chapter, sites are grouped into sections based on their focus and content. Within those sections, sites are listed in the order of their rankings. Sites that are equal in ranking are listed alphabetically, so that if three sites earned five stars, they are listed together in alphabetical order.

It is beyond feasibility to review every law-related Web site. This book is by no means comprehensive. Every effort has been made to include the best sites and to cover a cross section of the less than stellar contenders. Undoubtedly, I will later learn that I have missed some that I should not have.

I avoid the obvious. For example, I cover FindLaw as an index, but I do not mention it for every topic area even though it has a section for every topic area.

Most importantly, I rate sites from the overarching perspective of their usefulness to legal professionals. Had I been writing this book for a different audience, I might have rated some sites differently. A site might be truly outstanding in terms of overall design and content, but have so little relevance to the practical applications of day-to-day law practice that it does not rate five stars.

Some Housekeeping

This book is not an introduction to using the Internet. It assumes the reader already has access to the Internet and at least some standard Internet browsing software such as Internet Explorer, Netscape Navigator, Mozilla or Opera.

The book contains many references to documents' being in Adobe Acrobat format. These documents carry the file-name extension ".pdf" for portable document format. Courts, in particular, often use this format to publish their opinions because it exactly replicates the appearance of the printed document. In order to view a document in this format, you must first install Acrobat Reader, a "plug-in" or add-on to your Web browser. You can download this software for free from Adobe's Web site, www.adobe.com.

The book also reviews sites that include video or audio components, often delivered in a "streaming" format that requires special software. If your computer is running recent versions of either the Microsoft Windows or Apple operating system, you should already have this software. Some video and audio components call for the RealOne Player, which you may not already have. This, too, is available free as a download that you can obtain at Real.com, www.real.com. You will find that Real sells an advanced version of its software, but the free version is all you need.

A Word About URLs

All Web sites are identified by their Internet addresses, called URLs, or Uniform Resource Locators, which usually look something like "http://www.americanlawyermedia.com." As a style convention, I have left off the "http://" at the beginning of most URLs, because most browsers no longer require this to be typed. However, if the URL does not begin with "www," then I have left the http prefix to identify what follows as a URL.

When hunting for information on the Web, remember that these URLs are essentially just names for hierarchical file structures, much like what you would find on your own computer. If you see a URL such as "www.american-lawyermedia.com/cases/mostrecent.htm," the slashes tell you that "cases" is a subdirectory under the higher level "americanlawyermedia.com" directory, and that "mostrecent.htm" is a file within that subdirectory. If you go to that URL and receive an error message or a "file not found" message, don't give up—just move back up the file ladder by removing everything after the final slash, which should bring you to the "cases" page. If that still doesn't work, remove "cases" and go to the site's main page. Often, the resource you are trying to get to has moved to a new location within the Web site. By starting back at the main page, you may be able to work your way forward and find it.

Sometimes, the easiest way to find something on the Web is to guess its URL. Most commercial or business sites end in the .com domain, government sites end in .gov, and colleges and universities end in .edu. So, if you are looking for the Web site of American Lawyer Media, guess what—it is www.americanlawyermedia.com. If you are looking for the National Labor Relations Board, sure enough, it is www.nlrb.gov.

There is also a convention for finding state government sites. In almost every case, you can get to a state's main Web page using the URL "www.state.XX.us," replacing the XX with its postal code. Thus, the URL for Massachusetts state government is www.state.ma.us. From a state's main page, you usually can find links to its legislature, its judiciary and its executive branch agencies.

As a medium for legal research, the Web is not much different from a bricks-and-mortar library. Consider me a librarian, happy to help guide you to what I consider to be the best available resources. But take some time to wander around and explore on your own. You are likely to find something you consider even better than what I've pointed out, and you might even have some fun along the way.

Let me know what you find. Send me your favorite Web sites and other comments at rambrogi@legaline.com.

Chapter 2

Search Sites: Finding Needles in the Internet Haystack

―――――――――――――― Chapter Contents ――――――――――――――

Crawlers
Indexing the Web
Metasearchers
Government
People Finders

―――――――――――――――――――――――――――――――――――――――

There is a lot of information out there in Cyberspace—if only you can find it. Estimates put the Web's publicly available contents at more than 4 billion pages, and that does not even begin to count the contents of private databases available by way of the Web.

Yet organization of the Internet remains anarchic, to say the least. The resource you need could as easily be on a major university's Web site as on some high school kid's home page.

When it comes to sorting out this tangle, the Web has seen major strides in relatively little time. As recently as the mid-1990s, the best ways to find resources on the Internet were Archie and Veronica—not the comic strip characters, but somewhat archaic software programs that allowed you to search the Internet for particular files.

Today, there are so many tools to help you search the Web's vast resources that you could spend a fair amount of time just searching for the right searcher. But be on notice: searching the Web is still far from precise. A 1999 article in the journal *Nature* estimated that search engine accuracy has been getting worse, not better, to the point that no engine indexed more than 16% of the estimated size of the publicly accessible Web. Search engines all claim to do much better, of course, but precise measurements are impossible. A superior site for learning everything you ever wanted to know about Internet searching and search engine rankings is Search Engine Watch, http://searchenginewatch.com.

What follows is a guide to these search tools. The list is not exhaustive, but offers an introduction to the three major types:

- *Crawlers.* Also known as "spiders," these constantly scour the Web in an effort to create searchable catalogs of everything out there.
- *Indexes.* These are directories of Web sites, usually arranged hierarchically by category.

- *Metasearchers.* These allow you to use several search tools from a single location or in a single search and to receive blended results.

We also look at specialized tools to help you search the vast network of government resources on the Web and "people finders" to help you find individuals' addresses, phone numbers or e-mail addresses.

Crawlers

Think of crawlers as little Web-surfing robots, gathering copies of everything they find into an enormous database. That database becomes a searchable index of almost everything available on the Web. Significantly, when you use one of these tools, you are searching *copies* stored in a single database, not the actual Web site. The accuracy of these search engines depends on how thorough they are in combing the Web to find documents to bring back to their database, and in how frequently they refresh their stores.

Here are some of the most popular crawlers:

★★★★★ AlltheWeb.com, www.alltheweb.com

AlltheWeb is one of the most comprehensive and freshest search engines. It scans the entire Web every seven to eleven days to ensure that its content is up to date and to eliminate broken links. In addition to searching billions of Web pages, it can also search hundreds of millions of multimedia, audio and video files. Use it also to search news stories from thousands of sources around the world.

★★★★★ Google, www. google. com

Google has become one of the most popular search engines, in part because of its unique Page Rank technology. Simply put, Google interprets a link to a Web page as a kind of vote for its quality cast from among the Internet's democratic masses. The more sites that link to a page, the more valuable it must be, Google reasons. Applying this technological premise, Google ranks

Google is one of the most popular and easy-to-use search engines.

search results based on what it believes will be the most valuable pages that match your query. Google also claims to be the most comprehensive search site, with a database of over a billion Web pages. There is more to Google than Web searching. Google Groups is a complete archive of discussions from Usenet—the Internet's original bulletin board—back to 1981. Need a medical illustration? Try Google Image Search, possibly the largest image bank on the Web. Google News delivers headlines from more than 4,000 sources.

★★★★★ Teoma, www.teoma.com

Teoma's aim is to deliver a higher degree of relevance in its search results than other search engines. Like Google, it ranks the relevance of pages through a sort of Web popularity contest, reading each link to a page as a vote for its quality. But while Google draws votes from all the Web, Teoma takes each page to a jury of its peers. That is, it first identifies other sites on the same topic, then analyzes how often those sites link to the page. Teoma calls this "subject-specific popularity." The idea is this: if you want to know the best Web sites for auto enthusiasts, you will do better by polling the sites of other auto enthusiasts than you will do by polling the Internet at large. This makes sense for lawyers. Of all the law-related sites on the Web, the best ones for lawyers are likely to be the ones that lawyers as a group most often link to, as opposed to those that non-lawyers find useful.

Teoma, which is owned by Ask Jeeves Inc., touts two other features: "Refine" and "Resources," both of which appear onscreen to the right of the search results. The Refine feature organizes query results into what Teoma calls "naturally occurring communities." Search "Labor Relations," for example, and Teoma will suggest categories such as the following by which you can refine the search results: Industrial Relations, Employment Relations, University Labor, Labor Law, Labor Relations Board, Management Relations and Supreme Court Collections. The Resources feature provides jumping off points to link collections elsewhere on the Web having to do with the query topic. As of 2003, Teoma had crawled more than 1 billion Web pages and indexed more than 500 million URLs. Teoma claims that although its index is smaller than those of other search engines, it has taken steps to eliminate spam and duplication, making it more precise.

★★★★ AltaVista, www.altavista.com

Introduced in December 1995 by Digital Equipment Corp., AltaVista was the Internet's first true full-text search service and long remained among the best. But starting in the late 1990s, it went through a series of identity crises and changes of ownership that diluted its effectiveness. In 2003, Overture Services purchased AltaVista with a commitment to reestablish its leading position among search engines. While it is still good, it is not up to par with Google or AlltheWeb.

★★★★ Ask Jeeves, www.ask.com

Plain English is what sets Ask Jeeves apart from other search engines. Users pose their search queries as questions in plain English and receive links to Web sites containing relevant information, services and products. Ask Jeeves' searches are driven by the Teoma search engine, discussed above.

★★★★ HotBot, www.hotbot.com

Originally created by the publisher of *Wired* magazine, HotBot, now part of the Lycos network, remains a Web search powerhouse. It is noteworthy for providing quick access to four major search engines: HotBot, Lycos, Google and Ask Jeeves. Search any of these by way of HotBot, although you cannot search all four at once in the way that a metacrawler would allow. HotBot is extremely easy to use, offering a simple, point-and-click interface, intuitive pull down menus, and the ability to use plain English terminology for constructing searches.

★★★★ Lycos, www.lycos.com

You know the drill: "Lycos, go get it!" Lycos is one of the oldest search engines, operating since 1994. Originally, it indexed only abstracts of Web pages rather than the full text. In recent years, it has undergone a redesign to become more of a topical index in the style of Yahoo. Its searches are powered by AlltheWeb.com.

★★★★ WiseNut, www.wisenut.com

WiseNut organizes search results into categories, which it calls its WiseGuide. These categories are generated on the fly using key words drawn from search results. A search for "Labor Relations" on WiseNut yielded four WiseGuide categories—Labor Relations, Human Resources, Industrial Relations and Other—and another nine subcategories, including Labor Relations Board, Industrial and Labor Relations, and Employee and Labor Relations. WiseNut is among the larger search engines in the size of its database, boasting some 1.5 billion documents. It was the first to offer a feature that other sites have since adopted: Sneak-A-Peak. When you search, each listed result includes the Sneak-A-Peak button. Click it and the listed site appears in a small window directly on the search results page, eliminating the need to repeatedly hit your browser's Back button as you view results.

Indexing the Web

★★★★★ Invisible Web, www.invisible-web.net

Much of the information stored on the Internet is invisible to search engines such as Google and AltaVista. This is because it is stored on data-bases that shut out search engine "spiders"—databases from universities, libraries, associations, businesses and government agencies. This directory, from the authors of the book *The Invisible Web*, is a guide to some of the best of these resources. From here, lawyers can find links to patents, land records, corporate filings, marriage registries, professional licenses and much more. Most sites listed are free.

★★★★★ MyWay, www.myway.com

Here is a search index that stands out for its feistiness, among other things. When it was introduced late in 2002, it challenged reigning Web index Yahoo with an ad campaign whose slogan was "Yahoo is toast." Its site replicates many of Yahoo's features, but—in contrast to Yahoo—it excludes banner and pop-up advertising, charges no fees for any of its search services, and has one of the simplest and least intrusive privacy policies found anywhere on the Web. A Web search using MyWay simultaneously searches, *inter alia*, Google, AltaVista, Ask Jeeves, and AlltheWeb.

★★★★★ Wayback Machine, www.archive.org

For a helping of 'Net nostalgia, set the Wayback Machine, Mr. Peabody, to the early days of the World Wide Web. The Internet Archive's Wayback Machine lets you see the Web as it is no longer. It contains more than 30 billion Web pages archived since 1996. Type in an address and be transported back in time. Great fun. But, for lawyers, also of real value, whether to research prior uses, unearth evidence or compile a history. Recently, the Wayback Machine added full-text searching to a substantial portion of its archive, so you can search not only for a Web page that no longer exists, but also for the text those pages contained.

★★★★★ Yahoo, www.yahoo.com

Yahoo is not a crawler, it is a directory, but it is the oldest Web directory and most likely the best known. It differs from crawlers in that it does not search for Web sites; it relies on users to submit sites. As a result, it is far from comprehensive. On the other hand, if Yahoo does not find a match in its directory, it automatically sends the search to Google to search other Web sites. Yahoo's strength is its well-organized and easy to use catalog of Web sites. You can search the catalog by key words, or simply browse. Generally, if you are looking for a specific business or law firm, or a type of entity that falls within a defined category, then Yahoo is the place to start.

Metasearchers

Think of these as one-stop shopping. They allow you to use several search engines from one location, and sometimes in one search.

★★★★★ Dogpile, www.dogpile.com

Part of the InfoSpace Network, Dogpile is a metasearcher that combs the most popular search engines—including Yahoo!, Google, AltaVista, Ask Jeeves, Teoma and others—to compile a list of matches for a user's query and then organizes the results by each individually searched resource.

★★★★★ Kartoo, www.kartoo.com

Kartoo is unique in that it returns search results visually in the form of a series of interactive maps. The relevance of different sites is shown in the size of the images depicting them, and relationships among the sites are mapped out by interconnecting lines.

★★★★★ MetaCrawler, www.metacrawler.com

One of the Internet's earliest "metasearchers," MetaCrawler sends your query to multiple search engines simultaneously, then organizes the results and displays them in a uniform format, ranking them by relevance. Efficiency is the key word here—with one search, MetaCrawler draws results from AltaVista, Yahoo, Google, Ask Jeeves, and other sites. MetaCrawler can also filter results by domain name (e.g., ".edu," ".com" and ".gov").

★★★★★ Search.com, www.search.com

Part of CNET's network of computing and technology resources, Search.com incorporates the metasearcher formerly called SavvySearch. Using Search.com, a single search can retrieve results from more than 800 search engines, Web directories, auctions, storefronts, news sources, discussion groups, reference sites and more. Results are initially sorted by source, but you can reorder them by relevance or date.

★★★★★ Vivisimo, www.vivisimo.com

This site takes its name from the Spanish word for "clever." True to its name, it is not really a search engine at all, in that that it does not crawl or index the Web. Rather, it is a software program that calls on other search engines, extracts the relevant information, and then organizes the results into a clear and hierarchical folder structure, much like the folders one would find in a Windows directory. Perform a search here and your results appear in the center of your screen as they would elsewhere. But to the left is a group of folders and subfolders into which Vivisimo has almost instantly organized the search results. A search for "Labor Relations" resulted in twenty-two top-level folders with names such as Industrial Relations, Human Resources, Labor Relations Board, Labor Studies and Laws. Click on Industrial Relations, and ten subfolders appear, including Research, Labor Laws and Department of Labor. The folders make it easier to zero in on the sites whose topics mostly closely match your query.

Government

The federal government's network of more than 20,000 Web sites is an invaluable source of primary and secondary legal reference information. Statutes, regulations, cases, court rules, agency policies, press releases, enforcement actions, official forms and a host of other official documents and publications make the U.S. government's "dot-gov" sites the most important domain for law-related research.

To help you find your way through this vast and valuable network, the following sites can help.

★★★★★ **FirstGov,** www.firstgov.gov

FirstGov is the official gateway to all U.S. government information on the Internet, connecting to more than 51 million pages on more than 20,000 federal, state, territorial and tribal sites. Launched in 2000, it was overhauled in 2002 to make it easier for users to find what they need. Links are organized by type of user (citizen, business, etc.) as well as by

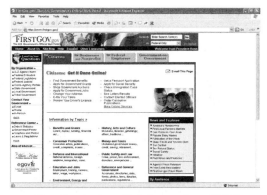

FirstGov is the official portal to all U.S. government information on the internet.

topics and common reference terms. You can also search within branches of government or browse a complete listing of federal agencies. FirstGov can be searched in its entirety using either a simple search box or an advanced search interface that allows greater refinement.

★★★★★ GPO Access, www.gpoaccess.gov

The Web site of the U.S. Government Printing Office, GPO Access provides free access to a wealth of federal information. Its coverage falls into three categories:

- Online, searchable databases of executive and legislative material, including the U.S. Code, the Federal Register, the Code of Federal Regulations, the Congressional Record, Commerce Business Daily, and much more.
- The Federal Bulletin Board, a collection of more than 7,500 files posted by federal agencies to provide free and immediate public access to federal information in electronic form.
- Search tools to help users find government information, including the Catalog of U.S. Government Publications, the Government Information Locator Service, and the Pathway Indexer, an index of more than 1,350 federal agency and military Internet sites.

In 2003, the site was extensively reorganized to make it easier to use. Now, materials are organized by branch of government and by topic, and searches can be conducted across multiple databases.

★★★★★ Science.gov, www.science.gov

Lawyers in a range of practice areas—from tort to IP to biotech and beyond—can attest that scientific research is often an important aspect of law practice. Such research became a bit easier in December 2002 when the federal government launched this gateway to science and technology information on the Internet. A collaboration among sixteen scientific and technical organizations from eleven major science agencies, the site indexes more than 1,000 government resources—technical reports, journal citations, databases, government Web sites and fact sheets—all available free. Agencies participating in the site are the Departments of Agriculture, Commerce, Defense, Education, Energy, Health and Human Services, and Interior; the Environmental Protection Agency; the National Aeronautics and Space Administration; the National Science Foundation; and the U.S. Government Printing Office.

★★★★★ U.S. Government Documents, www.columbia.edu/cu/lweb/indiv/usgd

Columbia University's Lehman Social Sciences Library hosts an extensive collection of current and historical government documents and also provides indexes of government documents elsewhere on the Web. Follow the link to "Subject Guides & Internet Resources" for a series of guides to federal, state and international documents. The site is comprehensive in its coverage and easy to use.

★★★★ FedWorld, www.fedworld.gov

FedWorld, created in 1992 by the National Technical Information Service, an agency of the U.S. Department of Commerce, is a service for locating U.S. government information online. It provides a gateway for searching federal job openings, Supreme Court opinions, scientific and technical publications, Internal Revenue Service forms and publications, and other government information. In addition, it hosts and provides access to several specialized databases. These include the World News Connection, a database of wage determinations under the Davis-Bacon Act, and the Federal Computer Product Center. FedWorld still also serves as a gateway to various older government file-transfer (or FTP) and telnet sites.

★★★ Regulations.gov, www.regulations.gov

The U.S. government launched this Web site in 2003 in order to make it easier for the public to participate in federal rulemaking. The site allows users to search for, review and comment on proposed rules that have been published in the Federal Register. Users can search for proposed regulations by keyword or by agency name. Regulations can be viewed in either HTML or PDF format. Once having read the proposal, a user can submit a comment using the provided form.

★★★ United States Government Manual, www.gpoaccess.gov/gmanual/index.html

The official handbook of the federal government, this is an in-depth guide to the organization and staffing of Congress, the courts and the executive branch. It also covers quasi-official entities, international organizations, boards, commissions and committees. The 2003-2004 edition can be searched in its entirety or browsed chapter-by-chapter in either PDF or plain-text format. Earlier editions starting in 1995 are also available here.

People Finders

It has never been easier to find someone. For lawyers, the implications of this are significant. Whether you are looking for lost heirs, material witnesses or just long-lost law school classmates, the Web makes it simple. Here are some of the Web's tools for finding people's locations, phone numbers and e-mail addresses.

★★★★★ Infospace, www.infospace.com

Infospace features an array of white and yellow page directories, maps and directions, e-mail directories, public records, city guides, and other listings. It includes reverse lookup.

★★★★★ Rootsweb Social Security Death Index, http://ssdi. rootsweb.com

Searched the phone and e-mail directories, but still no luck? Maybe the person you are looking for is dead. One way to find out is here, a database of deaths compiled from Social Security Administration records. Maintained by the genealogy site Rootsweb, this easy-to-use database includes more than 70 million records and is updated every month.

★★★★★ Search Systems, www.searchsystems.net

Claiming links to some 17,000 free sources of public records information on the Web, Search Systems is a top Web resource for finding official records and publicly available information. Operated by Pacific Information Resources, it includes links from throughout the world, although the greatest number come from the U.S. and Canada. Databases are organized geographically as well as by topic. Not all sites listed are free, but those that are not are clearly marked. What can you find here? You have to explore it to appreciate it, but among its listings are professional license registrations, corporate records, marriage notices, UCC filings, deed registries, birth and death records, lobbyist listings, physician disciplinary proceedings, and much more.

★★★★★ Switchboard, www.switchboard.com

How can a lawyer use Switchboard? Use it to search for a missing witness or locate a lost heir. Get the e-mail address of opposing counsel. Find a long lost law school pal. Create a map to an unfamiliar courthouse accompanied by detailed driving directions. Search for a particular business or search generally for all businesses in your area of a certain type. There are a number of white page directories on the Web, but Switchboard has consistently remained among the best. Switchboard includes a reverse phone number lookup.

★★★★ AnyWho, www.anywho.com

AnyWho is AT&T's directory of personal and business phone numbers. It includes reverse lookup—allowing a user to enter a phone or fax number and find out to whom it belongs.

★★★★ Cemetery Records Online, www.interment.net

This free site lists more than 3.5 million records from some 7,500 cemeteries throughout the world. It is fully searchable by surname or you can browse through the records for specific cemeteries.

★★★★ WhoWhere?, www.whowhere.lycos.com

On the Web since 1996, WhoWhere? is one of the original Web people finders, allowing users to search for someone's phone number, address and e-mail address. In 1998, it became part of the Lycos network. Its e-mail searches returned more limited results than other e-mail search tools we tested.

★★★ Telephone Directories on the Web, www.infobel.com/teldir

This is a directory of directories, listing some 400 Web white and yellow page directories online with listings from nearly 200 countries worldwide.

Chapter 3

Zeroing In: LawCrawler, Legal Indexes, Legal "Destinations," and Other Search Tools

---
Chapter Contents

Law Crawler
Legal Indexes
Legal "Destinations"
Other Search Tools

Legal research on the Web is not all that different from old-fashioned library research. The first time you tackle a topic, you most likely start with sources that are fairly broad in their scope—a card catalog, say, or an encyclopedia. As your search evolves, you narrow in on cases, treatises or reference books until eventually you find something on point. Having found the most relevant reference, the next time you come to the library you skip the card catalog and head straight to it.

The Web has scores of legal resources on point for particular topics. Once you find a site that has the information you need, you are apt to return to it again and again. But finding that site in the first place is not always easy. That is when you should turn to the Web's equivalent of the card catalog—one of the several sites that index the Web's legal resources so that you can more easily find them.

Most of these are organized by topic of law or type of resource. Thus, links might be arranged under "bankruptcy," "law schools" or "U.S. courts." Some legal indices simply list relevant links; others add brief descriptions or annotations.

This chapter looks at these legal research starting points, often called "portals" or "indexes." Think of a portal as a gateway to the Web, a site through which you find your way into the Web's vast network of resources. Usually, a portal offers others services as well, such as discussion forums, e-mail, and possibly goods for sale. Think of an index as a stripped down portal, organizing Web resources by topics, to help you zero in on the most relevant sites. But before we get to the portals, we start with the legal field's only Web search engine, a tool that does not simply organize links to legal Web sites, but that actually allows you to search the full text of legal sites on the Web.

LawCrawler

★★★★★ LawCrawler, http://lawcrawler.findlaw.com

Using a general Internet search tool to perform legal research is like looking for a needle in a haystack. These search engines are so good at what they do that your query might result in thousands of hits, which you must then sort through in search of pages relevant to your research. LawCrawler, a search engine sponsored by FindLaw, cuts the haystack to more manageable size.

Using the same search engine that powers Google, it scours only sites known to contain legal or government information. The result is a search that brings back more relevant results. And for even greater precision, LawCrawler allows you to limit your search to particular types of sites or databases, such as U.S. government sites, state sites, law schools, or Supreme Court opinions.

Legal Indexes

★★★★★ FindLaw, www.findlaw.com

It started in 1994 as a list of Internet resources prepared for a workshop of the Northern California Law Librarians. It grew over the years into a multi-faceted starting point for lawyers using the Web, boasting the highest level of traffic of any legal Web site. Following its purchase in January 2001 by West Group, FindLaw became more polished and diverse, but it is still free to use and remains the best starting point for finding legal information on the Web.

Its core remains The FindLaw Guide, a comprehensive index of links to resources in more than forty subject areas as well as to case law, codes, legal associations, law reviews and more. But beyond its index are a host of features. In addition to LawCrawler, discussed above, FindLaw's constantly growing library of court opinions and statutory codes features the most extensive collection of Supreme Court opinions available free on the Internet, dating back to 1893. FindLaw also collects opinions from all federal circuits and virtually all state supreme courts. It has expanded to offer legal news, real time SEC filings, community discussion areas and online continuing legal education. Its career center is home to law firm salary charts, legal job listings, personalized legal job placement services and the "Greedy Associates" message boards. It also offers information channels for law students, businesses and the public.

When West purchased FindLaw, it promised that everything that existed on FindLaw before would remain and continue to be free. West has stayed true to its word while adding valuable new features, including an extensive Corporate Counsel Center, an enhanced lawyer-search directory, an expanded jobs and career section, and more news and commentary.

★★★★★ Hieros Gamos, www.hg.org

One of the longest-standing and most comprehensive legal portals, Hieros Gamos boasts more than 2 million links. International in scope, it is organized under a detailed index of topics and sources. The front page opens with six "centers": Law Business, Law Events & Library, Law Practice, Law Student, Legal Employment and Law Consumer. Each center contains categories of related resources, allowing you to drill down through increasingly specific subpages. Besides the centers, HG also has general categories for U.S. law, international law, legal associations, bar associations and lifestyle. It provides quick links to directories of lawyers and law firms, experts and consultants, and court reporters. Topics suffer, if at all, from too much information, with long lists of links to international sites, country sites, state sites, commentary, cases and statutes, publications, CLE courses, and more. It even, somewhat superfluously, includes bibliographic references to non-Internet resources and publications. Hieros Gamos has long been a top destination for anyone seeking legal information on the Web.

★★★★ American Law Sources On-line, www.lawsource.com/also

Covering the U.S., Canada and Mexico, ALSO provides a comprehensive collection of links to free sources of law on the Internet, organized by jurisdiction. For each jurisdiction, ALSO provides links to sources of primary law—cases, statutes and regulations—then to commentary on the law, such as law reviews and books, and finally to practice aids, such as official forms or court information. ALSO is quite comprehensive in its scope, although not always entirely up to date in listing available resources.

★★★★ Best Guide to Canadian Legal Research, http://legalresearch.org

A surname, not braggadocio, led to the title of this site, but surname aside the name is not far off the mark. Catherine P. Best, a research lawyer with the Vancouver, B.C., firm Boughton and an adjunct professor of law at the University of British Columbia, authored this legal research tutorial. This is no mere collection of links; rather, Best enhances her links with in-depth discussions of the how and why of legal research, complete with step-by-step instructions on various types of electronic and statutory research. While the focus is Canadian law, the lessons are broadly applicable to researchers anywhere and the links cover a number of jurisdictions worldwide.

★★★★ Emory University School of Law, www.law.emory.edu

Emory was a leader among law schools in publishing on the Internet. It hosts case law collections for five federal circuit courts, and is home to the Federal Courts Finder, a map of the U.S. circuits with links to the sites containing each circuit's cases. It does not include federal district or bankruptcy courts. Emory's Electronic Reference Desk is an index to law-related resources on the Internet.

★★★★ LawGuru.com Multi Resource Legal Research, www.lawguru.com/multisearch/multimenu.html

LawGuru.com offers this tool for searching multiple Web sites using a single query. It allows multiple-site searches in four categories: state codes and statutes, state court opinions, federal court opinions, and federal courts and codes. To search state codes, for example, the user checks the states to be searched, types the query, and hits search. For each state selected, a new browser window opens displaying the results for that state.

★★★★ WashLaw Web, www.washlaw.edu

Brains over beauty. That might be the motto of WashLaw Web, from Washburn University School of Law in Topeka, Kansas. One of the earliest legal indexes on the Internet and still among the most exhaustive, it long ago abandoned any use of graphics for a straight text approach. Go to its page and there it is—a straight index of the topics it covers, from Alabama to Zip codes. Click on any topic to go to a page of links, some accompanied by brief descriptions of the site. If you prefer not to browse the topics, the entire site can be searched by key words. WashLaw shows some signs of fatigue, with some important newer sites missing and some dead links still there.

★★★ Arizona Lawyer's Guide to the Internet, http://home.earthlink.net/~jjfjr

Do not be fooled by the name—you do not need to be in Arizona to benefit from this site. It is a collection of links to Internet resources for legal and factual research. Unlike so many other such sites, this one, maintained by paralegal Jesse Frey, is selective and closely monitored. That means old or useless links are thrown out and new ones are added. Even so, several links were out of date when we last visited the site.

★★★ Law and Policy Institutions Guide, www.lpig.org

This index of legal resources on the Web is selective rather than comprehensive, listing only those sites that it finds to be "the most authoritative, timely and useful sources for legal research on the Internet." Links are organized into general categories, such as "U.S. Federal," "Global Legal,"

"Associations," and the like. Most links are annotated with descriptions of the site, although not from a critical perspective. The entire site is searchable.

★★★ The Law Engine, www.TheLawEngine.com

Consider this the little engine that could, a smaller, less powerful alternative to a diesel locomotive such as FindLaw. Its index of legal sites is nowhere near as extensive, but the focus here is on simplicity and ease of use. Its collection of links is organized into major categories, all of which are listed on one page. There is also a search page from which searches can be conducted on a number of major legal and non-legal search engines and indices.

★★★ Meta-Index for U.S. Legal Research, http://gsulaw.gsu.edu/metaindex

This page presents an array of search forms for many law and U.S. government sources; each form contains sample search criteria. From here, you can search for opinions of the U.S. Supreme Court and all federal circuit courts. A legislative section allows searching of the U.S. Code, as well as of bills and the full text of the Congressional Record. There are also search forms for federal regulations, people in law, and other legal sources. The site is provided by the Georgia State University College of Law.

Legal "Destinations"

★★★★★ Law.com, www.law.com

Law.com accurately describes itself as "first in legal news and information." Reacquired in 2002 by American Lawyer Media—from which it was spun off three years earlier—and redesigned in 2003, it is the backbone supporting a wide-ranging network of news and information resources and law-related directories and services. Law.com's central focus is legal news, drawn from ALM's roster of national and regional newspapers, magazines and newsletters. These include *The American Lawyer*, the *National Law Journal, Corporate Counsel, Law Technology News* and *IP Law & Business*, as well as *The New York Law Journal, Legal Times, Texas Lawyer* and *The Recorder* in San Francisco. While each publication has its own site within the Law.com network, Law.com distills the most important stories every day and delivers them through its free Newswire.

Special-focus areas of Law.com pull together news and information pertaining to particular topics. The Supreme Court Monitor tracks news and cases from the high court, while practice centers focus on business law, employment law, IP law, litigation and technology law.

In addition to news, Law.com offers information services such as VerdictSearch, a searchable database of verdicts and settlements; LawJobs, listing job openings from throughout the United States; and LawCatalog, an online bookstore for law-related publications. Other services here include online CLE and directories of expert witnesses and court reporters.

Law.com has become a premier destination for legal professionals on the Web.

★★★★★ Legal Information Institute, www.law.cornell.edu

A program of Cornell Law School, the groundbreaking Legal Information Institute pioneered legal publishing on the Internet. Started in 1992, its mission was to experiment with the application of hypertext technology to the publication of legal materials online. It established the first law site on the Internet in 1992 and the first legal Web site in 1993. To facilitate use of the Web site, it developed one of the first Windows-based Web browsers, called Cello. It quickly became the leading Internet site for distribution of U.S. Supreme Court opinions and later added decisions of the N.Y. Court of Appeals. Its hypertext version of the U.S. Code remains its most heavily used feature. Over the years, the LII has published a host of significant legal documents on the Web, including the Constitution, the Federal Rules of Evidence, and the Federal Rules of Civil Procedure. It also presents links to legal materials published elsewhere on the Web, organized both by topic and source. As a lawyer once put it to me, "They deserve a lifetime achievement award."

★★★★★ lexisONE, www.lexisone.com

From Lexis-Nexis comes this useful, free online legal resource, aimed at solo practitioners and small firms. Launched in July 2000, the site grew rapidly, then seemed to take a giant step backwards, trimming some sections. Today, the site's resources fall into five categories:

- *Free forms.* More than 6,000 legal forms, many from official sources, including an extensive collection of enhanced forms from Matthew Bender, all continuously updated and logically organized.
- *Free case law.* This free library of case law from Lexis includes U.S. Supreme Court cases since 1790 and selected federal and state cases

from January 1, 1998. LexisONE does not offer the full panoply of search capabilities offered through the paid Lexis database, lacking features such as Shepard's Citations and the Lexis Search Advisor.
- *Legal news.*
- *Legal Internet guide.* A well organized collection of links to legal resources on the Web—some 20,000 links in thirty-one categories, as of this writing.
- *Balancing life and practice.* An assortment of articles on careers, technology, travel, leisure and other topics.

Registration is required to access the site's features, but there is no charge to register. The entire site is easy to navigate and includes help files to assist you in using the site and making the most of its various features.

★★★★ Lawyers.com, www.lawyers.com

When Martindale-Hubbell introduced this consumer-oriented Web site, it presented it to lawyers as a vehicle to help them leverage the marketing power of the Internet and increase their exposure to consumers and small businesses in need of legal assistance. The site allows consumers to search a database of more than 440,000 lawyers and law firms using criteria such as location, lawyer or law firm name, areas of practice, and fluency in a particular language. In conjunction with this consumer site, Martindale-Hubbell offers Lawyer HomePage Plus, a service by which small-firm lawyers can create inexpensive Web sites linked to the Lawyers.com directory. The service, intended for solo and small firms, provides templates and hosting services to simplify the creation of a Web site, and then links the site to Lawyers.com. "Premium" Web sites, custom built for larger firms, are also offered.

In order to be listed in the Lawyers.com database or to be eligible to purchase a Web site through Lawyer HomePages, a lawyer or firm must have purchased a paid listing—or "Professional Biography"—in the Martindale-Hubbell Law Directory. Prices of such listings vary. This is unlike the company's Lawyer Locator (www.martindale.com), which includes the names of all listed lawyers, not just those who purchased enhanced listings. The main attraction, of course, is Lawyers.com, a site that both helps consumers find a lawyer and tutors them on the basics of law. It does this through five sections:

- *Find a Lawyer.* The center of the site is a database of more than 440,000 lawyers and law firms searchable by type of practice, location, language or attorney/firm name.

- *Get Legal Tips.* An outline of the key considerations and questions as well as guidance on fees, pro bono/legal aid and arbitration/mediation services.
- *Research Legal Topics.* A collection of articles, organized by legal topic, that provide an overview of U.S. law for individuals and businesses.
- *Ask a Lawyer.* A service by which users can pose general legal questions to a panel of lawyers.
- *Community.* Message boards and discussion forums related to law.

Other Search Tools

★★★★★ LawPeriscope, www.lawperiscope.com

When I first visited LawPeriscope, a site that profiles the nation's 300 largest firms using the firms' own Web sites, I was not impressed. Heck, I thought, anyone could pull together a bunch of links to someone else's site. Then one day I found myself at one of those large firm sites, trying to navigate my way to a particular piece of information, without success. I remembered LawPeriscope, and a few clicks later, I found what I was looking for. I have used it routinely ever since. The key is LawPeriscope's profiles—outlines of each firm that take the information on the firm's own site and organize it under a simple and uniform structure. For each firm, LawPeriscope lists offices, practice areas, attorneys, representative clients, seminars and events, publications and resources, and other features, linking directly to the full information wherever it resides on the firm's own site. The result is a well-organized resource, easy to use and worth a try.

★★★★★ LLRX.com, www. llrx.com

Since its creation in 1996, LLRX, an innovative Webzine for legal professionals, has remained on the cutting edge, spotting new trends, zeroing in on key developments, and often being first to report important news. Completely free, it is updated monthly with insightful feature articles and regular columns on legal research, technology and management. Contributors include law librarians, attor-

Used by Permission of LLRX™

LLRX keeps lawyers plugged in to the latest developments in legal research and technology.

neys and legal technology consultants. All of this is backed up by a rich archive of past issues and specialized research libraries and practice centers. For legal professionals serious about using the Internet, LLRX has long been the best guide.

★★★★★ The Virtual Chase, www.virtualchase.com

In July 1995, the American Association of Law Libraries' annual meeting was the venue for the launch of my former newsletter, "*legal.online*," the first periodical to cover the Internet for lawyers. One of the very first people to come by my booth and subscribe was Genie Tyburski, a law librarian at Ballard Spahr Andrews & Ingersoll, Philadelphia. A year later, Tyburski unveiled her own site, The Virtual Chase, and quickly made it a top destination for legal researchers. Sponsored by Ballard Spahr, Tyburski continues to add features that make this a truly useful site. A top feature is Tyburski's annotated guide to legal resources on the Web, distinguished in part by Tyburski's addition of dates to her annotations, so users know how recently they were written. Another feature is TVC Alert, a daily bulletin of research news, available on the Web site and by e-mail. Her skills as a librarian show in her many articles about research strategies, found under headings such as "How to Research" and "Information Quality," and tools such as her guide to researching businesses on the Web. A section for Internet trainers includes tutorials on Internet research. The Virtual Chase is a practical, interesting and well-designed site for legal professionals.

★★★ University Law Review Project, www.lawreview.org

From here, you can conduct a full-text search of all law journals that are available on the Web. You can also peruse a list of all online journals, organized by topic and by law school, and follow the links to their individual Web sites. This site was set up by FindLaw and the Coalition of Online Journals, with help from Verity, the Australasian Legal Information Institute, the Legal Information Institute at Cornell, Stanford University, JURIST—The Law Professors' Network, and many law schools and journals throughout the world.

Chapter 4

Bankruptcy Lawyers Indebted to the Net

―――――――――― **Chapter Contents** ――――――――――

Bankruptcy Law
Guides to Bankruptcy Practice
Tools for Bankruptcy Lawyers

The Internet is far from bankrupt when it comes to resources relating to the laws regulating insolvency and corporate reorganizations. The Bankruptcy Code and Rules, bankruptcy court decisions, current news, educational materials, and even current case documents and notices are available online. Here is a guide to finding bankruptcy law and information on the Internet.

(For a guide to finding bankruptcy court opinions on the Web, see Appendix II.)

Bankruptcy Law

★★★★ Official Bankruptcy Forms, www.uscourts.gov/bankform

Offered on the Web by the Administrative Office of the U.S. Courts, this is a complete library of official bankruptcy forms available to be downloaded or viewed online. Documents are in Adobe Acrobat format.

★★★★ U.S. Bankruptcy Code, http://www4.law.cornell.edu/uscode/11

The Legal Information Institute at Cornell Law School provides this hypertext version of the federal bankruptcy law.

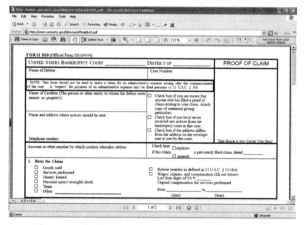

This proof of claim is among the official forms available online from the U.S. courts.

Guides to Bankruptcy Practice

★★★★★ American Bankruptcy Institute, www.abiworld.org

This organization of more than 7,500 insolvency professionals—including bankruptcy judges, attorneys, trustees, accountants and others—has long claimed that its Web site is "the premier site for bankruptcy information on the Web." Over the years, its claim has continued to hold true. The site features a wealth of bankruptcy information, including breaking news in the field, updated daily; bankruptcy statistics; legislative news; and articles from its weekly newsletter, *Cracking the Code*, and its periodical, *ABI Journal*. It also includes full text bankruptcy decisions, fully searchable and sorted by selected Circuits or by state. A library section contains analyses of significant cases written by ABI members. Some sections of the site are restricted to ABI members, but the bulk of the resources are free to anyone.

★★★★★ Bankruptcy Basics, www.uscourts.gov/bankbasic.pdf

Published in June 2000 as a public service by the Bankruptcy Judges Division of the Administrative Office of the U.S. Courts, this seventy-two-page pamphlet covers liquidations, individual bankruptcies, reorganizations under Chapter 11, farm and municipal bankruptcies, and the Securities Investor Protection Act. It includes a glossary of bankruptcy terminology.

★★★★★ Bankruptcy Bulletin, http://www.weil.com/wgm/CWGM Pubs.nsf/Bankruptcy

A monthly newsletter from lawyers at the international law firm Weil, Gotshal & Manges, Bankruptcy Bulletin is a timely and well-written review of new developments in bankruptcy law and practice. Each month's issue includes up to four articles analyzing recent court decisions and statutory developments. The January issue each year presents a more substantive review of major developments during the preceding twelve months. Issues beginning with December 1997 are available.

★★★★★ The Bankruptcy LawTrove, www.lawtrove.com/bankruptcy

The Bankruptcy LawTrove is possibly the most comprehensive collection on the Internet of links to bankruptcy-related resources. Maintained by the Boston law firm Swiggart & Agin, it provides links to bankruptcy legislation, regulations, courts and cases; other bankruptcy law Web sites; government resources related to bankruptcy; and vendor pages offering products and services for bankruptcy lawyers. Besides links, the site includes Agin's answers to frequently asked questions about bankruptcy.

★★★★★ Commercial Law League of America, www.clla.org

The CLLA has the timeliest and most thorough legislative updates in the bankruptcy field of any site we have visited. Dispatches are current to the day and link to full-text documents, when available elsewhere on the Web. Representing professionals—mostly attorneys—who specialize in collections, creditors' rights and bankruptcy, the CLLA encourages the development and adoption of ethical and fair practice standards in the field. Its site includes the texts of these ethical codes and standards of practice, and allows visitors to search for a CLLA member, each of whom must subscribe to these standards. Search options include location, name and company.

★★★★★ LexisNexis Matthew Bender, http://bender.lexisnexis.com

LexisNexis Matthew Bender is publisher of the authoritative treatise, *Collier on Bankruptcy*, and of a suite of related bankruptcy publications, including the *Collier Bankruptcy Practice Guide*, the *Collier Bankruptcy Manual*, and the weekly *Collier Bankruptcy Case Update*. Full access to these and other publications is available online through the LexisNexis research service. If you are not a Lexis subscriber, you can purchase access to the bankruptcy library for one day at a cost of $76 or for a week for $130.

★★★★ Bankruptcy Alternatives, www.berkshire.net/~mkb

Mory Brenner, a lawyer based in the Berkshire Mountains of Western Massachusetts, publishes this site that, while at first glance appears amateurish, is deceptively deep with information focused on exploring not just bankruptcy, but alternatives such as a debt workout or full payment of debts. Brenner has prepared fairly detailed FAQs on a number of aspects of bankruptcy and workouts. He also provides a brief but practical collection of links to bankruptcy resources elsewhere on the Web, as well as links to alternative sources for mortgages, automobile loans and commercial loans.

★★★★ Bankruptcy: An Overview, www.law.cornell.edu/topics/bankruptcy.html

This is a general introduction to bankruptcy law and related Internet resources presented by the Legal Information Institute of Cornell Law School. A brief textual introduction to this area of law is accompanied by links to federal bankruptcy statutes, pertinent sections of the Code of Federal Regulations, the Federal Rules of Bankruptcy Procedure, recent U.S. Supreme Court decisions involving bankruptcy, selected state laws, and other Web resources. A good place for basic bankruptcy information.

★★★ Bernstein Law Firm, www.bernsteinlaw.com

A Pittsburgh law firm concentrating on the representation of creditors in collections and bankruptcy, Bernstein Law Firm offers a noteworthy collection of its lawyers' articles on bankruptcy topics. The highlight is Bernstein's *Dictionary of Bankruptcy Terminology*, an alphabetical guide to terms commonly used in bankruptcy.

★★★ National Association of Consumer Bankruptcy Attorneys, http://nacba.com

The NACBA is an organization of more than 1,300 lawyers who concentrate on representing debtors in consumer bankruptcies. Its Web site provides an overview of the organization and its officers and a calendar of scheduled events. A "news" page links to news stories of interest to bankruptcy lawyers, although the most recent link was one year old on our last visit. A legislative section was more up to date. NACBA members with a password can log into a restricted area of the site, which includes a bulletin board for posting messages to others. The site includes a short selection of links for bankruptcy lawyers.

★★ Bankruptcy in Brief, www.moranlaw.net

Targeted at debtors and creditors, this California law firm's site contains a basic guide to bankruptcy law and procedure. In simple text, it discusses whether to file bankruptcy, options for a failed start-up, creditors' rights, and other topics. It includes a glossary of bankruptcy terms. Not much here for lawyers already knowledgeable about bankruptcy law.

★ Bankruptcy Developments Journal, www.law.emory.edu/BDJ/bdjhome.htm

A publication of Emory University School of Law, this law journal's Web site has general information about the journal and its editorial board, but no full text articles.

★ University of Arizona College of Law Online Bankruptcy Course, www.u.arizona.edu/ic/law/bankruptcy.html

Law Professor Bill Boyd's online bankruptcy course, first published on the Web in 1994, appeared on a recent visit to be undergoing an overhaul. Intended to cover Chapters 7, 11 and 13, only the discussion of Chapter 7 remains, and it has some holes. A discussion of Chapter 13 has disappeared and been replaced by an "under construction" note. On several visits to this site over the years, I've always found the section on Chapter 11 to be under construction.

Tools for Bankruptcy Lawyers

★★★★★ **Bankruptcy Data. com,** www.bankruptcydata.com

Whether you are a bankruptcy professional or an interested investor, you will find Bankruptcy Data.com to be a useful reference source. It provides data on all publicly traded companies with total assets of at least $10 million that have filed for bankruptcy, have defaulted on publicly held debt, or have proposed a distressed exchange offer since

BankruptcyData.com provides timely and detailed data on public bankruptcies.

1986. You can search the database using any combination of company name, business type, assets and bankruptcy start date. Once you locate a company, you can purchase reports that range from simple synopses for $5 to detailed profiles for roughly $40. A full report typically includes complete information on the company, the bankruptcy filing, financials, news stories and creditors. Also available for purchase for each company are update services and reports summarizing details of the company's bankruptcy or reorganization plan. The site also delivers daily bankruptcy news briefs. Rather than pay by the view, you can opt to subscribe to the site, at prices that range from $500 to $5,000 a year.

★★★★ **BankruptcyClearinghouse.com,** www.bankruptcyclearing-house.com

This site, launched in 2003, promises one-stop shopping for bankruptcy court data nationwide, providing access to bankruptcy filings from courts in all fifty states, the District of Columbia and Puerto Rico. Data for most courts dates back to January 1, 1997, and is current to within a few days. Users can pay by the search, at $1 each, or have unlimited searches for a flat rate of $50 a month. The service allows you to prepare custom proof-of-claim forms and save them to use again later.

★★★★ BankruptcySales.com, www.bankruptcysales.com

Bankruptcysales.com is a Web site where bankruptcy trustees, debtors in possession, and others post listings of assets being offered for sale from bankruptcy estates. Distinguishing this site from others listing assets for sale is that it is a joint venture of the American Bankruptcy Institute and the National Association of Bankruptcy Trustees, two highly regarded organizations. Members of either organization can post listings here for free; others must pay $100 to post. The fee is per visit, not per posting, and allows multiple postings on a single visit. The site is updated daily with new postings. Assets are listed by category and the descriptions can be viewed by anyone.

★★★★ Internet Bankruptcy Library, http://bankrupt.com

The Internet Bankruptcy Library is a one-stop shopping site for the bankruptcy professional. It offers a variety of original materials and links to other online materials. Among the resources offered here: news from the bankruptcy world; information on discussion groups and mailing lists focusing on particular troubled companies; archives of T&W Newswire, a bankruptcy related news and announcement mailing list; data on distressed securities; bankruptcy and insolvency resource materials; an international directory of bankruptcy and insolvency professionals; directories of bankruptcy conferences, organizations and publications; and other information.

★★★★ U.S. Trustee Program, Department of Justice, www.usdoj.gov/ust

The U.S. Trustee Program is a component of the Department of Justice responsible for overseeing the administration of bankruptcy cases and private trustees. The program consists of twenty-one regional trustee offices nationwide and an Executive Office for U.S. Trustees in Washington, D.C. This site contains information about the program and the federal bankruptcy system. It includes a guide to each of the regional offices and links to their Web sites. It also includes directories of private trustees throughout the U.S. Of particular interest to lawyers are its substantive handbooks and reference materials for cases under Chapters 7, 12 and 13 of the Bankruptcy Code. The reference materials include forms, suggested questions and answers for trustees, and rules. The site also houses the full text of administrative decisions issued by the Program regarding private trustees.

★★★ National Association of Bankruptcy Trustees, www.nabt.com

The National Association of Bankruptcy Trustees was formed in 1982 to address the needs of bankruptcy trustees throughout the country and to promote the effectiveness of the bankruptcy system as a whole. The majority of its members are Chapter 7 trustees who primarily oversee liquidations; its members also include trustees under Chapters 11, 12 and 13. For bankruptcy professionals, the site is noteworthy for its calendar of scheduled bankruptcy sales and its listing of bankruptcy property up for bid. Sales are listed by category of goods, i.e., financial notes, heavy equipment, personal property, etc.

★★ Huntington Legal Advertising, www.legalnotice.com

Based in Beaverton, Oregon, Huntington Legal Advertising specializes in legal-notice advertising for bankruptcies, class actions and other legal proceedings, using the Internet as well as traditional print and broadcast media. Its Web site is a brochure for its services, and includes links to a handful of notice sites it has created on the Web for specific class actions.

★★ Poorman-Douglas Legal Services, www.poorman-douglas.com

Poorman-Douglas provides data processing services in bankruptcy cases and class action lawsuits. Its services include database management, distribution of notices by mail and in newspapers, advertising, claims processing, balloting, tabulation and reporting, locator services, 800 number creditor/claimant hotlines, and disbursement. Its Web site provides descriptions of these services, and a small, revolving collection of articles and white papers on topics such as automated document storage.

★ 411Bankruptcy, www.411bankruptcy.com

411Bankruptcy is a directory of bankruptcy attorneys. It allows users to search for a bankruptcy attorney in a particular locale by entering the ZIP code. Lawyers can list themselves in their specific ZIP code for free or in all ZIP codes within their county for $59.95 a year.

Chapter 5

Corporation Law and Corporate Governance

―――――――――――――――――― Chapter Contents ――――――――――――――――――

Statutes, Rules and Forms
Courts and Cases
Practice
Contracts
Limited Liability Companies
Company Information
Membership Organizations
Related Resources

――

A corporate lawyer I know complains that the Web has no truly top-notch sites devoted to supporting the day-to-day work of practitioners in this field. Sure enough, the best sites in this area tend to be narrow in their focus—Delaware cases or forms of contracts, for example.

In part, the problem may be that corporation law is one of those areas that tends to cross the boundaries of several practice areas—employment, contracts, securities, real estate and intellectual property, to name just the obvious. Thus, no site for corporate lawyers can fully address in a cohesive and comprehensive manner everything they would find to be important and relevant.

For this very reason, readers of this chapter should also be sure to read the other chapters that relate to their practice. In particular, the chapter on securities law includes several important sites that, had they not fallen there, would have been included here. The most important of these to any corporate lawyer is the Web site of the Securities and Exchange Commission, www.sec.gov, and the EDGAR database of corporate filings available there.

That said, here is a look at sites focused primarily on corporation law.

Statutes, Rules and Forms

★★★★★ **Delaware Division of Corporations,** www.state.de.us/corp/default.shtml

According to this site, more than 500,000 companies are incorporated in Delaware, including 58% of the Fortune 500 and 50% of U.S. publicly traded companies. For others wanting to follow suit, this site is where to find every-thing needed to incorporate in Delaware. It includes the state's corporation law, all necessary forms, a schedule of fees, and a complete description of the procedure for incorporating.

★★★ **State Corporation and Business Forms,** www.findlaw.com/ 11stategov/indexcorp.html

The legal portal FindLaw assembled these links to Web sites containing official state corporate and business forms.

★★★ **State Corporation Statutes,** www.law.cornell.edu/topics/ state_statutes.html#corporations

This page provides links to each state's corporation laws on the Web, cour-tesy of the Legal Information Institute at Cornell University.

Courts and Cases

★★★★★ **Delaware Corporate Law Clearinghouse,** http://corpo-rate-law.widener.edu

This Web site provides access to filings and opinions from the nation's premier trial court for corporation law, the Delaware Court of Chancery. The site includes opinions, briefs, com-plaints, settlements, motions and other documents filed in the Court. Coverage begins from March 1999 and includes only opinions from cases that the Court has coded as "corporate matters" on its docket. The site also provides general informa-tion about and a history of the

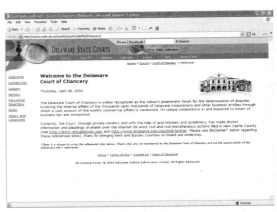

Delaware's Chancery Court is the preeminent trial court for corporate law.

court. The Clearinghouse is a cooperative project of the Court, the Widener University School of Law Legal Information Center, and Stanford University School of Law.

★★★ **Delaware Court of Chancery,** http://courts.state.de.us/chancery

This is the official home page of the preeminent trial court for corporation law. It includes the Court's opinions, as well as its rules, selected forms and other information about the Court. The Court is working with private vendors to make its docket information available online for a fee.

Practice

★★★★★ **FindLaw Corporate Counsel Center,** http://corporate.findlaw.com

FindLaw's Corporate Counsel Center is the most broad-ranging free resource for corporate counsel on the Web, with current news, in-depth articles, substantive documents, court filings and opinions, and links to related resources. The site is organized primarily by industries and practice areas, each with a primary page that links to articles, news, recent lawsuits and research tools. A section devoted to business contracts provides hundreds of full-text contracts, organized by industry, by company, and by type.

★★★★★ **LeapLaw,** www.leaplaw.com

Launched in November 2002, this subscription "knowledge base" is targeted at corporate associates, in-house counsel and small law firms. Developed by a former corporate paralegal in Massachusetts, LeapLaw positions itself as a sort of virtual paralegal, providing access to tools and information that will help a lawyer "leap" to completion of a task. It does this primarily through a database which it says contains more than 2,000 corporate terms and definitions, more than 800 legal forms, another 800 sample corporate votes, a collection of "best practices" guides, and links to outside sources of information. LeapLaw's focus is corporation and business law, but it includes materials pertaining to related fields such as securities, employment, intellectual property and tax. As of this writing, subscriptions cost $150 a month, $400 a quarter, or $1,500 a year. There is an extra cost to download certain model legal forms.

★★★★ **Corporate Counsel,** www.corpcounsel.com

The Web site of *Corporate Counsel* magazine, published by American Lawyer Media, it includes selected full-text articles from the magazine, the annual general counsel compensation survey, reports of major deals and suits, comings and goings among corporate counsel, and other news briefs.

★★★★ Corporate Crime Reporter, www.corporatecrimereporter.com

The Corporate Crime Reporter is a legal newsletter that highlights recent news items about ongoing corporate crime prosecutions. The site includes full transcripts of interviews with prominent lawyers and full-text documents from cases in the news. The site serves as a companion to the Corporate Crime Reporter newsletter, published forty-eight times a year in Washington, D.C.

★★★★ corporate.martindale.com, http://corporate.martindale.com

In-house counsel are the intended users of this site, from Martindale-Hubbell. Entirely free after registration, it features a glorified version of the Lawyer Locator, where users can add private notes to lawyers' listings. The site includes access to the Law Digest, summarizing the laws of all fifty states and eighty foreign countries. Also here are databases of ADR providers and expert witnesses.

★★★★ DuPont Legal Model, www.dupontlegalmodel.com

When DuPont's legal department showed that it could both cut costs and achieve greater success, its formula came to be known as the DuPont Legal Model and was widely emulated by other companies' law departments. This site is a complete guide to the model and its implementation. It includes a library of articles, descriptions of initiatives taken with DuPont, and lists of the law firms and service providers that serve as DuPont's strategic partners.

★★★★ IncSpot, www.incspot.com

IncSpot is a suite of online corporate tools for customers of Corporation Service Company ("CSC"), a Wilmington, Delaware provider of registered agent, incorporation, document filing and retrieval, qualification, and other corporate services. Services available through IncSpot include:

- Records management. Manage company records and compliance with corporate filing requirements.
- Delaware e-Filing. Track and file annual reports, tax returns and related matters.
- UCC and lien tools. Search, prepare and electronically file UCC Article 9 forms and motor vehicle and real estate liens.
- Name management. Manage and track corporate names, doing-business-as names, domain names and trade names.
- Litigation and service of process management.

★★★★ RealCorporateLawyer, www.realcorporatelawyer.com

From RR Donnelley Financial, this site is designed for securities lawyers who practice in the area of corporate finance. It features Securities and Exchange Commission daily briefs, harvested from the SEC's own Web site, reports of SEC and related regulatory developments, current news about corporate finance, and in-depth articles contributed by lawyers who practice in the field. A monthly webzine provides a more in-depth look at SEC and corporate finance news.

★★★★ SocraticLaw, www.socraticlaw.com

Launched in March 2003 by a former Delaware trial lawyer, this service provides full-text searching of transcripts of trials related to corporate and securities law, bankruptcy and intellectual property. Its database includes trial transcripts obtained from court reporters or transcribed from copies of audio recordings obtained from the courts. The database has transcripts from the Delaware Chancery Court and Delaware Supreme Court and will soon include the U.S. District Court for Delaware. Eventually, the company will add transcripts from state and federal courts outside Delaware. Transcripts can be searched by court, judge, lawyer, party, expert witness, case citation, case number, date of proceeding, type of action, statute and legal issue. An initial consultation concerning a research project is free, after which it costs $250 to initiate a research project and between $3 and $5 per page for the results.

★★★ TheCorporateCounsel.net, www.thecorporatecounsel.net

From the publisher of *The Corporate Counsel* and *The Corporate Executive* newsletters, this site provides current news and analysis of corporate and securities law. Unfortunately, to access most of the information, you must be a subscriber to one of the print newsletters or purchase a Web-only subscription for $625 a year.

Contracts

★★★★★ Contracting and Organizations Research Initiative, http://cori.missouri.edu

Operating on the premise that research on contracting is stymied by a lack of available contracts, the CORI project at the University of Missouri, Columbia, is working to create a digital collection of contracts and make them available over the Internet. The collection so far contains more than 10,000 contracts, drawn primarily from filings with the Securities and

Exchange Commission's EDGAR database, where company filings frequently include contracts of interest to investors. CORI downloads, extracts and categorizes these contracts and makes them available via a full-text search and retrieval system. Users can search the library by full text or according to contract type. Contracts available so far encompass mergers and acquisitions, employment, finance, joint ventures, leases, licenses, purchases, joint ventures, agriculture and underwriting. In addition to the digital contracts, CORI has a collection of hard copy contracts, including HMO-physician agreements, sports stadium leases, container shipping contracts, and more. These contracts are described at the site and can be ordered by e-mail.

Limited Liability Companies

★★★★ **Callison on LLCs,** www.faegre.com/firm_practice_detail. asp?practiceid=5#articles

J. William Callison, partner in the Denver office of the law firm Faegre & Benson, is a nationally recognized authority on limited liability companies. He wrote the treatises *Limited Liability Companies: A State-By-State Guide to Law and Practice*, published by West Publishing in 1994, and *Partnership Law and Practice: General and Limited Partnerships*, published in 1992 by Clark Boardman Callaghan. Although you cannot read these treatises here, his law firm's Web site does offer *Formation, Operation And Taxation Of Limited Liability Companies And Limited Liability Partnerships*, an eighty-nine-page manual prepared for the Colorado Society of Certified Public Accountants. Also here is Callison's article, "Blind Men and Elephants: Fiduciary Duties Under the Revised Uniform Partnership Act, the Uniform Limited Liability Company Act, and Beyond," first published in 1997 in the Journal of Small and Emerging Business Law, as well as a sample LLC operating agreement.

★★★ **LNET-LLC,** http://groups.yahoo.com/group/lnet-llc

This is the Web home of LNET-LLC, an e-mail discussion list on limited liability companies, limited liability partnerships and other unincorporated business entities. The list's membership ranges from lawyers to certified public accountants, and includes professors, law students and graduate students in accounting. You can read list messages here, but cannot post messages without first joining the list. Besides providing information on subscribing to and participating in the list, its site hosts a small library of documents and links concerning LLCs, LLPs and other unincorporated entities.

★★★ Lnet State Pages, http://c2.com/w2/bridges/LnetStatePages

This is a collection of links, organized by state, to resources about limited liability companies and partnerships. Links include state statutes, filing requirements and other useful information. Part of the Bridges project,[1] the site is organized as a "wiki," in which any visitor can modify or create pages. This means that the site's users and visitors also contribute to its upkeep.

Company Information

★★★★★ Corporate Information, www.corporateinformation.com

Corporate Information got even better in 2000, when it merged with the Wright Research Center. CI provides a comprehensive set of well-organized links to business research information on the Web. It has a search engine with links to more than 350,000 company profiles located at other sites, plus its own research reports on more than 15,000 companies. Wright publishes detailed research information on more than 20,000 companies worldwide, including more than a decade of historical data. The CI Web site combines these resources to enable multi-faceted research into companies and industries. Users can search for information on a specific company, of course, but they can also research any of thirty industries in some sixty-five countries. Research also can be performed by country or by U.S. state. Other useful tools include a currency rate calculator and a page explaining the meaning in foreign countries of the letters that follow a company's name.

★★★★★ Hoovers Online, www.hoovers.com

Hoovers' "company capsules" provide essential information on more than 50,000 public and private companies, including current financials and key competitors. Subscribers receive access to in-depth company information, including historical financials, reports on the competitive landscape, and overviews of products and operations. A basic "Hoover's Lite"

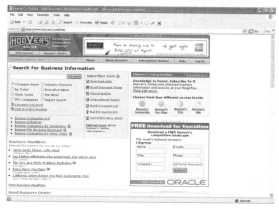

Hoovers reports on more than 50,000 companies.

---

[1] See Chapter 24 *infra*.

subscription for an individual is $399 a year, with advanced subscriptions available to corporate and business customers.

★★★ Annual Report Gallery, www.reportgallery.com

The Annual Report Gallery, from Cornerstone Investor Relations, indexes more than 2,200 annual reports, covering almost all of the Fortune 500 companies. The gallery is not itself a source of these reports; rather, it links to the reports contained on the companies' own Web sites. Companies are listed alphabetically. For each, the Gallery includes a link to the company's annual report, a link to its home page, a link to a stock tracker, and a brief corporate and earnings profile. The Gallery maintains partnerships with sites that provide annual reports from countries outside the U.S. and provides links to those sources. It also provides general financial links.

Membership Organizations

★★★★★ American Corporate Counsel Association, www.acca.com

Lots here, but you will have to be an ACCA member to have access to it all. The bar association of some 14,000 in-house lawyers, ACCA offers its members a diverse online reference source it calls the Virtual Library. Organized by topic of law and also searchable in full text, the Virtual Library includes hundreds of forms, articles, bibliographies and other practice materials. Supplementing this is a collection of "InfoPaks," packages of articles and materials that focus on the issues that corporate counsel most commonly face. The Virtual Library also includes case law, in the form of a searchable database of cases pertaining to in-house practice. Another feature available only to members is "MemberToMember," by which members can search for and consult with other members who have expertise in particular matters. An in-house job listing service provides a searchable database of employment offerings for corporate counsel.

Those who do not belong to ACCA are not closed out entirely. They can use ACCA's well-organized collection of links to find corporation law resources elsewhere on the Web. Non-members have full access to a library of amicus curiae briefs ACCA has filed. They can also read about ACCA's efforts to increase diversity in the profession and to encourage *pro bono* activities. Of course, visitors can read up on ACCA in general, learn about its committees and officers, and check a schedule of its events.

★★★★★ National Center for Employee Ownership, www.nceo.org

Inc. Magazine called it "The single best source of information on employee ownership anywhere in the world." The National Center for Employee

Ownership is a private, nonprofit membership organization that provides information on employee stock ownership plans (ESOPs), common employee stock option plans, and employee participation programs. Its Web site features a library of articles that explain ESOPs and related employee ownership plans in a fair amount of detail. For those who want to read about the topic in greater depth, NCEO's site includes a catalog that describes and sells its various books and journals devoted to employee ownership. Lawyers, economists, consultants and various other authorities contribute a series of timely columns to the site. This is an excellent resource for anyone wanting to learn more about this subject.

★★★★★ Task Force on Corporate Responsibility, American Bar Association, www.abanet.org/buslaw/corporateresponsibility/home.html

In response to a series of corporate scandals in recent years, the American Bar Association appointed the Task Force on Corporate Responsibility. Its recommendations led to the ABA's adoption in 2003 of new lawyer conduct rules. The rules permit a lawyer to reveal confidential client information if the client is using the lawyer's services to commit a crime or fraud that would cause financial harm to others. They also permit a lawyer representing an organizational client to report up the corporate ladder violations by corporate officers of laws or legal duties that would harm the organization. This site includes the task force's complete report as well as details on the corporate responsibility rules. The site also provides access to a clearinghouse of ABA activities dealing with corporate responsibility issues, including programs, projects, articles, reports and publications.

★★★★ American Society of Corporate Secretaries, www.ascs.org

The American Society of Corporate Secretaries is a professional association of more than 4,000 corporate secretaries and others in the U.S. and Canada who are involved in such matters as corporate governance, records management, the regulation and trading of securities, proxy solicitation and other shareholder activities, and corporate administration. Only those members are allowed access to the most valuable parts of this Web site, such as its "Core Document File," a collection of internal and other corporate documents, many of them not publicly available, on nearly sixty topics provided on a current basis by companies chosen for their diversity in industry and size. Members also have access to the Society's general reference files, which include an array of annual reports, proxy statements, certificates of incorporation and bylaws, and to the shareholder proposal database, an index of shareholder proposals received by members' corporations, as well as companies' requests for SEC "no-action" letters and staff responses. Non-members visiting the site can learn about the Society's structure and membership, as well as its publications and events.

★★★★ Business Law Section, American Bar Association, www.abanet.org/buslaw/home.html

Corporation law, corporate governance and corporate practice are among the topics on the agenda of the Business Law Section of the American Bar Association. You will have to be a member of the Section to gain access to all of the substantive materials here. But anyone can read the articles from the current or past issues of *Business Law Today*, the Section's every-other-month news magazine, or abstracts of articles from the quarterly journal, *The Business Lawyer*. Elsewhere on the site, visitors can obtain general information about Section membership, events and publications. Drill down to the sites of the section's individual committees and task forces for resources relating to their work.

★★★ DiverseCounsel, www.diversecounsel.org

Dedicated to increasing the diversity of the legal profession "from the inside out," this site is sponsored by the American Corporate Counsel Association in cooperation with a number of other bar associations. Its primary feature is a searchable directory of minority outside counsel. The site also has a library of diversity resources and a collection of links to diversity-related Web sites.

★★★ InternationalCounsel.org, www.internationalcounsel.org

The American Corporate Counsel Association sponsors this site, which is a searchable directory of outside counsel located outside the United States. ACCA members can post recommendations of international outside counsel they have worked with.

Related Resources

★★★ FinWeb, www.finweb.com

This site tries to point to other sites that contain actual information on economics and finance-related topics. Annotated links to journals, working papers, databases, and other sources.

Chapter 6

Criminal Law and Justice Online

———————— Chapter Contents ————————

Evidence
Government
Practice Resources
Death Penalty
Law Enforcement
Associations

For criminal lawyers, the resources offered by the Internet range from the practical to the philosophical.

On the practical side are Web sites such as that of the U.S. Sentencing Commission, where you can find the complete text of the Sentencing Guidelines and a library of research and reports on mandatory sentencing, drug policy and related matters.

On the philosophical side are some of the sites devoted to topics such as juvenile justice or the death penalty.

In between are a host of useful and informative materials, ranging from crime statistics to brief banks to guides to forensic science and evidence. What follows is a guide to some of the best Internet resources for criminal lawyers.

Evidence

★★★★ **Federal Rules of Evidence,** www.law.cornell.edu/rules/fre/overview.html

From Cornell Law School's Legal Information Institute, a searchable database of the full text of the rules.

Government

★★★★★ **Bureau of Justice Statistics, U.S. Department of Justice,** www.ojp.usdoj.gov/bjs

An extensive and useful library of statistics about crime and victims, drugs, criminal offenders, the justice system, law enforcement, prosecution, courts and sentencing, corrections, expenditures, and other special topics.

★★★★★ Crime and Justice Electronic Data Abstracts, www.ojp. usdoj.gov/bjs/dtdata.htm

You want to show the jury the relationship between homicide rates and education levels in your state. Or maybe you need to tell the judge how many robberies were reported in your state each year since 1964. The Bureau of Justice Statistics of the U.S. Department of Justice has aggregated crime and justice data from a variety of published sources and made it available on the Web. Data is presented in spreadsheets to facilitate its use in analysis, graphing and mapping. The files contain thousands of numbers and hundreds of categories, displayed by jurisdiction and time. Wherever possible, the data is the most recent available. Sources for the data include BJS statistics on correctional populations and federal case processing, the Uniform Crime Reporting program of the FBI, and the Bureau of the Census.

★★★★★ Cybercrime, www.cybercrime.gov

Launched in March 2000 by the Computer Crime and Intellectual Property Section of the U.S. Department of Justice, Cybercrime provides information on the growing area of crimes related to the Internet, focusing on hackers and intellectual property crime. The site includes a variety of materials, such as press releases, speeches by Justice Department officials, Congressional testimony, and Justice Department reports. In addition, there is material to help the general public and law enforcement, including information on how to report Internet-related crime. Materials on the site are organized according to the legal or policy issues involved. Categories include investigating and prosecuting computer crime, protecting intellectual property rights, electronic commerce, free speech issues, searches and seizures of computers, encryption, privacy, and law-enforcement coordination.

★★★★★ Federal Justice Statistics Resource Center, http://fjsrc. urban.org

This online database from the Federal Justice Statistics Program contains comprehensive information about suspects and defendants processed in each stage of the federal criminal justice system. It includes data collected from the Executive Office for U.S. Attorneys, the Administrative Office of the U.S. Courts, the U.S. Sentencing Commission, the Federal Bureau of Prisons, the Pretrial Services Administration, U.S. Courts of Appeals, and the Federal Probation Supervision Information System, with coverage spanning the period from 1994 to the most recent data-reporting year. The site is useful for finding data about specific events and outcomes, such as the number of defendants prosecuted, convicted and sentenced in a given year. You can also download criminal justice datasets for more in-depth analysis. The Bureau of Justice Statistics of the U.S. Department of Justice funds the center, which is operated by the Urban Institute, an economic and social policy research organization.

★★★★★ Justice Information Center, www.ncjrs.org

This site of the National Criminal Justice Reference Service, the clearinghouse for the U.S. Department of Justice and the Office of National Drug Control Policy, lives up to its claim to be "one of the most extensive sources of information on criminal and juvenile justice in the world." The site's materials are organized by major categories, such as corrections, courts, crime prevention, criminal justice statistics, drugs, and juvenile justice. Within each category are libraries of documents and reports as well as links to related Web sites. Select "Drugs and Crime," for example, and you can download any of a number of reports and fact sheets on drug-related crime.

★★★★★ National Archive of Criminal Justice Data, www.icpsr. umich.edu/NACJD/index.html

This archive houses more than 550 data collections relating to criminal justice. The collection can be searched by key word, subject or title. There are a wealth of potentially useful reports and studies relating to sentencing, probation, jury selection and more. It is sponsored by the University of Michigan, the U.S. Dept. of Justice, and the Bureau of Justice Statistics.

★★★★★ U.S. Sentencing Commission, www.ussc.gov

If you practice criminal law in federal court, this site could prove indispensable. Even for those who practice only in state court, there is a wealth of useful information to be found here. Among the highlights are the complete text of the Sentencing Guidelines Manual, which can either be downloaded or viewed online in hypertext format, and a library of the commission's research and reports on such matters as mandatory sentencing and drug policies.

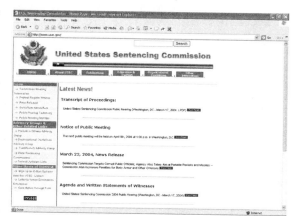

For criminal lawyers who practice in federal court, this site is indispensable.

★★★★ Bureau of Alcohol, Tobacco, and Firearms, U.S. Dept. of the Treasury, www.atf.treas.gov

Thought only the FBI had a most-wanted list? The ATF has one too, which you can see on its Web site, along with in-depth information about its role in policing not only alcohol, tobacco and firearms, but also arson and explosives. Sections describe each of these programs in detail. Also at the site are the full text of regulations enforced by the ATF, downloadable forms, and other information about the Bureau.

★★★★ Federal Bureau of Investigation, www.fbi.gov

Extensive information about the FBI and its operations, as well as about current and recent investigations. Topics include international crime, economic espionage, wiretapping, and electronic surveillance. Statistics from the Uniform Crime Reporting Program are available, as is information about the Integrated Automated Fingerprint Identification System, the National Crime Information Center, and, of course, the ten most-wanted list.

★★★★ U.S. Department of Justice, www.usdoj.gov

The DoJ calls itself "the largest law firm in the nation," and much of its work is criminal justice. Its site includes information on a number of criminal justice programs and initiatives and provides a gateway to the Web sites of DOJ's various divisions, including the Criminal Division and the Drug Enforcement Administration. Of particular interest to practitioners is the full text of the United States Attorneys' Manual.

★★★ JustNet, www.nlectc.org

The Justice Technology Information Network, part of the National Institute of Justice's National Law Enforcement and Corrections Technology Institute, is intended for law enforcement, corrections and criminal justice professionals. But its testing and evaluation reports on a range of criminal justice technologies—from body armor and autoloading pistols to handcuffs and police vehicles—could prove a useful source of background information for criminal lawyers.

★★★ National Institute of Justice, www.ojp.usdoj.gov/nij

The research and development agency of the Department of Justice, NIJ's mandate is "to prevent and reduce crime and to improve the criminal justice system." This site has information about research and projects in areas such as community policing, violence against women, get-tough "boot camps" as alternatives to prisons, and the increasing use of courts devoted exclusively to hearing drug cases.

★★★ Prosecutors on the Web, www.prosecutor.info

From the Eaton County, Michigan prosecuting attorney, this is a collection of links to Web sites maintained by prosecuting attorneys, district attorneys, attorneys general and U.S. attorneys nationwide. It is organized by state and includes federal and international listings, as well as links to prosecutors' associations. A useful compilation.

★★ White House Social Statistics Briefing Room, www.white-house.gov/fsbr/ssbr.html

Official government statistics, including crime statistics. Data and charts measure violent crime, homicides, property crime, drug arrests, correctional populations, and more.

Practice Resources

★★★★★ CrimeLynx, www.crimelynx.com

Designed for criminal defense lawyers, this site features four major compilations of links, covering legal research, forensics and expert witnesses, investigations, and criminal policy. The collections of links are fairly thorough, but are not annotated. They are intended to list only the best sites, not to be exhaustive. CrimeLynx also highlights daily news stories of interest to criminal defenders and provides links to various other news sources on the Web.

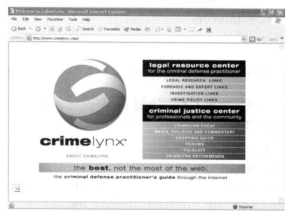

This useful site is unabashedly liberal in its perspective on criminal policy.

Unabashedly liberal in its perspective on criminal policy, the site features the e-zine "TalkLeft," offering commentary on crime-related political and justice news. In contrast to the e-zine is the site's shopping page, featuring links to books, videos, office supplies and more, all means of helping to support the site.

★★★★★ Criminal Defense Online, www.sado.org

Although its focus is Michigan, this is a useful and comprehensive site for criminal lawyers everywhere. Maintained by the Michigan State Appellate Defender Office, the site has criminal defense bulletins; a moderated newsgroup for defense attorneys; summaries of decisions on criminal law and procedure; newsletters; and links to other criminal law Web sites. The newsgroup and database are available only to criminal defense attorneys who register and pay an $80 annual fee.

The heart of this site is its criminal-defense database, which the SADO aptly describes as an online "motherlode." Among its contents are:

- Appellate briefs filed by SADO attorneys since 1992.
- Other pleadings, including trial motions and model appellate pleadings.
- Summaries of criminal opinions from the U.S. Supreme Court, the 6th Circuit Court of Appeals, the U.S. District Courts for Michigan, and Michigan state courts.
- Summaries and full text of unpublished Michigan Court of Appeals cases since 1990.
- Sample *voir dire* questions.
- Information on expert witnesses who work with criminal defense lawyers.
- Non-standard jury instructions.

Truly a comprehensive and invaluable site for criminal defense lawyers.

★★★★★ Criminal Justice Resources on the Web, www.criminology.fsu.edu/cj.html

Don't be put off by the animated cockroach crawling under Alcatraz on the opening page. This site, from a professor at Florida State University's School of Criminology, is the most extensive collection of criminal justice links on the Internet. It links include local, state, federal and international resources, police agencies, crime-related Web sites, juvenile delinquency, drug and alcohol information, and sites covering prisons and the death penalty, due process and civil liberties, forensics and education. There is even a collection of images relating to criminal justice. Browse links by subject or search the entire collection by key word.

★★★★★ Cybercrimes, http://cybercrimes.net

Cyber-stalking, hacking, cracking. These and other "cybercrimes" are the focus of a Web site from the University of Dayton School of Law and Professor Susan W. Brenner. Offering original articles, current news, and a collection of annotated links, the site looks at topics such as harassment, pornography, stalking, terrorism, piracy, and cryptography. It includes links to federal and state computer crime laws and to a host of related U.S. and international Web sites.

★★★★★ Federal Grand Jury, www.udayton.edu/~grandjur

This site is devoted to educating people about what grand juries are and what they do, on both the state and federal levels. It was created by Susan W. Brenner, professor at the University of Dayton School of Law and co-author of the book, *Federal Grand Jury Practice*, published by West Group. The site opens with general questions and answers about grand juries, illustrated with actual examples of grand jury documents such as an indictment, a report, and a transcript of a grand jury proceeding. Subsequent pages provide detailed information about federal and state grand juries, with a host of supporting documents and even photographs. The site even provides a multimedia presentation featuring photographs of an actual grand jury at work. Of course, the site includes links to other grand jury resources on the Web.

★★★★★ Illinois Appellate Defender, www.state.il.us/defender

Although of greatest use to criminal lawyers in Illinois, this practical Web site warrants a visit by anyone in this field. It has current and archived criminal case digests, summaries of legislation, death penalty materials, and an appellate handbook, among other items. A "brief bank" has no actual briefs, but summarizes the issues addressed in briefs filed in major appellate cases. The death penalty library includes a summary of issues decided by the Illinois Supreme Court in capital cases. Most of the site's materials can be downloaded in a choice of formats.

★★★★★ Sourcebook of Criminal Justice Statistics, www.albany. edu/sourcebook

This is the online version of the *Sourcebook of Criminal Justice Statistics*, a publication that brings together data about all aspects of criminal justice in the United States, presented in over 600 tables from more than 100 sources. The data is compiled by the Utilization of Criminal Justice Statistics Project at the University of Albany and published each year in hard copy by the Bureau of Justice Statistics of the U.S. Department of Justice. Although the book is published annually, it is updated on an ongoing basis. This Web site is regularly updated to reflect new data as it will appear in the next edition, so that it is always more current than the print version. Data is organized under six general headings: characteristics of the criminal justice system, public attitudes towards crime and criminal justice, nature and distribution of known offenses, characteristics and distribution of persons arrested, judicial processing of defendants, and persons under correctional supervision.

★★★★★ United Nations Office on Drugs and Crime, www.unodc.org

Consider this site a clearinghouse for the international exchange and dissemination of information on crime prevention and criminal justice. With sections on preventing drug abuse and reducing demand for illicit drugs; terrorism, corruption and human trafficking; treaties and global legal affairs; and statistics and analysis, this is a wide-ranging resource on international crime prevention and criminal justice. It provides extensive descriptions of U.N. programs and initiatives, backed up by the full text of treaties, conventions, action plans, reports, monographs, surveys, and a host of substantive documents. The site is well-organized and easy to navigate.

★★★★ ACLU Criminal Justice, www.aclu.org/CriminalJustice/ CriminalJusticeMain.cfm

There is much useful information to be found here, especially among the ACLU briefing papers, copies of selected ACLU legal documents, and other materials related to the protection of constitutional rights within the criminal justice system. On topics such as search and seizure, racial bias and the death penalty, the ACLU provides background materials from its case files, including press releases, court decisions, briefs, complaints and legislative documents.

★★★★ Anatomy of a Murder, http://library.thinkquest.org/2760/ homep.htm

By telling the fictional but legally accurate story of a criminal prosecution, this site offers a trip through the workings of the criminal justice system. It includes a glossary of legal terms and summaries of significant Supreme Court criminal rulings.

★★★★ Courts, Court Procedure, Evidence, Remedies, www.law. cornell.edu/topics/topic2.html#procedure

From Cornell's Legal Information Institute ("LII"), this site provides links to materials about courts, court rules, and court procedure.

★★★★ **Criminal Law and Procedure,** www.law.cornell.edu/topics/topic2.html#criminaljustice

Also from LII, this site provides links to materials relating to criminal law, criminal procedure, the death penalty, juvenile justice, and prisons and prisoners' rights. A useful starting point for legal research.

★★★★ **Criminal Law Resources on the Internet,** http://wings.buffalo.edu/law/bclc/resource.htm

This page provides an exhaustive collection of links to criminal law materials from the United States and throughout the world, with an emphasis on criminal codes, criminal procedure codes, and enforcement codes. Sponsored by the Buffalo Criminal Law Center at the State University of New York at Buffalo School of Law, it includes each state in the U.S. and countries from Argentina to Venezuela, providing criminal lawyers a useful shortcut to finding primary law on the Web.

★★★★ **FedCrimLaw,** www.fedcrimlaw.com

Devoted to federal criminal law, this site is sponsored by the publishers of *Punch and Jurists*, a weekly newsletter summarizing the most significant cases relating to the federal criminal justice system. Much of the site is restricted to those who pay the $199 annual subscription. For this, they get access to a database containing more than 6,000 full-text federal court opinions dealing with criminal law. Subscribers also obtain the full text of the weekly newsletter and access to resources such as model jury instructions and sample briefs. For non-subscribers, the free section provides excerpts from the newsletter and features such as "Crazy Cases," a collection of outrageous cases.

★★★★ **TnCrimLaw,** www.tncrimlaw.com

A collection of resources for Tennessee criminal defense lawyers, this simple site includes the state's rules of evidence and criminal procedure, updates on state legislation related to criminal law, and links to related state and national resources. It also includes more substantive materials, such as *The Manual on Recurring Problems in Criminal Trials*, a guide to the law governing many of the procedural matters that arise in criminal trials, originally prepared for the Federal Judicial Center.

★★★ **California Criminal Law Review,** www.boalt.org/CCLR

Students at the University of California at Berkeley's Boalt Hall School of Law have put together a completely online criminal law journal. The inaugural issue, published in February 2000, included articles on mental illness and the death penalty, and using international law to defend an accused. More recent volumes looked at consistency and fairness in sentencing, and theories of "virtual crime" (crimes committed using a computer), among other topics. Articles can be viewed in either HTML or PDF formats. References in footnotes are hyperlinked, when possible, to online sources of case law, statutes and journal articles. The articles are practical and nicely presented.

★★★ International Journal of Drug Testing, www.criminology.fsu.edu/journal

First published early in 2000, the International Journal of Drug Testing is devoted to publication of scientific research, technical applications, policy analysis and other issues related to drug testing. It is jointly sponsored by Florida State University and the University of South Florida, St. Petersburg. Full-text articles available online include "The Further Mismeasure: The Curious Use of Racial Categorizations in the Interpretation of Hair Analyses" and "An Analysis of Firefighter Drug Testing Under the Fourth Amendment."

★★★ Recovered Memory Archive Project, www.brown.edu/Departments/Taubman_Center/Recovmem/Archive.html

Can traumatic childhood events be forgotten and then remembered later in life? This site seeks to demonstrate that they can, by collecting and documenting cases of recovered memory. The site describes cases drawn from legal proceedings, scientific or academic studies, and elsewhere, in which lost childhood memories came back many years later. It includes a library of full-text articles, studies and research on the topic. If you have a case involving recovered memory, this site is likely to contain useful information.

★★ CriminalDefense.com, www.criminaldefense.com

On first click, this site looks promising, with a legal research section and a "Criminal Justice Knowledgebase." The research section is useful insofar as it provides search links to other legal Web sites. But try to search for articles or other resources within this site and the results are disappointing. The so-called knowledge base is a small collection of poorly edited articles, all at least a year old as of this writing. It appears the site's primary reason for being is as an attorney directory, but even there it fails. A search for a criminal defense lawyer in my state, for example, resulted in eight names—only four of whom were listed as criminal defense practitioners. The others included an IP lawyer, a sports lawyer and a private investigator. Listings provide no information about the lawyer, only an e-mail link.

★★ National White Collar Crime Center, www.nw3c.org

The National White Collar Crime Center—or NW3C as it calls itself—is a federally funded organization devoted to supporting law enforcement agencies involved in the prevention, investigation and prosecution of high-tech and economic crime. Together with the FBI, it helped establish the Internet Fraud Complaint Center. Its Web site has general information about initiatives in which it is involved, as well as a small collection of links to related resources. Plans are under way to add to the site a Cyber Resource Center, devoted to cyber crime, cyber security and cyber terrorism.

★★ Truth in Justice, www.truthinjustice.org

Truth in Justice is a non-profit organization devoting to freeing innocent men and women convicted of crimes they did not commit, and to preventing wrongful convictions. The Web site explores various cases of persons eventually freed from prison or still serving time. It includes resources that explore the reliability of eyewitness identifications and junk science.

★ gunlaws.com, www.gunlaws.com

Bloomfield Press, the Phoenix, Arizona publisher of *Gun Laws of America*, hosts this site, offering links to each state's laws on firearms and concealed weapons. The site includes general information about the company's books and articles on gun laws and ownership.

Death Penalty

★★★★★ Capital Defense Network, www.capdefnet.org

This resource-packed site provides support for federal capital defense counsel and habeas corpus assistance and training through detailed litigation guides, an appellate brief bank, summaries of cases since 1988 involving the death penalty, various facts and figures about death penalty trials, recent developments in capital cases, seminar materials and more.

★★★★★ Capital Defense Weekly, http://capitaldefenseweekly.com

This practical site offers several useful resources. Begin with "Capital Defense Weekly," its newsletter analyzing current court opinions and news developments relating to capital punishment. That is supplemented by the CDW blog,[1] with daily updates on capital cases. Then there is its Brief Bank,

---

[1] For more about blogs, see Chapter 27 *infra*.

a collection of appellate briefs in capital cases culled from various sources. The Brief Bank also includes selected motions and other pleadings, and various practice guides and manuals. The site includes ample collections of links, one specific to death penalty cases and another to more general reference materials. This useful site is hosted by Karl R. Keys, a lawyer in Bloomsbury, New Jersey.

★★★★ **Death Penalty Information Center,** www.deathpenaltyinfo.org

A large collection of research materials and issues analysis makes this a useful site, even though its audience is the media and the public, not practicing lawyers.

★★★ **The Justice Project Campaign for Criminal Justice Reform,** www.cjreform.org

Keeping innocent people off death row is the aim of this site and its sponsors. It provides support for and information about the proposed federal Innocence Protection Act, backed up by Profiles of Injustice, true stories of innocent people who spent time on death row. Other sections provide guides to legislation and excerpts from Congressional testimony.

★ **Death Penalty Resource Page,** www.romingerlegal.com/death-penalty.htm

A collection of links to Internet sites relating to the death penalty, created by the Web design company Rominger Legal Services, this site does not take a position for or against capital punishment, but provides links to a variety of resources from cases and brief banks to speeches and historical documents. The site is out of date, with several dead links.

Law Enforcement

★★★★★ **Zeno's Forensic Page,** http://forensic.to/forensic.html

A complete and well-organized list of resources for forensics, including a list of various research organizations and their specialties. The site includes sections for forensic sciences, forensic medicine and forensic psychiatry. This is one of the most complete lists of forensics links available on the Web as well as one of the most up-to-date.

★★★★ CopNet, www.copnet.org

This site offers an international collection of law enforcement links. While many links focus on police work, there are useful resources for lawyers involved in criminal justice. Links are divided between official police agency sites and other resources of interest to police. Snoop around and see what you can find.

★★★ Coplink.com, www.coplink.com

Lawyers engaged in criminal law, personal injury and other fields that involve them in police practices and procedures will find a useful set of links in this site, which is targeted at law enforcement personnel. "Coplink.Com" has compiled a comprehensive collection of links to law enforcement agencies and support services. They are organized under operational headings such as Narcotics, Traffic, Forensics and Crime Prevention. All links can be searched by key words. The site also includes message and discussion boards restricted to members of the law enforcement community. While here, you can listen to police radio scanners for New York, Dallas, San Diego and a handful of other cities.

★★★ Crime Scene Investigation, www.crime-scene-investigator.net

An overview of guidelines for crime scene response, collection and preservation of evidence and crime scene photography, with articles by police experts and links to related resources.

Associations

★★★★★ National Association of Criminal Defense Lawyers, www.criminaljustice.org

The NACDL's Web site is designed as both a public forum on criminal justice matters and as a private online service for NACDL members. The public part of the site features a wide-ranging array of information, including current NACDL news releases, legislative alerts, ethics opinions, and selected, full-text articles from current and past issues of NACDL's magazine, *The Champion*. The site takes an in-depth look at key criminal justice issues, providing news, articles and Web links. A members-only section includes a brief bank, a membership directory, and various practice aids.

★★★★★ National Legal Aid & Defender Association, www.nlada.org

NLADA's membership includes both civil and criminal lawyers representing indigent clients, so criminal lawyers will want to jump right to the section of the site labeled "Defender Resources." Here they will find NLADA's E-Library, an information clearinghouse containing substantive legal documents as well as information about program management, delivery of services, technology, training and conferences, government relations and communications. The site also includes a forensics library, with information on forensic science for criminal defense attorneys. A number of other features make this a useful and practical site.

★★★★ American Non-Governmental Organizations Coalition for the International Criminal Court, www.amicc.org

AMICC's name may be unwieldy, but the site it launched in 2002 is not. It is a comprehensive repository of information about the United States and its uncertain relationship with the International Criminal Court. In support of its goal to have the U.S. ratify the Rome Statute that created the ICC, AMICC devotes this useful and informative site to news, background and policy analysis.

★★★★ Criminal Justice Section, American Bar Association, www.abanet.org/crimjust/home.html

This site provides general information about the Section, its committees and events, including the annual meeting, criminal justice news, and upcoming seminars. The site's most substantive feature is the text of the ABA's Criminal Justice Standards, which cover topics such as discovery, guilty pleas, speedy trials, mental health and appeals. The site is home to the ABA's Juvenile Justice Center, a clearinghouse of information on juvenile justice and defense.

★★★ National District Attorneys Association, www.ndaa.org

The NDAA's Web site provides general information about the NDAA and its publications and programs. But it also serves as home to the American Prosecutors Research Institute, which provides a range of research and training materials on major program areas. These materials cover DNA forensics, gun violence, "community prosecution," child abuse, juvenile justice, traffic law, violence against women and white-collar crime. These materials help make this a substantive and useful site for prosecutors.

★★ Association of Federal Defense Attorneys, www.afda.org

Most of this site is restricted to members, who have access to a newsletter, research materials (including case summaries and a brief bank), a document library, information about training, and a legislative advocacy network. New users can register for a one-day pass.

★★ The Defender Association, www.defender.org

As this is the Web site of the Seattle, Washington public defender's office, the focus is Washington state law. But several segments of the site, devoted to special projects on the death penalty, juvenile justice, racial disparity and juvenile delinquency, make it worth a visit for anyone involved in these issues.

★ National Criminal Justice Association, www.ncja.org

The NCJA is the Washington, D.C.-based special interest group that represents states on crime control and public safety matters. The NCJA's work focuses primarily on helping develop and implement national policy in the criminal justice field and on helping states address criminal justice-related problems. Its Web site provides general information about association membership, events and publications. It includes highlights from recent issues of the NCJA's newsletter, *Justice Bulletin*, although full text is available only to members.

A Rich Vein of Environmental Resources

If you think you've had some bears for clients, consider British Columbia lawyer Ben van Drimmelen, whose Web address told it all: barristers4bears.com. Sure enough, at that site, no longer available, there was his photo, right on the front page, arms around a particularly grizzly professional acquaintance.

Van Drimmelen was not trapped in the claws of an unfortunate walk-in. To the contrary, this former forester and biologist was putting his training to good use, concentrating his practice—and his one-time Web site—on laws concerning natural resources such as fish, wildlife, forests and water.

Van Drimmelen reports that he intends to revive his site someday. Meanwhile, here is a look at some of the other sites on the World Wide Web devoted to environmental law.

Focus on the Law

From a practitioner's standpoint, many of the most useful sites are those specifically devoted to the topic of environmental law. Of these, some of the best have been created by lawyers or firms who practice in the field.

★★★★★ Envinfo.com, http://envinfo.com

The Morgan, Lewis & Bockius law firm sponsors this collection of environmental law information resources. Its most outstanding feature is the annual Environmental Deskbook, prepared by the firm's Environmental Practice Group as a convenient reference source for its clients, particularly client attorneys and others who are involved in environmental regulatory matters. Each Deskbook features articles on recent trends in environmental law, as well as updated versions of its regular annual sections: a regulatory calendar of selected environmental compliance deadlines, citations to federal environmental regulations, a description of the firm's environmental practice, an overview of federal environmental statutes, and an in-depth look at California and Florida environmental programs. Envinfo.com also serves as home to the "Information Network for Superfund Settlements," a service dedicated to the exchange of practical information concerning implementation of the Superfund program. The Network maintains a wide-ranging collection of EPA guidance documents, administrative orders and other relevant materials.

★★★★★ Environmental Law Net, http://lawvianet.com

David S. Blackmar, an environmental lawyer with Murtha Cullina LLP, Boston, created this rich and wide-ranging site in order to better serve his clients, who include general counsel, in-house attorneys and corporate environmental managers. He divides the site between two sets of resources: legal information libraries and "community resources." The libraries are really just collections of links to material elsewhere on the Web, but it is a thorough and well-organized set of links. It includes federal, state, international and tribal laws and regulations; court and agency decisions; agency documents and databases; resources for environmental compliance; materials relating to enforcement and litigation; and resources having to do with environmental aspects of real estate and corporate transactions. The community part of the site includes a daily news section, with press releases and other news compiled from various sources, and a "desk reference" of Internet tools useful to environmental lawyers. This is an ambitious and useful site.

★★★★★ North American Commission for Environmental Cooperation, www.cec.org

Created by Canada, Mexico and the United States under the North American Agreement for Environmental Cooperation, the CEC's goal is to help prevent potential trade and environmental conflicts, and to promote the effective enforcement of environmental law. A highlight of its resource-rich Web site is its detailed, treatise-like outline of North American environmental law, describing the laws of Canada, Mexico and the U.S. and providing links to original source materials. A newsletter and current news headlines review recent developments related to the North American environment.

★★★★ Pesticide.net, www.pesticide.net

This is a one-stop resource for up-to-date news, legal and regulatory information on conventional pesticides, bio-pesticides and antimicrobial pesticides. Maintained by the Lake Ridge, Virginia law firm Wright & Sielaty, this virtual library is comprehensive and current. Documents are indexed by topic, with sections for laws and legislation, regulations, court cases, guidance and policy, enforcement documents, registration forms and files, current news, news releases, Federal Register notices, and other topics. Much of the library consists of indexes of links to free sources elsewhere on the Web— in particular, the EPA itself—but the library offers the advantage of pulling it all together.

★★★★ Schnapf Environmental Law Information Resource Center, www.environmental-law.net

New York environmental lawyer Lawrence P. Schnapf, author of *Environmental Liability: Managing Environmental Risk in Corporate and Real Estate Transactions and Brownfield Redevelopment*, published by Lexis Law Publishing, hosts this site, which focuses on environmental law in New York, New Jersey and Connecticut, but covers federal and other state issues as well. It includes links to selected state environmental laws and a compendium of state sites having to do with brownfields and voluntary cleanup. A section on EPA guidance documents and regulations provides up-to-date links to documents on the EPA site and elsewhere. Smaller sections cover a variety of other environmental law topics.

★★★ Roger Beers' Environmental Litigation Pages, www. rbeerslaw.com

Oakland, California, environmental lawyer Roger Beers maintains this site, featuring a collection of his many articles on a wide variety of environmental law topics, including attorneys' fees, biological resources, discovery in environmental litigation, procedural obstacles, solid waste disposal, workplace exposure, and more. Unfortunately, most of the articles are at least two years old, and Beers warns that some are more than a decade old, so they may not reflect the current state of the law. Most of the articles indicate the date they were published or last updated.

★★ Cameron May, Environmental Law Publications, www. jus.uio.no/lm/index.html

For books about environmental law, visit this London-based publishing company specializing in international trade and international environmental law. Cameron May publishes the journals "International Trade Law Reports," "The Global Anti-Dumping Handbook," "International Trade Corruption Monitor," the "International Sanctions Reporter" and "Environmental Taxation & Accounting." You can peruse its catalog of books and journals online. It does not allow for secure ordering and payment through its Web site, but will accept orders by e-mail.

★★ Rocky Mountain Mineral Law Foundation, www.rmmlf.org

Organized in 1955, the Rocky Mountain Mineral Law Foundation is an educational organization providing seminars, courses and books on the legal aspects of issues affecting mineral and water resources. Headquartered in Denver, Colorado, it is a cooperative project of law schools, bar associations and industry associations. Its Web site serves primarily as a catalog of upcoming courses, describing them and listing the faculty, although there is no vehicle for registering online. The site includes a catalog of publications and articles offered by the foundation, although, again, there is no way to order these online. The foundation provides the full text online of its two newsletters, *Mineral Law Newsletter* and *Water Law Newsletter*.

Public Interest Advocacy

Public interest advocacy has long been a central focus of groups devoted to protecting the environment, as they have taken their battles to the courtroom and the legislature. Several groups either devoted to legal advocacy or for whom it is a key issue have established sites on the Internet.

★★★★★ Environmental Defense, www.environmentaldefense.org

With more than 300,000 members, Environmental Defense is a national non-profit organization that makes use of science, economics and law to address environmental issues. Its site is deep with fact sheets, primers, reports and analyses of major environmental topics. No mere collection of links, this site provides a rich research library, with full text reports on an array of topics compiled by a staff that includes more than seventy-five full-time lawyers, scientists and economists. Topics range from how hog lagoons in North Carolina are threatening public health to how to select seafood in an environmentally responsible way. Beyond reports, the site includes testimony and filings before regulatory agencies and other bodies, newsletters, press releases, and other documents.

★★★★★ Greenpeace International, www.greenpeace.org

Greenpeace may well be the epicenter of international environmental activism. Its wide-ranging and comprehensive Web site reflects that position. It serves as the umbrella for national and local Greenpeace organizations worldwide, all of which have their own distinct sites. It houses an archive of resources and materials posted to the Web dating back to 1994. There is detailed information on its various campaigns relating to toxics, nuclear waste, marine life, genetic engineering, and other issues. All of this is frequently updated with news and other features.

★★★★★ Natural Resources Defense Council, www.nrdc.org

This is a site deep with layers of informative and practical resources. There are sections for each major environmental topic: clean air and energy, global warming, clean water and oceans, wildlife and fish, parks and forests, toxic chemicals, nuclear weapons and waste, and cities and green living. Within each of those sections are even deeper layers of subsections with information on specific aspects of the topic. A legislative section includes in-depth legislative analyses, reports and testimony. Throughout the site are current news articles and legislative bulletins. *Onearth*, the NRDC's quarterly magazine, is here in full. Topping off the site is a collection of links to other environmental resources on the Internet.

★★★★★ Sierra Club, www.sierraclub.org

With more than 600,000 members, the Sierra Club is a leading environmental organization. Its site includes selected articles from its publications and information on its various programs. It also houses archives of the Club's legislative-alert mailing list. Its up-to-the-minute site offers news and detailed reports on its current campaigns and political activities.

★★★★ Center for International Environmental Law, www. ciel.org

CIEL is a non-profit, environmental law firm based in Washington, D.C., the focus of which is on international and comparative environmental law and policy. Its work encompasses policy research and publication, advice and advocacy, education and training, and support for institutions. The site, updated frequently, offers descriptions of CIEL programs, online newsletters, and other original materials. Among the topics it covers are biodiversity, climate change, human rights and the environment, trade and the environment, and organic pollutants. Of particular interest is its Law and Communities Program, which focuses on how environmental laws, as written and enforced, often fail to protect citizens and resources in rural areas in developing countries.

★★★★ Earthjustice Legal Defense Fund, www.earthjustice.org

Earth Day 1998 was the launch date for this Web site, from the environmental law firm formerly known as the Sierra Club Legal Defense Fund. Featuring striking nature photography and compellingly written text, the site provides details about the ELDF's key program areas as well as a docket of current cases. Action Alerts assist visitors in sending e-mail to lawmakers on various environmental issues.

★★★★ Environmental Law Institute, www.eli.org

This site is home to the *Environmental Law Reporter,* a subscription periodical, available both in print and online, that provides current, in-depth reports on environmental law, including court decisions, legislative news and regulatory updates. A free trial is offered to non-subscribers. ELI's site also includes general information about the organization, which describes itself as seeking to advance environmental protection by improving law, policy and management. Of particular interest is ELI's library of research reports and briefs, which you can purchase here in hard copy or download for free in Adobe Acrobat format.

★★★★ World Wildlife Fund, www.wwf.org

This is the umbrella site for the WWF's global network of conservation organizations. The site offers ample news and publications related to protecting wildlife—its one fault may be that its scope is too broad, leaving the visitor uncertain where to start. This is an interesting site for those concerned about wildlife, but it offers little overall of substance for lawyers.

★★★ Environmental Law Alliance Worldwide, www.elaw.org

The Environmental Law Alliance Worldwide—or E-Law, as it calls itself—is a network of more than 300 environmental advocates from sixty countries. Its members include public interest lawyers, scientists and other environmental advocates. From its Web site, you can review a list of its organizational members, read about some of its key court victories, and review .pdf versions of its newsletters reporting environmental law news and activities of its members. The site includes an extensive collection of links to international environmental laws and legal resources.

★★Burning Issues, www.webcom.com/~bi

Burning Issues is a group involved in fighting pollution caused by smoke from wood-burning stoves, wood-burning ovens in restaurants, and outdoor burning of wood debris. Its modest Web site includes reports on legal developments, links to studies and policy reports, and news stories.

★★ EcoNet, www.igc.org/home/econet/index.html

Once a comprehensive, substantive Web site with news, action alerts, feature articles and extensive links, EcoNet is now only a shadow of its former self, with a half-dozen links and a small collection of recent news articles.

News

Keeping current with the latest developments in environmental law is crucial. Here are sites that help.

★★★★★ Planet Ark, www.planetark.org

Calling itself "[y]our daily guide to helping the planet," Planet Ark offers World Environment News, daily environmental updates from Reuter's News Agency featuring full-text news stories on environment-related topics from throughout the world. Visitors to the site can sign up to receive the daily headlines via e-mail. An ancillary feature is Reuters Environment News Pictures, with photographs from throughout the world. Both the news and photo archives are searchable. The site also hosts the Australian Broadcasting Corporation's radio program World Environment News, a weekly review of major stories. The Australia-based Planet Ark Environmental Foundation sponsors the site.

★★★★ Capitol Reports Environmental News Link, www.caprep.com

Environmental News Link is a free, daily environmental news service. The front page lists news items in brief, with links to longer stories. A separate news digest page organizes news by topic. The site also provides extensive links to legislation, court decisions and agency actions, both federal and state, relating to environmental law.

★★★★ Environmental News Network, www.enn.com

ENN reports environmental news seven days a week, and its site is updated throughout the day. Its core is ENN Daily News, original news reports produced by ENN's own staff of reporters. Supplementing this is the ENN World

Wire, a package of news gathered from news services such as Reuters, AP and others. ENN Direct allows ENN affiliates to submit press releases and have them posted directly online. Along with these news products is a selection of audio and video programming and a daily ENN news webcast.

★★ Endangered Species & Wetlands Report, www.eswr.com

This monthly print newsletter covers the Endangered Species Act, wetlands and private property rights issues. It focuses on Congress, the federal courts and federal agencies. The Web site provides only the front pages of recent issues, published online in .pdf format. The site's "Federal Register Report," updated daily, links to Federal Register notices from the Fish and Wildlife Service and the National Marine Fisheries Service.

Government

★★★★★ Agency for Toxic Substances and Disease Registry, www.atsdr.cdc.gov

This agency's purpose is to prevent exposure to hazardous substances from waste sites, unplanned releases, and other sources of pollution. Among the most useful features of its site are HazDat, a database of hazardous substances and their health effects, and "ToxFAQs," short summaries about hazardous substances excerpted from ATSDR Toxicological Profiles.

★★★★★ California Environmental Resources Evaluation System, http://ceres.ca.gov

The California Environmental Resources Evaluation System—or CERES—is an information system developed by the California Resources Agency to facilitate access to a variety of electronic data regarding the state's environmental resources. Its goal is to improve environmental analysis and planning by integrating information from multiple sources and contributors. It is an attractive and well-organized site, with information organized in multiple ways, allowing visitors to browse by geographic area, theme, data type and organization. A section devoted to environmental law includes the full text of applicable state and federal laws and regulations, selected court opinions, and special focuses on water law and policy and land use law. Included is a library of documents for state government attorneys, with information on public records, open meetings, administrative law and the state legal system.

★★★★★ **Environmental Protection Agency,** www.epa.gov

From acid rain and agriculture to wastewater and wetlands, the one indispensable government resource for the environmental lawyer is the Web site of the Environmental Protection Agency. This well-designed and easy-to-navigate site is home to the full text of laws and regulations, press releases, newsletters, and other EPA documents. It has complete

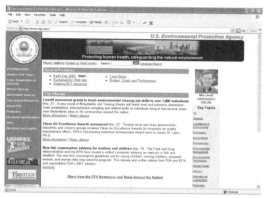

The Environmental Protection Agency includes the full text of laws and regulations.

information on agency programs, offices and publications. Use the site's "browse" feature to bring up a list of every covered topic and its related resources.

★★★★★ **U.S. Department of Agriculture,** www.usda.gov

When we think USDA, we think farms. But did you know that Smokey Bear works for the USDA? Its Forest Service is responsible for protecting the nation's 192 million acres of national forests and rangelands. And you probably did not know that the USDA's Natural Resources Conservation Service oversees some 3,000 conservation districts across the U.S. Its Web site has extensive information on these programs and more, along with agency reports, news releases, speeches and the comprehensive Agriculture Fact Book.

★★★★★ **U.S. Department of the Interior,** www.doi.gov

The Interior Department is the federal agency responsible for the management of more than half a million acres of federal lands, including the entire National Park System and vast tracts of federal lands, mostly in the western regions of the country. DOI is also responsible for enforcing laws that protect nearly 2,000 threatened and endangered species and that govern the management of national wildlife refuges. Its divisions include the Bureau of Indian Affairs, the Bureau of Land Management, the Bureau of Reclamation, the Fish and Wildlife Service, the U.S. Geological Survey, the Minerals Management Service, the National Park Service, the Office of Surface Mining and the Office of Insular Affairs. Its site has a broad collection of resources relating to preserving and protecting natural resources.

★★★★ EnviroMapper, www. epa.gov/enviro/html/em/ index.html

Created by the Environmental Protection Agency, EnviroMapper is sort of a road map for the environment. You can use it to map out environmental information on drinking water, toxic chemical releases, air quality, hazardous waste, water discharge permits, and Superfund sites. Start with a map of the U.S., then zoom in as close as you like.

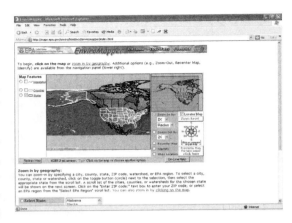

The EPA's EnviroMapper targets the location of Superfund sites in any area of the U.S.

Lawyers can use EnviroMapper for various purposes: locate a tax incentive zone for a Brownfield, view information on EPA-regulated facilities in your vicinity, or obtain environmental statistics and profiles.

★★★★ Enviroene, http://es.epa.gov

Technically part of the EPA site, this is really a Web site unto itself. It is an attempt to provide a single repository for information and databases relating to pollution prevention, compliance assurance, and enforcement. In addition to a wealth of information on these topics, Enviroene also provides access to funding, grants and environmental research publications.

★★★★ U.S. Department of Energy, www.energy.gov

Here you can find scientific and technical information relating to sources of energy and their impact on the environment. The site includes extensive information on nuclear waste and environmental safety and health. There is also information on the DOE's own environmental cleanup activities.

★★★★ U.S. Fish and Wildlife Service, www.fws.gov

Part of the Department of the Interior, the Fish and Wildlife Service's site has extensive information on its many programs relating not just to fish and wildlife, but also endangered species, wetlands and coastal ecosystems. Follow the "Law Enforcement" link for the text of statutes, administrative regulations, treaties, executive orders, interstate compacts and memoranda of agreement enforced by or relating to the Service.

★★★★ U.S. Geological Survey, Water Resources of the U.S., http://h2o.usgs.gov

Extensive data and publications about U.S. and state water resources.

★★★ NASA, Destination: Earth, www.earth.nasa.gov

NASA's focus may be outer space, but its "Destination: Earth" project is using information gathered from out there to help predict how weather and climate will affect the environment down here. A fascinating site to explore, although with only marginal usefulness to the practice of environmental law.

★★★ U.S. Department of Justice, Environmental and Natural Resources Division, www.usdoj.gov/enrd

With more than 600 employees, the Division is involved in more than 10,000 open environmental cases and describes itself as "the nation's environmental lawyer." Its Web site describes the Division's organization and features a library of legal documents, including model consent decrees and proposed consent decrees for certain CERCLA actions. Also here are Division press releases and selected guidance and standards documents in full text.

★★★ U.S. EPA Online Library System, www.epa.gov/natlibra/ols.htm

This is the virtual "card catalog" for EPA's library network. Use it to locate EPA books, reports and audiovisual materials. You can search several library collections, including the EPA's comprehensive National Catalog and various specialized catalogs. Once you locate a publication you want, you may have to visit the nearest EPA library to obtain it. This site includes complete information on where and how to obtain these publications.

Laws and Treaties

★★★★★ Environmental Treaties and Resource Indicators, http://sedac.ciesin.columbia.edu:9080/entri/index.jsp

This site allows you to query various databases in order to determine specific information about environmental treaties. For example, you can determine which treaties are in force for a particular country, or which treaties govern a particular subject. You can also browse treaties by title. All the treaties are available in full text. The site is operated by the Consortium for International Earth Science Information Network.

★★★★ Globelaw, www.globelaw.com

This storehouse of international environmental materials is now the home of much of the material formerly housed by Greenpeace International at its now defunct Multilateral Environmental Treaties site. Composed of original documents and links, is a comprehensive index to environmental law resources on the Web. It provides a guide to finding multilateral treaties, conventions and laws both specific to environmental law and on broader matters of international law. It also lists resources on specific topics such as climate change, nuclear testing, toxic waste and biodiversity. Included are selected court and arbitration opinions on key environmental topics.

★★★★ Legal Information Institute's U.S. Code, www. law.cornell. edu/uscode

Cornell University's Legal Information Institute's hypertext U.S. Code includes complete U.S. environmental laws. Major laws found there include:

- CERCLA (Superfund), http://www.law.cornell.edu/uscode/42/ch103. html
- Clean Air Act, http://www.law.cornell.edu/uscode/42/ch85.html
- Clean Water Act, http://www.law.cornell.edu/uscode/33/ch26.html

★★★ Pace Virtual Environmental Law Library, http://joshua. law.pace.edu/env/vell6.html

Created in 1998, this site offers an exhaustive collection of links to U.S. and international laws, treaties and other primary sources of environmental law. Unfortunately, it appears as though the site is no longer maintained. While much of the site remains current and useful, some links use out-of-date URLs and others point to sites that no longer exist.

★★ Environmental Law Centre, University of Victoria, www. elc.uvic.ca

This student-run law clinic at the University of Victoria, Canada, recently began posting to its Web site research memoranda its students and staff have prepared on a range of environmental law and public policy topics. The site also has a small collection of environmental law links.

★ **WetLands.com,** www.wetlands.com

Hosted by a private environmental services company, this site offers the text of selected federal wetlands regulations and proposed regulations. When last visited, some parts of it had not seen updates in several years.

Law Reviews

★★★ **Environmental Law,** www.lclark.edu/org/envtl

Established in 1969, this law review claims to be the oldest one dedicated solely to environmental issues. It is published quarterly by students at Northwestern School of Law at Lewis & Clark College in Portland, Oregon. Although tables of contents for issues back to 1995 are available on this site, full text of articles begins in 2000 with volume 30—a special thirtieth anniversary issue on the development of environmental law over those three decades. The most recent year's issues are available only through a link to WestLaw, which requires a WestLaw subscription.

★ **The Environmental Lawyer,** www.law.gwu.edu/stdg/envlwr

The Environmental Lawyer is a law review published as a joint venture between the American Bar Association's Section of Natural Resources, Energy, and Environmental Law and the George Washington University Law School. The Web site provides only abstracts of articles, no full text. Even worse, they are undated, showing only the volume in which they appeared, the title and the author. Nothing on the site keys volume numbers to dates, so one is unable to determine the age of an article.

Other law reviews that focus on environmental law include:

- **Colorado Journal of International Environmental Law & Policy,** www.colorado.edu/Law/cjielp. No text available online.
- **Duke Environmental Law & Policy Forum,** www.law.duke. edu/ journals/delpf. Full text articles.
- **Ecology Law Quarterly, University of California Berkeley,** www.law.berkeley.edu/journals/elq. Tables of contents only.
- **Fordham Environmental Law Journal,** http://law.fordham.edu/publications/index.ihtml?pubid=100. Tables of contents and selected abstracts.
- **Georgetown International Environmental Law Review,** www.law.georgetown.edu/journals/gielr/. Selected abstracts only.
- **Hastings West-Northwest Journal of Environmental Law and Policy,** www.uchastings.edu/wnw. Tables of contents.

- **Journal of Environmental Law & Litigation,** www.law.uoregon. edu/~jell. No articles or abstracts. Only information on subscribing to the Journal and contacting its editors.
- **New York University Environmental Law Journal,** www.law. nyu.edu/ journals/envtllaw/. Full text articles.
- **Oxford University Journal of Environmental Law,** www3.oup. co.uk/ jnls/list/envlaw. Full text of articles since 1996 is available.
- **Pace Environmental Law Review,** www.law.pace.edu/pelr/index. html. Tables of contents are provided, but not full-text articles.
- **Tulane Environmental Law Journal,** www.law.tulane.edu/tuexp/ journals/enviro/index.html. Tables of contents only.
- **Villanova Environmental Law Journal,** http://vls.law.vill.edu/students/orgs/elj. No articles online, but the site provides details on subscribing and submitting articles, and contact information for the editorial board.

Non-Legal Resources

These sites offer scientific or technical information related to the practice of environmental law:

★★★★★ Scorecard, www.scorecard.org

Scorecard might just be the Erin Brockovich of the World Wide Web. Who knew that the rural, seaside county in which I live ranked among the worst 20% of all counties in the U.S. for air quality? Scorecard knew. Type in a zip code to find complete information on air pollution, water contamination, Superfund sites, toxic chemical releases, and other environmental horrors for your location. Run by the folks at Environmental Defense, www.environmentaldefense.org, Scorecard integrates more than 300 governmental and scientific databases to create a potent weapon for local environmental activists.

★ Environmental Information Resources, www.gwu.edu/ ~greenu/ index2.html

This site, published as part of a partnership between the EPA and George Washington University, appears not to have been updated since July 1997. It provides an extensive collection of links to environmental resources on the Internet, organized by subject, name or country. Unfortunately, many of the links are dead.

Membership Organizations

★★★ **American Bar Association, Section of Environment, Energy and Resources,** www.abanet.org/environ

Here you will find general information about this ABA Section, including a calendar of events, a roster of committees, descriptions of committee activities, and information on Section publications. The section has some twenty-five committees, on topics from agricultural management to water resources, and each committee's newsletter is available through the Section's publications page.

Estate Planning with Help from the Web

If the only certainties in life are death and taxes, then it is easy to understand the value of an estate planning lawyer, whose job it is to apply the laws governing both.

For the lawyers who toil in this field, the Internet offers a way to research tax and probate laws, keep current with new developments, and even obtain sample estate plans.

While there are a surprisingly large number of estate planning sites on the Web, the unfortunate fact is that the bulk of them are aimed at consumers and offer little of use to professionals. This chapter includes a sampling of those consumer sites, but concentrates on sites useful to the estate planning professional.

Starting Points

Sometimes, getting started is the hardest part of legal research. These sites serve as roadmaps to the many estate planning materials available on the Internet.

★★★★★ **Estate Planning Law Materials,** www.law.cornell.edu/topics/estate_planning.html

If it is law you are seeking, the place to start is the Cornell University Legal Information Institute's page. Here you will find hypertext versions of Subtitle B of Title 26 of the United States Code, covering federal estate and gift taxes, as well as the related provisions of the Code of Federal Regulations. Also available are recent U.S. Supreme Court cases related to estate and gift taxes, and the texts of the Uniform Probate Code, Uniform Principal and Income Act, Uniform Trusts Act and Uniform Fiduciaries Act. The LII also includes links to state probate, property and tax statutes.

★★★★★ Estate Planning Links Web Site, www.estateplanninglinks.com

This may well be the most extensive collection of links to Web sites relating to estate planning, estate and gift tax, other taxes, elder law, probate, trusts, charitable planning and philanthropy, estate planning software, and related issues. Originally compiled in 1995 by Dennis M. Kennedy, then a trusts and estates lawyer in St. Louis, Missouri, it is now maintained by Dennis Toman, an elder-law attorney in Greensboro, North Carolina.

★★★★★ Legal Research for Estate Planners, www.jasonhavens.net

This is a comprehensive, well-organized and up-to-date collection of links to estate planning resources on the Web. Created by Jason E. Havens, an estate planning lawyer in Destin, Florida, this annotated guide covers both national and state-specific sites and also indexes sites by topic and type of resource.

Lawyer Resources

Far too many estate planning sites on the Web focus on consumers, offering the why and how of financial planning. More valuable to lawyers are the sites that track current legal developments, provide in-depth analysis and offer practice-proven tips. The following fit that bill, or at least try to.

★★★★★ The Tax Prophet, www.taxprophet.com

The Tax Prophet is San Francisco lawyer and columnist Robert L. Sommers. Sommers writes prolifically for the *San Francisco Examiner* and elsewhere on a variety of tax topics, estate planning among them. His Web site, collecting his many columns and scholarly articles, is popular among professionals and consumers alike. From the main page, follow the "Estate Planning" link to find his articles on estate and gift-tax planning and asset protection.

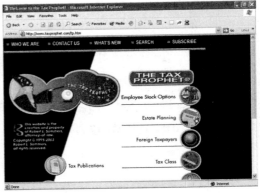

Estate planning is among the Tax Prophet's topics.

★★★★ RIA, www.riahome.com

This publisher of tax research products and software, created from the merger of Research Institute of America and Warren, Gorham & Lamont, maintains a sizable catalog of estate planning products. Some are in print or on CD-ROM, but many are also offered in formats that RIA delivers via the Web, meaning that you can retrieve them from anywhere you have access to the Internet. These Web products include the monthly newsletter, "Estate Planner's Alert"; the more analytical "Estate Planning Journal"; the book, "Estate Planning Law & Taxation"; and several others. Although on the Web, they are not free. An annual subscription to "Estate Planner's Alert", for example, was $185. RIA offers free trials of some of its Web-based products and free demos of others. To find these estate planning materials from the home page, follow the link to "Estate Planning Research."

★★★★ Trusts and Estates.net, www.trustsandestates.net

There is something unassumingly homespun about this site, from Fort Worth, Texas, estate planning lawyer Noel C. Ice. Take, for example, the front page link to a photo of a bucolic, snow-capped mountain, titled "Where I Would Rather Be." But beneath the amateurish façade of this site, there is real substance. Ice has authored a virtual treatise on distributions from qualified plans and IRAs, which is available here in toto. He also offers a complete series of "nutshell" guides to estate planning topics, written for non-lawyers. A variety of other articles fill out the site, some written for lawyers, others for consumers.

★★★ CCH Federal and State Tax, http://tax.cchgroup.com

Follow the "Estate Planning" link for this tax and business law publisher's catalog of print and electronic products on estate planning. Its online offerings include CCH Solutions for Financial Planning, a Web-based library written by financial planning experts that includes analysis and guidance, practical observations and advice, sample forms and documents, checklists, and more. Also featured is the Financial and Estate Planning Library, a comprehensive, online library that combines electronic versions of several CCH publications to provide daily news, in-depth analysis, expert commentary, full-text laws, financial calculators, interactive tax forms, and other practical features.

The site offers complete information on pricing of these products, any of which can be purchased directly through the site.

★★★ **Hale and Dorr Private Client Bulletin,** www.haledorr.com/ practices/prac_publications.asp?groupID=7

Formerly titled "Trusts and Estates Bulletin," this newsletter from the Boston-based law firm Hale and Dorr publishes articles focusing on current developments of interest to trusts and estates lawyers. This site includes all issues since 1994.

★★★ **Michigan Probate & Estate Planning Journal,** www.icle.org/ sections/probate/journal/about.htm

This quarterly journal from the State Bar of Michigan publishes articles that are of interest to estate planners outside as well as in Michigan. Complete issues are available dating back to 1995, all in PDF format.

★★★ **SeniorLaw,** www.seniorlaw.com

SeniorLaw is described as a Web site where senior citizens, their families, attorneys, social workers and financial planners can access information about elder law, Medicare, Medicaid, estate planning, trusts, and the rights of the elderly and disabled. Hosted by the New York City law firm Goldfarb Abrandt Salzman & Kutzin, it features collections of links to both elder law resources and elder law attorneys on the Web. The site is periodically updated with news about changes in the law and important court rulings. A small library features articles on elder law.

★★★ **Trusts & Trustees,** www.trusts-and-trustees.com

Trusts & Trustees is a Web site about international trusts from the publishers of the journal of the same name. In addition to a selection of full-text articles on the uses and formation of international trusts, the site includes case notes, opinion and trend articles analyzing developments in trust law, and book reviews. For the most part, the full-text articles come from older issues of the journal; for more recent issues, only summaries of articles are available. Also included are summaries of court decisions, although these, too, are from older issues. You will have to buy a subscription to see the most recent articles and cases. Throughout, the focus is on the law of the United Kingdom, where the journal is published.

★★ **National Directory of Estate Planning,** Probate & Elder Law Attorneys, www.search-attorneys.com

This directory lists estate planning, probate and trust attorneys throughout the U.S. and Canada. It can be searched by location, attorney name or firm name. Each listing provides basic information about the firm and a link to its Web site. Lawyers can add their own listings at no charge.

★ **Estate Planning Legal Research Guide,** www.law.ukans.edu/library/este_res.htm

From the University of Kansas School of Law, this is a simple card-catalog style listing of treatises on the topic of estate planning, with a handful of links thrown in for good measure.

Associations

Bar association sites vary in substance and depth. Some provide only general membership information, while others strive to provide deeper levels of information useful to their members. In the field of estate planning, several of the "associations" are really something different—networks of attorneys that resemble franchises, brought together under a single company that provides marketing support and practice materials.

★★★★ **National Academy of Elder Law Attorneys,** www.naela.com

The National Academy of Elder Law Attorneys is an organization of lawyers who concentrate in legal issues affecting the elderly and disabled, including estate planning, guardianship and conservatorship, public benefits, and health care planning. NAELA divides its Web site into a restricted area for members and a public area. The public area has several useful features. For those seeking a lawyer, NAELA provides a directory of its members, which can be searched by lawyer name, firm name, location or area of specialization. NAELA's collection of links is particularly well done, with each link annotated with a brief description. The private members' area contains a member directory, publications, special-interest group sections and other academy information.

★★★ **American Bar Association Section on Real Property, Probate and Trust Law,** www.abanet.org/rppt/home.html

This site offers general information about Section activities, membership and publications. It has the full text of *Probate & Property*, its bimonthly magazine, although access to many articles is restricted to Section members, while only selected articles are available to non-members. It also has the tables of contents of *Real Property, Probate & Trust Journal*, although, again, full text of the articles is available only to Section members. Visitors can browse a catalog of estate planning books published by the ABA and make purchases online. Rounding out the site are information on Section-sponsored e-mail discussion lists and a small collection of links. As is often the case with ABA sections, the more you drill down through the committee and subcommittee pages, the more you will find in the way of useful articles and reports.

★★★ American College of Trust and Estate Counsel, www.actec.org

ACTEC limits part of its Web site to its members. The public area provides a well-organized collection of links to estate planning and other Internet resources. It also has the tables of contents from its newsletter, but no ability to retrieve the full text of any article. A public area membership section allows anyone to search for ACTEC fellows by name or location.

★ American Academy of Estate Planning Attorneys, www.aaepa.com

The American Academy of Estate Planning Attorneys is more akin to a franchise company than a legal association. It provides lawyers with systems and products aimed at helping them start and build an estate planning practice. Members receive instruction in marketing, public relations, technology and practice building as well as various tools to support these efforts. This is AAEPA's public Web site, largely a sales and marketing brochure aimed at attorneys who might be interested in becoming members. For attorneys who do join, AAEPA has a separate, password-protected site with practice-building ideas, articles on legal trends, a member discussion board, online ordering of AAEPA products, registration for AAEPA events, and links to other estate planning sites.

★ Estate Planning Partners, www.estateplanningpartners.com

This is the home page of Integrity Marketing Solutions, a marketing and practice development firm for estate planning lawyers. Brochure-like in its format, it gives an overview of the firm's services and products.

★ National Network of Estate Planning Attorneys, www.netplanning.com

The National Network of Estate Planning Attorneys is a network of estate planning law firms. Lawyers who join this organization obtain assistance in setting up and marketing an estate planning practice. Its Web site is divided between a section for consumers and one for lawyers. The consumer section provides general information about estate planning and allows visitors to request a referral to an estate planning lawyer. The lawyer section has general information about the services NNEPA provides and the procedures for becoming a member.

Consumer Resources

The majority of estate planning sites on the Web cater to consumers. Usually hosted by lawyers or financial planners, these sites offer information as an attraction, in the hope that visitors who peruse them might also retain their host's services. Some of these sites are useful to lawyers as well, providing attorneys who are unfamiliar with the finer points of estate planning with easily understood overviews, and sometimes focusing on somewhat esoteric matters for which information is not easily available.

★★★★ Crash Course in Wills and Trusts, www.mtpalermo.com

What started as an outline by Kentucky lawyer Michael T. Palermo for an adult education class at a local community college evolved into this fairly detailed, hyperlinked manuscript covering the basics of estate planning. Browse the table of contents for specific chapters or flip page by page through the entire work. This award-winning site has been online for several years, but Palermo keeps it current with updates reflecting developments in the law. Although targeted at consumers, the site is sure to be of value to lawyers as well.

★★★★ Viatical Settlements, www.viatical-expert.net

What, you may ask, are viatical settlements? Sometimes called "accelerated death benefits," they come into play when the terminally ill sell their death benefits to investors to raise cash for medical expenses, living costs, or whatever else. Gloria Grening Wolk, a financial planner, social worker and advocate, has written two guidebooks on viatical settlements, one for the terminally ill and the other for investors. This is her site, with information both on her book and on the general topic. For investors, she names names, listing viatical companies that are licensed by state authorities as well as those that are "on the hot seat"—the subjects of state enforcement actions or private lawsuits. Wolk also provides an overview of state viatical licensing laws and other practical information.

★★★ CourtTV's Wills of the Famous, www.courttv.com/legal-docs/newsmakers/wills

From Babe Ruth and Shoeless Joe Jackson to Joe DiMaggio, from Marilyn Monroe to Princess Diana, from Elvis and Lennon to Jerry Garcia, their wills are all here. Entertainment value, sure, but there are lessons in estate planning here as well, as the wealthy and famous maneuver to avoid the death tax.

★★★ Layne Rushforth's Estate Planning Pages, http://rushforth.net

Nevada lawyer Layne T. Rushforth offers this collection of articles, news, memoranda and forms on basic and advanced estate planning topics. The articles, written for non-lawyers, cover general topics such as estate reduction, irrevocable trusts, charitable trusts and asset protection.

★★★ Nolo Press, Wills and Estate Planning, www.nolo.com/category/ep_home.html

From the California-based publisher of self-help legal books and software comes this useful site, where consumers can find answers to frequently asked questions on various estate planning topics. In addition to a variety of FAQs, the site includes the Nolo *Encyclopedia*, with detailed articles on topics such as "What Kind of Estate Plan Is Right For You?" Also, Nolo's "Auntie Nolo" features plain English answers to visitors' legal questions on estate planning and other issues.

★★ Law Office of Emanuel Haas, http://counselornet.com/emhesq

New York lawyer Emanuel Haas provides a collection of FAQs for consumers on estate planning topics.

★★ Robert Clofine's Elder Law and Estate Planning Page, www.estateattorney.com

Devoted to providing estate, tax, elder law and related financial planning information for consumers, this site was created by Robert Clofine, a Pennsylvania lawyer. The articles collected here, although modest in number, are more informative than many similar offerings on other lawyers' Web sites and include timely updates.

★★ SaveWealth.com, www.savewealth.com

The Preservation Group, a financial services company, sponsors this site, aimed at providing families with information on how to build and preserve wealth. It includes a fairly detailed guide to estate planning, written in easily understood terms, that covers introductory questions and more advanced topics such as different types of trusts. However, the site provides no clear direction on how to obtain professional assistance in estate planning matters.

★ Artful Dodger's Guide to Planning Your Estate, www.thawley.com

The subject of this site is described as "The only book on estate planning guaranteed to keep you entertained." Written by California lawyer Thomas

Hart Hawley as a guide to "anyone who has acquired even modest wealth," the book can be sampled here through brief excerpts. The site includes ordering information.

★ Wealth Transfer Group, www.wealth-transfer.com

This Florida consultancy serves only clients with estates in excess of $10 million. The main attraction of its Web site is its newsletter archives, which offer articles useful to professionals and non-professionals alike. Unfortunately, the archives are not searchable, so must be browsed issue by issue, and are not regularly updated with new articles.

Attorney Virginia L. Weber, www.virginiaweber.com

A simple FAQ on estate planning is about the only feature of this San Diego, California, lawyer's site.

State-Specific Sites

★★★★ California Estate Planning, Probate and Trust Law, www.ca-probate.com

California lawyer Mark J. Welch created this site, which he later sold to its current operator, the Castleman Law Firm, Pleasanton, California. Although oriented to consumers, the site also offers much for lawyers, regardless of whether they live in California. Unfortunately, what was once one of the best estate planning sites on the Web is now becoming slightly out of date, with some expired links. Among the site's features are an analysis of estate and gift tax aspects of the 1997 Budget Act; a collection of articles by Welch, Lorin Castleman and others; a forms library; and links to other estate planning sites. Probably the most popular feature is the site's collection of links to wills on the Web—a collection that includes the wills of celebrities such as Princess Diana, Jacqueline Kennedy Onassis, Elvis Presley and Marilyn Monroe as well as those of ordinary people, in some cases dating to the fifteenth and sixteenth centuries.

★★★★ Pennsylvania Estate and Trust Cybrary, http://evans-legal.com/dan

This is the Web site of Philadelphia lawyer Daniel B. Evans. An active member of and frequent author for the American Bar Association's Real Property, Probate and Trust Law and Small Firm Management sections, Evans' Web site contains the text of a number of useful articles on estate planning, practice management and legal technology.

★★★★ Texas Probate Web Site, www.texasprobate.com

Maintained by Glenn M. Karisch, a partner with Barnes & Karisch, Austin, Texas, Texas Probate is focused on helping lawyers keep current with estate planning and probate law in Texas. It grew out of Karisch's efforts to track and report on probate legislation in the state, and the legislation section remains a primary feature, with up-to-date information on legislation affecting estate planning, probate law and trust law. Legislative coverage includes bill tracking, analysis, final versions and an end-of-session wrap-up. A collection of links, originally prepared by Karisch for a presentation at the 1999 annual meeting of the American College of Trust and Estate Counsel, includes his annotations, with the best earning his "four chili pepper" rating. Rounding out the site are libraries of forms and articles on Texas estate planning and probate law.

★ Massachusetts Estate Planning Forum, www.elderlaw.com

This a collection of brief, consumer-oriented estate planning FAQs from the law firm Feigenbaum & Uddo.

Software

Companies that design software for estate planning lawyers sometimes offer samples for downloading from their Web sites. We have visited a few of those sites, but have not sampled the software.

★ Cowles Legal Systems, www.cowleslegal.com

Cowles Legal Systems designs software for estate planning lawyers. From its Web site, you can view demonstration versions of its various products for trusts, wills and estates.

★ Leimberg & LeClair, www.leimberg.com

Leimberg & LeClair publishes books, software and audiotapes for estate planning professionals. Its Web site allows you to browse its catalog of products.

Discussion Lists

Need a quick answer to a question about the finer points of estate planning? Two e-mail discussion lists focus on this topic. From these Web sites, you can find out how to join, read and search archives of previous postings.

★★★★ ABA-PTL Archives, http://mail.abanet.org/archives/aba-ptl.html

The "PTL" is for probate and trust law; the "ABA" is for American Bar Association. This site is home to the archives of this e-mail list, which is sponsored by the Real Property, Probate & Trust Law Section of the ABA and devoted to discussion of estate planning and administration. Founded in 1995, ABA-PTL is one of the longest-running discussion lists for lawyers. Here, you can peruse all the messages that have been posted to the list. If you want to post your own, you will have to subscribe first. To do that, click on the "join the list" link and follow the instructions.

★★★★ Gift-pl archives, www.listserv.iupui.edu/archives/gift-pl.html

This is home to the archives of discussions from the Gift-pl e-mail list, devoted to the topic of gift planning. It includes the full text of every message posted to this list since May 1996. The list had some 2,000 subscribers as of August 2000, most of whom were professionals and development officers in planned giving throughout the U.S. and Canada, as well as a number of attorneys and accountants.

Chapter 9

Family Feuds: Divorce, Custody and Child Support

Family law—divorce and child custody—may be the most ubiquitous field of law practice. That makes it all the more surprising how few family law resources there are on the Internet of true usefulness to practicing lawyers.

Although there are thousands of law firms with their own Web sites, it seems that only a relative handful of them concentrate on family law practice. And where, for other fields of law, significant libraries of online resources continue to be developed, there remains little of significance to the family practitioner.

This is not to say that there is a scarcity of sites devoted to divorce and children, but the greater number of them are targeted to non-lawyers who are seeking support while going through a divorce or who want to handle the legal process of divorce on their own. These sites tend to be of little practical use to lawyers, providing only general reviews of law and practice that would be elementary to a lawyer.

Still, as with anything else on the Internet, there is more than immediately meets the eye. Here is a review of family law sites on the Web.

Divorce and the Law

★★★★★ DivorceNet, www.divorcenet.com

DivorceNet started out in 1995 as a means of showcasing the Newton, Massachusetts, family law practice of Sharyn T. Sooho. It quickly grew into one of the most comprehensive family law sites on the Web and remains so today. Its popularity came in large part from its early incorporation of an "interactive bulletin board," where visitors could post messages, questions and announcements and others could respond. That original discussion board has evolved into a selection of some twenty topical discussions devoted to matters such as domestic violence, child support, parental abduction, stepfamilies, and others. There are also discus-

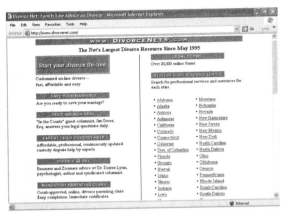

DivorceNet is one of the most comprehensive family law sites on the Web.

sion boards for each state and even a live chat room. Postings tend largely to come from people seeking answers to legal questions, and lawyers are often among those responding. Beyond the bulletin boards, DivorceNet includes a separate page for each U.S. state. Each of these pages provides a summary description of the state's divorce laws, with links to full-text statutes in most cases; listings of family law attorneys and support services in the state; selected articles; child support calculators; and links to related state resources. DivorceNet also contains back issues of its electronic newsletter, "The Family Law Advisor"; a divorce law dictionary; and "answer desks" for questions on law, relationships, taxes and psychology.

★★★★ Uniform Matrimonial, Family & Health Laws Locator, www.law.cornell.edu/uniform/vol9.html

Cornell Law School's Legal Information Institute has a site to help you locate state laws on the Internet that correspond to uniform matrimonial, family and health laws. Examples of the references here include: Uniform Adoption Act, Uniform Alcoholism and Intoxication Treatment Act, Uniform Child Custody Jurisdiction Act, Uniform Civil Liability for Support Act, Uniform Divorce Recognition Act, Uniform Duties to Disabled Persons Act, Model HealthCare Consent Act, Uniform HealthCare Information Act, Interstate Family Support Act, and the Uniform Controlled Substances Act. For each uniform law, the locator provides links directly to the corresponding state statute.

★★★ Divorcesource.com, www.divorcesource.com

Designed to serve as a comprehensive divorce information network for both professionals and the general public, Divorcesource.com may prove somewhat disappointing to lawyers, but sufficiently full of information to keep consumers browsing for some time. In organization and content, it strives to be a mega-site for matters relating to marriage and divorce. All of its information is organized both by state and under generic topics such as "Affairs & Divorce," "Children & Divorce," "Grandparent Issues," and several more. Its section, "Cases of Interest," will likely intrigue lawyers. It compiles significant cases both by the topics they address and by the states from which they came. Thus, you could click on "Discovery" to see cases on that topic, or select "Alabama" to see all cases from that state. These are digests of decisions only, not full text. Visitors can obtain more information about these cases by purchasing a site subscription, which starts at $8.95 for three days. Also of interest to lawyers is Divorcesource.com's overview of divorce laws by state. Each state page gives a brief overview, covering residency requirements, grounds for divorce, alimony, child custody, and other legal basics. State-specific pages include these legal overviews plus various articles about the process of divorce and related issues, and a locator for finding family lawyers, counselors, mediators and other professionals. The professionals listed are all paid advertisers. Also listed for each state are links to relevant state resources. The site includes various bulletin boards and chat rooms, with most messages coming from people going through problems related to divorce, support or custody.

★★★ Unmarried Couples and the Law, www.palimony.com

Maybe the only Web site devoted to palimony and related issues, this is sponsored by Goldman & Kagon, the Los Angeles firm that handled the famous palimony defense of actor Lee Marvin. The site has a small collection of short articles on general topics of living together, such as estate planning and same-sex couples. It also has articles specifically focused on the Marvin case, including tips on defenses and discovery in such cases. A Resources page lists links to Web resources related to unmarried couples.

Child Custody

Child custody is sometimes the most bitterly fought aspect of a divorce. For lawyers involved in custody disputes, there are several sites with useful resources.

★★★★ Children's Rights Council, www.gocrc.com

The Children's Rights Council is an organization that believes, "The best parent is both parents." Its site includes information about current legislation relating to child custody and support, and has the full text of related federal bills. One section provides a state-by-state survey of laws providing for joint custody. A library includes a bibliography of research on joint custody and shared parenting. The site also has the text of the Children's Bill of Rights. A connected site, "Info 4 Parents," provides articles and resources on shared parenting targeted towards never-married and single parents.

★★★★ National Center for Missing and Exploited Children, www.missingkids.org

Custody battles sometimes lead to parental kidnapping. If you face such a case—or any case involving the abduction or sexual exploitation of a child—you will find helpful information offered by the National Center for Missing and Exploited Children, a nonprofit agency that works to locate and protect missing and exploited children. NCMEC provides assistance to parents, children, law enforcement, schools, and others in recovering missing children and raising public awareness about ways to prevent child abduction, molestation, and sexual exploitation. The site includes a library of useful publications and extensive information on the group's work within the U.S. and internationally.

★★ Central Missouri Child Advocacy Law Center, www.rollanet.org/~childlaw/main.htm

This is another one of those sites which, although focusing on a particular state, offers resources of interest to anyone in the field. Operated by a Missouri nonprofit that provides guardian ad litem services in child abuse and neglect cases, much of the site is devoted to Missouri law and procedure. But of broader interest is the *Guardian Ad Litem Online Handbook*, a work in progress compiling references from throughout the nation. It includes standards and guidelines from other jurisdictions as well as articles on such topics as detecting child sexual abuse and communicating with a child. Although the site is no longer kept up to date, it remains a useful resource.

★ Child Custody and Divorce: Free Legal Advice, www.childcustody.net

Michigan lawyer James Whalen put together this fifty-chapter guide to divorce and child custody in Michigan, with more chapters in the works. It is written in a folksy style for non-lawyers. He has also assembled links to various states' divorce laws, although the links are out of date, with several leading to pages that have moved or cannot be found.

★ **Professional Academy of Custody Evaluators,** www.pace-cus-tody.org

PACE is a private, nonprofit organization devoted to registering custody evaluators based on specific criteria, and disseminating information concerning the education, training, and experience of registered evaluators. Its site provides a state-by-state directory of custody evaluators who have met its criteria. Its site also includes an archive of newsletter articles concerning custody. One such article, for example, was "Factors Affecting Children's Power To Choose Their Caretakers In Custody Proceedings." The site also contains information on materials and resources to be used in evaluating custody. There are links to related sites.

★ **The Psychologists' Custody Strategies,** www.custodycenter.com

Do you know the fourteen "key behaviors" that distinguish parents who do well in custody disputes from who do not? Can you identify the single biggest mistake a father in a custody dispute can make? The answers to these questions and many others are promised in a book marketed through this site. Two psychologists who specialize in custody matters wrote the book, with different versions for men and women. The site houses nothing beyond its sales pitch.

Child Support

★★★★★ **Federal Office of Child Support Enforcement,** www.acf.dhhs.gov/programs/cse/index.html

If you represent a former spouse who is owed delinquent child support, there are several sites with information about relevant laws and collection procedures. A good starting point is the site of this agency of the U.S. Department of Health and Human Services. It offers detailed profiles of each state's child support enforcement laws, with specific information on support guidelines, income withholding, establishment of paternity, statutes of limitations, international reciprocity, age of majority, and modification of orders. CSE also provides links to each state's child-support enforcement agency. The site includes libraries of policy documents, news releases, and the full text of federal laws and regulations relating to child-support enforcement.

★★★★★ **National Electronic Child Support Resource System,** http://ocse.acf.dhhs.gov/necsrspub/

Created by the Federal Office of Child Support Enforcement, NECSRS is a searchable, electronic index of federal, state and local resource materials related to child support. The index can be searched by key words or browsed by topic or type of resource. Documents include administrative, legislative and judicial materials, as well as a variety of reports and guides.

★★★★★ **Support Guidelines.com,** www.supportguidelines.com

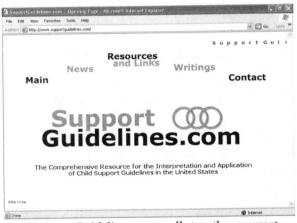

Support Guidelines.com pulls together support laws from throughout the U.S.

This site offers a vehicle for researching child support laws nationwide. Its highlight is access to the full text of the child support guidelines of all fifty states and the District of Columbia. It includes links to other Web resources for family law research, as well as to child support calculators available online. Laura Wish Morgan, owner of Family Law Consulting, Charlottesville, Virginia, and chair of the Child Support Committee of the Section of Family Law of the American Bar Association, maintains the site. The site includes the complete first chapter of her treatise, *Child Support Guidelines: Interpretation and Application,* published by Aspen Law & Business. She also provides digests of recent cases concerning child support as well as a more in-depth monthly article.

Violence, Abuse and Neglect

★★★★★ **American Bar Association Center on Children and the Law,** www.abanet.org/child/home.html

Sponsored by the ABA's Young Lawyers Division, the Washington-based Center on Children and the Law is one of the ABA's largest-staffed programs and hosts one of its busiest Web sites. Within the site are sections devoted to a number of specific issues, such as child and adolescent health, child protection, foster care, court improvement, parental kidnapping, juvenile courts, and others. The site includes selected articles from the Center's periodicals, such as the monthly "Child Law Practice." It also provides the full text of numerous reports and legal materials, as well as the complete 1992 manual, "Working With The Courts in Child Protection."

★★★★★ Women's Law Initiative, www.womenslaw.org

This site is a nationwide resource for women who are victims of domestic violence. It explains, for every state in the U.S., how to get a restraining order, and provides the applicable statutes and court forms. It includes a number of articles on domestic violence, and provides links to state and local domestic-violence resources.

★★★★ American Bar Association Commission on Domestic Violence, www.abanet.org/domviol/home.html

This site gets right to the point, opening with a collection of links to key resources for victims of domestic violence along with key phone numbers for anyone needing shelter or referral to a lawyer. Also on the site are a range of training materials for lawyers and others on domestic violence, a model code on domestic and family violence, and links to a number of related Web sites.

★★★★ National Data Archive on Child Abuse and Neglect, www.ndacan.cornell.edu

If you are unfortunate enough to have a case involving allegations of child abuse or neglect, you may want to explore the research data available from the National Data Archive on Child Abuse and Neglect. Its primary activity is the acquisition, preservation and dissemination of high quality datasets relevant to the study of child abuse and neglect. At its Web site, you can browse a catalog of available datasets and place an order for any you would like to purchase, at a cost of $75 per dataset. Several of the datasets' user guides are provided for free here, in either hypertext or Adobe Acrobat format. One guide likely to be of broad interest among lawyers in this field is *Sensitively Assessing Children's Testimonial Competence*, a research project that examined the most sensitive means by which to measure children's competency to take an oath that they will testify truthfully.

★★★ American Bar Association Steering Committee on the Unmet Legal Needs of Children, www.abanet.org/unmet/home.html

In 1993, an ABA working group issued the report, "America's Children at Risk: A National Agenda for Legal Action," which exhorted lawyers to devote their skills to the legal needs of children. An outgrowth of that working group, the Steering Committee on the Unmet Legal Needs of Children, is charged with facilitating the ABA's efforts to implement the report's recommendations. The primary feature of its site is *A Directory of Pro Bono Children's Law Programs*, its guide to legal volunteer opportunities on behalf of children. The directory lists child advocacy programs across the nation, including volunteer projects, law school clinics and resource centers. Originally a hard copy publication, the directory is available in abridged format on the Web site. The complete directory can be downloaded from the site in Adobe Acrobat format. Besides the directory, the steering committee's page provides links to information on a handful of related ABA publications, most of which must be purchased in hard copy.

Parents' Rights

★★★★ DadsDivorce.com, www.dadsdivorce.com

Founded by a lawyer, DadsDivorce is a useful site for fathers facing divorce or child custody litigation. It features "Dad's Guide to Custody," adapted from *Civil War: A Dad's Guide to Custody*, the book written by the site's founder, Joseph Cordell, a lawyer in St. Louis, Missouri. An amateur military historian, Cordell uses analogies drawn from the real Civil War to illustrate this detailed guide to the legal aspects of divorce and divorce litigation. A companion online text offers a similarly detailed exploration of the financial issues faced by divorcing fathers. Lawyers will find useful the site's state-by-state guide to divorce and custody laws. For each state, the site provides both quick and detailed summaries of the laws as well as links to the full text of statutes and to pertinent administrative and judicial resources. A bookstore offers for sale hard copies of Cordell's book and others on the topic of divorce and separation, as well as "custody calendar" software for divorced fathers to track expenses, visitations and more.

★★ The Men's Issues Page, www.menweb.org/throop/index.html

Devoted to covering the several men's movements "encyclopediacally," this site is a collection of links and articles on topics ranging from domestic violence to romance and marriage. For domestic relations lawyers and their clients, the site has several areas of particular interest, including a collection of resources relating to false allegations of child molestation and abuse, and a "Single Dad Index" with an array of resources on child support, paternity, visitation, custody, alimony, divorce and missing kids. The site is no longer updated, but a note from February 2003 says it "is still a treasure trove of information."

Professional Associations

★★★★ American Academy of Matrimonial Lawyers, www.aaml.org

With more than 1,500 members, the American Academy of Matrimonial Lawyers is a national organization, based in Chicago, of lawyers who practice matrimonial law. Regardless of whether you are a member, you will appreciate the Academy's library of full-text manuals and pamphlets designed to help your clients understand the divorce process and its impact on children. The most substantive of these, *Divorce Manual: A Client Handbook*, outlines the legal steps involved in divorce, in clear language and in a manner that bridges state-to-state differences. Two other publications available here are *Stepping Back From Anger*, a parents' guide to easing the impact of divorce on their children, and *Making Marriage Last*, a booklet of pointers for preventing divorce. Other features of this site include news updates of interest to matrimonial lawyers, a modest collection of links, and general information about the Academy.

★★★ American Bar Association Section of Family Law, www.abanet.org/family/home.html

Unless you are a registered member of this ABA Section, its site has little in the way of substantive resources. There is the standard Section fare of committee rosters, membership information and a calendar of events. Likewise, there are descriptions and ordering information for *The Family Advocate*, the Section's quarterly magazine, and the *Family Law Quarterly*, a scholarly journal devoted to family law, but only limited access to selected full-text articles. Section members get entrée to a restricted area of the site, which includes a directory of members, ethics updates, and a client handbook.

★★★ National Court Appointed Special Advocate Association, www.casanet.org

For anyone who serves as a guardian ad litem or court-appointed special advocate, this is a useful Web site. Its Advocate's Library houses articles on abuse, addiction, adoption, advocacy, delinquency, juvenile justice, and several other topics. Elsewhere, the site offers a selection of guides and manuals for advocates to use.

★ International Academy of Matrimonial Lawyers, www.iaml.org

The International Academy of Matrimonial Lawyers describes itself as a peer-selected organization of the finest matrimonial lawyers in the world. Its Web site, on the other hand, is far from the finest, with the only information offered to non-members being listings of its officers and members, links to members' Web sites, and a calendar of events. A "News Updates" page had only one somewhat recent item Likewise, the site's links page had plenty of links, but hardly any focused on matrimonial law and several were out of date.

Adoption

★★★ Adoption Network, www.adoption.org

With sections for adoptees, birth parents and adoptive parents, the Adoption Network Web site is a worthwhile starting point for adoption-related research on the Web. It provides summaries of the adoption laws of each U.S. state, as well as of selected foreign countries, and includes links to U.S. laws and policy documents related to adoption. For adoptees searching for their birth parents, the site lists groups throughout the U.S. that will provide assistance.

For Your Clients

The bulk of the Internet's resources related to divorce and custody are not for lawyers, but their clients. These sites can be worth the bookmark, however. Some contain information you will want to share with your client, and some have information even you will find useful.

★★★★ KidsnCommon.com, www.kidsncommon.com

KidsnCommon seeks to help bridge the communication gap between divorced parents and enable them to address more constructively issues involving their children. Among its features are an interactive calendar accessible by both parents, a component for sharing documents, a bill sharing and payment service, access to free family and credit counselors, and other planning and informational resources. A thirty-day free trial is offered, after which the service costs $6.95 a month per parent or $11.95 a month for an entire family. Lawyers should consider whether this is a resource to which they might want to refer their clients. For lawyers who do decide to refer a client, KidsnCommon will return the favor by offering them free listings on the site.

★★★ DivorceLawInfo, www.divorcelawinfo.com

DivorceLawInfo is a family law self-help center for non-lawyers and pro se litigants. It provides state-by-state legal guides to marriage, divorce and child custody, as well as state-specific child support calculators. Begin by selecting a state, which takes you to a page containing links to state laws, courts, government agencies, bar associations and community resources related to divorce, custody and child support. DivorceLawInfo supplements this free information with a "bookstore" that sells legal forms and self-help books for individuals handling their own divorce.

★★★ Divorce Online, www.divorceonline.com

Divorce Online describes itself as "an electronic resource for people involved in, or facing the prospect of, divorce." It offers articles and information on divorce-related topics. It includes a referral list for locating a lawyer, but lists only a small number of lawyers in a handful of states.

★★★ Nolo Press, www.nolo.com

Nolo is a California publisher of self-help legal materials. Its Plain-English Law Centers are designed for non-lawyers, but even those admitted to the bar might find something useful in them. Nolo's site provides helpful FAQs on marriage and divorce, same-sex couples, domestic violence, divorce mediation, property division and alimony, and related topics.

★★ Divorce Helpline, www.divorcehelp.com

Divorce Helpline promises to offer "Tools to keep you out of court." Operated by a lawyer, the site includes "A Short Divorce Course," and several short articles, such as "How to do your own legal research" and "When legal separation is better than divorce." The site also has worksheets for organizing personal and financial information related to a divorce.

★★ DivorceSupport.com, www.divorcesupport.com

This site for non-lawyers offers a variety of state-specific divorce tools for purchase. Its catalog includes guidebooks, child support calculation reports, and divorce forms—both blank and prepared. Other items for sale include a divorce recordkeeping system and a divorce calendaring system. Its bookstore lets you buy or rent a variety of divorce-related books. Beyond the items for sale, the site gives a general state-by-state overview of divorce laws and hosts chat rooms and bulletin boards.

Support Services

★★★ Education Experts and Child Custody, http://childcustody.com

If you have a case of child custody in which the quality of different schools is an issue, this may be the site for you. It belongs to SchoolMatch, an organization that performs school evaluations and assessments. It maintains a database with assessments of every public school in the U.S. and more than 14,000 private schools. Its experts are available to provide testimony and assistance in case preparation. This Web site does not allow access to the SchoolMatch data. Instead, it serves largely as a brochure, describing the company's services and offering scenarios taken from actual cases in which it has been involved.

★ DivorceSearch.com, www.divorcesearch.com

This service searches divorce records anywhere in the U.S. You cannot search yourself—they do the searching for you. You can order a search through this site for $39.95, and have the results sent back to you within twenty-four to forty-eight hours. The same outfit will also search marriage, death and other vital records

Chapter 10

Protecting Intellectual Property:
Copyright, Patent and Trademark Law

─────────────── **Chapter Contents** ───────────────

Laws, Cases and Treaties
Practice Resources
U.S. Government Resources
Trademark/Patent/Copyright Searching
Related Resources
Associations
Journals/Articles

With its ease of duplicating and delivering words, sounds, pictures and data, the Internet has spawned a sprawling industry among lawyers and regulators seeking to protect and define intellectual property rights in a digital age. And just as it is raising new questions for IP lawyers, it is also helping to answer them through an array of governmental and private Web sites. In fact, the sheer number of IP-related sites may be the best measure of the importance of this area of law in today's world.

With so many sites devoted to copyright, patent and trademark law, it is surprising to discover how many of them are of high quality and true value to the practicing lawyer. Using the Web, lawyers can search patents, trademarks and copyrights throughout the world; police their clients' trade names and service marks; research primary source law such as statutes and treaties; and study secondary materials such as law reviews.

In fact, some of the most cutting edge material on intellectual property protection in the digital age can be found nowhere but on the Internet.

Here is a guide to IP resources on the 'Net.

Laws, Cases and Treaties

★★★★★ **Collection of Laws for Electronic Access,** http://clea. wipo.int

CLEA—the Collection of Laws for Electronic Access—is maintained by the World Intellectual Property Organization. It is a database containing all national laws relating to intellectual property, the texts of all treaties administered by WIPO, and bibliographic data concerning each legislative text and treaty. While the bibliographic data is in English only, the laws and treaties are available in French and Spanish as well. The system is remarkably simple to use, with a search bar and menu of contents on the left and results displayed in the center. Thus, you can simply click your way through the menu to a specific country, or perform a more complex search. Help is amply available throughout the site.

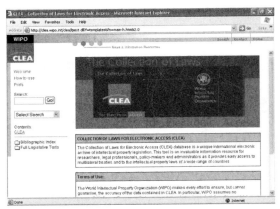

WIPO provides a database of all national and international IP laws.

★★★★★ Copyright and Fair Use, http://fairuse.stanford.edu

Sponsored by Stanford University Libraries, FindLaw and the Council on Library Resources, this is a useful collection of copyright law materials and links with a focus on primary source materials, including current legislation and recent cases. Of particular note is its case law section, which includes not only full text opinions, but, for some cases, briefs and analyses.

★★★★★ Intellectual Property Materials, www.law.cornell.edu/topics/topic2.html

Cornell Law School's Legal Information Institute has put together this site on copyright, patent and trademark law. It provides links to virtually all relevant primary source materials, including the U.S. Copyright Act, the Patent Act, the Lanham Act, federal regulations, the Patents Cooperation Treaty, the Paris Convention, the General Agreement on Tariffs and Trade, recent Supreme Court decisions, and the Berne Convention for the Protection of Literary and Artistic Works. It also provides a small but well-selected list of links to secondary sources. The combination of primary and secondary materials makes it a preferred site for starting research.

★★★★★ Uniform Domain Name Dispute Resolution Policy Database, http://udrp.lii.info

Decisions in domain name disputes are supposed to be available on the Internet, but they were difficult to track down, having been published on various sites with no easy search mechanism. This site, launched in 2003, offers a solution, providing free access to decisions issued in accordance with the Uniform Dispute Resolution Policy of the Internet Corporation for Assigned Names and Numbers (ICANN), www.icann.org.

As of this writing, the database includes more than 7,000 decisions involving nearly 12,000 domain names. The developers plan eventually to include all decisions. One novel feature of the tool is that it searches for names based on how they sound, rather than by their precise spelling. The UDRP database was jointly developed by the University of Massachusetts Center for Information Technology and Dispute Resolution, the Markle Foundation, Cornell University's Legal Information Institute and The Online Public Disputes Project.

★★★★★ World Intellectual Property Organization, www.wipo.org

WIPO is the U.N. agency responsible for the protection of intellectual property throughout the world. Its Web site provides background and texts of all major treaties and other forms of international IP protection. The site includes complete information on intellectual property in general, and on specific WIPO initiatives on dispute resolution, domain names, electronic commerce, biotechnology, and other current issues.

Practice Resources

★★★★★ All About Trademarks, www.ggmark.com

This site has one of the best overall collections of links to trademark resources, as well as some to general IP resources. Links are organized under general trademark resources, federal law and practice, state trademark laws, international trademark law, trademarks in Cyberspace, and trademark searching. There are also links to online journals and articles. Topping it all off are articles reviewing the basics of acquiring, protecting and using trademarks. For its list of links alone, this is a useful site for IP lawyers. It is maintained by Dallas, Texas, lawyer Gregory H. Guillot.

★★★★★ BitLaw, www.bitlaw.com

Created by Daniel A. Tysver, a partner with the Hopkins, Minnesota, IP firm Beck & Tysver, BitLaw has grown over the years from a compilation of legal resources related to computers and the Internet into a virtual online treatise on intellectual property and technology law. With over 1,800 pages covering patent, copyright, trademark and

BitLaw is a virtual treatise on intellectual property and technology law.

Internet law, the site is a combination of original essays and hyperlinked resources. Tysver's exploration of each topic begins with an executive summary followed by increasingly deeper layers of more detailed discussions. He supplements these essays with the full text of significant copyright decisions, hypertext versions of federal IP laws and regulations, general discussions of various legal issues, and a good collection of links. He also provides official forms and sample contracts.

★★★★★ Creative Commons, http://creativecommons.org

You do not have to be an IP lawyer to be familiar with the phrase, "All rights reserved." But what if the creator of a work of intellectual property wants to reserve only some rights? This is the operating thesis of Creative Commons, a trailblazing project with roots in the Berkman Center for Internet & Society at Harvard Law School and the Stanford Law School Center for Internet and Society. It has developed a Web application that allows creators to dedicate their work to the public domain or license it on terms less restrictive than those traditionally encountered in copyright licenses, allowing certain uses on certain conditions. Creative Commons licenses are designed to cover creative works such as Web sites, scholarship, music, film, photography, literature and courseware.

★★★★★ Intellectual Property Law Web Server, www.patents.com

One of the longest-standing IP law resources on the Web, this site skips the pointless graphics and goes right for the meat. Sponsored since 1993 by the law firm Oppedahl & Larson—formerly of New York, now in Colorado—the site includes a collection of IP law FAQ pages, with answers that are informative and useful. Although the focus is patents, there is also information on copyrights, trademarks, trade secrets, computer law, and "weblaw," as well as information on domain name litigation in which the firm is involved.

★★★★★ Intellectual Property Mall, Franklin Pierce Law Center, www.ipmall.fplc.edu

This is a comprehensive, "one-stop shopping" site for links to IP resources on the Internet. Many of the links include thorough annotations, making them more useful than most. But links are not all you will find in this wide-ranging IP resource. Among the varied resources at this site are a library of faculty research papers on IP topics, a collection of IP moot court briefs from award-winning teams, federal IP jury instructions, copies of USPTO patent examinations, and a tutorial on patent searching via the Internet.

★★★★★ **Intellectual Property Rights Helpdesk,** www.ipr-help desk.org

The who, what, where and how of European IP law and practice is the theme of this comprehensive site, maintained by the European Community's Research and Development Information Service. The Helpdesk provides broad information on European IP law, with sections focusing on copyright, inventions, designs and other IP issues. It includes an extensive collection of practice guides and working papers.

★★★★★ **Law.com IP Law Practice Center,** www.law.com/jsp/pc/ iplaw.jsp

Law.com's IP practice center is a part free, part subscription service providing news, court opinions, in-depth analysis and practice pointers. Its practice-specific news articles, updated daily, are gathered from American Lawyer Media's chain of national and state publications. IP case opinions are culled from the Supreme Court, all the federal circuit courts, and state appellate courts. Subscribers also receive a weekly e-mail alert containing the latest news and cases.

★★★★★ **Links to Patent and Other Intellectual Property Information Resources,** www.bl.uk/services/information/patents.html

The Patents Information Service of the British Library's science, technology and business wing hosts this site, a guide to patent and IP resources on the Internet. Its collection of links concentrates on databases, particularly those that are free but also those that require subscriptions. For other types of resources, it favors links to British and European resources over those in the U.S. Some of the links are annotated, particularly those that point to databases, while other links are not. The collection of database links is extensive, as are sets of links to ancillary resources such as government patent offices and patent classification schemes. Included among the links are national and regional patent laws, patent treaties, and international sources of information on patent litigation. This is a thorough assembly of links, including many to resources not generally included in other collections of IP links.

★★★★★ **Mayall's IP Links,** www.mayallj.freeserve.co.uk

There are two very good reasons to visit this site, from U.K. patent attorney John Mayall. The first is for its collection of IP links. It may well be the best, most thorough collection of IP links, all thoroughly annotated. It includes links to the patent databases of virtually every country in the world, to patent databases for specific technologies, to patent offices of many countries, and to non-patent prior art databases. Much the same is true for trademarks: links to trademark databases and trademark offices throughout the world. Most international IP laws covering patents, trademarks and copyrights are included, as are IP treaties and conventions. The site also includes links to databases for determining the status of a patent or trademark. There are even links to sites that can help track current IP-related lawsuits in the United Kingdom. As if these many libraries of links were not enough, a final category is for links classified as "None of the Above."

The second reason to visit is to download and learn to use PatSee Patent Downloader. This is software—developed, as it happens, by Mayall's brother—that manages the process of downloading patents from the Internet, automating many tasks, speeding download times, and delivering high quality images. PatSee actually hunts various Web sites for the patent you want, and then, when it finds it, downloads it page by page in .pdf format. PatSee is "shareware," meaning you can try it free, and then pay for it only if you like it.

★★★★★ Trade Secrets Home Page, www.rmarkhalligan2.com/trade

Chicago lawyer R. Mark Halligan's Web site avoids flashy graphics in favor of an abundance of content, most of it original, in-depth articles written by Halligan. Whether you are new to IP law or an experienced practitioner, you are likely to learn something from this site, which includes current news, summaries of nearly 500 recent cases involving trade secrets, summaries of recent cases involving IP protection on the Internet, full text laws, and much more.

★★★★★ WIPO Arbitration and Mediation Center, http://arbiter.wipo.int

Through its Arbitration and Mediation Center, the World Intellectual Property Organization offers arbitration and mediation services for the resolution of international commercial disputes between private parties. With an emphasis on technology, entertainment, and other disputes involving intellectual property, the center has become the leading provider of dispute resolution services in the area of Internet domain names. It also works with specific industries to develop dispute resolution schemes tailored to meet their specific requirements. WIPO's site includes the complete texts of its arbitration and mediation rules, schedules of fees and sample contract clauses. With regard to domain disputes, the site provides a list of all domain cases filed with the center and the full texts of all decisions handed down under its dispute resolution policy. Those interested in becoming WIPO neutrals can obtain information here on how to apply.

★★★★ Intellectual Property Law, www.intelproplaw.com

There are four main sections to this site: links to IP resources, forums for discussing IP issues, current IP news, and listings of IP jobs. Links are organized into separate pages for patent, copyright and trademark. The collection is somewhat cursory but includes most key sites. The forums are in bulletin board format and appeared to be heavy with non-lawyers asking general IP questions. The news section is a simple grid by which visitors can quickly search online news sources such as Reuters and Google News for IP-related stories. The jobs section listed a number of available positions and also lawyers seeking employment.

★★★★ International Legal Protection for Software, www. fenwick. com/docstore/publications/ip/software_chart_2003.pdf

From the Silicon Valley law firm Fenwick & West, the site analyzes software protection under the patent, copyright and trade laws of seventy-two countries. Its prime feature is a chart listing the protections available in each country. The chart indicates whether software is within the subject matter protected under each country's copyright and patent laws, and shows the country's memberships in international conventions and bilateral agreements. The site includes a regularly updated collection of articles on topics related to international software protection. It merits stars for content, usefulness, ease of use and innovation.

★★★★ KuesterLaw, www.kuesterlaw.com

This site claims to be one of the most comprehensive resources on the Internet for information related to technology law, and in particular to intellectual property law. At one time it was, but in recent years it has failed to keep up with new sites and new developments. Hosted by Jeffrey R. Kuester, a lawyer in Atlanta, Georgia, the site offers background on intellectual property law; the text of cases, statutes, and bills; and intellectual property law resources. It remains a useful starting point for IP research on the Web.

★★★★ PatentCafé.com, www.patentcafe.com

The first-time visitor is sure to feel overwhelmed by the menu of features available through PatentCafé.com. Laying claim to being the leading business-to-business portal for patent, trademark and copyright directories, information, advice and networking, it offers sections for inventors, small businesses, IP professionals, corporate intellectual asset managers, and even kids. For lawyers, the site's "Patent Cafe" magazine features news articles and in-depth analysis of IP law.

★★★ IP Law & Business, www.ipww.com

This is the companion Web site to *IP Law & Business*, a magazine published by American Lawyer Media (the company that published this book). Targeted to in-house legal professionals and outside attorneys responsible for protecting and managing corporate intellectual property assets, the site features selected stories from the magazine, which is a streamlined version of the magazine formerly titled *IP Worldwide*. It includes IP Watch, a daily selection of intellectual property news.

★★★ The Copyright Website, www.benedict.com

Intended for laypersons, this site covers the fundamentals of copyright law. It also features "Famous Copyright Infringements," with graphic and audio samples of alleged misappropriations of music, lyrics, art and other creations. It merits stars for design, innovation and ease of use.

★★ Copyright Resources Online, www.library.yale.edu/%7Eokerson/copyproj.html

From the Yale University Library comes this collection of links relating to copyright issues, with an emphasis on copyright protection of materials used by students and faculty in the context of academia. The index is divided into two sections: University Copyright Resources and Non-University Intellectual Property Resources. The links include annotations of varying lengths. The site appears not to have been updated since 2000.

★★ EFF "Intellectual Property Online: Patent, Trademark, Copyright" Archive, www.eff.org/pub/Legal/Intellectual_property

A hodgepodge of articles, treaties, other source documents, white papers, briefs and other documents relating to IP, the Internet and electronic media, collected by the Electronic Frontier Foundation. A rich library, poorly organized, it earns stars for content and usefulness.

★★ National Writers Union, www.nwu.org

Online headquarters for this labor organization of freelance writers, the site includes current news and archival documents relating to the IP rights of freelancers, both in print and online. Among these documents is a recommended policy for publishers to follow in purchasing electronic rights from an author, and form freelancer contracts covering both print and electronic media. It includes an extensive section devoted to *Tasini v. New York Times*, the case involving freelancers' copyrights in work reused electronically.

★ Institute of Art and Law, www.ial.uk.com

This UK-based institute is dedicated to increasing public knowledge concerning the contribution of law to the development of cultural tradition. It produces the quarterly magazine *Art Antiquity and Law,* publishes various books on art and law, and organizes regular seminars. The site describes available products and upcoming seminars, but offers no substantive articles.

U.S. Government Resources

★★★★★ U.S. Patent and Trademark Office, www.uspto.gov

If you are searching for patents and trademarks, why not start at the source? The USPTO provides complete, online access to both its patent and trademark databases, each accessible through a range of sophisticated search options.

For patents, the USPTO provides access to its database of issued patents, with full text starting from 1976 and full page images all the way back to 1790. It also provides access to a database of patent applications published since March 15, 2001. Users can search either database by a variety of parameters or by using Boolean phrases. A manual search feature allows users to construct more complex searches, combining elements such as field searching, date-range searching, word truncation, and phrase searching.

For trademarks, the USPTO's Trademark Electronic Search System—or TESS—officially replaced the USPTO's somewhat antiquated Trademark Search Database on September 30, 2000. TESS allows anyone to search and retrieve trademark application and registration information via the Web, using the same text and image database provided to examining attorneys via the X-Search system. Users have four options for searching: a basic search form; a structured-form search, the simplest for novices; an advanced free-form search, enabling users to enter more complicated searches; and a "browse dictionary," allowing users to scan through the search indices to see indexed terms around a specific search term and providing the counts of occurrences for those indexed terms. Users can toggle between the three search forms during the search session. An initial search results in a menu listing, for each match, the word mark, its serial number, and a live/dead indicator. These, in turn, link to more detailed records. A search for "lawyer" returned 789 records.

Besides searching trademarks, you can also use the USPTO's site to file them. The Trademark Electronic Application System permits users to fill out and submit trademark applications over the Internet. Using TEAS, the user is able to fill out an application form and check it for completeness via the

Web. The user can then submit the application electronically to the USPTO or print it out for mailing. Electronic filers must pay by credit card or have a USPTO deposit account. If the mark uses a stylized design or logo, the filer will have to attach an image file in "gif" or "jpg" format. The TEAS system provides step-by-step instructions for completing a trademark or service mark application form properly. It also provides access to information about USPTO procedures and practices.

Of course, the USPTO's site also has loads of general information, including downloadable forms, general patent and trademark information, speeches and press releases, information about patent law changes, notices of legislation, and official gazette notices.

★★★★ U.S. Copyright Office, http://lcweb.loc.gov/copyright

This is home for information on copyright registration, with all required forms available for download. From this site, you can access (via telnet) the archaic Library of Congress Information System (LOCIS), which includes a searchable library of Copyright Office records from 1978 to the present. You can also obtain information on the beta CORDS system for electronic registration of copyrights via the Internet.

LOCIS contains records on materials registered for copyright since January 1978, including books, films, music, maps, sound recordings, software, drawings, posters, sculpture, and other materials. LOCIS also includes documents relating to copyright ownership, such as name changes and transfers. However, LOCIS was developed in the 1970s and seems prehistoric by today's standards for searching and accessing data online. It is anything but user friendly, requiring an understanding of archaic keyboard commands and search techniques.

The Copyright Office Web site also offers three experimental alternative databases "for short, simple searches and occasional users."

Trademark/Patent/Copyright Searching

★★★★★ MicroPatent, www.micropatent.com

MicroPatent is a company that offers both patent and trademark searching, as well as file histories and related services. Its primary components are:

- PatentWeb, providing full-text coverage of U.S. patents granted since 1836, U.S. published applications since 2001, European granted patents since 1991, European published applications since 1978, Great Britain published applications since 1916, German granted patents since 1989, German published applications since 1989, and Japanese published applications since 1976. Search full text for $95 a day, or search abstracts, bibliographic data and front-page drawings for $40 a day.

- Trademark.com, accessible through the MicroPatent main page or directly at www.trademark.com, allows full text searching of federal, state and common law trademark collections, as well as of top-level domain names and trademark files from Canada, WIPO, Europe and the United Kingdom. It also offers access to U.S. prosecution and trademark file histories. Other services include industry alerts and brand tracking. A twelve-hour search costs from $50 to $100, depending on the scope.

- FaxPat, available directly at www.faxpat.com, provides copies and file histories of U.S. and foreign patents, trademarks and copyrights. Documents can be ordered through its Web site and delivered electronically, by fax, or in hard copy. The site offers complete information on services and prices.

★★★★★ Delphion Intellectual Property Network, www.delphion.com

Originally created by IBM, this database was long available for free but now requires a subscription. It contains the complete text and images of all U.S. patents issued since 1971, as well as full images back to 1790. It also provides full text of all U.S. patent applications since March 2001. In addition to U.S. patents, Delphion provides:

- European patent applications. Bibliographic text and full document images of applications for European patents published by the European Patent Office since 1979 and full text since 1987.

- European patents granted by the European Patent Office. This includes bibliographic text and full document images of patents issued since 1980 and full text since 1991.

- Japanese patent abstracts. This database includes Japanese unexamined patent applications in English for both Japanese and non-Japanese priorities. At press time, representative first pages were available, beginning from 1976 and updated monthly.

- PCT publications. PCT publications are those issued by more than 100 member countries, including the U.S., under the WIPO Patent Cooperation Treaty. The collection includes bibliographic text and full text from 1978.

- INPADOC Family and Legal Status. Produced by the European Patent Office, the "INPADOC" patent collection contains information from sixty-five patent offices showing patents from the same "family," or involving similar claims, as the one being searched. INPADOC also includes information from twenty-two patent offices reflecting the legal status of a particular patent. Both family and legal status documents are combined in this single database, which dates back to 1968 and is updated weekly.

- German patent applications and patents granted, with full text beginning in 1987 and bibliographic text and images from 1968.
- Images for Swiss patents issued since 1990.

Delphion offers a number of sophisticated searching and viewing options. A subscription for unlimited access to all the databases costs $200 a month. A $95 a month option is more affordable but restricts access to some of the databases to a pay-for-use basis.

★★★★★ esp@cenet, http://ep.espacenet.com

Hosted by the European Patent Office, esp@cenet is the gateway to a network of patent databases in Europe and worldwide. The free service allows users to search for information about published patent applications from more than seventy countries. Patent documents contained in the database are in their original language. They can be searched by publication number, application number, priority number, publication date, applicant's name, inventor's name, technical field, or title text. Results list full bibliographic details, plus an image of each of the pages.

The service can also be used to find English-language abstracts of documents in the EPO's in-house databases of some 30 million patent documents from throughout the world. Much of this data goes back to 1970. These searches display the bibliographic data and an English language abstract for each document. If available, drawings and full text are also provided.

★★★★★ European Patent Office, www.european-patent-office.org

The EPO grants patent protection in nineteen member European states using a centralized application procedure. Its site includes a searchable database of European patent attorneys, full text copies of decisions from the EPO's boards of appeal, a database of European Patent Convention documents, and the EPO official journal. More importantly, the EPO hosts esp@cenet, described above.

★★★★★ Thomson & Thomson, www.thomson-thomson.com

The IP research company Thomson & Thomson offers Saegis, its multifaceted Web-based trademark service. Saegis is not just for research. As the

company accurately puts it, it is a complete online workflow solution helping users manage everything from the initial screening of a name to the
policing of a registered mark. It begins with the screening tool Thomson calls
Trademarkscan. It will automatically create search queries, or you can customize it to perform more specific searches. The results of your search are
displayed on screen and then saved in your own "inbox" for future reference.
Once you've screened the name, Saegis helps you surf the Web to determine
if the name is being used online and to screen for common law uses of the
name. You can then go on to order a full search from Thomson, which will
deliver the results to your same inbox. Combining these results, Saegis provides various tools to help you investigate potential conflicts via the Web.
The investigation done, it provides forms and resources to help you prepare
your opinion for presentation to your client. Once the name is cleared for
use, Thomson's Trademark Alert helps you police it by monitoring newly
filed and newly published trademarks.

★★★★ Patent Searching, www.tip.net.au/~rossco/psearch.htm

This unpretentious site is a comprehensive collection of links to Internet
patent searching. It comprehensively links government and commercial
patent sites, with descriptions of the type of information available at each
and a useful chart comparing the coverage and features of each database.

★★★★ STN on the Web, http://stnweb.cas.org

STN is an online technical and information service for scientists, engineers and information professionals. It offers access to a collection of more
than 200 in-depth databases in science and technology, including several
general and specialized patent databases. It is operated in North America by
Chemical Abstracts Service, a division of the American Chemical Society.
Pricing varies widely depending on the database being searched, but a full
price list can be downloaded in Adobe Acrobat format.

★★★ CCH Corsearch, www.cch-corsearch.com

CCH Corsearch was formed in early 2000 when the publishing company
Wolters Kluwer purchased Corsearch Inc., a trademark research service, and
merged it with its own CCH Trademark Research Corporation. The online
service offers a variety of differently priced packages allowing users to search
federal, state, Canadian and Mexican trademark data. For non-subscribers,
the Web site offers little detail about these services and little else of interest.

★★★ GetThePatent.com, www.getthepatent.com

This patent searching service promises to deliver complete, multi-page USPTO and European patent documents to your desktop via your Web browser, using a compressed file format that speeds download time. It delivers patents as a single file containing all of the patent pages. Its archive contains patent images for all USPTO, EPO and WIPO patents, as well as the national publications of Austria, Belgium, Canada, France, Germany, Great Britain, Japan, Spain and Switzerland. It also contains the full text and bibliographic information for all U.S. patents issued since 1976. In addition, it includes complete patent images for all utility patents issued by the U.S. since 1836. Several subscription options are offered. Infrequent users can pay $2.99 per patent with no other subscription fee. A subscription of $19.95 a month covers twenty patents a month with extra patents $1.99 each. The most expensive package is $89.95 a month, which covers 150 patents.

★★★ QPAT-WW, www.qpat.com

QPAT is a full text database of U.S. and European patents maintained by Questel-Orbit, an international online information company and member of the France Telecom Group. It includes the full text of all U.S. patents issued since October 1971, as well as full text European patent applications since 1978 and patents since 1991. It also includes PCT applications since 1978 and French patents from 1966. It Pluspat provides access to more than 46 million patent documents, including English language abstracts for more than 12 million patents worldwide. The databases include full-page images of most of the patents. Copies of an entire patent can be downloaded in .pdf format. Pricing information is available only by contacting one of the sales offices listed at the site.

★★★ Software Patent Institute, www.spi.org

This site offers free access to the SPI's database of software technologies. The database is unique in that it seeks to complement rather than compete with other online databases. In place of patents and current trade information, it compiles descriptions of software technologies from sources not readily available online or in electronic form. Source documents include computer manuals, older textbooks and journal articles, conference proceedings, and computer science theses. The database includes more than 104,000 excerpts from almost 1,500 documents. SPI says the database should be useful in tracking whether a proposed technology has already been developed in one form or another. The site appears to be updated only sporadically.

★★★ TM Web, www.tmweb.com

Self-described "Home of the $25 Trademark Search," this site allows online ordering of trademark searches from the Canadian company Arvic Search Services. There are no do-it-yourself search tools here, although Arvic does provide a basic overview of how to use the Web to perform a common law search, explaining that "[t]here is no need to pay us for searches you can perform on your own." The $25 search actually now costs $42.80 in Canadian dollars, which is about $31 in U.S. currency, and is only a pre-screen, searching both U.S. and Canadian trademark databases for possible conflicts. The schedule of fees tops out at about $180 for an extended search together with a professional opinion on the registrability of the mark. Arvic's site, although not exceptional in any way, stands out for its frankness and clarity, with a clear price schedule, samples of its products, and various guides to help visitors understand both its products and trademarks in general.

★★ Government Liaison Services, www.trademarkinfo.com

This Arlington, Virginia intellectual property research firm allows free searching of U.S. trademark registrations via its Web site. Searches return a list of matching word marks and the international classification numbers into which the marks are categorized. Searching is rudimentary and useful only as a general pre-screening tool. The site is primarily devoted to advertising the company's paid services for searching patents, trademarks and copyrights.

Related Resources

★★★★★ Patenting Art and Entertainment, www.patenting-art.com

Aimed at artists, entertainers, lawyers, executives and investors, this site focuses on using patents to protect art and entertainment creations. The site is entertaining as well as informative, with a gallery of images and text from art and entertainment patents as well as a database of art and entertainment patents from around the world. It includes overviews of patent law and the patent system, as well as information on legal resources. The site is maintained by Gregory Aharonian, editor of the Internet Patent News Service.

★★★★ Bad Patents, www.bustpatents.com

Should the U.S. Patent and Trademark office be issuing more than 20,000 new software patents every year? Gregory Aharonian, editor and publisher of the electronic Internet Patent News Service, thinks not. Aharonian—who also maintains the Patenting Art and Entertainment site discussed above—created this site to help lawyers and companies cope with the snowballing number of legal problems that he believes will result from tens of thousands of questionable patents. He begins with a collection of articles and studies that examine why the Patent Office issues bad patents in the first place. He follows that with a focus on bad software and technology patents, gathering a library of critiques, articles and legal documents intended to illustrate the flood of software patents and the problems they create. He includes an archive of software and Internet patents that were subsequently invalidated. Aharonian also looks at biotechnology and "bioinformatics" patents, pulling together various studies, statements and press clippings. To close his case, he presents various studies and documents relating to the economics of patent acquisition, litigation and licensing. Completing the site is Aharonian's collection of links to useful Web sites for inventors and lawyers and a photographic tour of the USPTO headquarters. While at the site, sign up to receive the free, daily electronic newsletter. This is a unique, thoughtful and useful site.

★★★★ Copyright Clearance Center Online, www.copyright.com

Whether you are looking for authorization to make a photocopy or an annual license to reproduce a copyrighted work, the Copyright Clearance Center is the place to turn. The world's largest licensing agent for text reproduction rights, the CCC allows registered users of its Web site to obtain permissions and authorizations directly online.

★★★★ MarkWatch, www.markwatch.com

MarkWatch is a service that monitors what is being said on the Internet about a particular product or brand and polices the Internet for unauthorized uses of a trademark or copyright. Its computers scan the Internet full time, in search of clients' names, brands and trademarks. It searches Web pages, Usenet message groups, domain registrations, and news stories. Then, once a week, it provides its clients with a report on any new or changed references to the monitored names. The report includes a description, an excerpt surrounding the reference, and a URL for linking to the original material.

★★★ Liblicense, www.library.yale.edu/~llicense/index.shtml

Yale University maintains this site, designed a resource for librarians to help them understand the unique issues related to licensing digital information. It offers a model licensing agreement, along with detailed analyses of common terms and standard clauses that generally appear in licensing agreements. The site also serves as home to the liblicense electronic discussion list, with information on subscribing and archives of past discussions.

★★ Master-McNeil, www.naming.com

If you need a name, here is where to turn. This company's forte is thinking up names. The site includes "A Glossary of Naming Terms," and a list of some of the names the company created.

★ Anti-Copyright, www.mayhem.net/copyrightfr2.html

Home page of the "Digital Pirate," whose motto is "I scan, therefore I am." A site for copyright anarchists.

★ DakaTec, www.dakatec.com

DakaTec specializes in trademark and patent drawings. Its site offers samples of its work and information on its services.

Associations

★★★★★ American Intellectual Property Law Association, www.aipla.org

AIPLA is a 10,000-member national bar association the members of which include lawyers in private and corporate practice, government service and teaching. Its Web site provides a wide range of information about IP law and practice, as well as general information about the association, including a meetings calendar, committee reports, its alternative dispute resolution functions, an update on continuing legal education, and information about membership. The site includes a library of amicus briefs AIPLA has filed in various trademark and IP cases, and testimony it has submitted with regard to various legislative and rulemaking initiatives. A library includes articles on AIPLA's ADR procedures and model patent jury instructions.

★★★★★ Intellectual Property Owners, www.ipo.org

Although it counts attorneys among its members, the IPO is not a bar association, but a group of manufacturers, organizations and individuals dedicated to protecting the rights of IP owners. Highlighting its Web site is its daily news service—reports from the courts, Congress and elsewhere on developments in IP law and related issues. Reports on court decisions often include the full text of the actual decision. A section of the site, "IP in the

Courts," pulls together in one location news reports of court rulings from the past year and the actual rulings. Also here are amicus briefs filed on behalf of the IPO and a small library of other briefs and selected court orders. From the site, visitors can register to have the daily news reports delivered to them via e-mail.

★★★★ International Trademark Association, www.inta.org

This international association of trademark owners and associated professionals has created a Web site that goes beyond the usual association fare of membership information, event listings and publication sales. Sure, those elements are all here, but they are accompanied by many pages of useful information. Much of the information is directed at non-professionals, such as the "TM Basics" page with FAQs and articles covering trademark basics. A section expressly for lawyers includes the ITA's collection of amicus briefs and a guide to using ADR in trademark and unfair competition matters. An interesting feature is the Trademark Checklist, a compilation of some 3,000 registered trademarks and service marks, created to assist journalists, editors and others with proper trademark usage.

★★★ Intellectual Property Law Section, American Bar Association, www.abanet.org/intelprop/home.html

For the most part, this site is devoted to general information about the Section, describing its committees, listing upcoming meetings, and housing a catalog of its publications. The section's Intellectual Property Newsletter is included in full text. A page on current legislation provides useful descriptions and analyses of bills pending before the U.S. Congress, and another section provides recently filed amicus briefs.

★★ Domain Name Rights Coalition, www.domain-name.org

Founded in 1996 by a party to a domain name dispute and two of his lawyers, the DNRC has continued as an advocacy group for entrepreneurs and small businesses on domain name issues. Much of its work has been directed against various domain name dispute resolution policies and laws, which DNRC contends interfere with First Amendment rights. Read all about it at this site, which includes the texts of DNRC's amicus briefs, its officers' testimony before various legislative and rulemaking bodies, position papers, press releases and other documents.

Journals/Articles

★★★★★ **Harvard Journal of Law & Technology,** http://jolt.law.harvard.edu

Devoted to the legal implications of emerging technologies, including IP issues, JOLT publishes the full text of all articles online starting with volume one in 1988 and continuing to the most recent issue.

★★★★★ **Richmond Journal of Law and Technology,** http://law.richmond.edu/jolt

This groundbreaking journal was the first law review to publish exclusively online. Its premier issue, in 1995, featured two seminal articles on IP in the Internet age: Dan L. Burk's "Trademarks Along the Infobahn: A First Look at the Emerging Law of Cybermarks," and I. Trotter Hardy's "Contracts, Copyright and Preemption in a Digital World." In the years since, it has continued to stay ahead in analyzing emerging trends in technology law.

★★★★ **Journal of Technology Law & Policy,** http://journal.law.ufl.edu/~techlaw

Students at the University of Florida's Levin College of Law publish this electronic journal devoted to the law and policy of technology. It includes the full text of all articles it has published since 1996.

★★★ **Intellectual Property and Technology Forum,** www.bc.edu/iptf

News and articles relating to intellectual property and technology law are the focus of this online publication created by law students at Boston College Law School. IPTF publishes current news as well as in-depth scholarly articles from student authors, professors and practicing lawyers. Topics include traditional intellectual property areas as well as technology law issues such as encryption, Internet privacy, telecommunications, biotechnology, and medical ethics.

★★ **IDEA: The Journal of Law & Technology,** www.idea.fplc.edu

Students at Franklin Pierce Law Center publish this print and electronic journal devoted to IP law throughout the world. No articles are available online.

★★ **Journal of Intellectual Property Law,** www.law.uga.edu/jipl

Published by students at the University of Georgia School of Law, this claims to be the first student-edited law journal devoted solely to the field of intellectual property law. Full text articles are available from 1993 to 1999, but more recent issues have not been posted to the site.

★ The Patent Jury Forum, www.jurytrials.com

This is an electronic journal "dedicated to the improvement of jury trials in patent infringement litigation." Its two issues online—both from 1997—contain various articles on patent cases and litigation and on jury practice in general. The site appears to have been abandoned, and its links to downloadable materials, such as jury instructions from actual cases, are dead.

Chapter 11

Labor Links: Employment Law on the Web

Federal and state laws governing labor and employment touch virtually all areas of law practice. Whether your concentration is corporate law or personal injury, tax or insurance, you are sure to encounter the statutes that govern everything from payment of wages to job safety to retirement benefits.

When questions of labor and employment law arise, the Internet is certain to hold the answer. Executive branch and independent agencies alike are on the Web, providing laws, regulations, administrative rulings, interpretive documents, field manuals, and more. Other sites—sponsored by law schools, law firms, bar associations and others—offer guides to practice and procedure in the field.

Here is a tour of those sites, starting with the megasite of the U.S. Department of Labor, with stops along the way at sites of independent entities such as the National Labor Relations Board and the Equal Employment Opportunity Commission, and at non-government sites offering either a general overview of the field or focusing on a specific practice topic, and concluding with sites of state labor agencies.

United States Department of Labor

★★★★★ The U.S. Department of Labor, www.dol.gov

The U.S. Department of Labor is host to a multi-layered Web site that serves both as its own home page and as an umbrella for the sites of each of the DOL's agencies, all organized in a common format.

From the home page, www.dol.gov, you can access information about programs, regulations and data for the entire department. It includes links to each DOL agency, general information about the DOL and the laws it administers, and the text of related laws and regulations. A series of interactive "e-laws" are designed to serve as "advisors" on topics of interest to employees and employers.

Beyond the DOL home page, each division has its own Web site that can stand alone as a distinct site. Generally, if you are seeking information about a specific entity, you should start with that entity's page. If you do not know which division has what you need, start with the DOL home page and work your way down.

Other DOL Web sites are:

★★★★★ Bureau of Labor Statistics, www.bls.gov

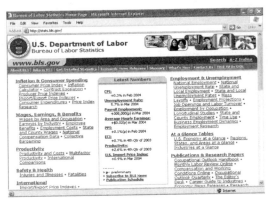

The definitive source for a diverse array of data. Topics include prices and living conditions, employment and unemployment, compensation and working conditions, productivity and more. Here you will find the Consumer Price Index and the Producer Price Index. Visitors can view commonly requested data reports or formulate their own queries by type of data, region and time period.

The BLS is the definitive source for economic and employment data.

This is also where on the Web to find the highly regarded BLS publication, *Monthly Labor Review*. The journal features research in a variety of labor-related fields, including the labor force, the economy, employment, inflation, productivity, occupational injuries and illnesses, wages, prices, and more. The site presents abstracts of each article and offers full-text downloads in Adobe Acrobat format. Articles are archived to 1988.

★★★★★ Employee Benefits Security Administration, www.dol.gov/ebsa

Responsible for protecting pension, health and other employee benefit plans, the EBSA has a broad-ranging site with information for employees, employers and legal professionals. It includes an extensive library of materials aimed at assisting businesses with compliance, as well as a complete library of federal laws and regulations.

★★★★★ **Employment Standards Administration,** www.dol.gov/esa

The ESA is composed of four major program offices:

- *The Office of Federal Contract Compliance Programs*, which administers the anti-discrimination provisions pertaining to government contractors and subcontractors.
- *The Office of Labor-Management Standards*, which enforces provisions of the Labor-Management Reporting and Disclosure Act and various other laws primarily related to promoting internal union democracy and the financial integrity of unions.
- *The Office of Workers' Compensation Programs*, which administers three major disability compensation programs.
- *The Wage and Hour Division*, responsible for enforcing the wage, hour and child labor provisions of the Fair Labor Standards Act as well as several other programs covering farm labor, family and medical leave, immigration and polygraph testing.

Its Web site offers complete information on all these programs, including statutory and regulatory provisions. Special pages are devoted to the minimum wage, sweatshops, and the Family and Medical Leave Act.

★★★★★ **Occupational Safety and Health Administration,** www.osha.gov

OSHA provides a wealth of information related to workplace safety and health. Included are the text of the Occupational Safety and Health Act of 1970, information on how and where to file an OSHA complaint, OSHA standards and regulations, OSHA's Field Compliance Manual, Federal Register notices related to OSHA, and OSHA directives. There is also a collection of publications on topics from asbestos to underground construction hazards, and downloadable software to help in OSHA compliance.

★★★★ **Mine Safety and Health Administration,** www.msha.gov

MSHA's site includes the full text of the Federal Mine Safety and Health Act, MSHA regulations, and a library of documents regarding mine safety and health. Also here are statistics on mine fatalities, injuries and accidents. A "Kid's Page" has information for children of mine workers.

★★★★ **Office of Administrative Law Judges,** www.oalj.dol.gov

The Labor Department's ALJs hear cases arising from more than eighty labor statutes, including cases involving black lung and longshore workers' compensation, civil rights, alien labor certification, whistleblower complaints, minimum wage disputes, migrant farm laborers, child labor and mine safety. The OALJ's Web site allows you to search its docket to determine whether a decision has been issued in a case and, if so, where to find the decision online. The site also includes specialized libraries of decisions in particular types of cases, such as black lung and contract appeals. The site also includes an assortment of ALJ benchbooks, guides to administrative practice and procedure, and standards for citation of ALJ opinions.

★★★★ Wirtz Labor Library, http://library.dol.gov

The Department of Labor's library, established in 1917, is one of the oldest Cabinet-level libraries and is internationally recognized for its excellent collection of historic materials. The most compelling reason to visit its Web site is its searchable card catalog, which includes all holdings added to the library since January 1975 as well as selected special collections. (Those seeking earlier card catalog entries will have to visit the library in Washington.) Elsewhere on the site, visitors can read about the library's history, holdings and special collections, and find links to other sites related to labor law and labor history.

★★★★ Women's Bureau, www.dol.gov/wb

Devoted to advocating on behalf of working women, this bureau's Web site is home to a variety of reports, publications and statistics on fair pay, gender-based discrimination, child care, working women's health, and related issues.

★★★ Benefits Review Board, www.dol.gov/brb/

The BRB hears appeals of workers' compensation claims arising under the Longshore and Harbor Worker's Compensation Act and the Black Lung Benefits amendments to the Federal Coal Mine Health and Safety Act of 1969. The site includes the full text of all published and unpublished black lung cases issued since 1989 and all longshore decisions since 1986. The site also offers an outline of current circuit court case law, as well as the full text of BRB's Black Lung and Longshore deskbooks.

★★★ Office of the Solicitor, www.dol.gov/sol

The Solicitor is the Department of Labor's chief legal officer, responsible for enforcing laws governing such diverse matters as fair labor standards, workplace safety and retirement benefits. The site provides a well-structured guide to the various laws and regulations enforced by the Department of Labor. Another useful feature is a library of briefs filed by the Solicitor in OSHA, fair labor practices and benefit security cases.

★★ Bureau of International Labor Affairs, www.dol.gov/ilab

International economic, trade, and immigration policies affecting American workers are the focus of this bureau. The Web site includes a collection of reports on international child labor and foreign labor trends. It also provides information on its various programs and activities and the laws and regulations it administers.

★★ Employees' Compensation Appeals Board, www.dol.gov/ecab/

This board is responsible for deciding appeals from the Office of Workers' Compensation Programs involving claims under the Federal Employees' Compensation Act. Its Web site provides the full text of all decisions issued since 1993 and headnotes from decisions beginning in 1988. The site also provides the text of the applicable law and regulations and a description of board procedures.

★★ Veterans' Employment and Training Service, www.dol.gov/vets

VETS helps veterans, reservists and National Guard members in securing employment and in enforcing their employment-related rights. Its site includes information about the laws VETS enforces, its programs, and a reading room of Freedom of Information documents.

Other Executive Agencies

★★★★★ National Institute for Occupational Safety and Health, www.cdc.gov/niosh/homepage.html

Part of the Centers for Disease Control and Prevention, NIOSH is responsible for conducting research and making recommendations for the prevention of work-related illnesses and injuries. The site is home to a number of databases with information relating to workplace safety, including the "Pocket Guide to Chemical Hazards" and the "Registry of Toxic Effects of Chemical Substances." It also features an extensive library of full-text documents, including alerts, manuals and hazard reports.

★★★★★ Social Security Administration, www.ssa.gov

A comprehensive site, with virtually everything you might want to know about the Social Security laws and benefits and the agency that administers them.

★★★★★ U.S. Department of Justice, Americans with Disabilities Act Home Page, www.ada.gov

The DOJ enforces the ADA as it relates to the employment practices of state and local governments. Employment lawyers will find much of use at its Web site. Among the highlights are the full texts of settlement and consent agreements resulting from ADA litigation, the full text of briefs filed by the DOJ in ADA cases, regular status reports covering not just DOJ enforcement actions but also related court decisions, and a library of ADA regulations and technical assistance manuals.

★★★ U.S. Office of Personnel Management, www.opm.gov

OPM administers the federal employment merit system for testing, recruitment and promotions. Its site includes the regulations, news releases and agency information. Of greater interest is its current listing of all available federal jobs. It also provides current salary and wage schedules.

Independent Agencies

★★★★★ Federal Labor Relations Authority, www.flra.gov

The FLRA is responsible for adjudicating federal sector labor disputes. Its Web site includes both the full text and summaries of all its decisions since 1994, as well as the full text of all court opinions pertaining to the FLRA. Decisions are organized by citation (e.g., "53 FLRA 70") and name, and also can be searched by key word. Supplementing the collection of court decisions is a library of briefs filed by the FLRA's Office of the Solicitor in litigation involving the FLRA. Also here are final actions of the Federal Service Impasses Panel, guidance memoranda and policies issued by the general counsel, and general information about FLRA offices and procedures.

★★★★★ National Labor Relations Board, www.nlrb.gov

The NLRB site includes decisions and orders issued by the Board since 1984, as well as regional director and administrative law judge decisions. They are in Adobe Acrobat format, so you will need the Adobe reader to view them, which you can obtain free at: www.adobe. com. The NLRB site also has the NLRB's *Weekly Summary*, a publication that summarizes all published NLRB decisions in

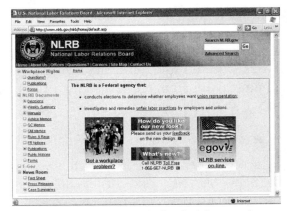

The NLRB's site includes decisions and orders issued by the Board since 1996.

unfair labor practice and representation cases, and which lists all decisions of NLRB administrative law judges and directions of elections by NLRB regional directors. The full text of the Board's rules and regulations is avail-able at the site, as are press releases and public notices.

★★★★ Equal Employment Opportunity Commission, www.eeoc.gov

The EEOC's site includes the full text of the laws it enforces, various fact sheets on such topics as filing a charge, recent press releases, and general information about the EEOC's organization and offices. Various publications are available to be downloaded, including EEOC enforcement guidelines on a number of topics.

★★★★ Federal Mediation and Conciliation Service, www.fmcs.gov

The FMCS is an independent agency providing arbitration and mediation for public, private and federal sector labor-management disputes. Its Web site includes information on FMCS services and has various forms and pub-lications that can be downloaded. It also provides online mediation through its program called Technology Assisted Group Solutions, or TAGS.

★★★★ Merit Systems Protection Board, www.mspb.gov

Established by the Civil Service Reform Act of 1978, the MSPB decides appeals from federal employees of removals and other major personnel actions. The Web site includes the full text of all its decisions since 1979. Decisions are searchable by key word, but not indexed by name or number. The site also provides summaries of recent decisions. MSPB forms and pub-lications can be downloaded from the site in Adobe Acrobat, Microsoft Word or HTML format.

★★★ Pension Benefit Guaranty Corporation, www.pbgc.gov

The PBGC is a federal corporation established by Title IV of the Employee Retirement Income Security Act to encourage the growth of defined benefit plans, ensure payment of benefits, and monitor pension insurance premi-ums. Its site includes final and proposed rules and regulations, technical updates, opinion letters, and interest rate information. It also has a library of forms related to plan terminations and other events.

★★★ Railroad Retirement Board, www.rrb.gov

The RRB is an independent federal agency charged with administering retirement-survivor and unemployment-sickness benefits for railroad work-ers and their families under the Railroad Retirement and Railroad Unemployment Insurance Acts. Its Web site includes information about benefit programs, cost-of-living reports, statistical information regarding benefits, information about taxation of benefits, and various publications and news releases.

★★★ U.S. Office of Special Counsel, www.osc.gov

OSC is an independent federal agency charged with investigation of alleged prohibited personnel practices and Hatch Act violations in the federal government and litigation before the U.S. Merit Systems Protection Board of cases arising out of these investigations. It also investigates cases involving the denial of federal employment to veterans and reservists. Its site includes detailed descriptions of prohibited personnel practices and OSC responses, Hatch Act do's and don'ts, and whistleblower information.

Other Government Resources

★★★★ DisabilityInfo.gov, www.disabilityinfo.gov

This comprehensive site collects disability-related information from throughout the federal government. Its employment section includes information on interviewing and recruiting, job accommodations, federal contracting, and laws and policies.

★★★ Federal Bulletin Board, http://fedbbs.access.gpo.gov

Operated by the Government Printing Office, this is an alternative site for many government documents. For labor lawyers, it includes full-text decisions of the Federal Labor Relations Authority and the Merit Systems Protection Board, both of which also have their own home pages offering the same decisions.

★★★ U.S. Senate Committee on Health, Education, Labor and Pensions, www.senate.gov/~labor http://health.senate.gov

This site provides information on the status of bills and resolutions referred to the committee, a schedule of committee hearings, a roster of committee members, and recent press releases.

Associations and Unions

★★★★★ American Arbitration Association, www.adr.org

ADR was being used to resolve labor disputes long before it swept over the rest of the legal field. Labor and employment disputes still make up a significant portion of the business of the American Arbitration Association. At the AAA's Web site, you will find all AAA rules, case processing information, the full texts of federal and state arbitration laws, sample forms and clauses, and full-text versions of AAA publications.

★★★★★ International Labour Organization, www.ilo.org

Founded in 1919, the ILO is a UN agency the mission of which is to promote social justice and internationally recognized human and labor rights. It formulates international labor standards in the form of conventions and recommendations, setting minimum standards of basic rights in areas such as freedom of association, the right to organize, collective bargaining, abolition of forced labor, equality of opportunity and treatment, and other standards regulating conditions across the entire spectrum of work-related issues. It provides technical assistance on labor law and industrial relations throughout the world. Its site is deep with content reflecting its work. Featured are two databases, one devoted to international labor standards and another containing national laws on labor, social security and related issues. The site serves as the umbrella for the ILO's many departments and programs, each with its own reservoir of information and resources.

★★★★★ Labor Research Association, www.laborresearch.org

Labor Research Association is a New York City-based nonprofit research and advocacy organization that provides research and educational services for trade unions. Its Web site is chock full of news, data and research regarding unions, the economy and politics. It combines news and research from throughout the Web with its own analyses and reports and selected full-text background documents to provide a thorough picture of the state of organized labor throughout the world. Topics include current organizing efforts, strikes, and contract negotiations; economic data covering employment, prices, wages and more; political issues such as ballot initiatives; legal opinions from the NLRB and the courts; and safety and health. A site rich in practical content, whether you represent unions or employers.

★★★★★ Section of Labor and Employment Law, American Bar Association, www.abanet.org/labor/home.html

This might have been just another bar association page, with its offerings of general information about the section, describing its committees, activities and meetings, but a partnership with BNA Books elevates this site to a higher level of practicality. Follow the link to "Publications and Papers," which will take you to the BNA-sponsored documents library, a repository of full-text journals, newsletters, committee reports and other section documents. Here you can find the full text of the section's highly respected journal, The Labor Lawyer, and a variety of topical newsletters, all in Adobe Acrobat format. From here, you can also get information on and purchase books produced jointly by the ABA and BNA, such as the definitive labor law treatises, *The Developing Labor Law* and *How Arbitration Works*.

★★★★ AFL-CIO, www.aflcio.org

This site is a complete guide to the organization that represents more than 13 million U.S. workers and is made up of sixty-four different unions. Lawyers will be most interested in the several sections of this site that address the organization's legislative agenda.

★★★★ National Right to Work Legal Defense Foundation, www.nrtw.org

The foundation is a nonprofit organization devoted to fighting compulsory union membership in the U.S. The site features a number of FAQs and briefing papers with information on workers' rights to avoid union membership and withhold union dues. A news section highlights current cases in which the foundation is involved, while an archive provides links to cases won by the foundation in the Supreme Court and federal courts of appeals. The site also provides links to relevant federal labor laws, state right-to-work laws, and other related resources. A map of the United States highlights states with right-to-work laws and links to the text of each state's law. Overall, this is an informative site that does a fair job of dealing with a sometimes controversial issue.

★★★ National Employment Lawyers Association, www.nela.org

Founded in 1985, the National Employment Lawyers Association is composed of lawyers who represent employees in cases involving employment discrimination, wrongful termination, employee benefits and other employment-related matters. NELA has a membership of more than 3,400 lawyers in all fifty states and the District of Columbia, as well as more than sixty state and local affiliates around the country.

NELA members can use this site as a gateway to access NELANet, a members-only electronic information-sharing network. For non-members, the site is somewhat sparse, largely devoted to promotional material about the organization and its conferences and products. It does include an up-to-date review of legislative and public-policy issues of interest to NELA, but a link to "Cases Around The Nation" offers only a sample of a database available to members. A page of links has only a handful of employment-specific resources salted with general legal sites.

Primers and Overviews

★★★★★ Cornell University School of Industrial and Labor Relations, www.ilr.cornell.edu

Cornell's ILR school is the nation's only institution of higher education offering a full four-year undergraduate program in industrial and labor relations, as well as various advanced degree programs. For practitioners, the most useful part of its Web site comes from its Catherwood Library. Its fully searchable electronic archive includes a range of materials relating to employer-employee relationships, including key government documents and public policy papers, all available free of charge. The library's Kheel Center features labor history materials. Also available through the ILR site is its journal, Industrial and Labor Relations Review. Although the full text is not here, the site includes each issue's table of contents and synopses of articles.

★★★★★ Institute of Industrial Relations, www.iir.berkeley.edu

Part of the University of California at Berkeley, the IIR supports multi-disciplinary research about labor and employment relations, hosts various faculty-run research centers, and sponsors several community service programs, including the California Public Employee Relations program, the Center for Labor Research and Education, and the Labor Project for Working Families. It publishes the academic journal Industrial Relations: A Journal of Economy and Society, and houses a research library that collects a wide array of information about work, organizations and labor issues. Its Web site includes a wealth of information about and created by these various programs. A highlight of the site is its Labor Research Portal, an extensive guide to labor resources on the Web. For labor relations lawyers, the site's Labor Contracts Database serves as an online clearinghouse for the complete text of union contracts.

★★★★★ Legal Information Institute, www.law.cornell.edu/topics/topic2.html

Cornell Law School's LII features a series of "law about" primers, overviews of a variety of legal subject areas. Its employment topics include collective bargaining, employment discrimination, unemployment compensation, workers' compensation, and workplace safety. For each subject, there is a textual introduction and a collection of links to primary and secondary resources elsewhere on the Web.

★★★★★ Ross Runkel Employment Law Page, www.lawmemo.com

Ross Runkel, professor of law emeritus at Willamette University College of Law, edits this site. It features summaries from his two e-mail newsletters, "Employment Law Memo," containing summaries of recent developments in employment discrimination, employment law and labor law, and "NLRB Memo," with summaries of decisions by the NLRB. Also at the site are "unofficial" home pages for the EEOC and the NLRB, each providing a fairly detailed overview of the agency, its governing law and regulations, and its work. Topping off the site is a directory of employment lawyers by state and a small collection of links. The case summaries were current to the day.

★★★★★ Workplace Fairness, www.workplacefairness.org

This the new Web site from the organization of the same name, devoted to providing information, education and assistance to individual workers and their advocates nationwide. It is affiliated with the National Employment Lawyers Association, a national organization of lawyers who represent employees in cases involving employment discrimination, wrongful termination, employee benefits, and other employment-related matters. The site is well done and informative, with pages providing fairly detailed information on hiring, termination, discrimination, harassment, wages and hours, unemployment, workers' compensation, health and safety, and other work-related issues. A feature entitled "This Week in the Courts" provides circuit-by-circuit summaries of recent United States Supreme Court and federal appellate court decisions affecting workplace rights.

★★★★ Labor and Employment Laws of the 50 States, www.law.cornell.edu/topics/Table_Labor.htm

From Cornell's Legal Information Institute, a thorough collection of quick links to state labor laws and agencies. Nothing fancy, but a useful time saver.

★★★ Law At Work, www.lawatwork.com

Assembled by Richard L. Connors, a management-side employment lawyer in Overland Park, Kansas, this site brings together links to a number of resources pertaining to employment and labor law issues. Links are organized by topic and jurisdiction and include both federal and state sources. State links focus on Kansas, Missouri and Nebraska. This is a simple but useful and well-organized collection of links.

★ **National Employment Law Institute,** www.neli.org

A continuing education organization focusing on employment law, NELI's Web site lists its program and publication offerings and information on how to register or purchase.

Focused Sites

Focus on Discrimination

★★★ **DiscriminationAttorney.com,** www.discriminationattorney.com

Sponsored by a Beverly Hills law firm, this site describes itself as a guide for lawyers and nonlawyers alike to the field of employment law and other areas of civil rights law. It is nicely designed and contains simple but informative FAQs on such topics as sexual harassment; age, race and disability discrimination; and whistleblowing. With the articles geared to non-lawyers, it offers little of use to practicing lawyers.

Focus on Employee Benefits

★★★★ **Employee Benefits Legal Resource Web Site,** http://benefit-sattorney.com

Carol V. Calhoun, a Washington, D.C. lawyer, sponsors this site, which includes a broad assortment of resources relating to benefits law. The most useful feature is its library of research links, which is actually jointly sponsored by Calhoun and another employee benefits Web site, BenefitsLink, www.benefitslink.com. The collection of links is wide-ranging and well-organized. Also at the site are message boards on benefits-related topics, a list of state retirement system Web sites, and information on finding a job in the employee benefits field.

Focus on Whistleblowers

★★★★ **National Whistleblowers Center,** www.whistleblowers.org

The purpose of this center is to support litigation on behalf of employee whistleblowers, to educate the public about employees' rights with regard to disclosing violations of law, and to provide referrals to lawyers qualified to represent whistleblowers. The site includes a timely news section, a guide to the legal protections for whistleblowers, and information on specific cases, issues and industries. Attorneys can register at the site to be considered for case referrals.

★★ Qui Tam Information Center, www.quitam.com

The site focuses on actions by those who have blown the whistle on government contractors. It presents a fairly cursory overview of the law in this field.

Focus on Disability Law

★★★★★ Job Accommodation Network, www.jan.wvu.edu

With a focus on accommodation of disabilities in the workplace, this comprehensive resource includes original materials along with a rich collection of links to disability-related legal resources elsewhere on the Web. Sponsored by the Office of Disability Employment Policy of the U.S. Department of Labor, it is operated in conjunction with the International Center for Disability Information at West Virginia University. Among the resources it contains are the text of the Americans with Disabilities Act of 1990, ADA regulations, accessibility guidelines, technical assistance manuals, and extensive libraries of ADA-related information. Its collection of links includes an assortment of medical and employment resources as well as legal sites.

★★★★★ Disability and the Workplace: An Internet Primer, www.ilr.cornell.edu/library/subjectGuides/disabilityAndTheWorkplace. html

From the Catherwood Library at Cornell University's School of Industrial and Labor Relations, this research guide is an exhaustive collection of links to Internet resources related to disability and the workplace. Links are annotated and organized by subject.

★★★★ Pike Institute on Law and Disability, www.bu.edu/law/pike

A program of Boston University School of Law, the Pike Institute supports education, research and public service activities concerning disability law. For practitioners, the site offers *Disability Law Highlights*, a monthly online newsletter summarizing recent court decisions, newly filed court cases, administrative actions, and legislation affecting people with disabilities. The site includes the complete text of the institute's book, *Estate Planning for Parents of People with Disabilities*, and also offers the book in audio format.

Focus on Overtime

★ The Overtime Law Page, www.overtimelawpage.com

A San Diego law firm hosts this site, which is primarily a marketing brochure for the firm accompanied by a simple FAQ on overtime law.

State Labor Agencies on the Web

Federal labor agencies are not alone online. Virtually all the agencies charged with enforcement of state labor laws also have sites on the Internet. They are:

- **Alabama Department of Industrial Relations,** www.dir.state.al.us
- **Alaska Department of Labor,** www.labor.state.ak.us
- **Arizona Industrial Commission,** www.ica.state.az.us
- **Arkansas Department of Labor,** www.ark.org/labor
- **California Department of Industrial Relations,** www.dir.ca.gov
- **Colorado Department of Labor and Employment,** www.coworkforce.com
- **Connecticut Department of Labor,** www.ctdol.state.ct.us
- **Delaware Department of Labor,** www.delawareworks.com
- **Florida Department of Labor and Employment Security,** www.fdles.state.fl.us
- **Georgia Department of Labor,** www.dol.state.ga.us
- **Hawaii Department of Labor and Industrial Relations,** http://dlir.state.hi.us
- **Idaho Department of Labor,** www.labor.state.id.us
- **Illinois Department of Labor,** www.state.il.us/agency/idol
- **Indiana Department of Labor,** www.state.in.us/labor
- **Iowa Workforce Development,** www.state.ia.us/iwd
- **Kansas Division of Employment and Training,** http://entkdhr.state.ks.us
- **Kentucky Labor Cabinet,** www.labor.ky.gov
- **Kentucky Labor-Management Relations & Mediation,** www.labor.ky.gov/lmr/index.htm
- **Louisiana Department of Labor,** www.ldol.state.la.us
- **Maine Department of Labor,** www.state.me.us/labor
- **Maine Bureau of Employment Services,** www.mainecareercenter.com
- **Maine Labor Relations Board,** http://janus.state.me.us/mlrb/homemlrb.htm
- **Maine Workers' Compensation Board,** www.state.me.us/wcb
- **Maryland Department of Labor, Licensing and Regulation,** www.dllr.state.md.us
- **Massachusetts Department of Industrial Accidents,** www.state.ma.us/dia
- **Massachusetts Division of Employment and Training,** www.detma.org

- **Massachusetts Workers' Compensation Advisory Council,**
  www.state.ma.us/wcac/wcac.html
- **MassJobs Council,** www.massworkforce.org
- **Michigan Department of Consumer and Industry Services,**
  www.cis.state.mi.us
- **Minnesota Department of Labor and Industry,**
  www.doli.state.mn.us
- **Mississippi Employment Security Commission,**
  www.mesc.state.ms.us
- **Missouri Department of Labor and Industrial Relations,**
  www.dolir.mo.gov
- **Montana Department of Labor and Industry,** http://dli.state.mt.us
- **Nebraska Department of Labor,** www.dol.state.ne.us
- **Nebraska Commission of Industrial Relations,**
  www.nol.org/home/NCIR
- **Nevada Department of Employment, Training & Rehabilitation,**
  http://nvdetr.org
- **New Hampshire Employment Security,** www.nhes.state.nh.us
- **New Hampshire Public Employee Labor Relations Board,**
  www.state.nh.us/pelrb
- **New Jersey Department of Labor,** www.state.nj.us/labor
- **New Jersey Public Employment Relations Commission,**
  www.state.nj.us/perc
- **New Jersey Workforce,** www.wnjpin.state.nj.us
- **New Mexico Department of Labor,** www.dol.state.nm.us
- **New York Department of Labor,** www.labor.state.ny.us
- **North Carolina Department of Labor,** www.dol.state.nc.us
- **North Dakota Department of Labor,** www.state.nd.us/labor/
- **Ohio Bureau of Employment Services,** www.state.oh.us/obesNO
- **Ohio Department of Commerce, Division of Labor and Worker
  Safety,** www.com.state.oh.us/laws/default.htm
- **Ohio State Employment Relations Board,** www.serb.state.oh.us
- **Oklahoma Department of Labor,** www.okdol.state.ok.us
- **Oregon Employment Department,** www.emp.state.or.us
- **Pennsylvania Department of Labor and Industry,**
  www.dli.state.pa.us
- **Rhode Island Department of Labor and Training,**
  www.dlt.state.ri.us
- **South Carolina Department of Labor, Licensing and Regulation,**
  www.llr.state.sc.us
- **South Dakota Department of Labor,** www.state.sd.us/dol

- **Tennessee Department of Labor,** www.state.tn.us/labor-wfd/
- **Texas Workforce Commission,** www.twc.state.tx.us
- **Utah Labor Commission,** www.ind-com.state.ut.us
- **Vermont Department of Labor and Industry,** www.state.vt.us/labind
- **Vermont Labor Relations Board,** www.state.vt.us/vlrb/index.htm
- **Virginia Department of Labor and Industry,** www.dli.state.va.us
- **Washington Department of Labor and Industries,** www.lni.wa.gov
- **Washington Public Employment Relations Commission,** www.perc.wa.gov
- **West Virginia Bureau of Employment Programs,** www.state.wv.us/BEP
- **Wisconsin Department of Workforce Development,** www.dwd.state.wi.us
- **Wyoming Department of Employment,** http://wydoe.state.wy.us

Chapter 12

Net Law: The Internet's Rules of the Road

─────── **Chapter Contents** ───────

Starting Points
Keeping Up with Case Law
Civil Liberties
Scholarly Pursuits
Focus On . . .
Membership Organizations
Law Journals

The Internet has spawned a field of law all its own. Internet law is a dynamic, malleable, uncharted area of practice, where the rules have yet to be firmly defined. Not really even a distinct area of law, it is actually an amalgam of theory and practice drawn from many fields—a mixture made up of parts taken from intellectual property, civil liberties, tort, criminal, property, telecommunications, international trade, commercial and conflicts law.

For the lawyers who labor in this field, Internet law requires them to remain acutely ahead of the game, able to keep on top of the latest legal developments and respond in a digital instant. Internet law also mandates, perhaps more so than any other field, that its practitioners remain generalists, able to sort through and recognize the array of legal issues that can arise in Cyberspace.

Where better to keep up with the latest developments in Internet law than the Internet itself? The Web is home to many sites devoted to understanding and keeping up with this fast-paced field.

Starting Points

★★★★★ BitLaw, www.bitlaw.com

Created by Daniel A. Tysver, a partner with the Hopkins, Minnesota, IP firm Beck & Tysver, BitLaw has grown over the years from a compilation of legal resources related to computers and the Internet into a virtual online treatise on intellectual property and technology law. With over 1,800 pages covering patent, copyright, trademark and Internet law, the site is a combination of original essays and hyperlinked resources. Tysver's exploration of each topic begins with an executive summary followed by increasingly deeper layers of more detailed discussions. He supplements these essays with the full text of significant copyright decisions, hypertext versions of federal IP laws and regulations, general discussions of various legal issues, and a good collection of links. He also provides official forms and sample contracts.

★★★★★ CyberLaw@Sidley, www.sidley.com/cyberlaw/cyberlaw_new.asp

From the technology and e-commerce practice group of Sidley Austin Brown & Wood, an international law firm with more than 1,400 lawyers worldwide, CyberLaw@Sidley is a truly practical site combining daily news coverage with in-depth feature articles and analysis. The news comes via links to other media sites, with a half-dozen or so headlines added every business day and older stories maintained through an archive. New feature articles are regularly added, with all articles organized under topics that include banking, copyright, domain names, e-commerce, encryption, legislation, privacy and others. A collection of links to Cyberlaw sites is also organized by topic, and some are annotated. The collection could use some updating, as a few of the links are dead.

★★★★★ GigaLaw.com, www.gigalaw.com

Although it bills itself as a general legal information site for Internet and technology professionals, Internet entrepreneurs and the lawyers who serve them, GigaLaw most closely resembles an online magazine, a kind of e-zine for e-law. Featuring regular columnists, in-depth articles and daily news, GigaLaw provides current coverage and considered analysis of issues at the convergence of law and

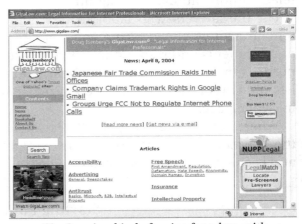

GigaLaw is a kind of e-zine for e-law, with daily news and in-depth features.

technology. Douglas M. Isenberg, an Atlanta lawyer and former journalist, publishes and edits the site, with articles contributed exclusively by lawyers and law professors. Although GigaLaw's articles cover the gamut of Internet law's hot topics, they also veer into areas not so commonly covered, such as "The Importance of Web Access for the Disabled," and "Age Discrimination

Law for High-Tech Companies." The site includes forums for posting messages and questions about an array of Internet law topics.

★★★★ Computer Professionals for Social Responsibility, www. cpsr.org

CPSR is a public-interest alliance of computer scientists and others concerned about the impact of computer technology on society. Follow the "Topics" link and explore CPSR's broad-ranging collection of articles and links focusing on a variety of topics that include "cyber-rights," computer crime, censorship and free speech, intellectual property, the environment, gender, privacy, and the workplace. The site includes extensive archives of materials going back to 1995. While most of the site appears to be current, some links are out of date and some pages badly need updating.

★★★★ Ultimate Internet Law Meta-index, www.imparl.net/ weblaw.html

This is a page of links, nothing more, but a good one—an index of links to other sites that themselves index links to Internet law resources on the Web. Steven D. Imparl, the Chicago lawyer who maintains the site, says that his goal is "to make this page the best meta-index on Internet law in the world." Imparl's collection is not exhaustive, but it succeeds in selecting sites that are useful. Imparl also does a good job keeping the site up to date.

★★★ Cyberlaw Encyclopedia, www.gahtan.com/cyberlaw

Toronto lawyer Alan Gahtan maintains this "encyclopedia," really a collection of roughly 1,200 links to resources elsewhere on the Internet, organized under an index of more than fifty topical headings. One aspect of Gahtan's collection that distinguishes it from other portals is the large number of court opinions to which it directly links. Pick a topic—say, copyright—and you will find links to cases that set precedents in that area. Unfortunately, a large number of these links—particularly links to court cases—no longer work. Despite this flaw, Gahtan's well-organized collection of links remains sufficiently thorough to maintain its usefulness to lawyers attempting to find answers to questions of Internet law.

★★★ E-Law, www.Loundy.com

David J. Loundy is a Chicago lawyer who also happens to be an Internet maven and a proficient writer. He writes a monthly technology law column for the *Chicago Daily Law Bulletin*, all of which columns (dating back to 1994) are on his Web site. Loundy tackles issues such as "meta tags"—words hidden in a Web page to help draw traffic that some lawsuits allege are used in a way that violates trademark law—as well as Internet fraud, spam and encryption, all in an informed and thorough style. Unfortunately, the frequency of his writing tapered off in recent years, so most of the articles are from prior to 2000.

Keeping Up with Case Law

★★★★★ **Perkins Coie Internet Case Digest,** www.perkinscoie. com/casedigest/default.cfm

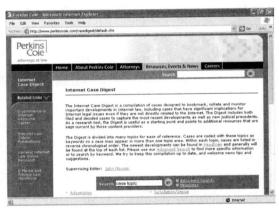

The Internet Case Digest, from the Seattle-based law firm Perkins Coie, is a compilation of U.S. and international court cases of especially high interest that address specific issues of Internet-related law, or that, although not directly related to the Internet, have significant implications for Internet legal issues. Although not the only site to track Internet law cases, Perkins Coie's stands out for a number of reasons, including its

The Internet Case Digest is a timely and comprehensive collection of case law.

broad scope and its up-to-the-minute timeliness. A unique feature is that case summaries include links not just to the full text of the opinion, but also to news reports about the case. Digests include both filed and decided cases in order to track not just new precedents but new developments as well. Digests are organized under topical headings, and the same case may appear under more than one topic. Within topics, cases are listed in reverse chronological order. Jump to "Headlines" to find the most recent additions and developments. Follow the "Advanced Search" link to search the site by key word, case name, court, date or other parameters.

★★★★★ **Phillips Nizer's Internet Library,** www.phillipsnizer.com/ internetlib.htm

Martin H. Samson, a partner with Phillips Nizer, New York City, created and maintains this top Internet law resource, collecting and analyzing the case law that is shaping the development of this field. Cases cover the gamut of Cyberlaw topics, including trademark and copyright infringement, dilution, defamation, click-wrap and shrink-wrap agreements, use of meta tags, links and frames, jurisdiction, spam, e-mail and First Amendment issues arising out of governmental regulation of the Internet, among others. Samson provides a brief synopsis of each case, with a link to a more in-depth analysis and, in many cases, the full text of the opinion. Users can browse the cases by subject matter, scroll through a list of all cases, or search their full text with key words. One shortcoming is that the site does not allow a user to see only the most recent cases, so a regular visitor has no way to view only what is new since the last visit. To make up for this, Phillips Nizer offers an e-mail alert to new cases.

Civil Liberties

★★★★★ Center for Democracy and Technology, www.cdt.org

An important site for anyone concerned about civil rights in Cyberspace, this is the Internet home of the Center for Democracy and Technology, a public interest organization "advocating for civil liberties in new computer and communications technologies." Covering such topics as free speech, data privacy, government surveillance, cryptography, domain names and terrorism, CDT combines in-depth analysis with up-to-date headline news and legislative tracking to serve as both a resource for research and education and a springboard for political action.

★★★★★ Chilling Effects, www.chillingeffects.org

When Internet expression meets with a cease-and-desist demand, for guidance look to a site devoted to the legal protection of online speech. Launched in 2002 by the Electronic Frontier Foundation and four law schools, it publishes actual cease-and-desist letters annotated with comments on the applicable law. Topics include linking, fan fiction, parody and criticism, copyright and trademark.

★★★★★ CyberSLAPP, www.cyberslapp.org

The founders of this site believe that a new form of lawsuit called a "CyberSLAPP" threatens to overturn the promise of anonymous online speech and chill the freedom of expression that is central to the online world. CyberSLAPP cases typically involve a person who has posted anonymous criticisms of a corporation or public figure on the Internet. The target of the criticism then files a frivolous lawsuit so that it can issue a subpoena to the Web site or Internet service provider involved and obtain the identity of the anonymous critic. Sponsored by a coalition of civil liberty and privacy groups, this site includes a collection of legal briefs and court opinions in cases in which Internet speakers were sued for their online speech or where subpoenas were requested to obtain the identities of online speakers.

★★★★★ Electronic Frontier Foundation, www.eff.org

Dedicated to protecting rights and promoting freedom in the electronic frontier, the Electronic Frontier Foundation, since its creation in 1990, has been at the forefront of cases involving civil liberties, privacy and freedom of expression in the arena of computers and the Internet. The EFF played critical roles, both as plaintiff and advocate, in *ACLU v. Reno*, the landmark lawsuit that successfully struck down portions of the Communications Decency Act. It tackled encryption restrictions in *Bernstein v. Department of State*. It established the blue ribbon campaign to promote free speech on the Internet. Its Web site features complete information on all of its projects and legal proceedings in which the EFF was involved. It also houses an enormous archive of documentary resources and legal materials, compiled over the course of the many campaigns in which it has been involved.

★★★★★ Electronic Privacy Information Center, www.epic.org

Founded in 1994, EPIC's work in the emerging arena of online civil liberties quickly made it a leading public interest advocacy organization. During its relatively brief life span, it has helped uncover Carnivore, the FBI's controversial Internet monitoring system; helped ease government restrictions on the use of encryption; and played a central role in *ACLU v. Reno*, the case that declared unconstitutional key portions of the Communications Decency Act. EPIC continues to be at the forefront of protecting civil liberties, and its Web site reflects that, with a range of current-awareness information on litigation, legislation and policy initiatives affecting free speech, privacy and other key areas, as well as a comprehensive archive of documents on free speech, computer security, freedom of information, cryptography and privacy.

★★★★ American Civil Liberties Union, Privacy and Technology, www.aclu.org/Privacy/PrivacyMain.cfm

When technology or the use of technology threatens civil liberties, the American Civil Liberties Union takes notice. These pages look at a range of issues at the intersection of technology and civil liberties, from government surveillance to Internet free speech. It reports on current ACLU cases in these areas and provides background legal and legislative materials.

Scholarly Pursuits

★★★★★ Berkman Center for Internet and Society, http://cyber.law.harvard.edu

Harvard Law School's Berkman Center is a research program founded to explore, study and help develop Cyberspace. Founded in 1995 as the Center on Law and Technology, it grew out of a seminar led by Harvard law professors Charles Nesson and Arthur Miller. In 1997, the Berkman family's gift of $5.4 million led to a name change and the appointment of Lawrence Lessig to the Berkman professorship. Today, the Center sponsors education programs and innovative projects devoted to understanding and furthering this evolving field. Its most cutting edge work may be in its open platform projects, aimed at democratizing systems of governance, law and education. An example of this is Openlaw, an experiment in crafting legal argument in an open forum, in which Berkman lawyers are developing arguments, drafting pleadings, and editing briefs in public, online. Non-lawyers and lawyers alike are invited to join the process by adding thoughts to the "brainstorm" outlines, drafting and commenting on drafts in progress, and suggesting reference sources. More recently, Berkman launched Weblogs at Harvard Law, a pioneering project to explore the potential benefits of Web logs ("blogs")[1] in educational and community-building contexts.

★★★★★ UCLA Online Institute for Cyberspace Law and Policy, www.gseis.ucla.edu/iclp/hp.html

Created in 1995, the Online Institute for Cyberspace Law and Policy provides resources for academics, lawyers, students and others. It features an extensive bibliography of books and journal articles in the field, with links to the actual works when they are available online. The site gives extensive coverage to controversial issues of Internet law, with sections devoted to topics such as file sharing and obscenity. An outline organizes major cases, statutes and other developments by their topics, with links to full text documents when possible, while a chronology traces key events in the development of Internet law during the decade of the 1990s. Rounding out the site is a library of articles by Internet law scholars and practitioners and a collection of links to Cyberlaw resources elsewhere online.

---

[1] For more about blogs, see Chapter 27 *infra*.

★★★ Berkeley Center for Law & Technology, www.law.berkeley. edu/institutes/bclt

Devoted to intellectual property and related fields of law as they intersect with business, science and technology, the Berkeley Center carries on a number of scholarly and research programs. Prominent among these are its conferences and lecture series on topics ranging from antitrust to digital music to patents. The Web site gives information on forthcoming and past programs, as well as providing an overview of the Center.

★★★ Cyberspace Law Institute, www.cli.org

The Cyberspace Law Institute was created to study and help develop "the new forms of law and law-making required by the growth of global communications networks and online communities." Early on, it was involved in pioneering projects merging law and the Internet, such as the Virtual Magistrate, the first program, now defunct, to attempt ADR online. Today, the CLI's site appears dormant, with an "under construction" note on the front page, but it retains its library of articles, papers and courses on Internet law, including the ambitious eighty-lesson course from 1999, "Cyberspace Law for Non-Lawyers." For lawyers, there are short courses such as, "Constructing a Company E-Mail Policy," and a full library of papers on Cyberlaw topics written by well-known scholars and practitioners in the field.

Focus On . . .

★★★★★ Computer Crime and Intellectual Property Section, www.cybercrime.gov

Launched by the U.S. Department of Justice in March 2000, the Computer Crime and Intellectual Property Section is a staff of federal lawyers who focus exclusively on the issues raised by computer and intellectual property crime. Their job includes advising federal prosecutors and law enforcement agents; commenting on and proposing legislation; coordinating international efforts to combat computer crime; litigating cases; and training other law enforcement groups. Their site covers topics such as encryption, electronic privacy laws, search and seizure of computers, e-commerce, hacker investigations, and intellectual property crimes. It provides in-depth coverage of these issues, with libraries of full text cases, laws and other documents from actual cases.

★★★★★ Cyberbanking and Law, www.cyberbanking-law.lu

Dedicated to electronic banking on the Internet and its legal implications, Cyberbanking and Law seeks to show, through examples and background materials, how electronic banking works and to explain its legal framework. Sponsored by the Economics Law Laboratory, Luxembourg, and the Institute for Computer Law, Saarbrucken, Germany, the site addresses the topic's technological and legal aspects in English, French and German. Features of the site include a periodic journal with in-depth articles on Internet banking, the full text of statutes and decisions relating to online banking from countries throughout the world, a library of research papers, and an annotated collection of links to sites dealing with electronic banking and payment.

★★★★★ Internet Corporation for Assigned Names and Numbers, www.icann.org

ICANN is a nonprofit corporation formed in October 1998 to manage the Internet's domain names and IP addresses. Its site provides detailed information on domain names and domain registration policies. A critical portion of the site for Internet lawyers is its section on resolution of domain name disputes. This section, of course, sets out the dispute resolution rules and procedures, but, perhaps more importantly, it tracks every domain dispute commenced under the rules, showing the date it was filed, its case number, the name in dispute and the final outcome, if any, along with a link to the full text of the decision or order, where available.

★★★★★ Uniform Computer Information Transactions Act, www.ucitaonline.com

2B or not 2B? That was the question that plagued the National Conference of Commissioners on Uniform State Laws in the late 1990s as its efforts to craft a Uniform Commercial Code provision on software licensing stirred controversy and debate within the legal profession and the technology industry. The end result was not a UCC provision at all, but the Uniform Computer Information Transactions Act, which the NCCUSL finally approved in July 1999. This comprehensive site provides detailed information on the drafting process and the final act, and tracks its status as state legislatures consider its adoption. Carol A. Kunze, a California lawyer who participated in the drafting process, maintains the site.

★★★★ Internet Jurisdiction, www.kentlaw.edu/cyberlaw

At first glance, a visitor to this site's fairly sparse front page might think there is not much here, and, judging by the name, assume the site is confined to issues of jurisdiction. The visitor would be wrong on both counts, for this is a site that is both broader and deeper than it appears. A joint project of Chicago-Kent College of Law and the American Bar Association, the site starts with a front page that lists fewer than a dozen articles and speeches on Internet law, several by Chicago-Kent's dean, Henry H. Perritt, Jr. But follow the link to "Project Documentation" for substantive articles providing overviews of jurisdictional issues in various countries and for various areas of law. Then go to the page listing the project's working groups. Each group has its own page, with its own collection of pertinent articles, court opinions, analyses, links and other materials. These groups address substantive topics including advertising, intellectual property, payment systems, privacy, gaming, sales of goods and services, securities and taxation, and each group is composed of prominent practitioners from throughout the U.S. The site could use a map or a search engine, but it is well worth exploring.

★★★★ The Link Controversy Page, www.jura.uni-tuebingen.de/bechtold/lcp.html

The Link Controversy Page is a comprehensive collection of links from sources throughout the world, intended to provide an overview of the legal—particularly copyright—problems of using hyperlinks to connect to images and text elsewhere on the Web. Links are mostly arranged by country, while a section devoted to specific linking cases collects links to news stories and articles pertaining to each case. Stefan Bechtold, a law professor at the University of Tuebingen, Germany, maintains the site. This is a useful resource for anyone exploring this issue, but beware: the site could use some updating, both in eliminating dead links and adding new sites.

★★ AdultWebLaw, www.adultweblaw.com

This site sells a set of legal forms and provides links to Web sites and articles related to the legal issues involved in hosting a Web site with adult content. It includes overviews of key legal issues relating to copyright and intellectual property, child pornography and obscenity, and provides links to international laws pertaining to sexual conduct.

Membership Organizations

★★★★ Computer Law Association, www.cla.org

Founded in 1971, the Computer Law Association is an international organization of lawyers involved in computer and communications technology. Its

Web site features an IT Resource Center, with books, articles, news, legal forms, and links to a range of related sites. Some of the material on the site is restricted to members, and other resources, such as the forms, must be purchased offline.

★★★ American Bar Association, Committee on Cyberspace Law, www.buslaw.org/cgi-bin/controlpanel.cgi?committee=CL320000

The ABA's Section of Business Law created this Committee in 1995 to address the growing use of the Internet to conduct business transactions. Since that time, it has established subcommittees and undertaken projects to explore such diverse topics as the corporate aspects of information technology, electronic commerce, electronic financial services, international transactions, intellectual property, and others. The Committee's Web site, a subsection of the Section of Business Law's site, provides information on subcommittees, task forces and working groups.

★★★ American Bar Association Section of Science and Technology Law, www.abanet.org/scitech/home.html

Digital signatures, e-commerce, Cybernotaries, computer crime—these are among the subjects the Section of Science and Technology Law finds itself focusing on nowadays. Notably, the Section produced the first comprehensive set of guidelines for the use of digital signatures, which it offers as a free download in a choice of WordPerfect or Microsoft Word formats. In addition, you can read all about the Section and its activities.

Law Journals

★★★★★ Journal of Online Law, www.wm.edu/law/publications/jol

This collection of scholarly essays is more a historical document than a law journal, preserved from a time when lawyers were just beginning to explore the law's parameters in Cyberspace. Until 2001, the Journal contained only seven articles, all from 1995 and 1996. But they were written by an esteemed group of early Internet law scholars and were among the first to explore questions that remain unanswered these several years later. Edited by I. Trotter Hardy, a professor at William & Mary School of Law, the Journal's contributors and advisors were lawyers who remain at the forefront of Internet law. Articles include Hardy's seminal "The Ancient Doctrine of Trespass to Web Sites"; "Cyber Payment Infrastructure," by Henry H. Perritt Jr.; "Cybertime, Cyberspace and Cyberlaw," by M. Ethan Katsh; and "Indecency, Ignorance and Intolerance: The First Amendment and the

Regulation of Electronic Expression," by Fred H. Cate. In 2001, one more article was added, exploring the constitutionality of anti-spam laws.

★★★★ Lex Electronica, www.lex-electronica.org

Lex Electronica is a bilingual electronic legal journal devoted to information technology law, published by the Public Law Research Center at the University of Montreal. Started in 1995, its articles explore privacy online, conflict resolution, encryption, e-commerce, telecommunications, and other information technology topics. Articles are available in English and French. The editors welcome the submission of articles for future issues, with complete submission guidelines described on the site.

Other journals with a focus on Internet law include:

- **Berkeley Technology Law Journal,** www.law.berkeley.edu/journals/btlj
- **Computer Law Review & Technology Journal,** www.smu.edu/~csr
- **The Cyberspace Law Journal,** http://raven.cc.ukans.edu/~cybermom/CLJ/clj.html
- **Harvard Journal of Law & Technology,** http://jolt.law.harvard.edu
- **IDEA The Journal of Law & Technology,** www.idea.fplc.edu
- **Intellectual Property Law Journal,** http://ubmail.ubalt.edu/~ubiplj
- **International Journal of Law & Information Technology,** http://www3.oup.co.uk/jnls/list/inttec
- **Journal of Information, Law & Technology,** http://elj.warwick.ac.uk/Jilt
- **Journal of Internet Banking and Commerce,** www.arraydev.com/commerce/JIBC/current.asp
- **Journal of Technology Law & Policy,** http://willow.circa.ufl.edu/~techlaw NO
- **Law on the Electronic Frontier: Table of Contents, Volume 2, Number 1, JCMC,** www.ascusc.org/jcmc/vol2/issue1
- **Michigan Telecommunication & Technology Law Review,** www.mttlr.org
- **Richmond Journal of Law & Technology,** http://law.richmond.edu/jolt
- **Virginia Journal of Law & Technology,** www.vjolt.net
- **West Virginia Journal of Law & Technology,** www.wvu.edu/~wvjolt

Virtual Realty: Real Estate Law on the Web

Conveyancing lawyers find themselves entangled in an ever expanding web of federal and state laws. Real estate practice today requires expertise in banking law, environmental regulation, civil rights, lending practices, taxation and more.

For those caught in this web, what better place to turn than the Web—the World Wide Web—where you will find a growing number of government and private resources related to real estate law and practice. Here is a guide to the best of what the Web has to offer.

Federal

★★★★★ Fannie Mae, www.fanniemae.com

The nation's largest source of home mortgage funds, Fannie Mae is a private corporation, federally chartered to increase the availability and affordability of housing. Its well-designed Web site has information for home buyers and lenders, as well as general financial information about the Fannie Mae corporation. It includes a complete library of downloadable mortgage documents, regular news updates, information on mortgage products and services, and the text of guide announcements and lender letters.

The site also now includes a consumer-oriented section called HomePath, which was a separate Web site until November 2002. It has information on buying or refinancing a home and tools designed to help users find a lender or mortgage. The site includes several mortgage calculators for helping consumers determine what price house they can afford, including the "true cost calculator" designed to help consumers determine the true cost of a mortgage by calculating down payment, interest rate and points, mortgage and title insurance costs, appraisal fees, and other factors. The site also includes a tool for searching for Fannie Mae properties for sale. Real estate lawyers will find this site useful mostly for the educational tools they can pass on to their clients, including a glossary of mortgage and finance terms.

★★★★★ eFannieMae.com, www.efanniemae.com

FannieMae launched this business-to-business companion site in 2002 for professionals involved in lending, mortgage brokering, and transactions involving mortgage-backed securities and debt securities. Subsections provide complete libraries of downloadable forms and documents, regular news updates, information on mortgage products and services, the texts of guide announcements and lender letters, and more.

★★★★★ Federal Deposit Insurance Corporation, www.fdic.gov

The FDIC's site has news of interest to the banking industry; federal banking laws and regulations; the full text of FDIC publications and articles, including a survey of the most important federal laws relating to banking; a number of statistical reports on banks and banking; the quarterly *Survey of Real Estate Trends*; and a host of other information for banking professionals and consumers. Real estate lawyers can use the FDIC's site to investigate a particular bank's financial condition or to review any of a number of statistical reports such as the FDIC's semiannual *Survey of Real Estate Trends*. The FDIC is in the real estate business as well. In its capacity as a court-appointed receiver, the FDIC liquidates a variety of assets, including real estate. Use the site's Real Estate Retrieval System to search for FDIC properties for sale nationwide. This is a well-designed site, rich in useful content.

★★★★★ Homes and Communities, www.hud.gov

The Web site of the U.S. Department of Housing and Urban Development is dense and multi-layered, deep with resources for consumers and professionals alike. Guiding visitors in is the well-designed front page The main navigation bar, a vertical strip to the left that remains a constant

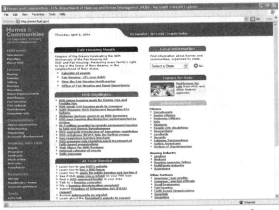

HUD's site is equally useful to professionals and first-time home buyers.

throughout the site, links to information organized under six main topics: HUD News, Homes, Communities, Working with HUD, Resources, and Tools. For consumers, the Homes section is likely to be of most interest, with pages devoted to buying, selling, renting and foreclosure. Lawyers are likely to be most interested in the Resources section, particularly its library. Jump to the section "Legal Information" to find administrative law judge decisions, legal opinions from HUD's general counsel, handbooks, regulations, notices and more. Other library sections cover topics such as fair housing, lead paint, labor relations and FOIA. Another navigation bar on the front page organizes the site not by topics, but by interest groups. Links lead to information designed for senior citizens, veterans, lenders, brokers, appraisers and small businesses, to name a few. Notably, one interest group absent from this list is lawyers.

★★★★★ HUDCLIPS, www.hudclips.org

This is the U.S. Department of Housing and Urban Development's official repository of policies, procedures, announcements and the like. Short for "HUD Client Information and Policy System," HUDCLIPS contains full-text searchable databases of all HUD handbooks; notices; mortgagee, preservation and Title I letters; U.S. Code Titles 12 and 42; Code of Federal Regulations Title 24; housing waivers; Office of General Counsel preservation documents; Federal Register notices; and more. The site also houses all HUD forms. Most come in PDF format, with some also in GIF format or as templates for Microsoft Word and Microsoft Excel. The PDF forms are "fillable," meaning you can call up a form such as the HUD-1 settlement statement and fill it out right from the site.

★★★★ The Federal Emergency Management Agency, www.fema.gov

FEMA's site is a general guide to the before and after of natural disasters—preventing them, preparing for them, mitigating loss from them, and dealing with their aftermath. The site provides information on the National Flood Insurance Program, the U.S. Fire Administration, housing recovery after a disaster, and FEMA mapping products. The library has downloadable forms, information on filing a flood insurance claim, and other useful articles. There is even a library of disaster photographs, with images of hurricanes, forest fires, avalanches, floods and tornadoes. The site is easy to use, offers many layers of practical information, and benefits from a much improved design that makes its many resources easy to locate and use. Unless you are a lawyer dealing with a disaster, there is not much here for you, but if you have clients recovering from disasters or living and working in disaster-prone areas, this site is invaluable.

★★★★ Freddie Mac, www.freddiemac.com

Freddie Mac is a private corporation created by Congress to support home ownership by purchasing mortgages and repackaging them into securities for sale to investors. Lawyers will find useful the current and historical prime mortgage rate information, as well as the various pages of information on mortgage and debt securities. All of Freddie Mac's mortgage documents are available to be downloaded, organized by state. The site also has press releases, information about secondary mortgages, and other information about the company's programs and services.

★★★ Department of Veterans Affairs, Home Loan Guaranty Services, www.homeloans.va.gov

This site includes complete information on VA-guaranteed home loans. Sections for consumers help them determine their eligibility for a VA loan. For lenders and real estate professionals, there is a guide to VA loans and a complete library of forms.

Practice Resources

★★★★★ Legal Information Institute, www.law.cornell.edu/topical.html

Cornell University's Legal Information Institute houses a collection of "law about" pages. Divided by subject, each gives a brief overview of the field of law and links to key references. For real estate lawyers, three of these pages are of greatest use:

- **Mortgage Law Materials,**
  www.law.cornell.edu/topics/mortgages.html
- **Real Estate Transactions,**
  www.law.cornell.edu/topics/real_estate.html
- **Real Property,** www.law.cornell.edu/topics/real_property.html

Each of these pages provides links to primary U.S. law governing the field and, notably, to the real estate statutes of each state. Each of these pages also includes links to recent decisions on the topic from the U.S. Supreme Court and the U.S. circuit courts of appeal.

★★★★ Americans with Disabilities Act Document Center, http://www.jan.wvu.edu/links/adalinks.htm

This long-standing site provides an extensive library including the ADA and regulations thereunder, technical assistance manuals and other documents. Although its major focus is the workplace, there are several documents in its collection of interest to real estate lawyers, among them the ADA Accessibility Guidelines issued by the Architectural and Transportation Barriers Compliance Board. A collection of links to other ADA resources includes many related to architecture and construction.

★★★★ Tenant.net, http://tenant.net

Tenant.net is an online resource for residential tenants, focusing on New York City and New York State. Although intended as a resource for tenants, lawyers in New York who practice landlord-tenant law will find the site's resources useful. These include summaries of New York Housing Court decisions since 1996, which can be browsed or searched by key words, and the full text of decisions issued between 1990 and 1994 by the New York Division of Housing and Community Renewal, Office of Rent Administration. The site also provides the full text of New York rent control and rent stabilization laws, and specific New York laws regarding real property, housing maintenance, zoning and multiple dwelling units.

★★★ AllRegs, www.allregs.com

AllRegs sells databases of current residential mortgage lending guidelines and forms. Its Web site offers a free, daily industry update, posting summaries of announcements from Fannie Mae, Freddie Mac, the FHA, the VA, and Ginnie Mae as they are released and archiving them for ninety days. If you prefer to receive the summaries by e-mail, you can subscribe using a form provided at the site. The site provides complete information on subscribing to AllRegs' fee-based products. Subscribers can link from the daily industry update to the full text of the update documents.

★★★ EIFS Legal Network, www.stuccolaw.com

EIFS (for Exterior Insulation and Finish System) is a kind of synthetic stucco used to cover the outside of homes, mostly in the southeastern U.S. This site focuses on litigation alleging that the product is defective, permitting water intrusion that can ruin a home. It is sponsored by a network of attorneys representing homeowners in EIFS-related litigation in six states and the District of Columbia. The site is oriented towards potential plaintiffs, and includes a detailed questionnaire visitors can fill out and send to the attorney listed for their state. For those new to the problem, the site includes a useful overview.

★★★ Preserve/Net, www.preservenet.cornell.edu

When you come to this site, created in order to serve as a comprehensive portal for preservationists, follow the "Legal" link to find a page of resources related to preservation law. It provides links to federal laws, regulations and executive orders, as well as to summaries of 135 preservation cases decided between 1966 and 1996.

★★ Construction Law Review, www.constructlaw.com

From the Philadelphia-based law firm Pepper Hamilton, this page features the Construction Law Review, covering legal developments of interest to the construction industry. The review is published only sporadically—when last visited, the most recent issue was more than a year old.

★★ Planners Web, www.plannersweb.com

This is the Web site of *Planning Commissioners' Journal*, a publication for non-professional planners who serve on city, county or regional planning boards, or who are active in dealing with local land use and community planning issues. Articles from the current and all back issues are available on the Web site, but only on a pay-per-view basis, allowing you to preview the first few paragraphs and then elect whether to pay the $5 or so to see the full text. You can search for articles using various parameters, or simply scroll through each issue's index. Beyond the journal, the site features the "Sprawl Guide," an annotated index of Web resources concerned with urban sprawl. A useful feature is a guide to finding planning reports from boards and commissions throughout the U.S.

★ Construction Law Center, www.constructionlaw.com

When a Web site claims to be "the center" for any area of law, it ought to deliver more than bare bones. This disappointing site is really just an advertisement for a Maryland law firm. Its only features are periodic articles on construction law, a page of links, and a page of construction humor.

Fair Housing

★★★★ National Fair Housing Advocate, www.fairhousing.com

The National Fair Housing Advocate is a resource designed to serve both advocates and the general public with news and information regarding the issues of housing discrimination. The Tennessee Fair Housing Council maintains the site, with financial assistance from the U.S. Department of Housing and Urban Development. For lawyers, the main appeal of this site will be its two databases of court and administrative decisions relating to fair housing. The fully searchable main database contains the full text of more than 2,200 fair housing cases, including comprehensive coverage of opinions issued by administrative law judges at HUD. The second database contains news reports and summaries of court cases related

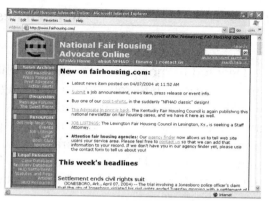

The National Fair Housing Advocate is for legal professionals and the general public.

to fair housing dating back to 1992. Another database available through the site tracks monetary settlements and court awards in fair housing cases. The site also provides a library of federal statutes and regulations relating to fair housing, including the Fair Housing Act, the Civil Rights Act of 1866, pertinent provisions of Section 504 of the Rehabilitation Act of 1973, the Community Reinvestment Act of 1977, and others. A separate section includes HUD guidance notices and memoranda. The group's newsletter, providing current coverage of fair housing cases, formerly produced in print, is now available only through this site.

★★★ The Fair Lending Guide Page, www.ffhsj.com/fairlend/fair.htm

The primary purpose of this site is to advertise *The Fair Lending Guide*, a book by the law firm Fried, Frank, Harris, Shriver & Jacobson that covers the Fair Housing Act, the Equal Credit Opportunity Act, and the Community Reinvestment Act. But the site is useful for offering the full text and archives of the Fair Lending Alert newsletter and a library of articles by FFHS&J lawyers on fair lending issues. The site merits stars for usefulness, content and ease of use.

★ Fair Housing Institute, www.mindspring.com/~fairhous/index.html

This private consulting firm features articles from its newsletter, "The Fair Housing Advisor," covering court decisions, legislative updates and more. It is described as quarterly, but when last visited the most recent article, flagged with the word "new" in red letters, was five years old.

Related Resources

★★★★ HSH Associates, www.hsh.com

Devoted to mortgage information, this is an extensive offering of current and historical data relating to mortgage rates. The site includes daily and weekly rates, market trends and forecasts, home equity rates, auto loan rates, and index rates for adjustable rate mortgages. There is also an assortment of financial calculators and a library of full text articles. A wealth of free information from HSH Associates, which is a financial publishing company, earns stars for content, usefulness, design and ease of use.

★★★ Interest.com, www.interest.com

Mortgage Market Information Services offers daily mortgage news, as well as a state-by-state guide to mortgage rates, broken down within each state by lender. Visitors can also use the site to shop for the best mortgage rate and to calculate the cost of a mortgage.

★★★ ired.com, www.ired.com

Calling itself the "International Real Estate Digest," IRED is a comprehensive site with a little something for everyone, lawyers included. The site's best feature is its links collection—it claims 25,000 links to real estate-related sites throughout the world. Among other features are columns on various real estate and environmental topics and news stories from the worlds of banking and real estate.

Law Firm Pages

★★★ Frascona, Joiner & Goodman, www.frascona.com

This Colorado law firm offers a broad array of articles on Colorado and federal real estate and construction law. Topics include brokerage law, real-estate contracts, finance, land use, leasing and titles.

★★★ NapaLaw.com, www.napalaw.com

Devoted to California real estate law, this site, sponsored by the Napa, California law office of Stephen J. Thomas, offers a variety of content, ranging from practical to entertaining. On the practical side, follow the "Forms & Updates" link to find current legal news and libraries of forms for a variety of real estate-related topics. The forms and updates library is fully searchable. On the entertaining side, there is Law Lite, a page devoted to real estate and legal humor. Unfortunately, the site is not kept current.

★★★ Real-Estate-Law.com, http://www.real-estate-law.com

Joshua Stein, a partner in the real estate practice group of Latham & Watkins, New York, maintains this site, which collects his articles about commercial real estate transactions and negotiations. Topics include hotels, insurance, leasing, letters of credit and mortgage lending.

★★★ Weiss & Weissman Real Estate Directory, www.wwlaw.com/re.htm

This California law firm has information on real estate transactions, taxation and ownership, with a focus on California and federal law. The site has a number of useful, general interest articles.

★ Realaw, hoohana.aloha.net/~realaw

The Honolulu firm Pitluck Kido Sato & Stone sponsors this site, which features news and articles on real estate law and a "law library" of Hawaii and federal resources. It appears largely out of date, with much of its content nearly five years old.

Title Companies

★★★★★ First American Corporation, www.firstam.com

Almost hidden within the First American site is an extremely useful resource for real estate lawyers, the Underwriting Library of First American Title Insurance. (From the main page, follow the link to "References/ Underwriting Tools.") Described as "the largest compilation of title material available on this planet," the library has several "volumes," including:

- Endorsement Manual, a library of endorsement clauses
- Title Insurance Forms, including a state-by-state guide
- Real Estate Practices, A State-by-State and International Guide,
- Publications and Articles
- The First American Financial Corporation Professional Services Guide

The third volume includes descriptions of each state's closing customs, documents of conveyance, documents of encumbrance, foreclosure procedures, and related information. The entire library can be viewed by table of contents or searched by key words. Besides the library, First American's reference section has other information useful to lawyers, including forms, manuals and treatises.

★★★★ TitleWeb.com, www.titleweb.com

TitleWeb is a portal and information center for lawyers, title agents, brokers, lenders, appraisers and anyone else involved in the title industry. Its greatest draw is its selection of news articles and feature columns. It features industry news, updated daily, with headlines, full text stories, lending rates and stock quotes. A selection of feature articles focuses on the Internet and e-commerce as they relate to the title insurance industry. The site also provides an "atlas" of links to related Internet sites, and a searchable directory of title companies across the U.S. The site is supported through advertising, so all its content is free.

Mortgage Guarantee Companies

★★★ Mortgage Guarantee Insurance Corporation, www.mgic.com

MGIC provides a variety of information for homebuyers, lenders and investors regarding its mortgage insurance products and services. Included here are its underwriting guidelines and detailed descriptions of its products.

Associations

★★★★ ABA Section of Real Property, Probate and Trust Law, www.abanet.org/rppt/home.html

The focus of this site is on general information about Section activities, committees, events and publications. It includes the tables of contents from the Section's Real Property, Probate and Trust Law Journal, but access to the journal's full text articles is restricted by password to Section members. The Section magazine, *Probate and Property*, is also available here in full text, with only selected articles restricted to members. Available to anyone are the electronic newsletters "E-State," for estate planners, and "E-Dirt," for real-estate lawyers. A useful feature of the site is a directory of lawyers in each state who are available for a fee to assist out-of-state counsel in preparing deeds and administering estates. Visitors can purchase CLE programs sponsored by the Section, either to view online or by video. For non-lawyers, the site includes general information about estate planning and real estate law.

★ ABA Forum on Affordable Housing and Community Development Law, www.abanet.org/forums/affordable

This site provides only general information about the Forum, listing its committees and divisions and offering a calendar of upcoming events.

★ **ABA Forum on the Construction Industry,** www.abanet.org/forums/construction/home.html

This simple site has only general information about the Forum, which was created in 1976 to address all aspects of law relating to construction

Chapter 14

Best Resources for Securities Lawyers

Chapter Contents

EDGAR and His Cousins
Practice Resources
Associations
State Securities Regulators

It started as a novel experiment, but its success helped pave the way for government information on the Internet.

In 1994, the nonprofit Internet Multicasting Service began offering the Securities and Exchange Commission's EDGAR database of corporate filings free via the Internet. A year later, as its funding was about to expire, IMS urged the SEC to continue where it would leave off.

At first, the SEC hedged, but in August 1995 it announced it would take on the task of providing free Internet access to EDGAR.

Thanks to the pioneering efforts of IMS, securities lawyers today can find a wealth of useful information free on the Internet. Here is a guide to the best.

EDGAR and His Cousins

★★★★★ Securities and Exchange Commission, www.sec.gov

The most important site for securities lawyers remains that of the SEC. It is the Internet home of EDGAR, the SEC's Electronic Data Gathering, Analysis and Retrieval system, through which companies file annual reports and other disclosure documents. Updated in real time, the database allows you to retrieve any document filed electronically with the SEC since January 1, 1994.

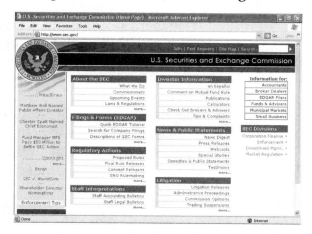

With its EDGAR database of corporate filings, the SEC is a key site for lawyers.

EDGAR archives can be searched for any information that might appear in a document's header. You can also search by company name. The site also houses current SEC rulemaking, SEC enforcement actions, and press releases and speeches.

★★★★★ EDGAR Online, www.edgar-online.com

Another top-notch destination for EDGAR research is EDGAR Online, although it suffers from a confusing case of multiple personality disorder. Several years ago, EDGAR Online, a subscription-based service, purchased Free Edgar, www.freeedgar.com, a free service, and then added IPO Express, www.edgar-online.com/ipoexpress, a related but still different service. If you go to EDGAR Online, you find no mention of Free Edgar, but go to Free Edgar and you find yourself frequently directed back into EDGAR Online. A visitor can become exhausted trying to sort through the differences between the sites, because nowhere on either site are the differences clearly explained.

As one might expect, the differences are in price and features. EDGAR Online requires a subscription, currently priced at $44.85 a quarter, while Free Edgar is, as the name suggests, free. Free EDGAR allows searches by company name and ticker symbol and shows the current day's filings. EDGAR Online allows more sophisticated full-text concept and keyword searching of the EDGAR database. Both services formerly offered a personalized, e-mail alert called Watchlist, but now that is available only through the paid service. In addition, EDGAR Online's "My EDGAR Online" feature allows you to create a portfolio of up to twenty-five companies, tickers, industries, regions and types of SEC data to track, with real-time e-mail notification of new filings matching your criteria.

EDGAR Online differs from its free cousin in these other extras:

- Word processing and spreadsheet capabilities that allow you to take data from any SEC document and import it into a Word, WordPerfect or Excel document.
- A hard copy option, providing printed, bound copies of any EDGAR filing, delivered to your office overnight.
- IPO Express, delivering e-mail notification of new public offerings.
- EDGAR Online People, for researching corporate directors and executives. Type in a name and obtain the person's salary, stock options, history of insider trading, and other information.

★★★★★ 10k Wizard, www.10kwizard.com

To search EDGAR in depth, steer clear of the SEC's second-rate search tools and instead try 10k Wizard. This better-than-EDGAR site combines real time access with full-text searching to create a superior EDGAR interface. Search for companies not only by symbol, as at the SEC site, but also by partial company name. You can search all filings in full text, allowing you to scan EDGAR for words, phrases and names. Users can develop and store their own portfolios of searches that monitor new SEC filings as they are received and notify the user by e-mail when a filing meets the search criteria. For large searches, 10k Wizard's XLS Snapshot converts your search results into a comprehensive Excel worksheet with live links to filings. The $150 a year subscription allows unlimited access and unlimited downloads.

★★★★★ SEDAR, www.sedar.com

SEDAR is Canada's answer to EDGAR. Short for System for Electronic Document Analysis and Retrieval, SEDAR is the system used for electronically filing most securities-related information with the Canadian securities regulatory authorities. Filing with SEDAR started Jan. 1, 1997, and is now mandatory for most reporting issuers in Canada. Complete information on the rules for electronic filing can be found on the site. Visitors to the site can search the entire database of filings, including all documents starting in 1997 and continuing up to the close of the most recently completed business day. If you prefer, you can browse a list of the most recent filings. Also here are profiles of all SEDAR public company and mutual fund filers. The site is well-organized and includes extensive explanatory materials, making it extremely easy to use.

★★★★ Livedgar, www.livedgar.com

This is a fee-based service from Global Securities Information for searching and delivery of EDGAR filings and other SEC information. Like other EDGAR search services, it features full-text searching, preformatted searching, and downloading of documents in word processing format. What distinguishes it from its competitors is that it includes more than just EDGAR. It lists all SEC filings dating back to 1967, provides more than 100,000 annual reports from 30,000 companies in 106 countries, includes the complete collection of SEDAR filings, and allows online access to paper filings such as no-action letters. The pay-as-you-go cost is $10 per log-on, then $1.75 a minute. GSI also offers flat-rate plans at negotiated rates. The site includes free SEC background information, such as the SEC Digest, the Securities and Exchange Act, and the SEC phone book.

Practice Resources

★★★★★ NASD Regulation, www.nasdr.com

The NASD's in-depth and well-designed Web site provides a general introduction to securities regulation as well as detailed information on practice and procedure. Among its features: reports of all enforcement actions NASD Regulation has taken since 1996; descriptions of arbitration and mediation procedures, including the NASD's arbitration code; and a guide to investor protection.

★★★★★ Securities Class Action Clearinghouse, securities.stanford.edu

Operated by Stanford Law School, this site provides detailed and timely information about securities fraud litigation for use by the legal community, investors and the media. The Clearinghouse publishes or links to the full text of more than 2,000 complaints, motions, judicial opinions, and other major class action filings and organizes them all under its own full-text search engine. From the site, you can register to receive automatic notices of litigation developments by e-mail. In addition to its full text offerings, the site includes analyses of complaints summarizing their major allegations, docket sheets from the Northern District of California, settlement documents, and links to related information. This is an extremely useful, informative and innovative site.

★★★★★ Securities Industry Association, www.sia.com

At the Web site of this association of investment banks, broker-dealers and mutual fund companies, lawyers will take the greatest interest in the regulatory and government relations sections. The regulatory section summarizes recent regulatory news and includes the texts of comment letters and exemption requests. More substantive overall is the government relations section, titled "On Capitol Hill," with detailed information on the SIA's legislative agenda, backed up by full-text supporting documents, testimony and legislative updates. There is also far more to be found at this comprehensive site, including briefing papers on key issues facing the securities industry and a library of publications.

★★★★★ Securities Law Homepage, www.seclaw.com

An extensive introduction to securities law, federal and state, written by Mark J. Astarita, a lawyer in New York City, as well as other information such as important court decisions and pending regulations. There is also a broker information center, an arbitration information center, and an investor information center. A comprehensive and well-constructed site.

★★★★ Bowne Newsletters, www.bowne.com/newsletters

Bowne publishes complimentary newsletters containing abstracts from legal and financial periodicals and articles from industry experts. These include the "Digest for Corporate and Securities Lawyers," the "Review for CFOs & Investment Bankers," and the "Bowne EDGAR & SEC Monitor Alert Service." These are provided in Adobe Acrobat format.

★★★★ Center for Corporate Law, www.law.uc.edu/CCL

Designed to be a repository of electronic data for corporate and securities lawyers, this site features *The Securities Lawyer's Deskbook*, containing the full text of the essential federal securities laws, regulations and forms. It includes the Securities Act of 1933 and associated rules and forms, the Securities Exchange Act of 1934 and associated rules, the Investment Company Act of 1940, and Regulations S-K, S-B, S-T and S-X. It is sponsored by the University of Cincinnati College of Law.

★★★★ Municipal Securities Rulemaking Board, www.msrb.org

The MSRB makes rules regulating dealers in municipal bonds, municipal notes and other municipal securities. Its site includes the full text of its rules, interpretive letters and interpretive notices, and posts any proposed or final amendments and additions to the rules. Also, dealers must report to the board all transactions involving municipal securities. At the site, visitors can search these reports and learn about the reporting process and its requirements.

★★★★ RealCorporateLawyer, www.realcorporatelawyer.com

From RR Donnelley Financial, this site is designed for securities lawyers who practice in the area of corporate finance. It features SEC daily briefs, harvested from the SEC's own Web site, reports of SEC and related regulatory developments, current news about corporate finance, and in-depth articles contributed by lawyers who practice in the field. A monthly webzine provides a more in-depth look at SEC and corporate finance news.

★★★ CyberSecuritiesLaw, www.cybersecuritieslaw.com

Current developments relating to securities regulation and the Internet are supposed to be the focus of this site, but the last update on a recent visit was nine months old. Edited by Blake A. Bell, a lawyer with Simpson Thacher & Bartlett in New York City, the site features the "CyberSecuritiesLaw Tribune," a newsletter featuring brief items about the field, as well as case and legislative alerts. A collection of links appears to be somewhat out of date.

★★★ Jefren Publishing Company, www.jefren.com

Free legal forms and news for securities and corporate lawyers are the focus of this site, sponsored by the publisher of *Proxy Statements: Strategy and Forms.* The forms, all samples taken from the book, can be downloaded for free in Adobe Acrobat format. The site also offers free access to its editorially enhanced, weekly version of the SEC News Digest. Jefren's editors organize the articles by subject area and make the text completely searchable.

★★★ Milberg Weiss Securities Class Action Designated Internet Site, http://securities.milberg.com

Created in response to a local rule of the U.S. District Court for the Northern District of California, this site is operated as a public service by the law firm Milberg Weiss Bershad Hynes & Lerach. It provides free access to hundreds of documents related to securities class action suits. Browse a list of cases or search by key words.

★★★ New York Stock Exchange, www.nyse.com

Little here relates directly to securities law, but there is much of interest to the securities lawyer, including current market information, a guide to member regulation and enforcement, the complete text of disciplinary and arbitration rules, a directory of listed companies with links to their Web sites, a glossary of financial terms, an archive of trading data, and a library of NYSE's periodicals and press releases.

★★★ North American Securities Administrators Association, www.nasaa.org

The NASAA represents state and provincial securities regulators in the United States, Canada and Mexico. Its recently expanded Web site includes information of use to professionals and consumers. A library section contains uniform forms, statements of policy, resolutions, model rules, state lists and proposals, model acts, jury instructions and reports. Other sections provide information on legislative initiatives, broker-dealer regulation and investment fraud.

★★★ Securities Fraud and Investor Protection, www.securities-law.com

Designed primarily for lay people, this site, from Boston securities lawyer Harry S. Miller, discusses causes of action, calculation of damages, and other topics also of interest to legal professionals. Articles offer little depth and the site is rarely updated.

★★ Annual Report Gallery, www.reportgallery.com

Just what its name suggests, this site collects annual reports—some 2,200 of them. They are indexed alphabetically by company name. The site does not archive the full text of these reports, but links to reports as posted on the particular company's Web site. There is no means to search the reports in full text. There is no way to tell how often, if ever, the site is updated, but at least some of the links are stale.

★★ Michael Huberman & Associates, Securities Consultants, www.ninthhole.com

From a California law firm that specializes in securities arbitration, this site provides general information for consumers on securities abuses and securities arbitration, but has little of use to the securities professional. Overdone golf course motif and banner advertisements add a nuisance element.

★ FinWeb, www.finweb.com

A out-of-date collection of links to general securities, economics and finance-related resources on the Web, collected and annotated by Louisiana State University Professor James R. Garven. Many of the links are dead and descriptions are stale.

Associations

★★★★ National Association of Bond Lawyers, www.nabl.org

For lawyers interested in learning about the NABL, its site offers the standard association fare, with general information about membership, events and publications. For others, the NABL hosts a useful resource library, providing access to a range of municipal finance background materials. Sources include government regulations, municipal industry documents, and various NABL documents such as policy statements, comment letters and seminar materials. A members-only section includes the quarterly newsletter, The Bond Lawyer.

★★ Business Law Section, American Bar Association, www.abanet.org/buslaw/home.html

General information about section membership, events and publications. Includes full-text articles from Business Law Today, the every-other-month section magazine, and abstracts of articles from the quarterly journal The Business Lawyer. Also includes committee reports.

State Securities Regulators

Most of the agencies responsible for enforcing state securities laws have Web sites, some with only general contact information and others with more extensive information. Here is where to find them.

- **Alabama,** http://asc.state.al.us
- **Alaska,** www.dced.state.ak.us/bsc/home.htm
- **Arizona Corporation Commission, Securities Division,** www.ccsd.cc.state.az.us
- **Arkansas,** www.arkansas.gov/arsec
- **California,** www.corp.ca.gov
- **Colorado Division of Securities,** www.dora.state.co.us/Securities
- **Connecticut,** www.state.ct.us/dob
- **Delaware,** www.state.de.us/securities/index.htm
- **Florida,** www.dbf.state.fl.us
- **Georgia Secretary of State Securities and Business Regulation Division,** www.sos.state.ga.us/securities
- **Hawaii,** www.state.hi.us/dcca/breg-seu
- **Idaho,** http://finance.state.id.us
- **Illinois,** www.sos.state.il.us/departments/securities/home.html
- **Indiana,** www.in.gov/sos/securities/index.html
- **Iowa,** www.iid.state.ia.us
- **Kansas,** www.securities.state.ks.us
- **Kentucky,** www.dfi.state.ky.us
- **Louisiana,** www.ofi.state.la.us
- **Maine,** www.state.me.us/pfr/sec/sec_index.htm
- **Maryland,** www.oag.state.md.us/Securities
- **Massachusetts,** www.state.ma.us/sec/sct/sctidx.htm
- **Michigan,** www.michigan.gov/cis/0,1607,7-154-10555---,00.html
- **Minnesota,** www.commerce.state.mn.us
- **Mississippi,** www.sos.state.ms.us
- **Missouri,** www.sos.mo.gov/securities/default.asp
- **Montana,** http://sao.state.mt.us/sao/securities/index.html
- **Nebraska,** www.ndbf.org
- **Nevada Secretary of State Securities Division,** sos.state.nv.us
- **New Hampshire,** www.nh.gov/sos
- **New Jersey,** www.state.nj.us/lps/ca/bos.htm
- **New Mexico,** www.rld.state.nm.us/Securities/index.htm
- **New York Department of Law, Bureau of Investor Protection & Securities,** www.oag.state.ny.us/investors/investors.html
- **North Carolina,** www.secretary.state.nc.us/sec

- **North Dakota,** www.ndsecurities.com
- **Ohio,** www.securities.state.oh.us
- **Oklahoma,** www.securities.state.ok.us
- **Oregon Division of Finance and Corporate Securities,** www.cbs.state.or.us/external/dfcs/index.html
- **Pennsylvania,** www.psc.state.pa.us
- **Rhode Island,** www.dbr.state.ri.us
- **South Carolina,** www.scsecurities.org
- **South Dakota,** www.state.sd.us/drr2/reg/securities/security.htm
- **Tennessee,** www.state.tn.us/commerce/securities/index.html
- **Texas,** www.ssb.state.tx.us
- **Utah Dept. of Commerce, Division of Securities,** www.securities.state.ut.us
- **Vermont,** www.bishca.state.vt.us/SecuritiesDiv/securindex.htm
- **Virginia,** www.state.va.us/scc/division/srf/index.htm
- **Washington,** www.dfi.wa.gov
- **West Virginia,** www.wvauditor.com
- **Wisconsin,** www.wdfi.org/fi/securities/default.htm
- **Wyoming,** soswy.state.wy.us/securiti/securiti.htm

For Tort Lawyers, A Web of Research

Personal injury lawyers are limited only by their imaginations in how they use the Internet. Through its vast resources, they can research a defective product, read up on a client's injury, or locate an expert witness.

What follows is a sampling of some of the best resources for personal injury lawyers on the Internet.

General

★★★★★ RAND Institute for Civil Justice, www.rand.org/centers/icj

Public policy think tank RAND's Institute for Civil Justice is devoted to study of the civil justice system. It is perhaps best known for its studies of trends in jury verdicts. But beyond verdicts, its research agenda underscores RAND's relevance to tort lawyers: administration of justice, alternative dispute resolution, automobile insurance, class actions and mass torts, environmental issues, expert evidence, law and health, product liability, and workers' compensation. In some instances, the reports that come out of these studies are available free, but in most cases, the report is summarized with information on how to purchase the full text from RAND. You can search for a report on ICJ's site by its title or browse available reports by topic.

★★★★★ TRIALSmith.com, www.trialsmith.com

The largest deposition bank on the Internet, TRIALSmith archives more than 150,000 deposition transcripts of experts, doctors and corporate representatives. Access is exclusively restricted to plaintiffs' lawyers, who also use it to exchange documents, tips and investigative tools. Search for an expert by name or keyword, and view any available deposition immediately online or download it to your computer. Formerly known as DepoConnect, TRIALSmith hosts more than 400 discussion lists with more than 60,000 lawyers participating. It is sponsored by more than fifty state and national trial lawyer associations and litigation groups. It offers a range of subscription plans at reasonable prices.

★★★★ Consumer Law Page, http://consumerlawpage.com

The Consumer Law Page offers an encyclopedic collection of articles and brochures of interest to PI lawyers and consumers. Topics include automobiles, insurance, product liability, toxic torts, and traumatic brain injuries. Among the articles here are "Product Liability: Preventing Deaths From Tire Explosions," "All-Terrain Vehicles: Deaths and Injuries to Children," "Breast Implants: Fact v. Fiction," and "Preparing the Defective Product Case." The site also has a extensive collection of links to consumer resources elsewhere on the Web. All of this is sponsored by the San Jose, California, firm Alexander, Hawes & Audet.

★★★★ Craig Ball's List of Helpful Links, www.craigball.com/links.html

Texas trial lawyer Craig D. Ball's collection of legal links are legend among tort lawyers. They include "Craig's Sampler of Informal Discovery Links," "Handy Terrific Links for Attorneys," and "Craig's Sampler of Demonstrative Evidence Internet Resources." Nothing fancy here, just a practical assortment of links from a practicing trial lawyer.

★★★★ Vacatur Center, www.andersonkill.com/Vacatur_Center/Vacatur_Center.asp

Are insurance companies paying off litigants to keep damaging precedent off the books? So says Eugene R. Anderson, whose Washington, D.C., firm Anderson Kill & Olick has created a Web site devoted to publishing vacated judicial opinions. Anderson charges that losing litigants—particularly insurance companies—often pay prevailing parties more than they won in court in exchange for their asking the court to vacate the judgment. This prevents other policyholders from using these decisions in future cases. Anderson Kill created its Vacatur Center to help preserve what it calls these "disappearing decisions." It encourages lawyers to submit their vacated decisions, which it will publish on the Web. By doing so, the firm hopes to end the practice of vacatur and preserve these precedents for others to use.

Organizations

★★★★★ Association of Trial Lawyers of America, www.atla.org

Access to the best parts of this Web site is restricted to ATLA members, but there is plenty of practical information here for non-members as well. The public portion includes "ATLA in the Courts," where you can find a library of amicus curiae briefs filed by ATLA and news of recent court decisions. The public area also includes factsheets and resource pages devoted to civil justice and issues such as malpractice. ALTA also provides general news about its activities in the courts and legislatures throughout the U.S. and a general overview of the association, its committees and its members. The restricted portion, which is free to ATLA members, features the ATLA Exchange, a full-text database containing deposition transcripts, court pleadings and other litigation information. The members' section also includes online discussion groups; a directory of ATLA members, which includes e-mail and Web addresses where available; the full text of ATLA periodicals such as *Trial* and the *ATLA Law Reporter*; the ATLA Job Bank, a free job listing service; and agendas and registration materials for ATLA seminars, "colleges" and conventions. The public site has general information about ATLA's litigation groups, while the restricted area has more detailed information.

★★★★★ Defense Research Institute, www.dri.org

For more than 21,000 defense, insurance and corporate counsel, the Defense Research Institute is the national bar association of choice. Much of its Web site is restricted to those members. Through this site, members can access the home pages of more than two dozen substantive DRI committees and sign up for any of a number of topical e-mail discussion lists. Members can view a complete library of DRI publications, including its monthly magazine, *For the Defense*, committee newsletters, and various in-depth articles. Members also can search DRI's expert witness database, with records on more than 50,000 plaintiff and defense experts. Searches result in listings showing the expert's profile and areas of expertise. For many of the experts, the database includes transcripts of depositions in which they participated, their resumes, or reports they authored. For anyone visiting the site, DRI offers general information about its organizational structure, membership and calendar of events.

★★★★★ e-DICTA, www.edicta.org

Launched in 2003, e-DICTA is the "mega site" of the Tort Trial and Insurance Practice Section of the American Bar Association. Part e-zine, part portal, it is a comprehensive and broad-ranging guide to resources on the TIPS Web site[1] and elsewhere on the Internet. It features an extensive collection of legal links, direct access (for TIPS members) to section newsletters, and pages devoted to emerging issues in tort litigation such as mold, medical malpractice and tort reform. Addition sections focus on legal technology, ethics, law students and young lawyers, and CLE. The front page includes legal news from selected law-related Web logs ("blogs").[2]

★★★★ American Bar Association, Tort and Insurance Practice Section, www.abanet.org/tips/home.html

TIPS describes its membership as eclectic—a mix of plaintiff and defense attorneys, insurance lawyers and corporate counsel. Its Web site is a bit eclectic as well, reflecting an ABA Section whose committees focus on topics ranging from admiralty to workers' compensation. As with the Web sites of most ABA sections, TIPS' site provides general information on membership, committee structures and coming events, as well as a bookstore from which visitors can purchase books and seminar materials. TIPS publishes two quarterly periodicals—*The Brief* magazine and Tort and Insurance Law Journal—but offers only synopses of articles online. It provides its newsletter, "TortSource," in its entirety in .pdf format.

★★★★ Trial Lawyers for Public Justice, www.tlpj.org

Created at the urging of consumer advocate Ralph Nader, TLPJ marked its twentieth anniversary in 2002. Specializing in public-interest litigation in such areas as toxic torts, the environment, access to the courts and discrimination, TLPJ celebrated its anniversary with a revamped Web site. The site already included descriptions of TLPJ's current caseload and a library of its briefs and legal filings. With the revamp, it expanded these features and added a public-interest database providing links to more than 2,000 Web resources, including legal research tools, law school public interest centers, places to find public interest law jobs, and, it claims, every legal aid, legal services and poverty law office in the U.S.

---

[1] See the immediately following listing.
[2] For more about blogs, see Chapter 27 *infra*.

★★★ ATLAmart, www.atlamart.com

Shopping for a law-related product or service? You might find it at ATLAmart, the online shopping mall sponsored by the Association of Trial Lawyers of America. ATLAmart lists companies offering software, marketing services, expert witnesses, demonstrative evidence, financial services and other products and services related to law office management and trial preparation. Companies pay to be listed and are organized under topical headings. Listings include links to e-mail and Web addresses where available.

Government

★★★★★ U.S. Consumer Product Safety Commission, http://cpsc.gov

With its focus on protecting the public from unsafe and defective products, the Web site of the Consumer Product Safety Commission is a treasure trove for product liability lawyers. Review the most recent product recalls, or search for recalls by product, company or even key words. Review statistical reports analyzing injuries caused by particular types of products as diverse as amusement rides and shopping carts. CPSC maintains an enormous publications library, searchable by topic, title or key word. Here you can find booklets on the hazards of lead paint in public playgrounds, preventing crib deaths and avoiding lawnmower injuries.

CPSC also operates a listserv that allows you to receive press releases, product recalls and other safety announcements by e-mail. To subscribe to this free service, you must use the sign-up form provided online at www.cpsc.gov/cpsclist.asp.

★★★★★ U.S. Department of Transportation, www.dot.gov

Trial lawyers will find this mega-site useful for its databases of laws, regulations, product recalls, safety notices and reams of other information from agencies under the DOT umbrella, including the National Highway Traffic Safety Administration, the Federal Aviation Administration, the U.S. Coast Guard, the Federal Highway Administration, and the Federal Railroad Administration. The site is home to the DOT's Docket Management System, an electronic, image-based database containing more than 800,000 pages of regulatory and adjudicatory information.

★★★★★ U.S. Food and Drug Administration, www. fda.gov

The FDA's Web site offers a wealth of useful information for personal injury lawyers. The site is divided among the major categories of products the FDA regulates: foods, human drugs, biologics, medical devices, radiation emitting devices, animal feed and drugs, and cosmetics. Each division is home to a variety of resources. Go to Human Drugs, for example, to review the latest drug approvals or to learn how to seek FDA approval to market a

The FDA provides safety information on food, drugs and medical devices.

new drug. The FDA also provides safety and recall information for products under its jurisdiction. The site includes current FDA news releases and information on related topics such as imports and toxicology.

★★★★ Web-based Injury Statistics Query and Reporting System, www.cdc.gov/ncipc/wisqars

In preparing a case for trial, a lawyer might want to determine how many bicyclists were killed by motor vehicles in her state between 1988 and 1998. Where should the lawyer turn? From the Centers for Disease Control, WISQARS—pronounced "whiskers"—provides online access to injury-related mortality data. Using mortality data from 1981 to 1999, it allows users to search and create reports in three categories. The first, mortality reports, lists numbers and rates of deaths for specific injuries, such as those from firearms, machinery, burns or motor vehicle accidents. The second, leading causes of death, can be used to determine the number of injury-related deaths relative to the number of other leading causes of death. The third, years of potential life lost, provides a measure of premature mortality for a specific population and range of years. For whichever type of report, users can search by state, gender, race and year. The service is easy to use and includes a thorough guide.

Product Safety

★★★★ Standards & Specifications, www.scholarly-societies.org/standards.html

Products liability lawyers should prepare themselves to settle in for many hours of surfing at this site, which provides links to more than fifty collections of full text professional standards and specifications, promulgated by organizations such as the Acoustical Society of America, American Institute of Aeronautics and Astronautics, American Iron and Steel Institute, American National Standards Institute, American Society of Mechanical Engineers, SAE International, and more.

★ Productslaw.com, www.productslaw.com

Intended as a collection of links to products liability news and resources on the Internet, this site, from a New York personal injury lawyer, suffers from a lack of updating. The most recent additions were nearly a year old, and the majority of links—many to news stories—were three or four years old. This is a simple, one-page list of links, organized under topics including breast implants, Agent Orange, tobacco, DES and medical malpractice.

Class Actions

★★★ ClassAction.com, www.classaction.com

This is described as a site where consumers can ask lawyers questions about class actions. It features a list of topics about which class actions are pending under five headings: Drugs, Medical, Consumer, Contamination and Jobs. Under each broader topic is a list of specific products or claims. For example, the Drugs heading includes Accutane, Baycol, Celebrex, and the like. Click on one of these product names for a quick overview of the litigation. At the bottom of each overview page is a form titled, "Have Your Case Evaluated." It appears that, by using the form, consumers can submit their questions to a lawyer. However, there is no mention anywhere of who the lawyers are or where they are located. While the site is clearly designed for non-lawyers, lawyers might find it useful as a quick reference on pending class actions.

★★ Classactionlitigation.info, www.classactionlitigation.com

Described as a legal research source for attorneys and a tool to help the public understand class action litigation, this site is primarily a collection of links to legal resources on the Web, some related to class actions, some to legal research in general. Before you can get past the front page, you have to assent to a disclaimer that nothing at the site is to be taken as legal advice. Once having gained entry, the site promises more than 10,000 links. While some relate to class action litigation in general and to specific cases, many are links to general legal sites, and several of those links were dead at last visit.

Daubert Sites

★★★★★ Daubert on the Web, www.daubertontheweb.com

The Supreme Court's 1993 decision in *Daubert v. Merrell Dow Pharmaceuticals* forever changed the rules on expert scientific testimony. Now, this useful Web site is changing how lawyers keep up with its progeny. Created by Philadelphia litigator Peter Nordberg, it offers more than 500 appellate cases, organized by circuit and field of expertise, along with a procedural guide to resolving Daubert challenges, practical trial tactics, and a work-in-progress treatise, "The Daubert Worldview."

★★★★★ The Daubert Tracker, www.dauberttracker.com

A lawyer preparing to qualify or challenge an expert at trial must answer a number of questions. What is the state of the case law under Daubert? How has the particular court or judge applied its teaching? How have courts ruled on this type of expertise? Has this expert ever come before a judge? But keeping up with the case law is no easy task. MDEX Online, a medical-legal consulting firm headquartered in Chicago, estimates there are more than 2,000 federal and 1,000 state cases interpreting and applying Daubert and its offspring, as well as thousands more state "gatekeeper" cases.

That is why MDEX developed this tool to help lawyers track these cases and, in particular, find out how specific experts or areas of expertise fared in the courts. Its central feature is a database of all reported cases under Daubert and its progeny, trial and appellate, backed up when available by full-text briefs, transcripts and docket entries. It also includes recent cases applying *Frye v. United States*, the 1928 Supreme Court decision requiring the exclusion of scientific evidence that is unproven or experimental, all state gatekeeper cases, and several thousand unreported cases.

The service, launched in August 2002, is composed of five distinct products:

- The searchable database of all reported cases.
- Core documents—docket sheets, briefs and transcripts—for each case.
- An e-mail update of new cases from the previous week.
- A quarterly journal with articles by trial attorneys, law professors, judges and experts.
- A series of "Web lectures" delivered by authorities on Daubert and scientific evidence.

A year's subscription is $495 with discounts for multiple users. You can instead purchase a two-hour session for $25 or a half-hour for $10. The full subscription includes the case law database, the e-mail update and the quarterly journal. Core documents and Web lectures cost extra. Briefs are $20 each for subscribers and $40 for others. Transcripts are $30 for subscribers and $60 for others. Documents and transcripts not in the database can be ordered for $35 to $60. Lectures are $60 to subscribers, $95 to others.

The Daubert Tracker is a useful tool for trial lawyers. It is easy to use and understand, and provides precise information about expert witnesses not easily found elsewhere. At $10 for a half-hour session, a lawyer would be remiss not to check an expert through the Daubert Tracker.

Skip Tracing

★★★ Skipease, www.skipease.com

The Internet took skip tracing from an art to a science. For lawyers, this made it much easier to locate missing witnesses, track down long-lost heirs and investigate opposing litigants. Skipease has culled the Web's most useful skip tracing tools and assembled them here. Using its links, you can research property ownership; Social Security numbers; death, birth and marriage records; professional licenses; and more.

★ Skip Tracing Tool Box, www.repo.org/WebFront/skip.html

"Skip tracing" is the art of finding "lost" people, be they witnesses, defendants, debtors or what have you. The Internet offers many tools to help locate someone. This site, maintained by the American Recovery Association, provides links to several of the most useful finding tools, including phone books, area code directories, ZIP code information, and others.

Motor Vehicle

★★★★★ Automobile Recall Database, www.nhtsa.dot.gov/cars/problems/recalls/recmmy1.cfm

From the Office of Defects Investigation at the National Highway Traffic Safety Administration, this database allows searches of automobile recalls by year, make or model. There are two ways to search the database. You can "drill down," starting with a model year, then selecting from a list of manufacturers that were subject to recalls in that year, then choosing a model and even a specific component. Alternatively, you can search directly for a specific vehicle by make, model and year. The result of a search is a complete report on the recall, detailing the number of units affected, dates of manufacture and other specific information, and providing a descriptive summary of the reasons for the recall and any actions that should follow from it.

★★★★★ Crashtest.com, www.crashtest.com

Although aimed at consumers, Crashtest.com, a site that draws together vehicle crash test data from several sources, is sure to be valuable for personal injury lawyers. The site compiles assessments of new and used cars generated by federal and insurance sources, allowing users to compare cars of different makes and years. Crashtest includes figures for side impact and full frontal collisions, frontal offsets, and head restraints, amounts paid by insurance companies for personal injury claims and collision damage, and death rates for different makes and models.

★★★★★ Fatality Analysis Reporting System, www-fars.nhtsa.dot.gov

From the National Highway Traffic Safety Administration, FARS provides data on all motor vehicle crashes in the U.S. that occur on public roads and result in fatality whether to a vehicle occupant or someone else. The hope is that by making this information easily accessible, it will help to improve traffic safety. FARS data covers all fifty states, the District of Columbia and Puerto Rico, and includes fatalities that occur within thirty days of the crash. Data is added annually, usually by Memorial Day of the following year. Users can query the data by a broad range of information fields, ranging from details about the individuals involved to information on traffic control devices at the accident scene. A "Query Wizard" offers a preformatted selection of common queries. A browseable and searchable reports library provides access to reports on crashes published by the NHTSA's National Center for Statistics and Analysis.

★★★★★ Insurance Institute for Highway Safety/Highway Loss Data Institute, www.hwysafety.org

Thankfully, what used to be two overlapping sites sponsored by the insurance industry finally merged into one. You can still use either URL, www.hwysafety.org or www.carsafety.org, or even a third, www.iihs.org—all bring you to the same place. It includes crash test ratings from forty m.p.h. frontal offset crash tests conducted by the IIHS Vehicle Research Center, as well as results of low-speed bumper tests. Search these by make or type of vehicle. Also here is a broad library of reports from IIHS research on issues relating to motor vehicle safety, ranging from aftermarket parts to urban crashes. The library includes state motor vehicle laws and fatality reports. Data is also provided on injury, collision and theft losses by vehicle. Among other features rounding out the site is the institute's newsletter, "Status Report," published ten times a year.

★★★★ Society of Automotive Engineers, www.sae.org

Whether your case involves cars, aircraft, trucks, off-highway equipment, engines, materials, manufacturing or fuel, this is the place to research technical standards and specifications. The Society of Automotive Engineers offers a wealth of information related to designing, building, maintaining and operating motor vehicles or craft for use on land or water or in the air. The Web site is home to complete libraries of standards and specifications, technical papers, books and professional periodicals.

★★★ Law Offices of Edward A. Smith, www.autoaccident.com

When they started handing out domain names, California PI lawyer Edward A. Smith must have been at the head of the line. But besides scoring "autoaccident.com," Smith has created a modestly useful site, noteworthy for its collection of links. Although the collection is small, it has a decided focus on sites useful to PI lawyers. Topics include safe cars, pedestrian injuries, brain injuries, and slip and fall injuries. Smith also offers a handful of PI checklists— steps an accident victim should take to preserve and collect evidence.

★★★ Traffic Accident Reconstruction Origin, www.tarorigin.com

Devoted to serving as a critical forum for ideas and techniques used in traffic accident reconstruction and to promoting excellence in the field, this Web site includes several useful and interesting features. In the library, you will find articles such as "Three Point Airborne Trajectory Analysis" and "Looking at Airbag Activation Sensors." A directory of experts lists names, specialties and e-mail addresses of accident reconstruction experts worldwide, while a directory of organizations lists groups and events. A unique feature is "Approach Angles," a page offering sets of facts concerning various hypothetical accident scenarios for which experts are invited to post their solutions. Lawyers who handle motor vehicle cases are certain to find information of interest on this site.

★★ Advocates for Highway and Auto Safety, www.saferoads.org

Advocates for Highway and Auto Safety, an alliance of consumer, health and safety groups and insurance companies and agents working together to make America's roads safer, offers a series of "fact sheets" on safety issues such as rollovers, child passenger safety, motorcycle helmets and safety belts. The site also provides information on the organization's federal and state lobbying efforts.

Aviation

★★★★★ Aviation Safety Data, http://nasdac.faa.gov

The Federal Aviation Administration provides through this site access to the principal federal databases relating to aviation accidents and safety. With others slated to be added over time, the eight databases available as of this writing were:

- The National Transportation Safety Board Accident and Incident Data System, the official repository of data from 1983 onward regarding aviation accidents and causes.
- The FAA Accident/Incident Data System, which is more extensive than the NTSB database because it includes records of potentially hazardous events that did not meet the NTSB's aircraft damage or personal injury thresholds, and because it includes data from 1978 onward.
- The Near Midair Collision System Database, involving incidents in which aircraft came within 500 feet or less of each other.
- NTSB Safety Recommendations to the FAA. These are recommendations made from 1963 onward as the result of NTSB investigations.
- Air Registry. An aircraft registry used to record and track civil aircraft registered in the U.S.
- Aviation Safety Reporting System. This system receives and analyzes reports of unsafe occurrences and hazardous situations.
- Bureau of Transportation Statistics. This data shows the amount of airline traffic and capacity.
- World Aircraft Accident Summary. Produced on behalf of the British Civil Aviation Authority, the summary provides details of all known major operational accidents worldwide.

The site also contains an aviation glossary, the text of FAA regulations, and links to other aviation sites.

★★★★ AirSafe.com, http://airsafe.com

AirSafe.com might better be called "Fear of Flying." Use it to search for airplane fatalities by airline, location or type of aircraft, or simply go to a list of all airline fatalities since 1970. (In fairness, there is also a list of airlines without fatalities.) Sections of the site are devoted to specific air crashes, while others offer tips on how to use the Web to investigate or find more information on a crash. Beyond fatalities, this consumer-oriented site offers information on airline service complaints, overbooked flights and flight delays. It provides advice on travel safety and help in overcoming fears about flying. Todd Curtis, a former airline safety analyst for Boeing and author of the book *Understanding Aviation Safety Data*, hosts the site.

Electromagnetic Fields

★★ **EMF Link,** http://infoventures.com/emf

EMF-Link strives to serve as a clearinghouse for information on the biological and health effects of electric and magnetic fields from sources such as power lines, electrical wiring, appliances, medical equipment, communications facilities, cellular phones and computers. Hosted by Information Ventures, a Philadelphia company that provides scientific consulting services and that publishes newsletters and journals on EMFs, the site describes itself as having thousands of articles on the topic. Full access to these articles is available only to subscribers to one of the company's other products. Non-subscribers are allowed limited access with some ability to search and retrieve articles.

Breast Implants

★★★ **Frontline: Breast Implants on Trial,** www.pbs.org/wgbh/pages/frontline/implants

On February 27, 1996, the PBS public affairs program *Frontline* broadcast its report, "Breast Implants on Trial." This site, the companion to that broadcast, has sections focusing on the legal, medical, corporate and personal aspects of the controversy. It includes the full transcripts of the closing arguments from Gladys Laas' 1994 jury trial against Dow Corning Corporation, in which she was awarded $5.2 million. It also houses various medical reports and medical journal articles on breast implants, and corporate documents from Dow Corning. The site is not updated.

★★ **David E. Bernstein's Breast Implant Litigation Home Page,** http://mason.gmu.edu/~dbernste/BreastImplants.html

David E. Bernstein, an associate professor at George Mason University School of Law, believes that breast implant litigation has been driven not by scientific evidence, but by politics, sensationalistic media coverage, and a contingency fee system that encourages speculative litigation. On this site, Bernstein provides links to scientific and medical reports concluding that there is no link between implants and systemic disease. He also offers his own articles on breast implants, tort reform and junk science.

Tobacco

★★★★★ **Inside the Tobacco Deal,** www.pbs.org/wgbh/pages/frontline/shows/settlement

This a fascinating Web site that tells the story of how two small town Mississippi lawyers took on the tobacco industry. Based on a Frontline documentary that aired May 12, 1998 on PBS, the site reconstructs the battle that started when Mississippi Attorney General Mike Moore joined with his "Ole Miss" classmate Dick Scruggs and sued tobacco companies on behalf of the state's taxpayers to recoup money spent on health care for smokers. The detailed site includes deposition excerpts, interview transcripts, an analysis of the criminal probe of the tobacco industry, an analysis of the tobacco deal, timelines of significant events, a discussion forum, links to related online resources, and a tobacco quiz. A complete transcript of the televised program can be downloaded.

★★★★★ **Legacy Tobacco Documents Library,** http://legacy.library.ucsf.edu

As part of the historic 1998 settlement among the tobacco industry and forty-six state attorneys general, tobacco manufacturers agreed to provide public access to industry documents produced through the discovery process. The settlement stipulated that the participating manufacturers would provide the public this access through a series of Web sites that the industry would maintain until June 30, 2010.

Fearing the eventual loss of public access to these documents, the American Legacy Foundation awarded $15 million to the University of California, San Francisco, to establish permanent Internet access to the documents and to develop a center for scholarly study of the material.

On January 31, 2002, the UCSF Library and Center for Knowledge Management unveiled the site that is to provide that permanent access, the Legacy Tobacco Documents Library. It houses more than 20 million pages of documents from tobacco industry files, many of them secret until uncovered in litigation, and stands as the world's largest public digital collection maintained by a library.

Ranging in date from the 1930s to the 1990s, the documents provide insight into tobacco industry marketing, research and development, cigarette analysis and design, and efforts to establish business in developing countries.

The library allows seven separate document collections to be searched through one easy-to-use interface. Users can perform simple or advanced searches, view documents in a variety of image formats, and collect their findings in a digital "bookbag" that they can download or e-mail. The site also provides information on topics related to the documents, such as the history of tobacco, litigation, tobacco use and health, and youth smoking.

★★★★★ **Tobacco Industry Documents,** www.cdc.gov/tobacco/ industrydocs/ index.htm

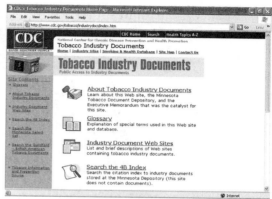

Providing the public with access to tobacco industry documents is the purpose of this site, sponsored by the Centers for Disease Control. The source for the bulk of this material is the Minnesota Tobacco Document Depository, reportedly the world's largest hardcopy cache of tobacco industry documents. With more than 27 million pages, the depository was created in 1995 to house documents from the trial in *Minnesota v.*

The Centers for Disease Control host this extensive cache of tobacco documents.

Philip Morris, Inc., and grew to include documents made public through other lawsuits as well as congressional investigations. This CDC site is organized into four sections:

- Industry sites. This section provides links to other Internet sites that have captured tobacco industry documents. Most of them are maintained by tobacco companies and mirror to some degree the contents of the Minnesota Depository. Users unable to obtain a particular document online through these sites can order it in hard copy from the Minnesota Depository.
- 4B Index. Tobacco company defendants created this site as a systematic way to access the documents that were released in the Minnesota litigation.
- Minnesota Select Set. This is a subset of roughly 380,000 pages of the total Minnesota Depository pages that were selected by lawyers as being key to the trial. They are available both as images of the original documents and as searchable text files scanned from the documents.
- Guildford-British American Tobacco Documents. Another subset of the Minnesota collection, these are some 7,000 documents chosen by lawyers for having the greatest relevance to the Minnesota trial and the population of that state.

★★★★★ **Tobacco Litigation Documents,** www.library.ucsf.edu/ tobacco/litigation

This site contains key litigation documents from the cases brought by the attorneys general and from similar actions against the tobacco industry. Now part of the UCSF collection, the collection was originally developed by the Tobacco Control Resource Center at Northeastern University, Boston. It was formerly on the Web under the name State Tobacco Information Center.

★★★★ **Tobacco BBS,** www.tobacco.org

Originally established in 1993 as a dial-in bulletin board system (BBS) and later migrating to the Web, this site focuses on a range of tobacco and smoking issues. It features legal, regulatory and health news and information, as well as a broad-ranging collection of links to tobacco resources and documents elsewhere on the Web.

★★★★ **Tobacco Control Resource Center,** http://tobacco.neu.edu

This site is home to the TCRC and the Tobacco Products Liability Project, projects of Northeastern University School of Law that provide support to products liability litigation against the tobacco industry and to legislative and regulatory initiatives to control the sale and use of tobacco. The site provides current news and analysis of tobacco-related litigation throughout the U.S., as well as libraries and archives of court opinions, litigation filings, industry documents, and news reports. It includes a collection of links to key tobacco sites on the Web.

★★★ **Coffin Nails: The Tobacco Controversy in the 19th Century,** http://tobacco.harpweek.com

Any lawyer who believes tobacco got its bad name only in the latter part of the twentieth century should visit this fascinating history of the tobacco controversy drawn from the pages of *Harper's Weekly* from 1857 to 1912. It shows that, as early as 1862, tobacco addiction was a recognized problem, with various "cures" offered to users. In 1867, the editor of *Harper's* identified the three major health dangers of tobacco use as cancer, heart disease and lung disease.

Chemicals/Allergies

★★★★ **Toxlaw.com,** www.toxlaw.com

A Web-based news and discussion forum for toxic tort litigators, Toxlaw features the Toxboard, an unmoderated, Usenet-style news forum where visitors can post and reply to questions or pass along news, press releases, comments or observations related to the field of toxic tort litigation. In addition to the general discussion forum, there are forums devoted specifically to discussions of sick building syndrome and multiple-chemical sensitivity. A useful feature of the site is ChemTracker, a tool for performing chemical, pathogen and allergen research over multiple Web sites, including those of the Centers for Disease Control and the National Institutes of Health.

★★★ Latex Allergy Links, http://latexallergylinks.tripod.com

Created by the parent of a child with latex allergy, this is a comprehensive, up-to-date listing of latex allergy-related sites on the Internet.

★★ Latex Allergy Information Resource, www.anesth.com/lair/lair.html

Based at the Department of Anesthesiology, University Hospitals of Cleveland, this simple site offers a tutorial for hospital staff with information and guidelines on caring for latex-allergic individuals undergoing surgery.

Medical

★★★★ Health Administration Responsibility Project, www.harp.org

This plaintiff-oriented site focuses on the liability of managed care organizations for the consequences of their decisions. Organized as a hypertext outline, it sets out theories of liability, sources of law and obstacles to trial. Major sections lead to detailed subsections. Citations to cases or statutes are linked to the full text. HARP also sponsors a listserv for discussion of these issues; information on subscribing is available at the Web site.

State Trial Lawyers' Associations

In addition to the national associations of plaintiffs' and defense lawyers, most states have their trial lawyers' groups. Their sites usually include information on their officers and members, their committees, calendars of events, legislative agendas, and local legal resources.

Alabama

- *Alabama Defense Lawyers Association*, www.adla.or
- *Alabama Trial Lawyers Association*, www.atla.net

Arizona

- *Arizona Trial Lawyers Association,* www.aztla.org

Arkansas

- *Arkansas Trial Lawyers Association,* www.arktla.org

California

- *Association of Defense Counsel of Northern California and Nevada,* www.adcnc.org
- *Association of Southern California Defense Counsel,* www.ascdc.org
- *Consumer Attorneys of California,* www.caoc.com
- *Consumer Attorneys of San Diego,* www.casd.org

Colorado

- *Colorado Defense Lawyers Association,* www.codla.org
- *Colorado Trial Lawyers Association,* www.ctlanet.org

Connecticut

- *Connecticut Trial Lawyers Association,* www.ct-tla.org

Delaware

- *Delaware Trial Lawyers Association,* www.dtla.org

Florida

- *Academy of Florida Trial Lawyers,* www.aftl.org
- *Florida Defense Lawyers Association,* www.fdla.org

Georgia

- *Georgia Defense Lawyers Association,* www.gdla.org
- *Georgia Trial Lawyers Association,* www.gtla.org

Hawaii

- *Consumer Lawyers of Hawaii,* www.clh.org

Idaho

- *Idaho Trial Lawyers Association,* www.itla.org

Illinois

- *Illinois Association of Defense Trial Counsel,* www.iadtc.org
- *Illinois Trial Lawyers Association,* www.iltla.com

Indiana

- *Indiana Trial Lawyers Association,* www.i-t-l-a.org

Kansas

- *Kansas Association of Defense Counsel,* www.kadc.org
- *Kansas Trial Lawyers Association,* www.ktla.org

Kentucky

- *Kentucky Academy of Trial Lawyers,* www.kata.org

Louisiana

- *Louisiana Trial Lawyers Association,* www.ltla.org

Maine

- *Maine Trial Lawyers Association,* www.mtla.org

Maryland

- *Maryland Trial Lawyers Association,* www.mdtriallawyers.com

Massachusetts

- *Massachusetts Academy of Trial Attorneys,* www.massacademy.com

Michigan

- *Michigan Defense Trial Counsel,* www.mdtc.org

Minnesota

- *Minnesota Defense Lawyers Association,* www.mdla.org
- *Minnesota Trial Lawyers Association,* www.mntla.com

Mississippi

- *Mississippi Trial Lawyers Association,* www.mstla.com

Missouri

- *Missouri Association of Trial Attorneys,* www.matanet.org

Montana

- *Montana Trial Lawyers Association*, www.monttla.com

Nebraska

- *Nebraska Association of Trial Attorneys*, www.nebraskatrial.com

Nevada

- *Nevada Trial Lawyers Association*, www.ntla.org

New Hampshire

- *New Hampshire Trial Lawyers Association*, www.nhtla.org

New Jersey

- *Association of Trial Lawyers of America*, New Jersey, www.atlanj.org
- *New Jersey Defense Association*, www.njdefenseassoc.com

New Mexico

- *New Mexico Trial Lawyers Association*, www.nmtla.org

New York

- *Injured Workers Bar Association of New York*, www.injuredworkers-bar.org
- *New York State Trial Lawyers Association*, www.nystla.org

North Carolina

- *North Carolina Academy of Trial Lawyers*, www.ncatl.org
- *North Carolina Association of Defense Attorneys*, www.ncada.org

North Dakota

- *North Dakota Trial Lawyers Association*, www.ndtla.com

Ohio

- *Ohio Academy of Trial Lawyers*, www.oatlaw.org
- *Ohio Association of Civil Trial Attorneys*, www.oacta.org

Oklahoma

- *Oklahoma Trial Lawyers Association*, www.otla.org

Oregon

- *Oregon Trial Lawyers Association*, www.oregontriallawyers.org

Pennsylvania

- *Pennsylvania Defense Institute*, www.padefense.org
- *Pennsylvania Trial Lawyers Association*, www.patla.org
- *Philadelphia Trial Lawyers Association*, www.philatla.org

South Carolina

- *South Carolina Defense Trial Attorneys' Association*, www.scdtaa.com
- *South Carolina Trial Lawyers Association*, www.sctla.org

South Dakota

- *South Dakota Defense Lawyers Association*, www.sddla.com
- *South Dakota Trial Lawyers Association*, www.sdtla.org

Texas

- *Texas Association of Defense Counsel*, www.tadc.org
- *Texas Trial Lawyers Association*, www.ttla.com

Utah

- *Utah Trial Lawyers Association*, www.utla.org

Vermont

- *Vermont Trial Lawyers Association*, www.vtla.org

Virginia

- *Virginia Association of Defense Attorneys*, www.vada.org
- *Virginia Trial Lawyers Association*, www.vtla.com

Washington

- *Washington Defense Trial Lawyers*, www.wdtl.org
- *Washington State Trial Lawyers Association*, www.wstla.org

West Virginia

- *Defense Trial Counsel of West Virginia*, www.dtcwv.org
- *West Virginia Trial Lawyers Association*, www.wvtla.org

Wisconsin

- *Civil Trial Counsel of Wisconsin,* www.ctcw.org
- *Wisconsin Academy of Trial Lawyers,* www.watl.org

Wyoming

- *Wyoming Trial Lawyers Association,* www.wytla.org

Chapter 16

Worldwide Commerce on the Worldwide Web

--- **Chapter Contents** ---

Just as the Internet has made the world seem smaller, it has fertilized the growth of global commerce. The ease of cross-border contact it has made possible has led to a surge in international trade.

For lawyers, this means that the law of international trade and the related field of international law can no longer remain the domains of a select few specialists. Clients large and small are taking their businesses to places they had never before imagined.

The Web's worldwide reach uniquely situates it to serve as a reference for the law of international trade. Sites from throughout the world provide substantive law and practical guidance.

International Law

★★★★★ **Cornell Law Library, International Resources,** www. lawschool.cornell.edu/lawlibrary/International_Resources/default.htm

The library at Cornell Law School maintains an unparalleled collection of resources and reference materials pertaining to international law and trade. It pulls them together here, providing easy access from a single page to the entire collection. From here, Cornell provides access to:

•   Foreign and International Law Resources on the Internet. This is a selective guide published on the Web by the library at Cornell Law School. It selectively collects and indexes Internet sites providing international laws and court decisions, documents, directories, trade information and statistics. Each listing includes a descriptive annotation. Sites were selected based on the reputations of the institutions maintaining them, the availability of primary and secondary sources in full text, and the uniqueness of the information. They are indexed according to both the jurisdictions and topics they cover.

- Cornell Legal Research Encyclopedia. Cornell's law librarians have compiled this detailed collection of legal resources organized by subject and country, and including many references for international law and trade. No mere collection of links, the compilation incorporates all available formats, including print, microfilm, CD-ROM, Westlaw, Lexis, and the Internet.
- International Court of Justice. Cornell hosts the official mirror site for the Americas, providing court documents and other information.
- Permanent Court of Arbitration. Cornell maintains this official documents site for the Permanent Court of Arbitration.
- International Labour Organization. Providing links to a Cornell-authored research guide, related Web sites, conventions, national labor legislation, the Digest of Decisions of the Freedom of Association Committee, Administrative Tribunal Decisions, and more.
- Global Legal Information Network. The Global Legal Information Network provides a database of national laws from contributing countries around the world accessed via a Web server of the U.S. Library of Congress. The database consists of searchable legal abstracts in English and some full texts of laws in the language of the contributing countries. It provides information on national legislation from more than thirty-five countries, with other countries being added on a continuing basis.
- UN21 Interest Group. Current and archived issues of the newsletter of the American Society of International Law.
- International Association of Law Libraries. The IALL is a worldwide organization of librarians, libraries and others whose work involves foreign and international legal resources.

★★★★ International and Foreign Law Resources, www.law.umaryland.edu/marshall/ElectronicResources/Subjects

A library of links to international and foreign law sites on the Internet, it is published by the Thurgood Marshall Law Library at the University of Maryland School of Law. The resource is intended to serve as a road map for locating international public and private law resources on the Internet and related, useful sites.

★★★ **Foreign and International Law,** www.willamette.edu/law/longlib/forint.htm

Willamette University hosts this international law page, a useful but not exhaustive collection of links to laws, treaties, organizations and other resources.

★★★ **Foreign and International Law Web,** www.washlaw.edu/forint

A service of Washburn University School of Law, this site offers a thorough collection of links to primary foreign and international legal resources, research aids, and related sites. The links are organized alphabetically by subject, author and country, and can be searched by key words.

★★★ **International Center for Not-for-Profit Law,** www.icnl.org

ICNL is an international organization that promotes legal reform on behalf of nonprofit organizations. Its Web site has a collection of full text articles on international nonprofit law and regulation. It features a searchable database offering access to documents from more than 160 countries having to do with legal, governance, taxation and regulatory issues involving nonprofits. The site also includes the full text of the quarterly International Journal of Not-for-Profit Law.

★★ **Center for International Legal Studies,** http://cils.net

Based in Salzburg, Austria, the center, through its Web site, offers complimentary subscriptions to "International Reports," its newsletter dealing with international business law topics. Published eight times a year, it is available only online and by email. Of the eight issues, four are special issues focused on banking, taxation, intellectual property and environmental law, and four are general issues dealing with various legal aspects of international business and investment. The Web site houses an archive of past issues and gives subscription information.

International Trade

★★★★★ **Global Competition Forum,** www.globalcompetitionforum.org

The International Bar Association hosts this site, the first to provide comprehensive access to the most current versions of the world's 100-plus competition laws, as well as more than 600 links to national competition authorities and international organizations with antitrust interests. The site also includes articles, speeches and commentary by experts in competition law enforcement and reform.

★★★★★ **Lex Mundi Guides to Doing Business,** www.lexmundi. com/publications/guides.html

Members of the Lex Mundi international law firm network contributed these comprehensive and frequently updated guides to doing business in more than sixty-seven countries, the European Union, and various U.S. states. Each guide is a detailed discussion of the jurisdiction's government and commerce, its investment framework, its rules for importing and exporting, forms of business organization, business-related laws, taxation, visas and other important topics.

★★★★★ **International Business Resources on the WWW,** http://globaledge.msu.edu/ibrd/ibrd.asp

Michigan State University publishes this extensive list of international business resources. The site includes links to international news sources and periodicals, government information from throughout the world, regional and country information, trade show listings, and even travel and culture resources. All links are annotated.

★★★★★ **International Trade Division, World Bank,** www.world-bank.org/trade

The best reason to visit this site is its extensive collection of working papers on international trade. Recent papers look at trade policies in electronic commerce, multilateral trade liberalization, exchange rates, export subsidies and much more. The site also provides primers on a number of trade topics, encompassing trade in goods and services, intellectual property rights, standards, trade and investment, government procurement, and competition policy. Another section examines the rules of international trade, discussing the policies of the World Trade Organization and other organizations. Completing the site are sections on export constraints and regional competitiveness.

★★★★★ **Lex Mercatoria,** http://lexmercatoria.org

Ancient when measured in Web years, Lex Mercatoria, created in 1993 by the University of Tromso, Norway, was one of the first legal sites of any kind on the Web and quite probably the first to focus on international trade. In July 2000, Lex Mercatoria was acquired by Cameron May, a legal publisher that specializes in international trade and international environmental law. Today, the site seems encyclopedic in scope, with comprehensive coverage of international trade, financial regulation, commercial law, intellectual property, maritime law, electronic commerce, and other related topics. The entire site is thoughtfully organized in a way designed to make its contents suitable for legal and academic writing and citation.

★★★★★ Mondaq Business Briefing, www.mondaq.com

This a service for professionals and business people involved in international trade and investment. The site provides global coverage of legislation and regulations, corporate finance, offshore finance, market analysis, economic analysis, risk management, property, consultancy, and worldwide business news. Coverage is supplied by lawyers, accountants, bankers and other professionals who enter into a marketing agreement with Mondaq to be contributors. Mondaq provides the same information to legal and business databases including Lexis-Nexis, Westlaw, Bloomberg and Dow Jones. Access to the site is free, although registration is required. Once registered, you can search archives of commentary and analysis on a range of issues, including international trade and finance, environmental law, employment law, Internet law, and much more.

★★★★★ World Trade Organization, www.wto.org

The WTO is the principal international body for setting the rules of trade between nations. WTO agreements form the legal ground rules for international commerce and for trade policy. Its site provides exhaustive information on specific trade topics such as goods, services, intellectual property, the environment, dispute settlement, and government procurement. It also includes an enormous library of trade documents and legal texts.

The WTO is the principal international body for setting the rules of trade between nations.

★★★★ eBusiness Lex, www.ebusinesslex.net

Calling it "the e-business legal portal," the European Commission's Enterprise Directorate General sponsors this site, a twelve-language Web portal containing information on the legal aspects of e-business, aimed specifically at small- and medium-sized European companies. The site contains information and resources on a range of issues, including contracts, online payments, privacy and data protection, and intellectual property rights. It includes a section containing European and national legislation relating to e-business. Law texts are shown in their original language, but an abstract is provided in the other languages of the site.

★★★★ G8 Information Centre, www.g8.utoronto.ca

This site is a collection of news articles, background information, research and academic papers, and other documents related to the G8—the group of world leaders who meet annually to deal with major economic and political issues. Maintained by the University of Toronto, it includes reports and agendas from meetings of the G8, as well as the G7 and the G20.

★★★★ Global Money, The Good Life and You, www.uiowa.edu/~erclog/webdex

Just what are the International Monetary Fund and the World Bank? University of Iowa Law Professor Enrique R. Carrasco and seven of his law students spent a year studying that question, out of which they produced this electronic book. The "e-book," as they call it, is intended to provide a basic understanding of the operations of the IMF and the World Bank and their roles in an increasingly global economy. The result is a comprehensive, balanced overview of international capital, written in a style that favors plain English over legalese.

★★★★ Legal Information Institute, International Trade Law, www.law. cornell.edu/topics/trade.html

From Cornell University's LII comes this collection of links to laws, treaties, government agencies, international organizations, and other sites related to international trade. Not a lengthy index, but a good starting point.

★★★★ Market Access Database, http://mkaccdb.eu.int

Operated by the European Commission, the Market Access Database is described as "the guide to cracking world markets." Its purpose is to provide up-to-date information about market access conditions in non-E.U. countries and to offer a systematic way for the European Commission to follow up on complaints from businesses about barriers to trade in non-E.U. countries. It features four primary sets of data: sectoral and trade barriers, applied tariffs, trade-flow statistics, and WTO bound tariffs. It also includes a guide to the General Agreement on Trade in Services, an exporters' guide to import facilities, and various market studies and reports.

★★★★ **Tools for Trade,** www.barnesrichardson.com/trade/trade.html

Lawyers will appreciate the useful Web site of the law firm Barnes, Richardson & Colburn, which provides both breaking news and more detailed analysis of developments in customs and international trade. A highlight is the firm's Daily Report, providing news of administrative actions that affect international trade. Unlike some sites that promise news, this one delivers, with a new report posted every day. Another feature of the site is summaries of important trade-related decisions of the U.S. Supreme Court, the U.S. Court of International Trade, and the Court of Appeals for the Federal Circuit. "International Trade Update," the firm's quarterly newsletter on developments in customs and international trade law, is here, although a new issue had not been posted for more than six months when we last visited. Articles by the firm's lawyers and a list of Web links round out the site.

★★★ **International Compliance Association,** www.int-comp.org

This Birmingham, England-based professional organization is dedicated to the furtherance of best compliance and anti-money-laundering practices in the financial services sector. Although access to much of the site is restricted to members, anyone can browse its useful collection of links to international regulators, law enforcement and financial intelligence units, financial oversight organizations, and other compliance-related sites.

★ **Cross Border Tax and Transactions,** www.crossborder.com

Published by an international tax lawyer in San Francisco, this site focuses on tax developments related to international trade and business. Its small offering of articles is stale, their dates mostly falling between 1995 and 1998.

★ **Regulatory and Trade Law Links,** www.cyberus.ca/~tweiler/webmark.html

An annotated collection of links to Internet resources, with an emphasis on Canada, the site is severely out of date.

★ **Trade Law Home Page,** www.tradelaw.com

From the Chicago law firm Riggle & Craven, a site that promises recent developments in trade law and links to other resources. The site is not well maintained or often updated.

Treaties and Conventions

★★★★★ Fletcher School of Law and Diplomacy, www.fletcher.tufts.edu/multilaterals.html

Tufts University's Fletcher School is host to The Multilaterals Project, an ongoing effort to publish multilateral conventions and other international instruments. The collection is organized by subject and also chronologically. The Trade and Commercial Relations section provides a wide array of full text documents, including the General Agreement on Tariffs and Trade, the treaty establishing the European Community, the Paris Convention for the Protection of Industrial Property, the Berne Convention for the Protection of Literary & Artistic Works, the WIPO Copyright Treaty, the UNCITRAL Draft Model Law on Electronic Commerce, and many others.

★★★★ Diplomacy Monitor, www.diplomacymonitor.com

As nations throughout the world increasingly use the Web to articulate diplomatic positions and mold global opinion on international issues, St. Thomas University School of Law launched Diplomacy Monitor. The site monitors this international output of communiqués, official statements, press briefings, position papers, interview transcripts and news releases from hundreds of Web sites operated by heads of state, ministries of foreign affairs, embassies, missions and even consulates, and channels it into a single information stream for scholars, diplomats, journalists, researchers and anyone else who is interested.

★ North American Free Trade Agreement, www-tech.mit.edu/Bulletins/nafta.html

The complete text of NAFTA, in hypertext, from *The Tech*, the student newspaper of the Massachusetts Institute of Technology.

U.S. Government Sites

★★★★★ Export.gov, www.export.gov

This site is the U.S. government's portal to all export-related information it makes available online. A substantial and wide-ranging site, it covers everything from the basics of exporting to the complexities of pricing, shipping and documentation. Of particular note is the site's Market Research collection, featuring country and industry market reports, trade agreements and statistics, project feasibility studies, and more.

★★★★★ International Trade Administration, www.ita.doc.gov

A branch of the U.S. Department of Commerce, the ITA's job is to encourage U.S. exports. Its site includes a substantial library of international trade information, organized by country, region and industry, as well as "assistance centers" focused on importing and exporting, trade information, and trade compliance. Of particular note are its country commercial guides—detailed guides to doing business in specific countries worldwide.

★★★★★ Safe Harbor, www.export.gov/safeharbor

The European Commission's Directive on Data Privacy prohibits the transfer of personal data to non-European Union nations that do not meet the European standard for privacy protection. Fearing that this directive could seriously hamper trade between the U.S. and E.U. nations, the U.S. Department of Commerce negotiated with the E.U. to create the Safe Harbor framework, enabling U.S. companies to be certified as being in compliance with the privacy directive. The Safe Harbor Web site provides a history and overview of the initiative, a library of related U.S. and E.U. documents, a Safe Harbor workbook, and instructions on becoming certified.

★★★★ Stat-USA/Internet, www.stat-usa.gov

This subscription service, operated by the U.S. Department of Commerce, provides a database of economic, business and international trade information produced by various arms of the U.S. government. Of particular interest is the National Trade Data Bank, which includes country commercial guides, market research reports, best market reports, and U.S. import and export statistics. Also useful is the International Trade Library of more than 40,000 documents. An annual subscription is $175. Non-subscribers may purchase individual articles.

★★★★ U.S. Commercial Service, www.export.gov/comm_svc

The U.S. Commercial Service is a branch of the U.S. Department of Commerce committed to increasing the number of U.S. firms, particularly small- to medium-sized firms, that benefit from international trade. The site includes information on market research, trade events, and exporting resources. Its most unusual feature is its matchmaking service for helping U.S. companies find international business partners. The Market Research section includes the complete set of Country Commercial Guides, prepared annually by U.S. embassy staff, which contain information on the business and economic situation of foreign countries and their political climates as they affects U.S. business. Also at the site is a calendar of trade events, both U.S. and international.

★★★★ U.S. International Trade Commission, www.usitc.gov

The USITC is an independent, quasi-judicial federal agency that provides trade expertise to both the legislative and executive branches, determines the impact of imports on U.S. industries, and directs actions against certain unfair trade practices, including patent, trademark and copyright infringement. The site provides the current USITC docket and calendar, including complaints and petitions that have been filed. It also provides a variety of economic reports on U.S. industries and the global trends that affect them.

★★★★ U.S. Trade Representative, www.ustr.gov

This executive branch office is responsible for developing and coordinating U.S. international trade, commodity and direct investment policy, and for negotiating with other countries on these matters. Its site includes a number of full text treaties and agreements, speeches on trade policy, press releases, and related information. Special areas of the site focus on such topics as the World Trade Organization and multilateral affairs, trade and the environment, monitoring and enforcement, world regions, and market sectors.

★★★ Private International Law Database, www.state.gov/www/ global/legal_affairs/private_intl_law.html

Created by the U.S. Department of State's office of the assistant legal adviser for private international law, this is a database of documents from the U.N. Commission on International Trade Law (UNCITRAL), the Hague Conference on Private International Law, the International Institute for the Unification of Private Law (UNIDROIT), and the Organization of American States. It includes a wide assortment of documents related to international trade and international business transactions. Documents can be read online or downloaded. However, a notice on the site stated that it was no longer being updated as of January 20, 2001.

The Americas

★★★★★ Foreign Trade Information System, www.sice.oas.org

The Trade Unit of the Organization of American States hosts this large collection of articles, trade agreements, legal texts, treaties and other documents. Materials are arranged under eight major sections: FTAA Process, with general information on the Free Trade Area of the Americas; Dispute

Settlement, with information on ADR procedures under agreements and treaties; Trade Agreements, with the full text of agreements between countries of the Western Hemisphere; Trade Forum, with articles, opinions and a calendar of events; Intellectual Property Rights, with the text of laws and regulations from OAS countries; Trade-Related Links; Summaries, short summaries of trade agreements; and Investment Treaties, with the full text of bilateral investment treaties between countries of the Western Hemisphere. The Trade Agreements area is organized into sections for multilateral agreements, bilateral agreements, regional-scope agreements, temporary, non-reciprocal agreements, and general association and cooperation agreements.

★★★★ Free Trade Area of the Americas, www.ftaa-alca.org

This site is an outgrowth of the 1994 Summit of the Americas and its plan to integrate the economies of the Western Hemisphere into a single free trade arrangement. It is an in-depth site that describes the origins and structure of the FTAA and houses the official documents, databases and reports of the organization and its various committees and working groups.

★★★★ National Law Center for Inter-American Free Trade, www.natlaw.com

The NLCIFT is a nonprofit organization devoted to facilitating the movement of goods, services and investment capital in the Western Hemisphere. The good news about its site is that it contains just about every resource you might want related to trade within the Americas. The bad news is that access to much of it requires an annual subscription, with packages starting at $595. For that, you get features such as Mexico's *Diario Oficial* (Mexico's equivalent to the Federal Register); the Inter-Am Database of the Americas, featuring legal and regulatory materials from throughout Latin America; the *Trade and Investment Law Bulletin*; and the biweekly *Inter-American Trade Report*.

United Nations

★★★★★ U.N. Commission on International Trade Law, www.un.or.at/uncitral

UNCITRAL is the U.N. branch devoted to harmonizing the law of international trade. Its site provides a complete collection of conventions, model laws, ratifications and amendments, case law, colloquium proceedings, and other documents. Visitors can access the site in their choice of English, French, Spanish or Japanese.

★★★★★ U.N. Convention on Contracts for the International Sale of Goods, www.cisg.law.pace.edu

Sponsored by Pace University School of Law, this is the U.S. home page of the CISG, the uniform international sales law that governs nearly two-thirds of all world trade. It is a comprehensive site, complete with the annotated text of the CISG, cases on the CISG, scholarly materials, and related documents and resources.

★★★★ International Court of Justice, www.icj-cij.org

Seated at The Hague, the International Court of Justice is the principal judicial organ of the United Nations, hearing cases on international law submitted by various states and offering advisory opinions on legal questions submitted by international organs and agencies. This site provides access to all of the Court's opinions since its formation in 1946 and provides its docket of current proceedings.

★★★ U.N. System Pathfinder, www.un.org/Depts/dhl/pathfind/frame/start.htm

The United Nations' Dag Hammarskjöld Library has created an online guide to finding "current, relevant and useful" publications from the many organizations that make up the U.N. The guide lists global studies and reports, handbooks and guides, bibliographies and indices, international statistical publications, compilations of treaties, resolutions and documents, as well as annual reports of U.N. bodies and specialized agencies. The site does not house any of the documents it lists—in fact, many are not available anywhere online. It provides links to those that are online and reference information for those that are not.

European Union

★★★★★ EUR-Lex, http:// europa.eu.int/eur-lex

EUR-Lex, an official European Union Web site, is the preeminent source for legislation in force in the E.U. as well as new legislation as it is enacted. The site has six major sections:

- Treaties, which has the 2002 Treaty on European Union, the 2002 Treaty establishing the European Community, the 2001 Treaty of Nice, and others.

- The *Official Journal*, published daily, containing new and draft legislation, notices and other information. In some cases, the E.U. publishes documents only in this electronic version of the journal, and not in print.
- Legislation, providing the electronic version of the legal acts in force set out in the *Official Journal of the European Communities*, along with the *Directory of Community Legislation in Force*.
- Drafts of legislation.
- Case law, providing access to recent case law of the European Court of Justice and the Court of First Instance.
- Parliamentary questions, providing materials on European parliamentary questions.

EUR-Lex is free to use, although users must register to use the Official Journal. The site is published in all eleven official E.U. languages.

★★★★★ Europa, http://europa.eu.int

The primary Web site of the European Union, Europa provides up-to-date coverage of European Union affairs and essential information on European integration. Through Europa, you can get access to all the information made available on the Internet by the institutions and bodies of the E.U., including the European Parliament, the Council of the Union, the European Commission, the Court

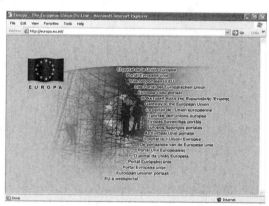

Europa is the official Web site of the European Union.

of Justice, the Court of Auditors, the Economic and Social Committee, the Committee of the Regions, the European Central Bank and the European Investment Bank. Designed with an extremely user-friendly interface, and offered in eleven languages, Europa has sections for those seeking basic information about the E.U. as well as for those conducting in-depth research.

Other Countries

★★★★★ Access to Justice Network, www.acjnet.org

The Access to Justice Network is a Web site devoted to Canadian justice and legal information. Sponsored by the Canadian Department of Justice, the University of Alberta and the University of Montreal, it offers a wealth of diverse information and resources. There are the requisite links to federal and provincial court opinions and statutes, but there are also connections to extensive databases of bibliographic information, a broad assortment of online publications for practitioners and consumers alike, directories of Canadian law firms and law societies, online conferences and open discussion forums. The entire site can be viewed in either English or French, and is well laid out and easy to move around in. This is one-stop shopping for Canadian legal resources.

★★★★★ Australasian Legal Information Institute, www.austlii. edu.au

This is to Australian law what Cornell's Legal Information Institute is to U.S. law—a comprehensive library of full text legal materials. It includes the full text of most Australian court decisions and legislation, a number of topical libraries and databases, and indexes of links to other Australian law sites. If you need Australian legal materials, look no farther.

★★★★★ British and Irish Legal Information Institute, www. bailii.org

From the same folks who sponsor the Australian Legal Information Institute, BAILII claims to be the most comprehensive collection of British and Irish primary legal materials on the Internet, with well over 475,000 searchable documents and 15 million hypertext links. BAILII's libraries of cases and legislation are divided among England and Wales, Ireland, Northern Ireland, Scotland and the United Kingdom. Its case law databases include decisions from the U.K. House of Lords, the England and Wales High Court and Court of Appeal, the Scottish High Court, the Northern Ireland High Court and Court of Appeal, and the Irish High Court and Court of Appeal. Statutes of the U.K., Ireland and Northern Ireland are provided.

★★★★ Chinalaw Web, www.qis.net/chinalaw

The mission of the Chinalaw Web, which is sponsored by the University of Maryland School of Law, is to provide information about Chinese law and the legal system in greater China. It covers the four legal jurisdictions in China: the People's Republic of China, the Republic of China on Taiwan, the Hong Kong Special Administrative Region of the People's Republic of China, and the Portuguese Colony of Macau. The site includes translations of Chinese laws and regulations from mainland China and Taiwan, Hong Kong and Macau, as well as more than thirty legal articles on various topics related to Chinese law. Laws are provided in both English and Chinese.

★★★ Legal Island, www.legal-island.com

This site is a collection of links to legal resources for Northern Ireland and the Republic of Ireland. Links are divided between northern and southern Ireland. Included are legislative sites, court opinions, law firms, legal publishers and related research sites. A simple site, but useful to anyone needing Irish law.

Other Resources

★★★★ U.N. Wire, www.unwire.org

This free daily news summary covers the United Nations, global affairs and international issues. It is sponsored by the United Nations Foundation and the Better World Fund. A sharp, newspaper-style layout and an index of news by topic make this an attractive site for news.

★★★ Embassy.org, www.embassy.org

Links to foreign embassies and international business centers, as well as a reference center and trade and commerce information. Operated by Stapleton-Gray & Associates.

Chapter 17

Virtual Justice: Resolving Disputes Over the Web

As use of the Internet to communicate and conduct business grew, disputes were inevitable. Thus it was that alternative dispute resolution took a foothold early on in the development of Cyberspace.

The range of potential disputes in the virtual world is as wide as in the tangible one—copyright or trademark infringement, misappropriation of trade secrets, defamation, fraud, deceptive trade practices, invasion of privacy—the list grows ever longer.

Early in 1996, operating on the assumption that disputes that arise online are best resolved online, a group of Internet trailblazers established **The Virtual Magistrate**, the Web's first forum for online arbitration and fact finding. Proceedings were to be conducted entirely by e-mail, and moderated by an impartial magistrate drawn from a pool of neutrals with experience in computer and Internet law.

The Virtual Magistrate came with a high pedigree, backed by the National Center for Automated Information Research, the Cyberspace Law Institute, the American Arbitration Association, and the Villanova Center for Information Law and Policy. But its first decision issued a few months later—an unenforceable default judgment against the non-participating America Online in favor of a complainant who was affiliated with the Virtual Magistrate—drew controversy, and the program by and large became dormant.

The Virtual Magistrate still lives on the Web, now "new and improved" and hosted by Chicago-Kent College of Law, at www.vmag.org. But while it appears largely inactive even today, plenty of other online ADR programs have sprung up in its wake. And beyond programs that provide actual online dispute resolution—or ODR as it has come to be called—many Web sites provide resources and materials about the use of ADR in the offline world.

So here is a look at what the Internet offers in the way of ADR resources. From educational materials to online dispute resolution, the Internet is home to an abundance of sites relating to this burgeoning field.

Online ADR

★★★★★ Cybersettle.com, www.cybersettle.com

Ever think that if you could cut through all the posturing and bureaucracy involved in insurance claims, you could settle them more easily? That is more or less the idea behind Cybersettle.com, an automated, online tool for resolving insurance claims. Either an insurer or a claimant can initiate the process. Cybersettle then invites the other party to participate. If it agrees, the two sides are given three opportunities—or rounds—to settle. For each round, each side submits an offer or demand. Software automatically compares these. If the offer and demand are within 30% or $5,000 of each other on any round, the claim is settled for the median amount. If an offer is the same as or greater than a demand, the claim is settled for the demand amount. Started by two former trial lawyers, Cybersettle now has the participation of a number of insurers and self-insured companies. Parties to a dispute pay only if they successfully reach a settlement. The fee ranges from $100 to $200, depending on the amount of the settlement.

★★★★★ iCourthouse, www.i-courthouse.com

iCourthouse is a sort of virtual judge and jury, providing jury trials via the Web. Parties submit opening and closing arguments, documentary evidence, and "testimony" (actually written statements), collected into a "trial book." Jurors—who can be any Web surfer who registers—select the cases they would like to decide from a docket of open cases. They review the contents of the trial books, and are able to post questions to the litigants. After all the jurors have rendered their verdicts, the parties receive a verdict summary that

iCourthouse is a sort of virtual judge and jury, providing jury trials via the Web.

includes the number of votes cast, the median award to the plaintiff, if any, and a compilation of juror comments about the case. The parties can choose whether the verdicts are to be binding or advisory. This, of course, assumes both parties agree to the proceeding in the first place, since, not being a real court of law, iCourthouse has no way to coerce defendants to participate.

Of far greater interest to lawyers is iCourthouse's JurySmart, a feature that allows lawyers to test the strengths and weaknesses of a case by previewing it to a pool of Internet jurors. Upon completion, they receive a written report of the results, which includes each juror's verdict, comments and questions, along with a profile that includes each juror's age, sex, occupation, education, and annual income. At a cost of $189 per report, this is an economical and effective way for lawyers to assess the merits of a case.

★★★★★ SquareTrade, www.squaretrade.com

When an eBay sale goes sour, the Web auction site refers its users to SquareTrade for help in resolving their disputes. SquareTrade uses unique technology together with a roster of more than 250 trained mediators to provide online dispute resolution. SquareTrade employs a two-tiered process. Parties to a dispute begin with the patent pending Direct Negotiation tool. The parties exchange messages regarding their positions using a secure case page hosted by SquareTrade. The Direct Negotiation tool suggests possible resolutions and helps parties work directly with each other towards resolution. If this first tier fails to resolve the dispute, the parties can request a mediator to assist them in coming to terms. All communication is done via the case page. Parties are charged nothing to use the Direct Negotiation tool. If they elect mediation, the cost varies depending on the Web business that referred them. For example, an eBay customer who files for mediation is charged $20.

General ADR Sites

★★★★★ ADR Resources, http://adrr.com

Dallas mediator Stephen R. Marsh hosts this surprisingly useful site. Although amateurish in appearance, it offers an array of information and resources that make it worthwhile for both ADR professionals and those seeking to learn more about the field. Start with Marsh's collection of essays, divided into four "volumes," each addressing successively more complex topics. The first, most general volume includes introductory materials as well as checklists for preparing for and appearing at a mediation. The second volume deals with more advanced or esoteric topics, such as the use of mediation in estate planning. The final two volumes focus on training and other issues. The Web site also carries a monthly newsletter, **Mediation**

On-Line, useful, among other reasons, for its regular updates of new Web sites related to ADR.

★★★★★ American Arbitration Association, www.adr.org

The AAA was a pioneer in the field of ADR, and its Web site is the preeminent ADR resource on the Internet. Here you will find information on ADR in labor relations, employment, commerce, the construction industry, and international disputes. The site has the text of AAA rules and samples of several AAA forms. It also includes a publications catalog, daily headlines from ADRWorld.com,

The American Arbitration Association site covers a wide range of ADR topics.

and a number of useful guides to ADR in various industries. The site's WebFile service allows parties to a dispute to file and track cases online.

★★★★★ Lovells International Arbitration Guide, www2.lovells.com/Arbitration/SilverStream/Pages/pgHome.html

The international law firm Lovells sponsors this free site devoted to providing practical assistance to clients and prospective clients who use arbitration to resolve disputes. It features the Drafting Engine, a tool that walks users through a step-by-step process resulting in a tailor-made arbitration clause. The Arbitration Guide also includes:

- Point-by-point guides to commencing and responding to arbitration proceedings.
- A cost calculator.
- The full text of the rules of the major international arbitration institutions and a comparative table of rules as well as national arbitration statutes and international arbitration conventions.
- A collection of links to international and national arbitration and ADR institutions, legal associations and online libraries.

Although the site is free, you will be required to complete a simple registration in order to gain access.

★★★★★ **ODR.info,** www.odr.info

This site, launched in November 2003, is the newest Web home of the Center for Information Technology and Dispute Resolution at the University of Massachusetts, Amherst. The center exists to explore the use of technology and the Internet in dispute resolution. Directed by UMass Professors Ethan Katsh and Janet Rifkin, the Center has been an innovator and leader in online dispute resolution since the early days of the Web. The center publishes a Web log ("blog")[1] about ODR as well as a monthly newsletter on the Web, *ODRMonthly*, and hosts an electronic discussion list about ADR, "dispute-res." The center consults with a range of organizations to assist them in developing their own online ADR programs and resources, and it has ongoing programs of study and research. Its site is home to a wide array of resources about ODR.

★★★★★ **Recent Developments in Dispute Resolution,** www.willamette.edu/law/wlo/dis-res

Here is help keeping up with the latest developments in dispute resolution. Every week, this newsletter arrives via e-mail, delivering news of court opinions, legislation, regulations, books and articles on the subject of ADR. It comes courtesy of the faculty and students at Oregon's Willamette University College of Law and its Center for Dispute Resolution. You can subscribe from the site, or, if you prefer not to receive the e-mail, you can read the current issue here, as well as all previous issues back to June 1997. Best of all, it is entirely free.

★★★★ **ADRWorld.com,** www.adrworld.com

ADRWorld.com tracks and reports breaking news in the field of alternative dispute resolution. It provides daily summaries and full text of court decisions related to ADR, and tracks legislative and regulatory developments in the field at the federal level and in all fifty states. Much of this is archived, creating a searchable, full text database of ADR-related court opinions, statutes, rules, policy documents and news stories. Summaries are free, but access to full text requires a paid subscription, which is $245 a year for a single user.

★★★★ **The CPR Institute for Dispute Resolution,** www.cpradr.org

An ADR information site and home page featuring information, publications and practice tools. Available through the site are articles on drafting

---

[1] For more about blogs, see Chapter 27 *infra*.

ADR contracts together with sample clauses, as well as sample articles from the Institute's publications on ADR practice and procedure. The site also includes the roster of the institute's 700 neutrals. The CPR Institute is a nonprofit alliance of corporations, law firms, academics and public institutions focused on new uses of ADR for business and public disputes.

★★★★ CR Info, www.crinfo.org

A confusing, almost intimidating, structure masks an exhaustive collection of conflict resolution resources. The site organizes its many resources into various "editions." There are "user editions" offering different routes into the site for adversaries, bystanders, students, educators, conflict resolution practitioners and researchers. Then there are separate "process editions" focusing on mediation, arbitration, negotiation, reconciliation, peacemaking and democratization. There are also "conflict editions" for different types of conflict: business, interpersonal, international, intergroup, environmental/public policy, legal/ADR and terrorism. Undoubtedly, these different groupings were designed to make the site more user friendly, but the result is just the opposite, leaving a first-time visitor uncertain where to start. Once you find your way in, however, the effort will prove worthwhile.

★★★★ RAND Institute for Civil Justice, www.rand.org/centers/icj

Think tank RAND has produced a number of studies relating to ADR. Follow the "Publications" link to find a searchable index of these studies, including abstracts and ordering information. Among the titles available from RAND are "A Research Agenda: What We Need to Know About Court-Connected ADR," and "Arbitration Agreements in Health Care: Myths and Reality."

ADR in Particular Fields

★★★★★ KluwerArbitration.com, www.kluwerarbitration.com

The publishing company Kluwer Law International hosts this fully searchable database of primary and secondary materials in the field of international commercial arbitration. The site assembles the full texts of commercial arbitration treaties, national arbitration laws, judicial decisions and arbitral awards, and model arbitration clauses for contracts. It also provides a guide to international arbitration institutions, including links to their rules. Information is included on identifying and selecting arbitrators and mediators to hear international disputes. Much of the commentary included in the site is drawn from Kluwer publications such as InternationalADR, Arbitration International, and Journal of International Arbitration.

★★★★★ **NASD Dispute Resolution,** www.nasdadr.com

The National Association of Securities Dealers operates the world's largest securities dispute resolution forum, focusing on monetary and business disputes between investors and securities firms. Its Web site provides an exhaustive overview of this process with general FAQs for those unfamiliar with the process, and more specific resources, such as rules and procedures, for ADR and securities professionals.

★★★★★ **WIPO Arbitration and Mediation Center,** http://arbiter. wipo.int/center/index.html

The Arbitration and Mediation Center of the World Intellectual Property Organization was established in 1994 to offer arbitration and mediation services for the resolution of international commercial disputes between private parties. It has come to play an important role in the development of the Internet and electronic commerce. In particular, it is a leading provider of ADR for disputes arising out of the use of Internet domain names. Its comprehensive Web site includes full information on these various programs, along with the full text of its rules, information on its services, recommended contract clauses and submission agreements, and listings of conferences and training programs.

★★★★ **Securities Arbitration,** www.seclaw.com/centers/arbcent.shtml

This is the arbitration center of SECLaw.com, a Web site devoted to securities law. The arbitration center contains articles offering an overview of the field, surveying typical issues in securities arbitrations, and reviewing the enforcement of arbitration awards.

★★ **Victim Offender Mediation Association,** www.igc.org/voma

This site provides general information about the association and the field of victim-offender mediation, as well as a collection of articles and links to other Web resources.

Private ADR Providers

★★ **JAMS,** www.jamsadr.com

A nicely designed Web site, but basically just a brochure for this private ADR company, which offers dispute resolution services throughout the U.S. The most useful feature is a database of its roster of ADR providers, allowing you to search by specialty or location. A selection of brief guides provides an overview of the ADR process.

★★ National Arbitration and Mediation, www.clicknsettle.com

For a few years, this company changed its name to clickNsettle and offered online dispute resolution along with traditional, live mediation and arbitration services. Now, it has reverted to its original name and discontinued its ODR service. Its Web site provides general information about its services and about submitting a case.

★ Global Arbitration Mediation Association, www.gama.com

As more and more companies spring up offering online dispute resolution, GAMA has gone in the opposite direction. It was one of the first organizations to offer arbitration of disputes over the Internet, allowing for complaints to be filed and served by e-mail, and holding "hearings" that consisted of affidavits and testimony submitted via either e-mail or Internet relay chat. Today, GAMA does none of that, instead offering only online directories of arbitrators, mediators and ADR organizations worldwide. Its directories seem woefully incomplete; a search for an arbitrator in Boston, for example, turned up only one listing, and for the entire state of Massachusetts only six listings.

★ The Janzen Group, www.businessmediators.com

This San Francisco-based company provides a range of ADR services and conflict management systems to businesses. It experimented for a time with online mediation, conducted via e-mail or on a private IRC channel, but it no longer offers that service. The Web site briefly describes the company and its principal mediators.

Studies and Training

★★★★ Program on Negotiation, Harvard Law School, www.pon. harvard.edu

A research center devoted to improving the theory and practice of conflict resolution, Harvard's Program on Negotiation provides professional ADR training, sponsors various publications, supports several research programs, and serves as a clearinghouse for ADR teaching materials and exercises. From its Web site, users can search the clearinghouse catalog and place orders to purchase any of its books, videos, simulations or other materials. The site offers information on two PON-sponsored journals, *Negotiation Journal* and *Harvard Negotiation Law Review*, but does not include full text articles. Finally, the site describes PON's various research projects and its professional training programs run by ADR dignitaries such as Roger Fisher, Frank E.A. Sander and Bruce M. Patton.

Membership Organizations

★★★★ Society of Professionals in Dispute Resolution, www.spidr.org

Formed in 1972, SPIDR is an international membership association committed to the advancement of the highest standards of ethics and practice for arbitrators, mediators and other ADR professionals. Prospective members can visit SPIDR's site to learn about its various subcommittees—or "sectors" as it calls them—devoted to such areas as online, commercial, environmental, family and consumer ADR. A publications section sells books, reports and conference proceedings, as well as audiotapes of conference programs. Special features include timely articles on current developments in ADR law and practice.

★★★ ABA Section of Dispute Resolution, www.abanet.org/dispute/home.html

The Section's Web site provides an overview of its committees and activities and a calendar of coming events. Also here is a collection of ADR standards and policies, such as the Model Standards of Conduct for Mediators, Family Mediation Standards and the Code of Ethics for Commercial Arbitrators. A page for law students highlights opportunities in ADR and offers an essay contest. Topping off this site is a modest collection of ADR links.

★★★ National Academy of Arbitrators, www.naarb.org

Only the elite among ADR professionals become members of the National Academy of Arbitrators. To be eligible merely to apply for membership, an arbitrator must have at least five current years of experience and have decided no fewer than fifty cases. This has helped establish the Academy as a leader in setting standards of ethics and professionalism. Its Web site provides an overview of the academy and its officers, as well as a directory of Academy members and the text of its code of professional responsibility.

Court and Government ADR

★★★★ ADR Resource Center, www.ncsc.dni.us/KMO/Topics/ADR/ADRsummary.htm

Part of the much larger Web site of the National Center for State Courts, the ADR Resource Center offers research and reports focused on the use of ADR in state court systems. Of particular use is its state-by-state contacts directory for court-affiliated ADR programs throughout the U.S. A section describing NCSC activities in the ADR arena provides a selection of full text articles and reports, as well as the transcript of a symposium on state court ADR sponsored by the Center and the *Cardozo Online Journal of Conflict Resolution*. The site also lists in bibliographic format the many materials that can be borrowed from the NCSC's library. Among these are a number of reports on and evaluations of court ADR programs throughout the U.S.

★★★★ Alternative Dispute Resolution: A Resource Guide, www.opm.gov/er/adrguide_2002/index.asp

The U.S. Office of Personnel Management publishes this detailed guide to ADR in the federal government. The publication surveys how the most common forms of ADR are being implemented in federal agencies, with an agency-by-agency review of current programs. The guide also provides a listing of training and resources available from government and non-government sources. It includes links to non-government ADR sites and provides a bibliography of related materials.

★★★★ Department of the Air Force, ADR Home Page, www.adr.af.mil

Virtually all federal government entities have Web pages of their own devoted to ADR, but the Air Force ADR page stands out as one of the best, in part because of its extensive collection of ADR links, most of them annotated with brief descriptions of the site. It includes not only government programs, but also private-sector programs and general ADR resources.

★★★ Federal Judicial Center, www.fjc.gov

The FJC includes a small library of publications examining the use of ADR in the federal courts, which you can read online or download in Adobe Acrobat format. Among the available titles are: "Voluntary Arbitration in Eight Federal District Courts: An Evaluation," a 1994 report on pilot court-annexed voluntary arbitration programs in eight federal district courts; "Court-Annexed Arbitration in Ten District Courts," a 1990 evaluation of pilot mandatory court-annexed arbitration programs in ten federal courts; "Alternatives to Litigation: Do They Have a Place in the Federal District Courts?" a 1995 paper addressing arguments for and against incorporating ADR programs into the case management procedures of federal courts; and "ADR and Settlement Programs in the Federal District Courts," a 1996 report that describes each federal court's alternative dispute resolution and settlement procedures.

★★★ **Interagency Alternative Dispute Resolution Working Group,** www.usdoj.gov/adr

A federal government working group established to promote and facilitate ADR in federal agencies, its Web site houses training materials and manuals to assist agencies in developing programs of their own. Anyone working to develop ADR programs or training would find many of the materials here to be of interest, particularly the Program Manager's Resource Manual, which includes chapters on designing, constructing and evaluating an ADR program.

Law Journals

★★ **Ohio State Journal on Dispute Resolution,** http://moritzlaw. osu.edu/jdr/JDRHOME.htm

The *Ohio State Journal on Dispute Resolution* is a student-edited publication of the Ohio State University College of Law and is the official journal of the American Bar Association's Section of Dispute Resolution. When the *Journal* introduced its companion Web site in 1997, the site included abstracts of recent articles and an index of all articles ever published in the *Journal*. The index remains, but the abstracts are gone, leaving only print subscription information for those wanting to read more.

Chapter 18

In Search of Ethics on the Internet

Chapter Contents

General Ethics Sites
Talking About Ethics
Ethics Codes and Opinions Available Online

Lawyers get a bum rap. Seen by many as ruthless and greedy, they practice perhaps the most ethical of professions. Bound by strict codes of conduct, almost everything they do—from counseling clients to marketing their firms—must conform to prescribed standards.

The Internet is critical to helping not just lawyers, but also the broader public, understand these rules more thoroughly. Codes of conduct and ethics opinions from a majority of states are available on the Web, and a growing number of ethics sites bring perspective to these standards.

General Ethics Sites

★★★★★ A Good Lawyer, www.agoodlawyer.com

Subtitled, *Secrets Good Lawyers [and their best clients] Already Know,* this is an online book written by McLean, Virginia, lawyer Stephen W. Comiskey. He describes it as "an intentionally brief book . . . to be used by lawyers to help fill in the gaps that we don't currently learn in law school . . . but that we need to know to practice law and to do it honorably." It is full of nuggets of wisdom such as, "Lawyers are the custodians of the ideals of our society," and "A trial is theater with consequences." You can download the book or read it online free. If you print it, Comiskey asks that you pay $10.

★★★★★ American Legal Ethics Library, wwwsecure.law.cornell. edu/ethics

From Cornell's Legal Information Institute, this digital library contains the full text of the codes or rules of professional conduct for most U.S. states, as well as the ABA's model code. Some are in hypertext format, others are included through links to state bar or court sites. In addition, major law firms are contributing narratives on professional conduct requirements in their respective states. Materials are organized by both state and topic, and all are fully searchable. As of September 2003, the narratives covered Arizona, Arkansas, California, Colorado, Connecticut, the District of Columbia, Florida, Illinois, Louisiana, Maryland, Michigan, New Jersey, New York, Ohio, Oregon, Pennsylvania, Rhode Island, South Carolina and Texas, with other states to be added.

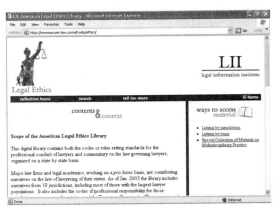

Cornell's American Legal Ethics Library includes most states' professional conduct rules.

The library's materials are organized both by state and topic, and all are fully searchable. Each element of the library is linked to the rest of the collection in multiple ways, permitting a user to track a specific issue or point from code to commentary in a single jurisdiction and to track the same question in materials from other jurisdictions.

★★★★★ Center for Professional Responsibility, American Bar Association, www.abanet.org/cpr/home.html

The Center's mission is to provide "national leadership and vision in developing and interpreting standards and scholarly resources in legal ethics," and its Web site addresses many of the profession's most cutting edge issues. Its sections on multidisciplinary practice and multijurisdictional practice are among the best resources on these topics anywhere on the Web. Its ethics section includes the full text of the Model Rules of Professional Conduct, annotated with comments and comparisons to the Model Code, as well as summaries of recent opinions of the ABA's Standing Committee on Ethics and Professional Responsibility. A service called "ETHICSearch" allows lawyers to e-mail their ethics questions and receive back citations to the authorities that should help them find the answers. Other features of the site include links to many states' professionalism codes and a variety of related documents.

★★★★★ Ethics and Lawyering Today, www.ethicsandlawyering.com

This monthly, electronic newsletter highlights important new cases, ethics opinions and other developments, often with links to full-text documents. It is published by William Freivogel, senior vice president, loss prevention, at Aon Risk Services, Chicago, and Lucian Pera, a lawyer in Memphis, Tennessee. The Web site includes current and past editions of the newsletter.

★★★★★ Freivogel on Conflicts, www.freivogelonconflicts.com

William Freivogel, who also maintains Ethics and Lawyering Today, publishes this "practical online guide to conflicts of interest for lawyers with sophisticated business and litigation practices." This is an online treatise discussing conflicts of interest in a range of scenarios and tracking current case law on the topic. It is a useful and informative resource, well worth exploring.

★★★★★ Legalethics.com, www.legalethics.com

A site of consistently high quality since its creation in 1995, it is devoted to helping legal professionals understand the unique ethical issues raised by the Internet. Its most useful service is in tracking and publishing state and local ethics rulings related to the Internet, organized by state. It maintains a comprehensive collection of links to ethics-related articles, other ethics sites, state ethics boards and related research sources. It

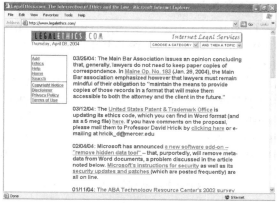

LegalEthics.com is devoted to the unique ethical issues raised by the Internet.

provides basic information on each state's ethics agency and rules of conduct and provides links to full-text rules and opinions where available.

★★★★★ Texas Center for Legal Ethics and Professionalism, www.txethics.org

This nonprofit organization, devoted to promoting lawyer ethics and professionalism, maintains a diverse and useful online library. Although of greatest use to lawyers in Texas, it also includes materials of broader interest. It offers two online courses on ethics and law practice. It has the complete text of the Texas disciplinary rules, together with tables comparing and cross-referencing them to the current and former ABA Model Rules. It has the full text of Texas Supreme Court Professional Ethics Committee opinions and a summary of court opinions related to the topic. Finally, there is an array of articles. All the online material is free and some can also be purchased in hard copy.

★★★★ American Judicature Society, www.ajs.org

The AJS is actively involved in promoting judicial ethics education as well as a fair and effective system of judicial discipline. Among the resources available through its Web site are a national directory of judicial conduct organizations, a clearinghouse service for data concerning judicial discipline, descriptions of courses available through its National College on Judicial Conduct and Ethics, and a selection of in-depth articles, such as "An Ethics Guide for Part-Time Lawyer Judges," and "Key Issues in Judicial Ethics."

★★★★ CrossingtheBar.com, www.crossingthebar.com

Thinking about moving to warmer climes? Ahh, but there's that nasty issue of bar admission. Here is help: a Web site that provides a state-by-state guide to reciprocity rules. Beyond reciprocity, it also includes rules for admission *pro hac vice*, rules regarding the unauthorized practice of law, special licensing procedures for corporate counsel, and information on how other professions deal with multistate practice. The site covers all U.S. states, territories and possessions. The site hosts a discussion forum for lawyers interested in multi-state practice issues, although it shows little activity.

★★★★ The Law Office Hornbook, www.hornbook.com

This is the online version of a quarterly periodical that focuses on malpractice avoidance, firm management and professional liability. The bars of Virginia, Hawaii, New Mexico and Arizona sponsor it as part of the risk management service they provide. Articles—expanded versions of those from the hard-copy edition—cover a range of ethics and professionalism topics.

★★★★ U.S. Office of Government Ethics, www.usoge.gov

The OGE is an executive branch agency established by the Ethics in Government Act of 1978. Its role is to prevent conflicts of interest on the part of government employees, and to resolve conflicts that do occur. Although not concerned strictly with legal ethics, the site hosts a wide-ranging library of resources relating to ethics in government and in general. The site includes a library providing or linking to the texts of applicable executive orders, statutes, regulations, advisory letters, "DAEOgrams" (OGE advisory memoranda to a "designated agency ethics official"), forms, publications, and other resource materials related to government ethics.

★★★ ABA/BNA Lawyers' Manual on Professional Conduct, www.bna.com/products/lit/mopc.htm

BNA provides Web access to current reports from this manual, updated every other week. It requires a paid subscription, but you can sign up online for a free trial and review a sample issue. Subscribers receive reports every two weeks, with e-mail alerts summarizing the highlights and linking to full-text articles and documents on the Web. Subscribers also get access to an archive of articles dating to 1998.

★★★ Association of Professional Responsibility Lawyers, www.aprl.net

APRL is a national organization of lawyers concentrating in the fields of professional responsibility and legal ethics. Its members include professors, bar counsel, legal malpractice litigators, in-house law firm ethics counsel, and the like. For non-members, the sole reason to visit this site is for its thorough library of links, which includes state ethics codes, ethics opinions, bar associations, and other sites related to ethics or malpractice.

★★★ Ethics and Standards for Arbitrators and Mediators, www.adr.org

The American Arbitration Association provides the complete text of its ethics codes governing arbitrators, mediators and ADR proceedings. Follow the link to "Rules and Procedures."

★★★ The Federalist Society, fed-soc.org

The Federalist Society for Law and Public Policy Studies is a group of conservatives and libertarians interested in the current state of the legal order. Its Professional Responsibility Group authors programs and sponsors seminars on various topics in the field. Some of these papers and programs are available on the Web site.

★★★ How to Succeed as a Lawyer, www.texasbar.com/members/buildpractice/boyd.asp

In the early 1960s, attorney Roland Boyd of McKinney, Texas, wrote a letter to his son offering tips on how to be a successful lawyer. When officials of the State Bar of Texas saw the letter, they prevailed upon him to allow the Texas Bar Journal to print it. Boyd agreed and it appeared in the November 1963 issue. Now the Texas bar makes it available on the Web.

★★★ James McCauley's Home Page, members.aol.com/jmc-cauesq/ethics

James McCauley is a lawyer in Richmond, Virginia, and ethics counsel for the Virginia State Bar. He is also a prolific writer of articles concerning legal ethics, several of which he includes on his site. The most ambitious is "Survey of the Law of Professional Responsibility in Virginia," which he and former Virginia Bar Counsel Michael L. Rigsby wrote for the *University of Richmond Law Review*. Other articles look at lawyers and the Internet, doctors and lawyers, Chinese walls, and whether accountants are practicing law. McCauley provides links to the complete text of the Virginia Rules of Professional Conduct and to charts and tables analyzing changes in the rules from Virginia's former Code of Professional Responsibility.

★★★ Legal Ethical Opinions Database, www.mcguirewoods.com/services/leo/

This site contains summaries of Virginia and ABA ethics opinions. The summaries are written by Thomas E. Spahn, a lawyer with the Richmond firm McGuireWoods. It is well-organized, allowing users to browse a table of contents or an alphabetical index, or to obtain the complete list of summaries arranged in chronological order.

★★★ National Association of Bar Counsel, www.nobc.org

NABC members may be considered the law enforcement officers of legal ethics. The highlight of the site has long been its semi-annual compilations of new court cases and ethics opinions involving attorney discipline. While NABC formerly made these summaries available to the public, in 2003 it restricted access to its members only. The only explanation is the following: "We regret to advise that the database of cases is now available only to members of the National Association of Bar Counsel." The site also includes the complete staff roster of every state ethics agency and a collection of links to notable ethics sites.

★★★ Paralegal Ethics, www.paralegals.org/Development/home.html

May a paralegal use that title when working in a corporation with no in-house legal supervision? The answer to this and other ethical questions facing paralegals can be found at this useful collection of resources devoted to the topic. Hosted by the National Federation of Paralegal Associations, the site includes the complete text of the NFPA's Model Code of Ethics and Professional Responsibility, its Guidelines for Rendering Ethics and Disciplinary Opinions, and several ethics and disciplinary opinions issued by the NFPA.

★★ The Ethical Spectacle, www.spectacle.org

Jonathan Wallace, a lawyer, software executive and writer, publishes this online journal, the purpose of which is "to shine a lantern on the intersection at which ethics, law and politics meet (or collide) in our civilization, particularly that part of it known as the United States of America." Little of it has to do with legal ethics per se. Articles by Wallace and others cover a range of social and international issues, all from a liberal-to-left perspective. Not a very practical site from a practice of law perspective, but an interesting place to browse.

★ Legal Ethics, www.ll.georgetown.edu/topics/legal_ethics.cfm

The law library at Georgetown University Law Center provides this cursory collection of ethics links and an ethics research guide.

★ Legal Ethics and the Practice of Law, www.mgovg.com/ethics

Charles F. Luce, Jr., a partner in the Colorado firm of Moye, Giles, O'Keefe, Vermeire & Gorrell and a lecturer in legal ethics at the University of Denver, offers a library of his articles on a range of ethics topics. While most focus on Colorado, many of the discussions are of broader interest. The most recent are from 1998, which makes this library slightly behind the times.

★ Legal Ethics Research Guide, http://ls.wustl.edu/Infores/ Library/ Guides/legalethics.html

Hyla Bondareff, research librarian at Washington University School of Law, wrote this guide to legal ethics research, which she most recently (as of this writing) updated in January 2002. Although it includes resources publicly available on the Web, many of its links are available only to users within Washington University, and others are to sites requiring a password. All in all, these restrictions make it of minimal usefulness.

★ National Action Plan on Lawyer Conduct and Professionalism, www.ncsc.dni.us/ccj/natlplan.htm

On January 21, 1999, following a two-year study, the Conference of Chief Justices adopted this study of lawyer professionalism. It proposes a plan intended to assist state appellate courts in providing leadership and support for professionalism initiatives. The entire plan can be downloaded in a selection of word processing formats and a summary can be read online.

★ NetEthics, www.computerbar.org/netethic/netnav.htm

The Computer Law Section of the State Bar of Georgia was one of the earliest bar entities to begin exploring the ethical implications of attorneys' using the Internet. Its NetEthics Committee maintains this online library of articles on Internet advertising, confidentiality and privilege. It also offers sample Web site disclaimers. The site appears to be out of date, with no new articles added for several years.

Georgetown Journal of Legal Ethics, www.law.georgetown.edu/journals/ethics

This site was created in 1996, neglected until 1998 when it got a minor facelift, and seems again to have been forgotten. It has no full text articles, but includes a list of all articles published in the *Journal* up to 1995.

Talking About Ethics

If you would rather talk about the topic of legal ethics than read about it, these discussion lists are for you. Two are e-mail lists to which you subscribe by sending an e-mail to the designated address. The third is a Web-based forum, meaning messages are posted on the Web for all to see.

Bioethicslaw-l is an e-mail list devoted to discussion of bioethics and the law. To subscribe, send an e-mail to: listserv@lawlib.wuacc.edu with the message, "subscribe bioethicslaw-L your first name last name." List discussions are archived at: lawlibdns.wuacc.edu/archive.html.

Legalethics-l is an e-mail list for discussion of general legal ethics, including issues involving the Internet. To subscribe, send an e-mail to listserv@lawlib.wuacc.edu with the message, "subscribe legalethics-L Your Name." List discussions are archived at: lawlibdns.wuacc.edu/archive.html.

Ethics Codes and Opinions Available Online

The Internet has evolved into a viable resource for research in legal ethics. Ethics codes of conduct and opinions from the bulk of the U.S. states are available on the Web. Following is a state-by-state guide to finding conduct codes and ethics opinions on the Web.

Alabama

- Rules, www.alabar.org/public/ropc.shtml
- Alabama State Bar Ethics Opinions, www.alabar.org/ogc/fopList.cfm

Alaska

- Rules: www.touchngo.com/lglcntr/ctrules/profcon/htframe.htm
- Opinions: www.alaskabar.org/index.cfm?ID=4665
- Alaska State Bar Rules: www.touchngo.com/lglcntr/ctrules/barules/htframe.htm

Arizona

- Rules: www.azbar.org/FindingLawyer/rules.asp
- Rules: www2.law.cornell.edu/cgi-bin/foliocgi.exe/az-code?
- Opinions: www.azbar.org/EthicsOpinions

Arkansas

- Rules: http://courts.state.ar.us/courts/cpc.html
- Rules: www2.law.cornell.edu/cgi-bin/foliocgi.exe/ar-code?
- Opinions: Not available

California

- Rules: www.calbar.org/pub250/crpc.htm
- Rules: www2.law.cornell.edu/cgi-bin/foliocgi.exe/Ca-code?
- Opinions: www.calbar.org/2pub/3eth/3ethndx.htm
- Opinions (Los Angeles County Bar): www.lacba.org/opinions

Colorado

- Rules: www.cobar.org/static/comms/ethics/rulesprof/rulprofc.htm
- Rules: www2.law.cornell.edu/cgi-bin/foliocgi.exe/co-code?
- Opinions: www.cobar.org/static/comms/ethics/fo_nondx.htm

Connecticut

- Rules: www.jud.state.ct.us/forms/rules.pdf
- Rules: www2.law.cornell.edu/cgi-bin/foliocgi.exe/ct-code?
- Opinions: www.ctbar.org (via Casemaker)

Delaware

- Rules: http://courts.state.de.us/supreme/rules.htm
- Opinions: www.dsba.org/ethics.htm

District of Columbia

- Rules: www.dcbar.org/for_lawyers/ethics/legal_ethics/index.cfm
- Rules: www2.law.cornell.edu/cgi-bin/foliocgi.exe/DC-code?
- Opinions: www.dcbar.org/for_lawyers/ethics/legal_ethics/index.cfm

Florida

- Rules: www.flabar.org/newflabar/lawpractice/Rules
- Rules: www2.law.cornell.edu/cgi-bin/foliocgi.exe/Fl-code?
- Opinions: www.flabar.org (follow "Regulation" link)

Georgia

- Rules: www.gabar.org/ogcrules.asp
- Opinions: www.gabar.org/ogcrules.asp

Hawaii

- Rules: http://mano.icsd.hawaii.gov/jud/hrpcond.htm
- Rules: www2.law.cornell.edu/cgi-bin/foliocgi.exe/hi-code?
- Ethics Commission Opinions, www.hawaii.gov/ethics/opinions/AO.htm
- Disciplinary Board Opinions, www.hsba.org/HSBA/Legal_Research/Hawaii/Disc/disc.cfm

Idaho

- Rules: www2.state.id.us/isb/rules/irpc/irpc.htm
- Rules: www2.state.id.us/isb/PDF/IRPC.pdf
- Opinions: Not available

Illinois

- Rules: www.state.il.us/court/SupremeCourt/Rules/default.asp
- Rules: www2.law.cornell.edu/cgi-bin/foliocgi.exe/Il-code
- Opinions: www.illinoisbar.org/CourtsBull/EthicsOpinions

Indiana

- Rules: www.in.gov/judiciary/rules/
- Opinions: www.inbar.org/content/legalethics/legalethics2.asp

Iowa

- Rules: www.judicial.state.ia.us/regs
- Opinions: www.iowabar.org/ethics.nsf

Kansas

- Rules: www.kscourts.org/ctruls/atrul.htm
- Opinions Not available.

Kentucky

- Rules: www2.law.cornell.edu/cgi-bin/foliocgi.exe/ky-code?
- Opinions: www.uky.edu/Law/kyethics

Louisiana

- Rules: www2.law.cornell.edu/cgi-bin/foliocgi.exe/la-code?
- Rules: www.lsba.org/Legal_Library/rules_of_professional_conduct_.asp
- Rules: www.ladb.org
- Opinions: www.ladb.org

Maine

- Rules: www.mebaroverseers.org
- Opinions: .www.mebaroverseers.org

Maryland

- Rules: www.law.cornell.edu/ethics/maryland.html
- Opinions (state bar members only): www.msba.org/memberonly/index.asp

Massachusetts

- Rules: www.state.ma.us/obcbbo
- Rules: www2.law.cornell.edu/cgi-bin/foliocgi.exe/ma-code?
- Opinions (Supreme Judicial Court): www.state.ma.us/obcbbo
- Opinions (Mass. Bar): www.massbar.org/publications/ethics_opinions/

Michigan

- Rules: www2.law.cornell.edu/cgi-bin/foliocgi.exe/mi-code?
- Opinions: www.michbar.org/opinions/ethics
- Opinions: www.adbmich.org

Minnesota

- Rules of Professional Conduct: www.courts.state.mn.us/lprb/conduct.html
- Rules on Lawyers Professional Responsibility, www.courts.state.mn.us/lprb/rules.html
- Minnesota Disciplinary Rules of Professional Conduct: www2.law.cornell.edu/cgi-bin/foliocgi.exe/mn-code
- Opinions: www.courts.state.mn.us/lprb/opinions.html

Mississippi

- Rules: www.mslawyer.com/mssc/index019.html
- Rules: www.mssc.state.ms.us/rules/default.asp

- Rules: www2.law.cornell.edu/cgi-bin/foliocgi.exe/ms-code?
- Opinions: www.msbar.org/opinidx.html

Missouri

- Rules: www2.law.cornell.edu/cgi-bin/foliocgi.exe/mo-code?
- Informal Advisory Opinions: www.mobar.net/opinions

Montana

- Rules: www.montanabar.org/attyrulesandregs/index.html
- Opinions: www.montanabar.org/ethics/index.html

Nebraska

- Rules: http://court.nol.org/rules/Profresp_31.htm
- Rules: www2.law.cornell.edu/cgi-bin/foliocgi.exe/ne-code?
- Rules: www.nebar.com/legalresources/code/index.htm
- Opinions: www.nebar.com/legalresources/opinions/index.htm

Nevada

- Rules: www.leg.state.nv.us/CourtRules/SCR.html
- Opinions: Not available.

New Hampshire

- Rules: www.courts.state.nh.us/rules/pcon/index.htm
- Opinions: www.nhbar.org

New Jersey

- Rules: www.judiciary.state.nj.us/rpc
- Rules: www2.law.cornell.edu/cgi-bin/foliocgi.exe/nj-code?
- Opinions: www.njlawnet.com/nj-rpc/lawlibrary.rutgers.edu/ethics/search. html

New Mexico

- Rules: Not available.
- Opinions (New Mexico bar members only): www.nmbar.org

New York

- Code of Professional Responsibility: www.nysba.org/Template.cfm?Section=Attorney_Resources

- Code of Professional Responsibility: www2.law.cornell.edu/cgi-bin/foliocgi.exe/Ny-code?
- Opinions: www.nysba.org/Template.cfm?Section=Ethics_Opinions

North Carolina

- Rules: www.aoc.state.nc.us/www/public/aoc/barrules.html
- Rules: www.ncbar.com/rules/rul_sup_rev.asp
- Opinions: www.ncbar.com/eth_op/ethics_o.asp

North Dakota

- Rules: www.court.state.nd.us/Rules/Conduct/frameset.htm
- Rules: www2.law.cornell.edu/cgi-bin/foliocgi.exe/nd-code?
- Opinions: Not available.

Ohio

- Rules: www2.law.cornell.edu/cgi-bin/foliocgi.exe/oh-code?
- Rules: www.sconet.state.oh.us/Rules/professional/
- Opinions: www.sconet.state.oh.us/BOC/Advisory_Opinions

Oklahoma

- Rules: www.oscn.net/applications/oscn/index.asp?ftdb=STOKRUPR &level=1=
- Opinions: Not available.

Oregon

- Rules: www.osbar.org/2practice/rulesregs/cpr.htm
- Rules: www2.law.cornell.edu/cgi-bin/foliocgi.exe/or-code?
- Opinions: www.osbar.org/2practice/ethics/ethicsops.cfm

Pennsylvania

- Rules: www2.law.cornell.edu/cgi-bin/foliocgi.exe/Pa-code?
- Opinions (Philadelphia Bar): www.philabar.org/public/ethics.asp

Rhode Island

- Rules: www2.law.cornell.edu/cgi-bin/foliocgi.exe/ri-code?
- Rules: www.courts.state.ri.us/supreme/disciplinary/rulesofprofessionalconduct.htm
- Opinions: www.courts.state.ri.us/supreme/ethics/ethicsadvisory-panelopinions.htm

South Carolina

- Rules: www.scbar.org/Rules_of_conduct/rules_of_conduct.htm
- Rules: www2.law.cornell.edu/cgi-bin/foliocgi.exe/sc-code?
- Opinions: www.judicial.state.sc.us//adv_opinion/index.cfm

South Dakota

- Rules: www2.law.cornell.edu/cgi-bin/foliocgi.exe/sd-code?
- Rules: www.sdbar.org/members/ethics/rules/default.htm
- Opinions: www.sdbar.org/members/ethics/default.htm

Tennessee

- Rules: www.tba.org/ethics2002.html
- Opinions: www.tsc.state.tn.us/opinions/Ethics/Ethics.htm

Texas

- Rules: www.lawlib.uh.edu/ethics www.law.uh.edu/ethics
- Rules: www2.law.cornell.edu/cgi-bin/foliocgi.exe/rpc-texas?
- Rules: www.txethics.org/reference_rules.asp?view=conduct&num=1.01
- Opinions: www.law.uh.edu/ethics/
- Opinions: www.txethics.org/reference_opinions.asp

Utah

- Rules: www.utcourts.gov/resources/rules/ucja/index.htm
- Rules: www.utahbar.org/rules/index.html
- Opinions: www.utahbar.org/opinions/index.html

Vermont

- Rules: www.brandsystems.net/vtbar/pdffiles/Vermontrulesof profes-sionalconduct.pdf
- Rules: www2.law.cornell.edu/cgi-bin/foliocgi.exe/vt-code?
- Bar Advisory Opinions: www.vtbar.org/static/vtbar/attorney_judic ial_resources/aeo_index_categories/advisory_ethics_opinion_index.php
- Professional Conduct Board Opinions: dol.state.vt.us/www_root/000000/html/decisions.html

Virginia

- Rules: www.vsb.org/profguides
- Rules: www2.law.cornell.edu/cgi-bin/foliocgi.exe/va-code?

- Opinions: www.vsb.vipnet.org/profguides
- Opinions: www.vacle.org/leos.htm
- Opinions: www.mcguirewoods.com/services/leo/

Washington

- Rules of Professional Conduct: www.courts.wa.gov/court_rules/?fa=court_rules.list&group=ga&set=RPC
- Rules of Professional Conduct: www2.law.cornell.edu/cgi-bin/foliocgi.exe/wa-code?
- Opinions: www.wsba.org/lawyers/ethics/default.htm
- Disciplinary Notices: www.wsba.org/lawyers/ethics/default.htm

West Virginia

- Standards of Professional Conduct: www.wvbar.org/BARINFO/standardspc/standardspc.htm
- Opinions: www.wvbar.org/BARINFO/wvlegalresearch/ethics/ethics.htm

Wisconsin

- Rules of Professional Conduct: www.courts.state.wi.us/html/rules/CHAP20A.HTM
- Rules of Professional Conduct: www2.law.cornell.edu/cgi-bin/foliocgi.exe/wi-code?
- Opinions: www.wisbar.org/ethop

Wyoming

- Rules: courts.state.wy.us/wyoming_court_rules.htm
- Opinions: Not available.

Chapter 19

CLE Online: Correspondence Courses for the Electronic Era

Chapter Contents

Online Providers
CLE Sites for Offline Seminars
CLE for Support Staff
Sites for CLE Information

You can really get an education on the Internet these days. No, not that kind. A legal education—continuing legal education, to be exact.

The Internet brings CLE to the lawyer's desktop—books, audio and video, even live "Webcasts," all delivered via computer. And many programs are accredited to meet state CLE requirements.

Here is a look at what is out there in online CLE. Our preference is online education—sites that provide CLE over the Internet. We also review some of the many sites that are simply online catalogs of offline seminars.

Online Providers

★★★★★ ALI-ABA, www.ali-aba.org

A CLE provider for half a century, ALI-ABA offers online education through its "Direct-to-Desktop CLE." These courses, each about an hour in length, combine streaming audio and printable written materials adapted from selected ALI-ABA lectures. A second line of enhanced courses combine streaming audio, dynamic slide presentations and graphics, printable written materials, and user discussion areas. These enhanced courses cost $69 each, while the audio courses are $49. The site also offers audio presentations on estate planning through its Audio Estate Planner Online. These programs cost $9.95 each. The site includes an extensive collection of articles and forms drawn from ALI-ABA magazines, sold either by the piece or by subscription. Finally, ALI-ABA offers simultaneous "Webcasts" of the satellite broadcasts it provides through the American Law Network. Beyond online CLE, the site allows visitors to sample, purchase and use a variety of publications. From ALI-ABA's library of CLE books and articles, users can browse available titles and preview excerpts. If you decide to purchase the title, you can use your credit card and download it immediately. ALI-ABA also offers free previews of entire chapters from recently published practice manuals, as well as free selections from such popular periodicals as The Practical Lawyer and The Practical Litigator.

★★★★★ CLE Online, www.cleonline.com

This innovative site presents CLE via the Web in the form of hypertext discussions that are "threaded" so that all replies follow the initial message in a grouped series. These are backed up by libraries of downloadable information. Many of its programs are produced in cooperation with the Texas Lawyer newspaper and the Houston Bar Association. Courses entitle lawyers to CLE credit in Texas, California, New York, Nevada, Tennessee and Vermont. Eligibility in other states depends on local rules. Because all seminars are presented in a textual format, users are not required to install any special audio or video plug-ins on their computers. The cost is $59 for a three-hour seminar or $25 for a one-hour program.

★★★★ Cognistar, www.cognistar.com

Cognistar stands out among online CLE providers for both its content and its technology. The courses if offers are original, developed and produced specifically for online learning. It uses nationally recognized instructors drawn from leading law firms and academic institutions. Its courseware is the most intuitive and user friendly I have seen. A user can choose among video, audio, and printable text modes. A panel to the right of the screen displays exhibits corresponding to the appropriate segment of the presentation. A notepad allows users to maintain personal notes on each course. Cognistar is accredited in several states and offers a broad-ranging catalog of courses. In April 2004 the company announced an alliance with LexisNexis for distributing iys programs through the LexisNexis Professional Development Center.

★★★★★ Defense Research Institute, www.dri.org/eseries/source/olcle/olcle_start.cfm

This organization of defense lawyers offers streaming video of its seminars via the Web. Topics focus on trial and appellate practice but also include corporate governance, civil rights, employment, ethics, and intellectual property, among others. Programs cost $100 for DRI members and $150 for nonmembers.

★★★★★ **Harvard Law School Forum,** www.law.harvard.edu/stu-dorgs/forum/index.html

If continuing legal education is about something more than mandatory credits, then its purpose may be—as Harvard Law School Dean James Landis said in 1946—to promote among lawyers "an aliveness to the world about them, its pressing issues and its challenges." This is the goal of the Harvard Law School Forum, an organization of students dedicated to bringing to their campus open discussion of a broad range of legal, political and social issues. Now, thanks to the Internet, the forum is bringing the actual audio recordings of more than forty years of those discussions to anyone who cares to listen. This is an awe-inspiring collection of speakers—you can listen to Eleanor Roosevelt's 1961 speech, "Unrest Within the Democratic Party," Jimmy Hoffa discussing Teamster area contracts in 1962; Martin Luther King, Jr. in 1962 on the future of integration; Timothy Leary in 1966 speaking on "LSD: Methods of Control;" and Dr. Wernher Von Braun in 1970 prognosticating on the topic "After the Moon—What?" More contemporary speakers include Rudolph Giuliani, Charlton Heston, Ralph Nader, Helen Thomas and Justice Department trustbuster Joel Klein. All of this is free, requiring only the free RealPlayer software.

★★★★★ **Institute of Continuing Legal Education,** www.icle.org

Michigan's ICLE was a pioneer in using the Internet to provide lawyers with easy access to CLE programs and materials. Its Web site features complete listings of its publications and courses available for purchase. The ICLE offers an extensive catalog of online courses, but these are available only to members of its "Partnership" program, which requires a one-year subscription with prices beginning at $395 for a sole practitioner. Beyond CLE, the ICLE site stands out for its Michigan legal library, including current court opinions, court rules and orders, and links to state law-related Web sites.

★★★★★ **Law.com Seminars,** http://store.law.com/seminars

Law.com sponsors more than 200 online CLE programs in three formats: streaming video, streaming audio, and text-based. Seminar content is produced by Law.com and American Lawyer Media as well as in conjunction with partners that include Law Journal Seminars, the Association of the Bar of the City of New York, the Center for Continuing Education, the Illinois State Bar Association, the Los Angeles County Bar Association, and others. Individual programs cost from $29 to $109 each; a year of unlimited access is $599.

★★★★★ LegalSpan.com, www.legalspan.com

LegalSpan is the technology engine behind the online CLE catalogs of some thirty state bar associations in the United States. Its Web site does not directly offer CLE, but instead links to the catalogs of each of its partners.

★★★★★ Practising Law Institute, www.pli.edu

A CLE provider since 1933, PLI has pushed full tilt into the electronic age with its series of MCLE-approved video programs available via the Web. All programs are recent, full, one- or two-day CLE courses, presented in their entirety, together with the course book. Each program is indexed for quick movement to individual presentations or particular topics. Each speaker's key points are bulleted and synchronized with the video. Course handbooks can be

This Practising Law Institute course includes streaming video and a course handbook.

downloaded and printed. Each program includes an online discussion forum and links to related PLI materials and related Web resources. Programs cost from $129 to $750 each, with a sample program available free. PLI also offers live, simultaneous Webcasts of many of its programs.

★★★★★ RutterOnline, www.rutteronline.com

Part of the West Group, Rutter provides online CLE in topics ranging from bankruptcy to substance abuse. Courses are presented in audio or video format, with newer courses using Windows Media format and older ones using RealPlayer. Course materials are provided in Adobe Acrobat format. Courses cost anywhere from $35 to $420, or you can purchase a pass allowing one year of unlimited access for $495. Visitors can try a seminar free for an hour. Participants are eligible to earn CLE credit in California.

★★★★★ Taecan.com, www.taecan.com

Taecan.com is a professional education company that provides online CLE, much of it designed in collaboration with state and local bar associations. Its partners include the Washington State Trial Lawyers, the Washington Law Institute, the State Bar of California, the Missouri Bar, the New York City Bar, the Houston Bar Association, the South Texas College of Law, the Florida Bar, the Los Angeles County Bar Association, and others.

Taecan offers accredited courses in Alaska, Arizona, California, Connecticut, District of Columbia, Florida, Hawaii, Illinois, Kentucky, Massachusetts, Maryland, Maine, Michigan, Missouri, Nebraska, New Jersey, New York, Ohio, South Dakota, Tennessee, Texas and Washington. Taecan offers a variety of accredited courses, each costing $25 to $50 per credit hour. Course materials are well-organized and include links to full text cases and statutes. Some courses are in audio format, others are text based.

★★★★★ West LegalEdcenter, www.westlegaledcenter.com

With more than 2,000 online CLE programs from more than seventy-five local, state and national providers covering virtually every field of law, this is a comprehensive source of online CLE. Programs are presented in either audio or video format. Prices for programs vary widely, depending on the source of the program and its format and length. The site includes a guide to state CLE requirements.

★★★★ ABA-CLE, www.abanet.org/cle/home.html

Online home of the ABA's Center for Continuing Legal Education, this site provides a variety of CLE programming directly online, as well as complete information on its more traditional products, from satellite seminars to books on tape. Also useful is its state-by-state summary of CLE requirements and information on the ABA Model Rule for Minimum Continuing Legal Education. Its primary online CLE components are:

- CLE Now!, a set of CLE recordings from nationally known lecturers—all for free. Listen to *Tips from the Top*, trial tips from some of the nation's best-known litigators; *McElhaney's Trial Notebook*, by Case Western Professor James McElhaney; or *Stopping Violence Against Women*. The lectures qualify for CLE credit in some states.
- ABA Connection, online recordings of the monthly, one-hour teleconference designed to provide practicing lawyers with substantive information on topical legal issues. Although the teleconferences are live, each is made available here for the following month, together with an online discussion area where Web listeners can continue the discussion.
- Webcasts of recorded programs, either in audio or video format, accompanied in some cases by electronic slides and in all cases by downloadable course materials. Subjects include commercial leasing, expert testimony, mortgage financing, discovery, and more.
- The Online Partner, a developing feature for providing CLE online using audio, video and text. One such program is titled "Ethical Considerations in Public Sector Law."

★★★★ **Continuing Education of the Bar, California,** http://ceb.ucop.edu

CEB has provided continuing education to California lawyers since 1947. Its Web site presents an almost dizzying catalog of books, live seminars, CD-ROMs and audio recordings, all available for purchase online. In addition, CEB delivers audio programs via the Web on all California required subjects plus business, employment, civil litigation, estate planning and real property. These use the RealPlayer software. They cost $35 an hour, with discounts provided to lawyers who purchase one of CEB's multiple program "passports."

★★★★ **LawCommerce CLE Center,** www.lawcommerce.com/cle

This site offers more than 200 online seminars covering most major legal subjects. Seminars are presented in either audio or video format. Prices start at $35 for a one-hour course. Written materials are provided in Adobe Acrobat format.

★★★★ **Massachusetts Continuing Legal Education,** www.mcle.org

The preeminent CLE provider in Massachusetts, MCLE's Web site is an electronic catalog, where you can search for, read descriptions of, and then purchase any of its many books, seminars, audiocassettes or CD-ROMs. You can also choose from a selection of streaming audio and video seminars, with prices starting at $49. In addition, MCLE offers articles and forms for sale through its site, all culled from its program materials. The site is well designed, allowing a visitor to browse by subject area or product type, or perform a full keyword search.

★★★★ **National Practice Institute,** www.npilaw.com

A CLE provider since 1976, this Minneapolis-based company produces online CLE with a twist—seminars broadcast live over the Internet. You need only have the Windows Media Player installed on your computer and a 56K or faster Internet connection, and you can participate in these seminars as they occur. NPI also puts on seminars on a variety of topics at a range of

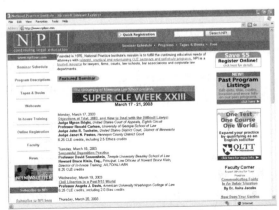

The National Practice Institute broadcasts seminars live over the Internet.

locations throughout the U.S., with complete schedules and information available through its Web site. There is a registration fee to attend one of NPI's Web seminars, but NPI offers a money-back guarantee that you will be satisfied.

★★★★ TennBar University, www.tennbaru.com

From the Tennessee Bar Association, this site provides online courses on a variety of topics, including bankruptcy, civil procedure, ethics, labor law and torts. Courses are designed to be about an hour in length and to be simple to navigate. They include links to full-text documents when available and e-mail access to all faculty.

★★★★ University of Texas School of Law Continuing Legal Education, www.utexas.edu/law/cle

UT School of Law includes online courses in the CLE it offers Texas lawyers. These courses are accredited in both Texas and California. Courses include audio lectures delivered via the Web, together with written materials offered either in HTML or PDF format. Some courses are also offered in video. Each course includes an interactive discussion board where participants can post questions and comments. A sample course allows visitors to try it out free. Prices start at $30, with most courses costing $75. The site also includes full information and registration materials for offline course offerings.

★★★ Indiana Continuing Legal Education Forum, www.iclef.org

The education arm of the Indiana State Bar Association, its Web site recently began providing a limited selection of online CLE. Although online programs are not eligible for CLE credit in Indiana, lawyers can try out one of these online courses, using audio, video and textual materials. The site provides complete information on "offline" courses and publications, and allows seminar registration and book ordering online.

★★★ TRT Continuing Legal Education, www.trt-cle.com

TRT provides Web-based CLE programming accredited in a number of states. Most of the online programs are on legal ethics, earn one hour of credit, and cost $75. TRT also provides CLE programs live and by teleconference. Its Web site provides complete information and pricing. Online courses are text-based, requiring registrants to read through the materials and participate in a course conference.

★★ Center for Continuing Legal Education, www.cce-mcle.com

This San Francisco CLE company offers eight California self-study cours-es online, covering substance abuse, sports law, bias in the legal profession, accounting and ethics. Read the article, then take a multiple-choice test to earn credit, at a price of $20 per test. CCLE produces live and audio programs for California and New York—you can read about them here and listen to samples.

CLE Sites for Offline Seminars

★★★★ Tennessee Commission on Continuing Legal Education and Specialization, www.cletn.com

From learning how to become certified as a specialist to finding a CLE course with just the number of credits you need, this is a useful Web site for Tennessee lawyers. You can search through all courses that have been approved for CLE credit in Tennessee in a number of ways, including by number of credits, location, date and subject. You can also review the state's rules on CLE and specialization. Finally, you can search for a lawyer who has been certified as a specialist in a particular field.

★★★ Kansas CLE Commission, www.kscle.org

This is the body that monitors CLE compliance and approves CLE pro-gramming in Kansas. Visit its Web site to view a current calendar of approved programs and to keep track of commission meetings and actions. At the site, lawyers can review the state's rules governing CLE or download forms to use for applying to receive CLE credit.

★★★ New Jersey Institute for Continuing Legal Education, www.njicle.com

New Jersey's ICLE is sponsored by the New Jersey State Bar Association, Rutgers University and Seton Hall University. It offers a number of live pro-grams covering a broad spectrum of legal topics. While it offers no online programs, it allows users to download .mpg audio files of selected programs for playback on a computer. From the site, you can select and register for a course or purchase a book or cassette.

★★★ SEAK, Inc., www.seak.com

SEAK provides seminars, publications and other resources focused on medical-legal issues, expert witnesses, workers' compensation, disability management and occupational health and safety. Much of SEAK's programming is targeted at physicians and experts, such as its "Law School for Physicians." For lawyers, SEAK sponsors three-day conferences on workers' compensation and occupational medicine and an occasional "Medical School for Lawyers." SEAK's Web site provides complete information on all its seminars and publications, as well as a handful of free articles and related resources.

★★★ TransMedia, Inc., www.objection.com

TransMedia, Inc. has developed what it claims are the first computer games ever to receive CLE certification. Designed exclusively for trial attorneys, these computerized trial simulations are approved for CLE credit in eighteen states. TransMedia offers four titles: "Objection!," a murder trial simulation; "Civil Objection! Autoneg," an automobile negligence case; "Civil Objection! SlipFall," a slip-and-fall case; and "Expert Witness!," a simulation focusing on the issues and procedures involved in using expert witnesses. You can purchase any of these games through the Web site for $99, or buy the complete set for $300. If you prefer to try the games out first, you can download demonstration versions. The site includes a complete guide to the states in which it has been approved for CLE credit and the types of credit available.

★★★ University of Mississippi, Center for Continuing Legal Education, www.ics.olemiss.edu/cle

The center coordinates seminars for lawyers, judges, paralegals and legal assistants in Mississippi. Its Web site provides a calendar of coming seminars, with detailed descriptions of each. Those who prefer can subscribe to the center's electronic mailing list and receive notices of new seminars by e-mail. The site includes the text of the state's rules and regulations for mandatory CLE.

★★ Texas Independent Bar Association, www.texindbar.org

In 1997, when the State Bar of Texas told Austin lawyers David A. Schulman and Roy Greenwood that they would have to pay expensive accreditation fees, it looked like they would have to shut down the two $50 CLE courses they had been offering for several years. But then Schulman learned that the bar did not require accreditation fees from local bar associations that did not charge their members to attend CLE seminars. Thus was born what was originally called "Dave's Bar Association," with annual membership dues of $100, payable in two installments at the time of each seminar. In the years since, Dave's Bar has expanded its course offerings and changed its name, and membership is now only $85 per year. Its Web site has a refreshingly homemade look, and descriptions of coming events and a roster of members.

★★ Maryland Institute for Continuing Professional Education of Lawyers, www.micpel.edu

MICPEL is an independent entity formed by the Maryland State Bar Association, the University of Baltimore Law School, and the University of Maryland School of Law, to provide continuing legal education in Maryland. Its site has no online course offerings, but does have its complete calendar of courses as well as its catalog of books. Visitors can register for a course or purchase a book through the site.

★★ National Institute for Trial Advocacy, www.nita.org

NITA is a non-profit, trial advocacy institute housed at the University of Notre Dame. Its Web site serves as an electronic catalog of its various CLE programs and publications. You can search for a seminar by date, location or topic, and then register for it using an electronic form. You can likewise search its selection of books and multimedia products by name, author or subject, and then purchase it online. The Web site includes background information on NITA and its specialized training programs for law firms and law schools.

★★ PACE Center for Continuing Legal Education, www.law.pace. edu/ccle/index.html

Pace University School of Law's Center for Continuing Legal Education organizes programs for attorneys in New York and elsewhere on various legal and practice topics. Its Web site provides a calendar of coming programs and lists audiotapes available for purchase. For reference, it includes the text of New York's CLE rules and regulations.

★★ Professional Education Systems, Inc., www.pesi.com

PESI provides continuing education to a range of professionals, among them lawyers, judges, paralegals and legal assistants. Its Web site has no online programming, but makes it simple to find one of PESI's national or local seminars. You can see a listing of all seminars by state, or search by topic. Seminar listings include detailed information and allow you to view the print brochure. You can register online.

★★ University of Washington CLE, http://uwcle.org

Here you can find schedules and descriptions of CLE programs available through the University of Washington School of Law.

★★ Washburn University School of Law, Seminars and Continuing Legal Education, www.washlaw.edu/postlaw/seminars.htm

Washburn provides a modest collection of links to CLE sites on the Web. The site links to the Washburn-hosted Web site of the Organization of Regulatory Administrators of CLE, or ORACLE, the national organization representing the forty jurisdictions with mandatory CLE. The primary feature here is a state-by-state guide to rules on mandatory CLE.

★ Center for Advanced Legal Studies, www.law.suffolk.edu/als

A program of Suffolk University Law School, Boston, Massachusetts, its Web site includes a calendar of programs and a catalog of course materials. There is no online content.

★ Courtroom Performance, www.courtroomperformance.com

These folks are trial preparation consultants who also offer trial advocacy courses. Their simple Web site is an electronic marketing brochure, with information about the company and its services, but little other content.

★ Foundation for Continuing Education, www.fce.org

The Foundation for Continuing Education provides continuing education programs for lawyers and accountants, mostly in Massachusetts. Its Web site provides a calendar of coming programs and a catalog of books.

★ Labor Arbitration Institute, www.laborarb.com

The LAI offers continuing education programs to labor and management advocates and attorneys on the subjects of labor law and labor arbitration. Its simple Web site describes upcoming programs and allows registration online.

★ Minnesota Continuing Legal Education, www.minncle.org

The Minnesota State Bar Association sponsors this site, which provides no online courses. It does include complete information about seminars and publications.

★ TaxForums, http://taxforums.com

TaxForums presents two seminars, one basic, one advanced, on tax planning for S corporations, LLCs and partnerships, at various locations around the U.S. Its simple site describes these programs and allows online registration.

All-In-One CLE, www.clelaw.com

This is a horribly designed, confusing Web site, apparently offering for sale "home-study" CLE courses for various states. There is no online content or online ordering, just general descriptions and a phone number to call for more information.

CLE for Support Staff

★★★★ NALACampus.com, www.nalacampus.com

Online education is available for paralegals, thanks to the National Association of Legal Assistants. The site offers twelve-hour courses in civil litigation, contracts, legal research, legal ethics, real estate, and intellectual property, among other topics, at a cost of $50 per course for NALA members and $75 for non-members. For each course, NALA provides a free "pre-test," designed to give an overview of the subject matter and to evaluate the user's level of knowledge. For those who continue on, each course is divided into four modules, each of which consists of a slide presentation—including both written and audio text—and a test. Users can move through these slides at whatever pace they prefer. As they complete each module, users take that section's test, and can go back to the module for further study if needed. At the end of the process, after completing all four modules, the user takes the final course test. Those who complete the process can earn credit towards continuing education requirements.

Sites for CLE Information

★★ Association for Continuing Legal Education, www.aclea.org

An organization of CLE providers, its Web site provides comprehensive information on its membership and committee structures. Other features include job postings for positions in CLE and a "members-only" area containing the ACLEA's newsletter and other materials.

Chapter 20

Managing and Marketing Your Practice with Help from the Web

Chapter Contents

Practical Resources
Bar, Legal Management, and Legal Marketing Associations
Law Firms
Management Consultants

Setting goals. Making rain. Appeasing clients. Taming technology. Supervising staff. Keeping books. Collecting accounts.

And you thought you would be practicing law!

For help in handling the managerial tasks that can deluge a law practice, turn to the Web. Bar associations, management consultants and others are there to help.

Practical Resources

The best sites on law office management and marketing pull together a variety of practical resources in a single destination. They offer how-to articles, war stories from lawyers in the trenches, links to other Web sites and useful products, and much more. Some of these sites focus narrowly on a single topic—spreadsheets or solos, for example—while others cover the gamut of issues that arise in the course of managing a law practice.

(Not rated) LawCatalog.com, www.lawcatalog.com

If you are reading this book, chances are you bought it here. American Lawyer Media's online catalog offers a variety of books, newsletters, audiotapes and other materials on law office management. This catalog allows you to browse or search titles and purchase them online. From the front page, start by clicking on the link "Law Office Management."

★★★★★ FindLaw Lawyer Marketing, http://marketing.findlaw.com

There once was a Web site called lawyermarketing.com, a useful and fairly extensive collection of links to information and resources on the Web related to legal marketing. Along came FindLaw, which acquired the site, added some links of its own along with a new design, and thus was born FindLaw Lawyer Marketing. The site includes links—many of them annotated—to books, articles, videotapes and audiotapes, Web sites, organizations and software. It also provides directories of marketing consultants and lecturers nationwide and information on CLE programs on marketing. One of the most comprehensive indexes for legal marketing on the Web.

★★★★★ Internet Marketing Attorney, www.internetmarketingattorney.com

Lawyer and marketing professional Micah U. Buchdahl operates this site, home of the annual Internet Marketing Attorney Awards, which reviews and scores the Web sites of each of the 250 largest firms in the United States. In 2003, Buchdahl added reviews of small- and mid-sized firms as well as international firms. Buchdahl also offers his annual Nifty 50—law firm Web sites that go beyond the basics of standard Web development.

★★★★★ Internet Tools for Lawyers, www.netlawtools.com

Who do the Internet experts respect for their Internet expertise? Well, Jerry Lawson for one. Lawson is principal of the consulting firm Netlawtools, Inc. and the publisher of this top-notch Web site. A practicing lawyer for more than twenty years, he is also a Web designer, Internet trainer and author of the American Bar Association book *The Complete Internet Handbook for Lawyers*. He

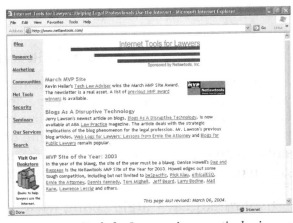

Internet Tools for Lawyers is a practical mix of articles, links and how-to guides.

writes about the Internet from the practical perspective of one who has actually practiced law and understands what lawyers need and want from the Web. His Web site is a mixture of articles, links, how-to guides, and more, all focused on lawyers' use of the Internet. Sections focus on legal research, marketing, online communities, helpful tools and security. Supplementing these sections are regular features, such as the monthly MVP highlighting the best legal Web sites; Net News, with links to news stories of particular interest to legal professionals; and *The Internet Roundtable*, in which

Lawson and others discuss topics of current interest. For any lawyer who wants to make more effective use of the Internet in his or her law practice, this site is well worth the visit.

★★★★★ The Law Marketing Portal, www.lawmarketing.com

This is the creation of legal marketing consultant Larry Bodine, former director of communications at Chicago's Sidley & Austin and, for those of us with longer memories, former editor in chief of the *ABA Journal*. The site is an outgrowth of an e-mail discussion list that Bodine created in 1996 where lawyers, law firm marketing directors and outside marketing consultants could compare notes and share information. It has evolved into a resource rich with information. Still home to the LawMarketing discussion list, it also features a library with articles by marketing experts from throughout the U.S. A job bank lists openings for marketing professionals, while a resource directory collects member recommendations for the best forms, consultants, photographers, restaurants, meeting places and just about anything else. A special "best of" feature extracts threads from the discussion list that focus on specific interests and concerns.

★★★★ Institute of Management and Administration Law Page, www.ioma.com/products/prod_catalog.php?chanid=7&sort=title

IOMA is a BNA-owned company that publishes newsletters on a range of management topics for a variety of industries. Its law page features one or two full text articles per month from each of three newsletters: *Law Office Management* and *Administration Report*, *Partner's Report for Law Firm Owners, and Compensation* and *Benefits for Law Offices*. IOMA archives all its newsletters in a searchable database, from which you can purchase specific articles for $10 each. From the law page, visitors can jump to other industry newsletters and to discussion groups on various management topics. If you prefer to search for articles from all of IOMA's newsletters, go directly to its Management Library, www.managementlibrary.com, where you can search a collection of more than 10,000 articles.

Bar, Legal Management, and Legal Marketing Associations

Two of the best sites on law office management come from associations representing the folks with the most direct experience, the Association of Legal Administrators and the Law Practice Management Section of the American Bar Association. Several other associations host sites with useful and practical information for lawyers seeking help with management and marketing.

★★★★★ Association of Legal Administrators, www.alanet.org

This is the online headquarters of this international organization of law firm managers. Like many association sites, it is divided between public areas and those for members only. The members-only areas contain many of the most practical features, including current industry news, document delivery and reference services, and a database of ALA members available for peer consulting in particular areas of expertise. Also for members are discussion groups devoted to general management, technology and human resources. For non-members, the greatest appeal of the site may be in its Job Bank and its Legal Management Resource Center. The former is a listing of positions wanted or available in legal management. The latter is a useful collection of links to legal and management articles and resources from the ALA and elsewhere on the Web.

★★★★★ Law Practice Management Section, American Bar Association, www.abanet.org/lpm

This may well be the most comprehensive site on the Web devoted to law office management. The LPM Section is the ABA's largest publisher of books, sponsor of its annual Techshow, and home to *Law Practice Management* magazine, *Law Practice Today Webzine*, and *Law Practice Quarterly* newsletter. The site combines these into something that is part library, part storefront. Shop its shelves of book titles or purchase Techshow course materials. Or browse its stacks of free resources, including an array of articles from its magazine and newsletter on marketing, management, technology and more; presentations and outlines from Techshow; and special focus sections on e-lawyering and rainmaking for women lawyers.

★★★★★ Solosez.net, www.solosez.net

The ABA Standing Committee on Solos and Small Firm Practitioners, sponsor of the Solosez e-mail discussion group, hosts this Web portal for solo and small firm practitioners. Its mission is to serve as a guide to the events, issues, resources and services that benefit solo and small firm practitioners across the USA and around the world.

★★★★ The Law Office Hornbook, www.hornbook.com

This is the online version of a quarterly periodical that focuses on malpractice avoidance, firm management and professional liability insurance. It is sponsored by the bars of Virginia, Hawaii, New Mexico and Arizona as part of the risk management service they provide. The articles at the site are described as being expanded versions of those from the hard copy edition.

Issues available online date from 1996. Each issue includes three to four articles—some in-depth, others simple updates—on topics such as client file retention, fee arbitration, trust accounts and attorneys' liens. A simple but informative site.

★★★ General Practice, Solo and Small Firm Section, ABA, www.abanet.org/genpractice

Lots to read here for managers of smaller firms, largely from the pages of the Section's eight-times-a-year magazine, *GP Solo*. Four issues each year focus on substantive legal topics and how best to manage a law practice; two issues are devoted to technology for solo and small firm lawyers; and two compile the best articles for solo and small firm lawyers from other ABA publications. Also at the site are selected articles from the Section newsletter, *Solo*, and the online publication, *Technology E-Report*.

★★★ LawNet, Inc., www.peertopeer.org

LawNet is an organization of technology users in the legal industry, made up largely of MIS directors, controllers, administrators and attorneys with an interest in technology. It publishes a quarterly newsletter as well as various white papers on topics such as litigation support and MIS hiring and retention. It also hosts special interest groups that focus on particular vendors. Its Web site offers information on all of these activities, as well as its newsletter articles and white papers.

★★★ Legal Marketing Association, www.legalmarketing.org

With nearly 2,000 members, Legal Marketing Association is a national organization dedicated to serving the needs and maintaining the professional standards of those involved in marketing for the legal profession. Like sites of many associations on the Web, the bulk of the Chicago-based LMA's site is given over to general information about membership, meetings and chapters. One distinguishing feature is the LMA's Job Bank, an online listing of positions available in law firm marketing and related professional service industries. The listings, which the LMA updates frequently, can be searched by location and job title. Another useful offering of the LMA's site is a selection of job descriptions for several marketing-related positions, which a law firm can adapt to its own needs. The site includes a Resource Center on legal marketing, but it is restricted to LMA members.

★★★ Toronto Law Office Management Association, www.tloma.on.ca

TLOMA is an organization of legal managers from more than 100 law firms in southern Ontario. Besides membership information and a calendar of events, its Web site includes the full text of its monthly newsletter, results of member surveys, and employment classifieds. Members can also access discussion groups and a membership directory.

★★ Florida Bar Law Office Management Assistance Service, www.flabar.org

From the main page, click on "Member Services" and then "LOMAS" for this service for members of the Florida Bar, which offers training in law office management through videotapes, books, manuals and on-site consultations. Its Web pages describe its services and provide ordering information. The site includes a handful of useful articles covering topics such as preparing a disaster response plan for a law office and "tricks" in Internet marketing, and also offers a selection of legal management forms and checklists.

Law Firms

A handful of law firms have Web sites devoted to management-related issues. These may be intended to promote a service or product, or simply to share insights.

★ Jay G. Foonberg, www.foonberglaw.com

When it comes to the basics of law firm management, Foonberg's the man. Thousands of lawyers preparing to hang out a shingle have studied his book, *How to Start and Build a Law Practice*. Many others have heard him lecture on management and marketing. It is disappointing, then, that Foonberg's Web site is nothing more than a sales pitch, where you can buy Foonberg's books and seminars, but find no practical articles or information.

Management Consultants

There is no shortage of consultants eager to help lawyers better manage and market their law practices. Not surprisingly, many of these consultants have found their way to the Web. But what is surprising is how many of these supposed experts in marketing and technology have sites that suggest a complete ignorance of the medium. Their sites are, overall, formulaic, uninviting and uninteresting, as if they all got together and agreed on a standard list of ingredients. Among these, there are no "five star" sites, and only a couple of any real usefulness.

(Not rated) Jaffe Associates, www.jaffeassociates.com

Because I work for Jaffe Associates, I cannot rate its site. But I can mention that this business consultancy for professional services firms has a Web site that includes an extensive library of articles about business development, media relations, creative services and Web design. A Tools section features glossaries on branding, media relations, technology and publishing as well as a collection of PR forms you can use.

★★★★ Altman Weil, www.altmanweil.com

Altman Weil is one of the oldest and best known management consulting firms for the legal profession, and its Web site has probably the largest library of articles on the topic. They cover law department and law firm management, outsourcing, alternative billing, technology, marketing, strategic planning, economic and financial management, human resources and organizational psychology. Of course, the site also has information about the company's services and publications and a "store" where you can purchase surveys, newsletters and other products.

★★★★ Hildebrandt, www.hildebrandt.com

Hildebrandt is a management consulting firm serving law firms, corporate legal departments and other professional services firms. The majority of the site is devoted to providing detailed descriptions of the firm's various areas of expertise and complete biographies of its consultants. Of most interest to those involved in law office management is the publications section, with a useful and timely collection of articles, advisories and white papers on practice management, strategy and planning, governance and management, and other topics.

★★★★ LawBiz, www.lawbiz.com

This is the Web site of the law practice management consulting firm Edward Poll & Associates. Poll has written four books and produces a series of monthly audiotapes on legal management, all of which can be purchased here—Poll even offers a handful of sample audiotapes that you can listen to online using RealPlayer. Poll is also a frequent contributor of columns and articles to a variety of legal periodicals, Also available here is Poll's monthly e-zine about law office management, and his Web site includes a sampling of recent articles.

★★★★ **Law Office Consulting Services,** www.lawofficeconsulting.com

If most marketing and technology sites suggest a complete ignorance of the medium, here is an exception. This simple, well-designed site offers a variety of features that provide good reason to visit as well as to come back a second time. Start with the "What's New" page, a monthly feature reviewing new developments in legal technology. Then follow the link to "Tips, Tricks & Traps," where you will find a monthly column offering technology tips for the law office. The site's "Top 100 Web Links" describes the firm's favorite sites for legal research, legal technology, and other legal resources. An archive offers back issues of both the What's New page and the Tips, Tricks & Traps column.

★★★ **Customer Focused Quality,** www.dbainc.com

A few years back, TQM—Total Quality Management—was all the rage in management advice. This site, from California-based consultants David Butler Associates, provides a library of general TQM articles, including this section on TQM for law firms. The articles, many written by legal consultant and former journalist Nancy Blodgett, have the ring of a Stephen Covey self-help book—Covey's name, in fact, is frequently invoked—but are backed up by real-life stories of law firms using these techniques.

★★ **Advocates Management,** www.advocates.com

The site of this Wisconsin law office management and marketing consulting firm has a look that screams "home made." Its only redeeming feature is a "topical index" of marketing terms and concepts, each linked to a page with a longer discussion of the term and what it means in the law office context. There are a few articles thrown in for good measure, as well as general information about the firm and its services.

★★ **The Hunter Partnership Alliance,** www.thescotthuntergroup.com

Devoted to "creating partnership in the workplace," this management consulting firm focuses on coaching people in management on how to encourage teamwork. The site offers a self-assessment questionnaire and a collection of articles from the motivational school of management advice.

★★ **The Law Practice Management Page,** www.weilandco.com/manage.html

Sponsored by the law practice management consulting firm John P. Weil & Company, this page offers a mixed bag of twenty-two articles on practice management, firm governance and compensation. The articles are general-ly well-written and informative. There is no indication whether or how often new articles are added, although the site seems to have changed little, if at all, over several years.

★ Bradley-Huggins Consulting Group, www.bhcgi.com

Although these folks claim to have been one of the first law firm consult-ing groups to establish a Web site, the site is none the better for age. It pro-vides only general information about the services provided by this national consulting company, and a handful of "news" items—stories and articles linked from other sites.

★ Client Focus, www.clientfocus.net

Client Focus is a management and marketing consulting firm in Granite Bay, California. Its site provides information about the firm's services, but not much else.

★ The Devil's Advocate, Legal Fee Management, www.devilsadvo-cate.com

The Devil's Advocate is a Virginia legal fee management and litigation consulting firm working on behalf of corporations, government agencies, law firms, insurance companies, and others. Actually a law firm, it handles disputes over legal fees, performs audits of legal bills, and provides expert testimony on billing practices. All of this is fully explained at its Web site, but there is little else here of any substance, save for a proposed "Client's Bill of Rights" and a sample "client-friendly billing agreement."

★ GAP Enterprises, www.gapent.com

If you enjoy sloganeering, visit the site of this New Jersey firm of manage-ment "solutionists" which provides "solutioning" and "cybersolutioning" to professional firms and businesses. The only items of general interest are a handful of articles about Sarbanes-Oxley compliance. In an apparent attempt to emphasize its global reach, the firm includes a page of greetings in more than 200 languages.

★ Italo Consulting, www.mindspring.com/~italco

You might think this site a bit odd right up front, when it asks anyone who reads its articles to send the company a check for $39 "on the honor system." And then there are its numerous audio clips that require a defunct plug-in to be played. You might even be put off by the site's promise that it "is a trove of invaluable advice that has helped numerous attorneys and law firms increase their profits by many thousands of dollars." Well, it's not exactly a trove, but there is some gold to be found in the site's twenty-four articles on law office management, all written by Atlanta consultant Art Italo.

★ The Lawcost Management Group, www.lawcost.com

In-house counsel and other purchasers of legal services are the target audience of this consulting firm, which is devoted to managing the cost of legal services. Its Web site is little more than a brochure describing its services. Almost hidden are a few articles on managing legal costs, ethics and legal fees, and the proper role of paralegals.

★ WJF Institute, www.wjfinstitute.com

The WJF Institute is a marketing training and consulting firm in Austin, Texas. It offers various training courses in client development, all of which are outlined on its Web site. Visitors will also find a collection of articles with titles such as "What Every Good Client Should Get From Every Good Lawyer." Unless you are interested in learning about this firm, you will find little of value at its site.

Chapter 21

The Public Good: Pro Bono and Public Interest

―――――――――――――― **Chapter Contents** ――――――――――――――

Promoting Pro Bono
National Support Organizations
A Narrower Focus
Membership Organizations

―――――――――――――――――――――――――――――――――――――――

Though often portrayed as greedy and self-serving, lawyers as a whole unselfishly and routinely provide their services on behalf of the poor and disadvantaged, understanding pro bono and public service work to be part and parcel of the privilege of practicing law. Some might donate a few hours here and there, counseling people on family law or helping a nonprofit with its legal affairs. Others devote their entire careers to public service, eschewing the higher-paying salaries of private practice to work at legal services offices or public interest advocacy groups.

For lawyers in public service, the Web has become a mainstream medium of communication. Many Web sites focus on particular areas of practice—housing, welfare or health, for example—providing practice guides, advocacy tools and legal updates to lawyers throughout the U.S. Other sites are broader in their reach, pulling together a wider range of information and resources of interest to legal services lawyers and public interest lawyers.

For the much larger number of lawyers for whom pro bono is a sideline rather than a career, an increasing number of Web sites are becoming available to help match them with opportunities in their home towns. More than just listings of pro bono opportunities, these sites provide resources to support pro bono work and often even assist in lining up mentors for less experienced lawyers.

The number of legal service and public service Web sites is large. This chapter looks at some of the sites that are national in their focus, together with selected more narrowly focused sites. Virtually every legal services agency in every state has a Web site, as do many bar-sponsored pro bono programs throughout the U.S. Space and time prevent including all of them here, but several of the sites below include comprehensive links to these many other Web sites.

Promoting Pro Bono

★★★★★ CorporateProBono.org, www.corporateprobono.org

CorporateProBono.org is an innovative program designed to match in-house counsel with pro bono opportunities in legal services and public interest programs. Created as a partnership between the American Corporate Counsel Association and the Pro Bono Institute at Georgetown University Law Center, CorporateProBono.org's hub is this Web site, launched on October 2, 2000, where corporate counsel may search for volunteer opportunities and locate tools, information and resources concerning pro bono participation. The site features a database of pro bono opportunities, which users can search by various parameters, including location, category, and even scheduling preferences. Supplementing this is a library of publications such as best practice guides and monographs, along with a practitioner network linking volunteers with experienced mentors. The site boasts a design that is both attractive and useable.

★★★★★ ProBono.net, www.probono.net

The most innovative sites create a genre all their own—one that, although new, seems immediately indispensable. When it launched in 1998, ProBono.net was such a site, developed as a means of enlisting Internet technology in efforts to increase the amount and quality of legal services provided to low-income individuals and communities. The site was spearheaded by Michael Hertz, a

ProBono.net employes Internet technology to enhance legal services for the poor.

lawyer with New York's Latham & Watkins, working under a fellowship from the Open Society Institute. Hertz remains with ProBono.net as its executive director. A number of law firms, legal services agencies and bar associations support the project.

ProBono.net functions as a kind of virtual network through which pro bono lawyers can exchange practice materials, volunteer opportunities and related information. The core of the site is its practice area and regional sections. Initially, it focused on New York City, for which it has seven distinct "communities"—Family Justice/Domestic Violence, Disability Rights,

Community Development, Criminal Appeals, Housing, Asylum Law, and Death Penalty. (Asylum Law and Death Penalty are actually *national* sections that are listed on each regional page.) Public interest organizations and a matched law firm host each of these practice areas and perform tasks such as updating the news and calendar pages, listing new cases that need attorneys, and screening area members. The New York section also includes Rochester, New York. Sections have also been created for Minnesota, San Francisco, Washington state, Washington, D.C., and Montana, and two national practice area sections have been added for asylum and death penalty cases. A notice on the site reports that another thirty regional sections are in development.

Each section provides training materials, listings of cases needing volunteers, message boards, practice materials and other resources. Lawyers interested in a particular section must first register in order to gain access, but there is no cost.

★★ Pro Bono Institute, www.probonoinst.org

Georgetown University Law Center's Pro Bono Institute is dedicated to exploring and identifying new approaches to the provision of legal services to the poor. Its Law Firm Pro Bono Project, a partnership with the American Bar Association's Standing Committee on Pro Bono and Public Service, works to support and expand the pro bono activities of the nation's largest law firms. Other programs work directly with legal services providers to enhance their services. The institute is a cofounder of Corporate ProBono.org, reviewed above. The Institute's Web site provides an overview of its activities, but few practical resources.

National Support Organizations

★★★★★ Center for Law and Social Policy, www.clasp.org

Part think tank, part advocacy group, CLASP is a national nonprofit organization with expertise in both law and policy affecting the poor. Through education, policy research and advocacy, CLASP seeks to improve the economic security of low-income families with

Part think tank, part advocacy group, CLASP focuses on law and policy.

children and secure access to our civil justice system by low-income persons. Its Web site features CLASP *Update*, a monthly report on welfare reform developments. It also maintains an extensive library of articles on legal services for the poor, child support enforcement, the Temporary Assistance for Needy Families block grant, and other topics. The site includes an overview of CLASP's national and state projects, as well as its organization and staff.

★★★★★ LStech.org, www.lstech.org

Recognizing that few legal aid programs have the budget to hire dedicated technology staff, LStech.org is a portal to technology services and information tailored to a legal aid audience. Funded by a Legal Services Corporation Technology Initiative Grant, it is operated as a partnership by the University of Michigan Law School, Legal Services of South Central Michigan, the National Legal Aid and Defender Association and the National Technology Assistance Project. Its most substantive section is its Tech Library, an extensive collection of articles on technology management, Web development, software, technology for advocates, telecommunications, networks, hardware and the Internet. Another section compiles information on technology projects implemented by poverty law programs throughout the U.S. The site includes online collaboration spaces, listings of tech jobs, and current technology news of interest to the poverty law community.

★★★★★ Sargent Shriver National Center on Poverty Law, www. povertylaw.org

The mission of the National Center on Poverty Law is to provide national leadership in identifying, developing, and supporting creative and collaborative approaches to achieve social and economic justice for low-income people. It is perhaps most widely known for its bimonthly legal publication, Clearinghouse Review, featuring in-depth articles and analysis on topics of interest to poor people's and public interest lawyers, including civil rights, family law, disability, domestic violence, housing, elder law, employment, health, and welfare reform. The hard copy Review publishes abstracts describing poverty law cases being litigated by legal aid advocates across the country. The Web site features these case reports in more depth. The full text of these cases is also available through the Center's Poverty Law Library—the Library includes more than 500,000 full text case documents, including pleadings and opinions from over 50,000 cases spanning thirty years.

Visitors to the site can read many of the case abstracts, but access to the full text of the cases and to articles from the Review requires a subscription. Two basic subscription levels are offered. For $350, a subscriber receives the Clearinghouse Review in print and Web access to the most recent three years of the review. Access to the library and older issues of the Review requires a separate, $200 annual subscription. Anyone can browse the case abstracts by area of law, search them by key words, or view only the most recently added cases. The Web site also offers a series of practice area pages focusing on food programs, health, housing, immigration and welfare. These pages feature recent news and links to relevant resources. A separate area of the site offers assistance in setting up legal "hotlines," and includes a useful collection of state-specific guides to frequently asked legal questions.

★★★★ Alliance for Justice, www.afj.org

The Alliance for Justice is a national association of environmental, civil rights, mental health, women's, children's and consumer advocacy organizations. At the top of its agenda is working to strengthen the capacity of public interest groups to influence public policy. To this end, its Nonprofit Advocacy Project produces legal guides to help nonprofits plan advocacy campaigns while navigating the laws that govern lobbying, fundraising and related issues. These guides can be ordered from the Web site, some for free, some for a fee. The Alliance also produces legal guides aimed at encouraging foundations to support nonprofits engaged in advocacy work. The Alliance's Judicial Selection Project monitors the judicial selection process nationwide, and, through this site, provides a database of federal judges that can be sorted by race, gender and court.

★★★★ Brennan Center for Justice, www.brennancenter.org

Named for the late Supreme Court Justice William J. Brennan, Jr., New York University School of Law's Brennan Center seeks to promote equality and human dignity through its work in three primary areas: democracy, poverty and criminal justice. Its programs tackle campaign finance reform, judicial independence and community justice, among other topics. In the legal services arena, it has produced a series of fact sheets, available on its Web site, designed to illuminate how restrictions on legal services programs interfere with zealous advocacy. Its Legal Services E-lert summarizes news articles and opinion pieces from the media that discuss legal services for the poor. It, too, is available here, along with an archive of past issues.

★★★★ Equal Justice Works, www.napil.org

Equal Justice Works, formerly known as the National Association for Public Interest Law, is the preeminent resource for law students and prospective law students interested in pursuing a career in public interest law. Founded by law students in 1986, NAPIL is dedicated to organizing, training and supporting public service-minded law students. Its Web site is a catalog of summer and year-round public service opportunities for law students, and also lists postgraduate fellowships and other public service opportunities for lawyers. In addition, the site offers guidance on choosing a law school and on financing a public interest education and career.

★★★★ Southern Poverty Law Center, www.splcenter.org

The Southern Poverty Law Center is a nonprofit institution that combats hate, intolerance and discrimination through education and litigation. Its Intelligence Project monitors hate groups and extremist activity throughout the U.S. Its Teaching Tolerance program supports educational efforts nationwide to tackle hate crime among young people. Through its Web site, visitors can read about the Center's current litigation and its courtroom victories over the years. The site includes articles from its quarterly publication, Intelligence Report, analyzing political extremism and bias crimes in the U.S. It provides list of hate groups categorized by type—e.g., Klan, skinhead, neo-Nazi—and searchable by state, and a similar list of "patriot" groups. There is also a list of hate incidents sorted by state. Details are provided on how to request the center's assistance and how to support its work.

★★★ Legal Services Corporation, www.lsc.gov

Legal Services Corporation is a private, nonprofit corporation established by Congress in 1974 to assure equal access to justice for all Americans. It does this primarily through its support of some 300 legal aid programs serving every county in the U.S. Through this Web site, users can read LSC's governing statute, bylaws and regulations, review its budget and case statistics, and see the text of its reports to Congress and testimony it has given to congressional committees. Visitors can locate local legal aid programs by clicking on a map of the U.S. or searching by county name.

★★ National Economic Development and Law Center, www.nedlc.org

The National Economic Development and Law Center, located in Oakland, California, is a multidisciplinary legal and planning resource center the mission of which is to contribute to the abilities of low-income persons and communities to realize their full potential. Its Web site describes its various programs and includes the full text of its monthly newsletter with articles about the Center's work.

★ Equal Justice Update, www.equaljusticeupdate.org (and another site of the same entity,

★ **National Equal Justice Library,** http://library.wcl.american. edu/nejl

The National Equal Justice Library, located at Washington College of Law in Washington, D.C., is an institution devoted to commemorating the legal profession's history of providing legal representation for those unable to afford counsel. It is co-sponsored by the American Bar Association, the American Association of Law Libraries and the National Legal Aid and Defender Association. For some reason, it has two very different Web sites, neither of which does justice to its lofty purpose. The first site, Equal Justice Update, is described as focusing "on programs not covered on the other Web site which reach beyond the walls of the library's physical facility as well as on items which require constant updating." The most substantive feature of this first site is its international legal aid collection, a library of materials about legal aid in countries outside the U.S. A feature of this collection is supposed to be an archive of decisions from other countries addressing equal access to justice, although it had only three cases on our most recent visit. The collection includes a small table comparing legal aid spending in selected countries, a bibliography of resources about international aid, and information on specific programs in a handful of foreign jurisdictions. The second site provides little content and when last visited appeared not to have been updated in several years.

A Narrower Focus

★★★★★ **Judge David L. Bazelon Center for Mental Health Law,** www.bazelon.org

A virtual tool chest for mental health lawyers is the best way to describe the Web site of the Bazelon Center, a legal advocacy center working on behalf of people with mental disabilities. Named for the federal appeals court judge whose decisions helped pioneer the field of mental health law, the Bazelon Center has assembled a site brimming with practical help for advocates, from current legislative and case law alerts to how-to handbooks. Its many resources are organized under key categories—elders, children, housing, involuntary commitment, mental health care, restraint, advance directives (i.e., legal documents prepared in advance, by persons concerned that they will be involuntarily committed for psychiatric reasons, to express choices about treatment), and others. Alerts bring this all up to date with in-depth analysis of recent developments. Rounding it all out is a detailed collection of disability and advocacy links, as well as a bookstore of Bazelon Center publications available for purchase.

★★★★★ National Immigration Law Center, www.nilc.org

The National Immigration Law Center is a national support center the mission of which is to protect and promote the rights of low-income immigrants and their family members. NILC staff specializes in immigration law, and the employment and public benefits rights of immigrants. The Center conducts policy analysis and social policy litigation and provides publications, technical advice, and training to a broad constituency of legal aid agencies, community groups, and pro bono attorneys. Its frequently updated Web site has a broad array of practical articles tracking the latest developments in immigration law and policy, as well as reports on recent court opinions.

★★★★★ Native American Rights Fund, www.narf.org

The Native American Rights Fund is a nonprofit organization that provides legal representation and technical assistance to Indian tribes, organizations and individuals nationwide. Its useful Web site has updates on pertinent cases as well as a court watch for pending matters. Sponsor of the National Indian Law Library, it offers a searchable version of the library's catalog, with descriptions of the more than 11,000 items in its collection. Through the library, the Web site provides various full text materials designed to assist tribal courts and advocates involved in Indian affairs. The site includes two full text periodicals, *Justice*, NARF's newsletter, and NARF Legal Review, its journal devoted to current legal developments, although when last visited neither had seen recent updates.

★★★★★ Pine Tree Legal Assistance, www.ptla.org

Maine's legal aid organization, Pine Tree Legal Assistance, publishes a Web site that stands as an example of what a legal services site can be. With materials in English and nine other languages, the site provides an array of materials so that Maine residents can learn about the law on their own. Under a grant from the Legal Services Corporation, it developed HelpMeLaw, www.helpmelaw.org, intended to be a comprehensive portal for low-income Mainers seeking legal assistance and information. But lawyers as far away as Hawaii will want to visit PTLA's site as well, primarily for its comprehensive collections of useful links. It features links to legal services organizations within the U.S., as well as a separate collection on legal aid organizations worldwide, covering, at last count, some thirty-four countries. Finally, "Around the Web in 80 Minutes" is an introduction to Internet legal research, including major subject areas and some not-so-common topics such as Native American law.

★★★★ First District Appellate Project, www.fdap.org

California's First District Appellate Project is a nonprofit, northern California law firm providing representation on appeal to indigent juvenile and adult defendants in criminal proceedings, and indigent minors and parents in dependency proceedings. The Web site features practical tools primarily for use by FDAP's panel of attorneys taking court-appointed cases from the California Court of Appeal. It includes pointers regarding research resources, information on courts and filing requirements, forms, checklists, and information on filing claims for compensation.

★★★★ National Consumer Law Center, www.consumerlaw.org

Lawyers involved in consumer fraud, debt collection, consumer finance, energy assistance programs and sustainable homeownership programs can find support at the Web site of the National Consumer Law Center. The NCLC provides legal answers, policy analysis and technical and legal support to legal services and private lawyers, state and federal consumer protection officials, public policy makers and others. Its Web site provides content for both lawyers and consumers. For lawyers, there is information on NCLC publications, newsletters and legal education programs. There is also information on the support services available to lawyers from NCLC. Consumers can visit the site to read any of a number of online pamphlets covering consumer law.

★★★★ National Health Law Program, www.healthlaw.org

The National Health Law Program is a public interest law firm that seeks to improve health care for America's working and unemployed poor, minorities, the elderly and people with disabilities. With sections devoted to an array of health advocacy topics, its Web site is a multifaceted resource. Its strongest suit, overall, is current awareness, with each topical section having a unique set of links to current news stories and legal and regulatory developments. Its various sections focus on advocacy, child health, consumer resources, immigrant health, managed care, Medicaid, Medicare, public accountability, racial and cultural issues, reproductive health, and state and regional issues. Within each section is a collection of full text articles and links to related resources elsewhere on the Web.

★★★★ National Housing Law Project, www.nhlp.org

The National Housing Law Project, a national housing law and advocacy center based in Oakland, California, works to advance housing justice for the poor by increasing and preserving the supply of decent affordable housing, by improving existing housing conditions, by expanding and enforcing low-income tenants' and homeowners' rights, and by increasing opportunities for racial and ethnic minorities. With a focus on the housing advocate, NHLP's Web site provides information in six primary categories: public housing, Section 8 housing, HUD rental housing, housing preservation, fair housing, and rural housing. Each of these categories, in turn, includes three types of resources: general authorities and information, information packets, and recent developments. The last of these offers current reports on legislation, litigation, regulations, HUD notices, and recently issued reports. As of this writing, the site seemed to be falling out of date, with no new information having been added for about a year.

★★★★ National Low Income Housing Coalition, www.nlihc.org

The NLIHC is dedicated to ensuring the availability of affordable housing. It carries out this mission through programs that focus on preservation, production, public housing, vouchers and "housing plus services." It has a range of materials of interest to housing advocates, but the most noteworthy may be its annually updated Advocates' Guide to Housing and Community Development Policy, which describes more than sixty housing-related programs, proposals and issues.

★★★ National Senior Citizens Law Center, www.nsclc.org

The National Senior Citizens Law Center advocates nationwide to promote the independence and well-being of low-income elderly individuals, as well as persons with disabilities, with particular emphasis on women and racial and ethnic minorities. Among its projects is a national technical assistance program for legal services, public interest and pro bono lawyers seeking to enforce federal rights against state governments and agencies. In conjunction with this, its Web site provides a regular review of significant cases on enforcing federal rights, with brief descriptions of each new case. The site describes periodicals and publications available for purchase from the Center, and includes a selection of recent news articles. Other pages describe the Center's programs and services.

★★★ Welfare Law Center, www.welfarelaw.org

The New York City-based Welfare Law Center works with and on behalf of low income people to ensure that adequate income support—public funding provided on the basis of need—is available whenever and to the extent necessary to meet basic needs and foster healthy human and family development. As part of its Project Fair Play, it monitors welfare-related litigation throughout the U.S., periodically reporting key case developments. A litigation docket of cases the Center was involved in had not been updated in a year. Still, the Center's site included some useful materials, including selected pleadings and a collection of analytical articles on topics such as child care and welfare, disability and welfare, food stamp access and Medicaid access.

Membership Organizations

★★★★★ **National Legal Aid and Defender Association,** www. nlada.org

A membership organization of lawyers providing civil legal services and criminal indigent defense, NLADA provides an informative resource for lawyers representing the poor. On the civil side, it tracks developments in our nation's capital related to legal services, and reports on recent cases involving Interest on Lawyers' Trust Accounts programs nationwide. NLADA members can read the NLADA Update, a twice-monthly publication that reports on news related to the delivery of civil legal services. On the criminal defense side, NLADA offers several members-only resources, including a forensics library and a database of management resources. NLADA's E-Library has both civil and criminal materials and is available to anyone who visits the site. Intended to serve as an information clearinghouse, it relies on member submissions for most of its content. The site also describes publications for sale through NLADA and lists future conferences and training programs.

★★★★ **Standing Committee on Pro Bono and Public Service, American Bar Association,** www.abanet.org/legalservices/probono/home.html

Whether you are a potential client looking for an attorney or a lawyer wanting to volunteer your help, you will find help here. For lawyers, this ABA committee offers a comprehensive list of pro bono programs, organized by state, as well as of volunteer opportunities. A Pro Bono Clearinghouse provides access to materials on developing, managing and promoting pro bono programs. Other sections contain links to pro bono resources within and outside the ABA. The site also contains information on pro bono conferences and related ABA services and publications.

Best Medical Sites for Trial Lawyers

A well-prepared trial lawyer might appear to know more about medicine than an M.D. Thorough understanding of a client's injury or disease is essential to success. While some of this medical knowledge comes from experts, much of it must be self-taught as the lawyer pores over medical journals and treatises.

For personal injury lawyers and others whose practices require medical research, the Internet is invaluable, providing access to the popular Medline database (a database of more than 11 million references to articles published in 4,300 biomedical journals) and a host of other medical libraries. Thousands of medical sites cover virtually every ailment, injury and body part, using everything from peer reviewed articles to detailed illustrations.

But beware bad advice. Perhaps nowhere more than in the field of medicine is the Internet rife with quacks. As with any medical information, know the source. That said, here are the best sites for lawyers to obtain medical information.

General Sites

★★★★★ American Medical Association, www.ama-assn.org

The AMA Web site has an extensive collection of resources and information regarding medical science and education. It includes a publications page, with abstracts and selected full text from JAMA (The Journal of the American Medical Association), and specialized archives devoted to specific areas of medical practice, such as internal medicine, ophthalmology, pediatrics, and women's health. The site also features various consumer services, including Physician Select, a searchable database with information on virtually every licensed physician in the U.S. and its possessions, and the Medical Group Practice Locator, a guide to finding medical group practices throughout the U.S.

★★★★★ MedicineNet, www.medicinenet.com

This free site is a dictionary of medical knowledge, with an alphabetical listing of diseases and their treatments; a similar listing of medications, their uses and side effects; and a dictionary of medical terms. Additional sections provide indexes of common symptoms and common medical procedures and tests. Doctors in active practice write all articles. A news section provides updates on current developments in healthcare.

★★★★★ MedScape, http://medscape.com

MedScape, designed primarily for health professionals, features a physician-optimized version of MEDLINE, the National Library of Medicine's database of bibliographic citations and author abstracts from more than 4,600 biomedical journals. MedScape also has content from more than fifty medical journals and textbooks, daily medical news by specialty, conference coverage, and continuing medical education. The site is free, but first-time visitors must register. Once registered, you can subscribe to "MedPulse," a weekly e-mail newsletter updating articles and news stories at the site.

★★★★★ Medterms.com, www.medterms.com

Part of the larger MedicineNet site, this free dictionary of classic and contemporary medical terms contains thousands of listings, many of which are more like encyclopedia entries than dictionary definitions. Written entirely by physicians, entries include not only standard medical terms but also pertinent scientific items, abbreviations, acronyms, jargon, institutions, projects, symptoms, syndromes, eponyms and medical history—a range of terms all having to do with medicine and the biomedical sciences. Users can browse the dictionary by alphabetical entry or conduct a keyword search.

★★★★★ Merck Manual of Medical Information, Home Edition, www.merckhomeedition.com

First published in 1899, *The Merck Manual of Diagnosis and Therapy* is the oldest continuously published general medical textbook in the English language and the most widely used medical textbook in the world. It covers almost every disease that affects humans in specialties such as pediatrics, obstetrics and gynecology, psychiatry, ophthalmology, otolaryngology, dermatology and dentistry, including conditions such as burns, heat disorders, radiation reactions and injuries, and sports injuries. This home edition, published for the general public, is based almost entirely on the text of *The Merck Manual* and retains its highly detailed, sophisticated medical information. It adds overviews of anatomy and physiology to help orient readers to the structure and function of specific organs. The Web site offers a choice of a standard, text based format, or an interactive version with photos, animations, videos and pronunciations.

★★★★★ Pain & the Law, www.painandthelaw.org

A joint venture of the Center for Health Law Studies at St. Louis University School of Law and the American Society of Law, Medicine, and Ethics, Pain & the Law is devoted to the legal issues associated with pain management and palliative care. Its primary sections are devoted to statutes and regulations, malpractice and civil actions, palliative care and criminal action, government entitlement programs, and agencies and organizations. Each of these sections includes primary materials along with links to related resources elsewhere on the Web. For example, the malpractice section includes descriptions of recent cases involving such issues as under- and over-medicating and failure to refer. It also provides links to relevant recent news stories and other online information. The statutes and regulation section provides access to state and federal legislation relating to pain, controlled substances and the like.

★★★★★ The Virtual Hospital, www.vh.org

The Virtual Hospital is an electronic health sciences library from the University of Iowa College of Medicine. It includes a section for the general public, but its larger purpose is to make the latest medical information available to practicing physicians. Included are multimedia textbooks, teaching files, clinical guidelines and assorted publications. Some databases are limited to University of Iowa students and faculty.

★★★★ Cochrane Library for Evidence Based Medicine, www.cochrane.org

Designed primarily for clinicians and researchers, the Cochrane Library focuses on organizing medical research to facilitate access to the accumulated "evidence" concerning the most effective treatments and practices. It features the Cochrane Database of Systematic Reviews, a collection of reviews of medical literature, with particular emphasis on randomized, controlled trials. It also includes the Controlled Trials Register, a bibliography of controlled trials. Although similar to Medline, the library is distinct in that it organizes information in a summary format, making it easier for researchers to find answers. A free trial is offered, after which a subscription is required.

★★★★ Global Lawyers and Physicians, www.glphr.org

Global Lawyers and Physicians is a nonprofit organization that focuses on health and human rights issues. It was founded in 1996 to commemorate the Nuremberg Code, which was developed by lawyers and physicians working together. GLP's goal is to reinvigorate the collaboration of the legal and medical/public health professions to protect the human rights and dignity of all persons. The site includes archival audio, film and photographs from the Nuremberg doctors' trial, a health and human rights database, and information on recent projects and activities concerning topics such as biomedical research, refugee health and patients' rights.

★★★ Administrators in Medicine, www.docboard.org

This simple site from the national organization of state medical board executives provides links to state medical licensing boards and to online sources of licensure information for specific physicians. In some cases, these sites also show whether a physician has been subject to professional discipline or to a malpractice claim.

★★★ MayoClinic.com, www.mayoclinic.com

From the respected Mayo Clinic in Rochester, Minnesota, this site is a collection of medical articles and resources all of which were developed or reviewed by Mayo staff physicians and researchers. With articles on a wide range of health topics, all material is dated so users can tell when it was placed on the site. Articles are written for the consumer and rarely lack the depth that a lawyer might be seeking in medical research. For more substantive information on medical research and clinical trials, jump over to Mayo's other site, www.mayo.edu, where you will find information for medical professionals on Mayo-sponsored research, education and patient care.

★★ LAWprn.com, www.lawprn.com

This site aims to provide physicians and health care professionals with quick access to "straightforward legal information." It promises an array of medical-legal resources, including 200 articles exploring significant legal and regulatory issues such as Medicare payment policy, medical liability, professional ethics, and the new privacy standards. A subscription-based service, the site also includes answers to questions of the week, intriguing court cases, and weekly news articles. According to a press release, subscribers may submit personalized questions to "Ask BJ"—lawyer B.J. Anderson—described as "one of the nation's premier health lawyers who has been answering doctors' legal questions for nearly 40 years." Anderson developed the American Medical Association's Health Law Division and was a regular contributor on law and medicine for the Journal of the American Medical Association. A basic subscription is $225 a year.

Index Sites

★★★★★ Medem, www.medem.com

Medem is distinguished by its backers, the nation's preeminent medical societies, which banded together to create this site out of concern over the lack of quality standards in online medical information. Featuring an extensive medical library, it aims to become the most comprehensive and trusted source of healthcare content on the Web. The societies that sponsor Medem are the American Academy of Ophthalmology; American Academy of Pediatrics; American College of Allergy, Asthma & Immunology; American College of Obstetricians and Gynecologists; American Medical Association; American Psychiatric Association; and American Society of Plastic Surgeons.

★★★★★ Medical Matrix, www.medmatrix.org

This is an encyclopedic collection of links to medical resources on the Internet. All linked resources have been peer reviewed, then annotated and given a rating of up to five stars. There are more than 6,000 links, organized into the following categories: disease and specialty, clinical practice, literature, education, health care professionals, and computers and technology. The site requires a paid subscription, which is $89 a year for an individual.

★★★★ Center for Health Law Studies, http://lawlib.slu.edu/healthcenter

Saint Louis University School of Law's Center for Health Law Studies is dedicated to health law and policy. It offers degrees in the field and publishes major health law journals. More important to practitioners, its Web site features a gateway to health law resources on the Web—a comprehensive collection of links to related legal and medical sites. Also here are abstracts from the center's quarterly *Journal of Health Law*. Unfortunately, full articles are available online only through links to the Lexis-Nexis database, which requires an account and password.

★★★★ Hardin MetaDirectory of Internet Health Services, www.lib.uiowa.edu/hardin/md/index.html

Hardin "lists the sites that list the sites," making it a preferred resource for starting research on a particular topic. It has no original information; rather, it provides lists of links to other sites each of which, in turn, has its own lists of links devoted to a particular topic. Hardin's list is alphabetical by specialty, from AIDS to toxicology. Hardin regularly checks back on the sites to which it links to make sure that the links remain up to date; those that do get Hardin's "Clean Bill of Health Award."

★★★★ MedExplorer, www.medexplorer.com

MedExplorer is a searchable collection of links to health and medical resources on the Web. It was started in 1996 by a paramedic and student at the University of Calgary who became frustrated with the many irrelevant sites he encountered when searching for medical information on the Internet. Today, it has grown to a sizeable and well-organized collection, making it a truly useful index for finding medical sites on the Web.

★★★★ Web Sites for Internists, www.acponline.org/computer/ccp/bookmark

A service of the American College of Physicians and American Society of Internal Medicine, Web Sites for Internists is an annotated guide to Web sites that physicians, and particularly internists, might find useful. It is selective rather than comprehensive, but not meant to serve as an endorsement of any site. New sites are reviewed and there is a searchable archive of older reviews. You can elect to view links with or without annotations.

★★★ HealthWeb, http://healthweb.org

HealthWeb provides links to medical information resources on the Web, but rather than attempt to be exhaustive, its staff evaluates links and selects only those it deems to be of high quality. Health science librarians and information professionals at leading academic medical centers in the Midwest, under the auspices of the University of Chicago, make the selections. Search the links by key word, or browse through categories that range from AIDS to women's health, and include diabetes, endocrinology, genetics, geriatrics and gerontology, osteopathic medicine, laboratory medicine and pathology, pediatrics, physiology, psychiatry and transplantation.

★★★ **Martindale's Virtual Medical Center,** www.martindalecenter.com/Medical.html

This is a true "mega-list" of links to medical information on the Web. It claims to contain links to 62,600 multimedia teaching files, 1,785 tutorials, 4,400 databases, 136,000 medical cases, 1,325 multimedia courses/textbooks, and thousands of movies. Links are not annotated or evaluated in any way, and the overall organization of the site can be somewhat confusing.

Government Resources

★★★★★ **Cancer.gov,** http://cancer.gov

From the National Cancer Institute, Cancer.gov provides a wide range of clinical and research cancer information. It covers a broad spectrum of topics, such as treatment options, clinical trials, ways to reduce cancer risk, and ways to cope with cancer. It also provides resources on support groups, financial assistance, educational materials, and more. All of the information on Cancer.gov is reviewed and continually updated by oncology experts based on the latest research in the field. The site includes PDQ, the NCI's cancer database, which contains peer-reviewed summaries of the latest information about cancer treatment, screening, prevention, care and clinical trials.

★★★★★ **Food and Drug Administration,** www.fda.gov

The FDA offers the trial lawyer a gold mine of information on its Web site, covering drugs, toxicology, cosmetics, foods, medical products, medical devices, and more. Hundreds of full text articles and reports are available.

★★★★★ **National Institutes of Health,** www.nih.gov

The medical research arm of the U.S. government, the NIH has the broad mission of seeking "new knowledge to help prevent, detect, diagnose, and treat disease and disability, from the rarest genetic disorder to the common cold." Its Web site is the virtual storehouse of that knowledge, with an array of health information libraries covering such topics as cancer, AIDS, women's health, and clinical alerts. While many of these libraries are oriented towards the public, others are tailored to research scientists, providing research news and information, online library catalogs and journals, and links to specific NIH research labs. Beyond itself being home to a wealth of health information, the site is also the hub linking the sites of the range of related institutes and organizations that comprise the NIH. These include the

National Cancer Institute, the National Eye Institute, the National Institute of Mental Health, the National Institute on Aging, and a host of others.

★★★★★ National Library of Medicine, www.nlm.nih.gov

What was already a great Web site became even better when the National Library of Medicine added free access to MEDLINE through its PubMed database. In addition to MEDLINE's bibliographic citations to more than 4,600 biomedical journals, PubMed includes 1.5 million citations from older journals published between 1953 and 1965, as well as other citations and journals.

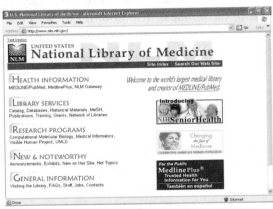

The NLM provides free access to MEDLINE and other medical databases.

The library also offers MEDLINEplus—the plus being a directory of health topics for consumers and professionals, with information on everything from aging and allergies to sleep disorders and STDs. You'll also find physician referral directories, medical terminology, and more.

The library, part of the National Institutes of Health, offers much more at its Web site than just MEDLINE. Of interest to lawyers who use demonstrative evidence is the page devoted to The Visible Human Project, which uses CAT scan images to create complete, anatomically detailed, three-dimensional representations of the male and female human bodies. There is complete information about the project as well as links to sites where Visible Human images can be explored online. Also available is a library of medical images that you can view online and from which you can order high resolution reproductions. Special libraries cover such topics as toxicology and environmental health.

★★★★ Centers for Disease Control and Prevention, www.cdc.gov

Two parts of this site will be of greatest interest to lawyers: "Health Topics" and "Data and Statistics." The first leads to various libraries of information on diseases, injuries and disabilities, health risks, specific populations and prevention. Many of these libraries are maintained by component agencies of the CDC, such as the National Center for Environmental Health and the National Institute for Occupational Safety and Health. The Data and Statistics part also leads to various collections of scientific data and health statistics, including the HazDat database of hazardous substance releases and health effects.

★★★★ ClinicalTrials.gov, http://clinicaltrials.gov

Developed as a collaboration of the National Institutes of Health, the National Library of Medicine and the Food and Drug Administration, this site offers information on more than 8,900 federal and private medical studies involving patients and others, primarily in the U.S and Canada but also at locations in more than ninety countries. The site is intended to provide patients, families and members of the public easy access to information about the location of clinical trials, their design and purpose, criteria for participation, and, in many cases, further information about the disease and treatment under study. There are also direct e-mail links to individuals responsible for recruiting participants for each study. The site emphasizes that it is completely confidential, requiring no registration or personal identification of any kind to access its information.

★★★★ Health.gov, www.health.gov

Sponsored by the U.S. Department of Health and Human Services, this site is a portal to the Web sites of federal health-related initiatives and activities.

★★★★ Healthfinder, www.healthfinder.gov

This site, from the U.S. Department of Health and Human Services, acts as a "gateway to reliable consumer health and human services information." It publishes no original content, but provides links to health resources on the Web available from U.S. government agencies and other agencies serving the public interest. The links can be browsed by topic or searched.

★★★★ National Center for Health Statistics, www.cdc.gov/nchs

This is the federal government's principal agency for tracking vital and health statistics, meaning that, for the fact seeker, there is a lot to be found here. It is a virtual "data warehouse" housing pallets full of data on births, deaths and disease, sliced and diced by gender, race, state, age and year. Follow the Fastats link to quickly find statistics organized by topic.

★★★★ PubMed Central, www.pubmedcentral.nih.gov

Sponsored by the National Institutes of Health, PubMed Central is a free archive of full text, peer-reviewed journal literature in the life sciences. Visitors can view abstracts of articles or their full text in a choice of HTML or .pdf formats. It includes dozens of journals, including *Arthritis Research*, various Biomed Central journals, *British Medical Journal, Breast Cancer Research, Critical Care, Genome Biology, Molecular Biology of the Cell,* and the *Proceedings of the National Academy of Sciences.*

★★★★ U.S. Department of Health and Human Services, www.hhs.gov

HHS is the umbrella over many health-related agencies. From its site, there are links to the Centers for Disease Control, the National Institutes of Health, the Agency for Toxic Substances and Disease Registry, the Substance Abuse and Mental Health Services Administration, and others.

Pharmaceutical

★★★★ PharmWeb, www.pharmweb.net

Started as a hobby by a British pharmacist in 1994, PharmWeb has grown into a significant repository of online pharmaceutical information and resources. It covers an array of general pharmaceutical information, and includes the World Drug Alert, which lists drug recalls, interactions, and related matters.

★★★★ RxList, The Internet Drug Index, www.rxlist.com

This easy-to-use site has a searchable index of drugs, describing their indications and side effects.

★★★ Drugfacts.com, www.drugfacts.com

Published by Facts and Comparisons, a division of Wolters Kluwer International Health & Science, Drugfacts offers paid access to the content of several highly regarded reference sources, including *A-Z Drug Facts, Medfacts,* and *The Guide to Popular Natural Products.* Other titles are also offered here on a subscription basis, including *Drug Facts and Comparisons, Drug Interaction Facts,* and the *Review of Natural Products.* Subscription prices vary depending on the product, but generally fall within the range of $150 to $450 a year.

★★★ United States Pharmacopeia, www.usp.org

If you have a case involving prescription drugs, you may want to visit the Web site of United States Pharmacopeia, an organization devoted to establishing "officially recognized standards of quality and authoritative information for the use of medicines and other health care technologies." The site has information on purchasing USP's *Drug Information,* a reference book with information on more than 11,000 generic and brand name drugs. But beyond online purchasing, USP's site offers useful free information. It features a searchable database of descriptions, precautions, proper use and side effects for more than 750 generic medicines. The site provides a variety of resources relating to standards development, quality review and patient counseling as they relate to drugs.

Mental Health

★★★★ American Psychological Association, www.apa.org

This site, from the American Psychological Association, features "PsycINFO," an electronic database of more than a million abstracts of psychological literature from 1887 to the present. Non-APA members can search PsycINFO for $11.95 for a twenty-four-hour-period.

★★★★ Internet Mental Health, www.mentalhealth.com

A self-described encyclopedia of mental health information, the site has information on each of the fifty-four most common mental disorders and each of the seventy-two most common psychiatric medications, an online magazine, and a page of links to other mental health sites. Information is fairly detailed, providing for each disorder its American description, its European description, treatment information, available research, information booklets, and magazine articles.

★★★ PsycLaw.org, www.psyclaw.org

Devoted to the interface between psychology and law, this site, hosted by the American Psychological Association, features various online resources and a catalog of other resources available only in print. A highlight is the library of APA amicus briefs, many only summarized, but some available in full text. News articles discuss recent legal developments and a links page connects to related online resources. The site includes abstracts of articles from the journal *Psychology, Public Policy, and Law*; APA members can view full-text articles.

★ Psychiatry.com, www.psychiatry.com

This site provides information about mental retardation and psychiatry, psychiatry and law, and geriatric psychiatry. There is a handful of substantive articles and a small collection of links.

Other Topical Sites

★★★★★ OncoLink, www.oncolink.upenn.edu

This award-winning site, sponsored by the University of Pennsylvania Cancer Center, is a thorough and well-organized library of information about cancer. In addition to being fully searchable, the site provides a variety of useful menus that help you quickly pinpoint information. Different menus sort information by disease or medical specialty. Others are devoted to cancer causes, screening and prevention; clinical trials; psycho-social support and personal experiences; and cancer FAQs.

★★★★ American Academy of Ophthalmology, www.aao.org

The Web site of the American Academy of Ophthalmology is a wide-ranging site for medical professionals and consumers. An education section features leading journals, peer-reviewed articles and case histories from a variety of sources. Other sections track state and federal legislative and government news of interest to this specialty. Consumers can use the site to search for an ophthalmologist by location, specialty or name.

★★★ American College of Gastroenterology, www.acg.gi.org

There is information here both for physicians and consumers. An interesting feature is the resource index of practice guidelines for gastroenterologists. For consumers, there is general information about common GI diseases.

★★★ DentaLaw Group, www.dentalaw.com

This site, from a consortium of trial lawyers who are also dentists, includes recent dental malpractice cases, a glossary of dental terms, and links to related dental and legal sites.

★★★ Neurotrauma Law Nexus, www.neurolaw.com

This site has general information on the legal aspects of brain and spinal cord injuries, descriptions of common injuries, and a glossary of terms.

★★★ Typing Injury FAQ, www.tifaq.com

If your client suffers repetitive strain injury, this site contains a variety of information about such injuries, resources for dealing with these ailments, and a broad description of products designed to reduce injury risk and symptoms. Sections cover medical resources, ergonomics, workers' compensation, disabilities, and much more. It includes a glossary of key terms.

★★ ACOR, www.acor.org

From this site, sponsored by the Association of Cancer Online Resources, you can search the archives of nearly 100 cancer-related Internet mailing lists. Topics covered by the lists include breast cancer, general cancer, leukemia, colon cancer, esophageal cancers, Hodgkin's disease, kidney cancer, sarcoma, lung cancer, melanoma, myeloma, ovarian cancer, testicular cancer and pediatric cancers. Also at the site are links to a number of patient-oriented Web resources.

★ Southern California Orthopedic Institute, www.scoi.com

At this site, you can get a basic introduction to orthopedic medicine and injuries.

Journals

★★★★★ New England Journal of Medicine, www.nejm.org

Considered among the preeminent medical journals, the NEJM is available in full text online, but only to print subscribers. A free subscription option provides access to articles online six months after publication. Non-subscribers can view each issue's table of contents and view abstracts of the articles. They can purchase individual articles for $10 each or purchase twenty-four hours' access to the entire site for $29. The most current issue is available on the Web every Wednesday at 5 p.m. EST. The subscriber archive includes past issues beginning with the first issue of 1993.

★★★★ Library of the National Medical Society, www.medical-library.org

From Current Clinical Strategies Publishing, this online library provides access to an assortment of medical journals, all for an annual subscription of $9.95. Available titles include Journal of Psychiatry Online, Journal of Emergency Medicine Online, Journal of Family Medicine Online, Journal of AIDS/HIV, Journal of Obstetrics and Gynecology Online and Journal of Pediatric Medicine Online.

★★★★ Priory Lodge Education Ltd., www.priory.com

Priory Lodge publishes international, peer-reviewed journals on a number of topics, including dentistry, psychiatry, chest medicine, general practice, pharmacy, veterinary medicine, anesthesia, and family practice. Each journal has its own Web site, which you can reach from this main page. At each Web site are scientific articles and news. Some also have pages devoted to readers' question or links to related sites.

Medical Illustrations

★★★★★ The Doe Report, www.doereport.com

Launched in February 2000, The Doe Report is a comprehensive medical demonstrative evidence resource, providing graphics, anatomical models and medical research. It contains more than 8,000 proprietary medical-legal exhibits that can be used in demand letters, settlement conferences, arbitration, mediation and trial. The site makes it extremely easy to find what you are looking for. It can be searched by key words, or you can browse by medical topic, medical specialty or body region. The site includes a medical reference library developed in conjunction with the National Institutes of Health with entries on the most common subjects covered in personal injury and medical malpractice law. Once you find an illustration you want, you can customize it by adding your client's name and a title. Prices for medical exhibits range from $99 for a small-format PDF to $399 for a 30" x 40" print. The company also produces custom graphics.

★★★★ LIDO.com, http://lido.com

If you use medical images in your trial practice, Lido.com is well worth a visit. It features a database containing more than 10,000 full-color, handcrafted medical illustrations and reusable exhibits. Each illustration or exhibit can be downloaded directly to the subscriber's PC, where it can be printed or added to a document or presentation. The entire collection of images is fully searchable. Results are displayed

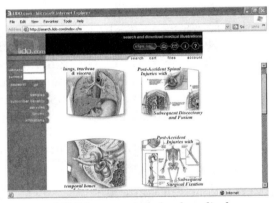

LIDO lets you download medical illustrations such as these samples.

as thumbnail-sized images. Clicking on one produces a larger preview. If it meets your needs, another click downloads it to your computer. The site offers tutorials to assist you in using the images to produce your own trial exhibits. It also provides referrals to medical illustration service providers. Each image costs $35.

★★★★ LifeART, www.lifeart.com

LifeART houses medical clip art, which can be searched and viewed through its site and downloaded in Windows- or Macintosh-compatible image files. Many images are offered in 3-D. Search for an illustration by key word or using drop-down menus for body part, body system or medical specialty. Results are displayed as thumbnail images. Click on one to view a larger version, along with a more detailed description of the image and its purchase price. Images can be purchased individually or as part of a larger specialty collection. Most individual images cost $29.95. LifeART is a division of the medical publisher Lippincott Williams & Wilkins.

★★★★ Whole Brain Atlas, www.med.harvard.edu/AANLIB/home.html

This visually fascinating site is a collection of images of normal and dysfunctional brains. View images of brains that have suffered strokes, tumors and Alzheimer's disease. Sponsored in part by radiologists and neurologists at Brigham and Women's Hospital, Boston, Harvard Medical School and the American Academy of Neurology, the site integrates images from magnetic resonance, X-ray computed tomography and nuclear medicine

★★ Human Anatomy On-Line, www.innerbody.com

This site combines more than 100 illustrations with animations and links to provide an interactive anatomy lesson. A fun but basic introduction to anatomy.

Chapter 23

Non-Legal Web Sites Can Help a Busy Lawyer

---------------------------- **Chapter Contents** ----------------------------

Reference Library
Public Records
Converters and Calculators
Office Help
Travel Help

How do you spell "relief"?

If you don't know, you can find out on the Internet, just by going to the online version of *Merriam-Webster's Collegiate Dictionary*, www.m-w.com. And if, once you've found the word, it's not the right fit, just click the "thesaurus" button to bring up a list of related words.

In fact, the Internet offers relief for all sorts of common questions and tasks that come up in a law office. You can send a package, book a flight, or locate a local courthouse.

Following are some of the non-legal sites that lawyers and other legal professionals are sure to find useful. We have avoided the well-traveled lists of search engines and directories in favor of sites that are slightly off the virtual beaten path.

Reference Library

★★★★★ Bartleby.com, www.bartleby.com

Bartleby.com's mission is to provide its patrons with free access to the most comprehensive selection of reference, verse, fiction and nonfiction works on the Web. Named for Herman Melville's *Bartleby, the Scrivener*, it publishes classic works of literature, nonfiction and reference on the Web, entirely free of charge. While lawyers may wish to spend their unbillable hours browsing Bartleby's collection of poetry, it is the reference collection they will find useful while on the clock. Among the titles it includes are the *Columbia Encyclopedia, Sixth Edition*; *The American Heritage Dictionary of the English Language,* Third Edition; *Roget's II: The New Thesaurus,* Third Edition; *Simpson's Contemporary Quotations*; and *The American Heritage Book of English Usage.* All of these can be searched by key words or browsed by their tables of contents.

★★★★★ **CIA World Factbook,** www.cia.gov/cia/publications/factbook

Find out just about anything about just about anyplace, courtesy of our national intelligence agency, the CIA. The Fact Book has maps, government information, geography, climate, terrain, population, mortality and literacy rates, and lots more for more than 260 different countries throughout the world. This formerly classified document was first made available to the public in 1975, and has been updated every year since. Lawyers can read about a country's constitution, legal system and judiciary.

★★★★★ **Martindale's The Reference Desk,** www.martindalecenter.com

What do you want to know? Whatever it is, you are likely to find the answer here. Exhaustive and up-to-date, Martindale's has thousands of links to everything from online calculators to worldwide postal information. Whether your question relates to medicine, science, air travel, business, computers or education, Martindale's has the links.

★★★★★ **Official City Sites,** http://officialcitysites.org

Official City Sites is a reference directory of officially sanctioned city, town, area, county, regional, Chamber of Commerce, Visitors Bureau, and related Web sites. Use it to find a local tax assessor, police department, or deed registry. Organized alphabetically by locality, it covers city sites in the U.S., Canada, Australia, France, Germany, Japan, New Zealand, the Netherlands and the United Kingdom.

★★★★★ **Oxford English Dictionary,** www.oed.com

The final word on the meaning and history of words is the Oxford English Dictionary. Comprising twenty volumes in print, it can be a bit cumbersome to carry around. The online version, introduced in March 2000, is far more convenient, can be searched with speed and ease, and is updated quarterly with at least 1,000 new entries and revisions. But one similarity the online version has with its print counterpart is that it is not free. A one-year, individual subscription is $295. Monthly subscriptions are available for $29.95. Network licenses start at $795. The print version, by comparison, costs $895. For those on the fence, the OED offers a free tour of its online edition.

★★★★ **Attorney's Toolbox,** www.macattorney.com/tools.html

California lawyer Randy B. Singer assembled this collection that he subtitled, "Cyberspace Tools For Attorneys and Legal Professionals." Using an outline of tasks lawyers commonly perform, Singer links to the sites that can help accomplish them. He covers discovery, legal research, trial preparation, office management and employment, linking to sources for experts and court reporters, background searches and company profiles, legal research and government information, and general office tools and virtual helping hands. Some of the links have become stale, but still a useful resource.

★★★★ DNS411, http://dns411.com

This universal domain name search tool searches all available domain registries, including country codes, new top-level domains, InterNIC handles and IP number block assignments. You can also use it to convert a domain name to its numerical IP address or convert a numerical address to its domain name.

★★★★ Nation Master, www.nationmaster.com

This site, home to a massive library of data on nations throughout the world, makes it easy to statistically and graphically compare nations based on your own specifications. Using a simple form, you can generate maps and graphs with ease on all kinds of statistics, selecting only the countries you want to include. If you would rather, you can simply browse the site's most popular graphs, with statistics showing the world's richest, most populous and most murderous nations.

★★★★ Research-It!, www.iTools.com/research-it

Every so often, you absolutely need to know the source of a quote or the birthday of a famous person. Here's the place to turn with those nagging little questions. It is actually a collection of search tools arranged in six categories: general search tools, language tools, research tools, financial tools, map tools, and Internet tools. Under the language category, there are dictionaries, a thesaurus, translators, conjugators, and anagram creators. The map section helps you find maps and driving directions. Under financial, you can compute currency exchange rates. This site is both useful and fun.

★★★★ U.S. Census Bureau's State and Metropolitan Area Data Book, www.census.gov/statab/www/smadb.html

Facts are a trial lawyer's tools, which makes the latest edition of the *State and Metropolitan Area Data Book* a valuable resource. It contains a variety of statistics on social and economic conditions at the state and local levels. Included are data on population, births and deaths, insurance coverage, housing starts, income, labor union membership, poverty levels, energy expenditures, manufacturing, and other topics. The Web site includes the complete text of the book, which can be viewed or downloaded in Adobe Acrobat format. It also presents several tables comparing state and local census and population statistics.

★★★ Acronym Finder, www.acronymfinder.com

Acronyms—where would lawyers be without them? But if you find yourself confusing the FCC with the UCC, turn to Acronym Finder, a database of more than 160,000 acronyms and their meanings. The site focuses on acronyms from technology, telecommunications, business, government and the military, but is by no means limited to those topics. For example, a search of "JD" yielded not only Doctor of Jurisprudence but also Jack Daniel's and John Deere. It works to find an acronym, as well. You've forgotten the federal agency that regulates securities. Type "securities" for a list of all acronyms that include that word.

★★★ Writers Free Reference, www.writers-free-reference.com

Writers Free Reference is a list of free reference tools useful to writers. It includes maps, encyclopedias, newspapers, quotations, people finders, heads of state, currency converters, grammar guides, anatomy texts, and more. The page is a simple list of references, followed by brief comments.

Public Records

★★★★★ American FactFinder, http://factfinder.census.gov

A service of the U.S. Census Bureau, American Fact Finder is designed to simplify census research. It makes it easy to find social, economic or housing characteristics for any location. Tools help you create various tables—either from predefined templates or using your own preferences—and generate maps illustrating data and statistics. Other sections allow you to research industry and business facts and economic

Ameican FactFinder makes it easy to find social, economic and housing data.

census data. American FactFinder allows you to access data using a variety of methods. Items labeled "quick" help you locate data or generate reports with only a couple of mouse clicks. Other methods help you perform more detailed research or construct more complicated queries.

★★★★★ Vital Records Information, www.vitalrec.com

Vital Records Information tells where to obtain vital records—birth, death and marriage certificates and divorce decrees—from anywhere in the U.S. It lists sources for each state, territory and county, and most cities and towns, along with contact, fee and ordering information. For records outside the U.S., the site lists links to foreign vital records sites. This straightforward site is designed with a nod towards genealogy, but it is one many lawyers are sure to find useful.

Converters and Calculators

★★★★★ Calculators On-Line Center, www.martindalecenter. com/Calculators.html

The most extensive collection of calculators you'll ever need, this site allows you to calculate everything from your personal net worth to the best distribution of grass seed over your lawn to your precise position on the surface of the globe.

★★★ Online Conversion, www.onlineconversion.com

What is your age in dog years? What is the driving distance between any two U.S. cities? How many pinches in a dash? You can convert just about anything to just about anything else at this site, home to more than 8,000 converters and calculators. Converters are organized by type, i.e., length, temperature, speed, volume, etc. This is a site that you will not think you need until you need it. In the meantime, you can have lots of fun.

Office Help

★★★★★ U.S. Postal Service, www.usps.com

In cyber lingo, we call it "snail mail," but since we all still use it every day, the USPS should definitely be on your bookmark list. Here you can use the Postage Calculator to compute the postage for any domestic mailing and some foreign addresses. You can track

The U.S. Postal Service Site offers law offices a variety of useful tools.

that Express Mail you sent yesterday. You can look up the Zip+4 code for any street address. The business section has mail forms for downloading in Adobe Acrobat format and an assortment of business publications online. Now you can even use the Postal Service Web site to pay bills online and create and send bulk mailings.

★★★★ FedEx Airbill Tracking, www.fedex.com/us/tracking

Not to be outdone by the Postal Service, Federal Express lets you track the status of your package any time of day, anywhere in the world. You can even follow your package's journey while it is in transit.

★★★★ Yale Web Style Guide, http://info.med.yale.edu/caim/manual/ contents.html

For lawyers who are considering designing their own Web sites, start here. This simple guide walks you through the process of designing a site that is pleasing to the eye and easy on the modem.

Travel Help

★★★★★ Hotels.com, www.hotels.com

Next trip out of town, book your hotel through Hotels.com, and likely save yourself some money. Launched in April 2002, this is a more user-friendly successor to a suite of sites started by Hotel Reservations Network, a hotel room "consolidator" that reserves rooms in bulk and offers them to consumers at below published rates. HRN's former sites, including HotelDiscounts.com and 180096hotel.com, will eventually be phased out, but users will find the same hotel bargains here. The one drawback is that you must prepay your room. But because HRN buys rooms in advance, it often has rooms still available when no one else does.

★★★★★ MapQuest, www.mapquest.com

It's 11 p.m. and you realize you have no idea of the location of the courthouse that you have to be in at 8:30 the next morning. No need to worry. Key in the address, and this site will create a detailed street map showing the precise location and provide you with precise driving directions. With one click, you can even see an aerial photo of the address. You can e-mail the map to your associate or download it to your Palm or other handheld. MapQuest's Road Trip Planner supplements maps and driving directions with information on hotels along the way and travel guides for your destination. MapQuest also has topographic maps and airport terminal maps.

★★★★★ MSN Maps & Directions, http://maps.msn.com

For many years, MapQuest's primary competitor was MapBlast!, owned by Vicinity Corp. When Microsoft Corp. bought Vicinity, it merged MapBlast! into its own MSN Maps. MSN Maps functions much like MapQuest, with one significant distinction. While MapQuest covers only the U.S., MSN Maps can provide detailed maps for Canada, Mexico and Europe as well, and atlas maps of the entire world.

★★★★★ Travelocity, www.travelocity.com

Can't drive to where you're going? Here's the place to book a flight, reserve a hotel room, and even get information on dining out. This site lets you check schedules and make reservations for 95% of all airline seats sold. Using the "Best Fare Finder," you can search for the lowest fares available between cities. You can also make reservations with some 47,000 hotels and more than fifty car rental companies. Destination guides offer photographs, travel guides, and things to do, including information on restaurants, museums, theaters, golf courses and more.

★★★★ Weather.com, www.weather.com

Whether you are traveling across country or just driving to your office, you will want to know the weather. Here is one of the best places to find what it will be. Key in a zip code and find out all about its weather, complete with maps and predictions.

★★★★ How Far Is It?, www.indo.com/distance

This site will calculate the distance between any two cities in the world. If they are both in the U.S., it will even provide detailed driving directions and draw a map showing the locations of each place.

★★ Local Times Around the World, www.hilink.com.au/times

You know how to get there and what the weather will be like, and you have booked a hotel room, but, what time will it be when you arrive? This guide finds the local time anywhere in the world.

The Not-So-Usual Suspects

Some of the Web sites that may be most interesting to legal professionals defy tidy categories. They are not about a particular topic of law. Some, in fact, are not about the law at all. Some are practical, some fun, others just plain different. Some, such as Yale Law School's Avalon Project, are the result of enormous scholarly and technological achievement. Others, such as the Anagram Genius, are practically useless but eminently entertaining.

These are the sites that, for lawyers, fall slightly off to the side of the information superhighway. Maybe for that reason, they are all the more worth a visit. So, with no particular criteria for selection, here are some sites worth wandering into.

Related to Law

★★★★★ **Bridges,** http://network-lawyers.org/bridges/HomePage

Bridges is a site unlike any other. It is an experimental, interactive, collaborative gathering place for lawyers, CPAs and other professionals. Key to its uniqueness is the ability to not merely read any page, but also add to it, as well as to create whole new pages. For example, starting with the home page, at the bottom is an "edit" link. Click on it, and up comes a form allowing you to add your own comments to the page. What is this good for? The most obvious application is for discussion groups, and Bridges is host to several, mostly focusing on taxation, employee benefits and technology. Beyond discussion groups is the Automation Guide project. In 1991, the American Institute of CPAs published the original guide to automating a tax practice. Realizing the need for an updated version, the AICPA turned to Bridges, where it opened the revision process to all members with access to the Web. Any member can read what has been written so far and contribute changes, ideas and updates. The interactivity of Bridges even allows any visitor to the site to add his or her own Web page. Bridges offers a glimpse into the future of lawyer-to-lawyer collaboration over the Internet.

★★★★★ Construction WebLinks, www.constructionweblinks.com

Created by the San Francisco-based law firm Thelen Reid & Priest, this site aims to be the definitive construction industry portal to the Web. It offers links to thousands of Web sites relevant to the construction and facility management industries. The site is organized into three primary sections: organizations, including trade organizations, government agencies and private businesses; industry topics, such as bidding opportunities, technical data, safety information, building codes and job opportunities; and resources, including online reference materials, travel information and news. All the links are annotated with a brief description of the site. You can explore the categories using the index of topics, or search them all by keywords. This is a well-done and comprehensive site.

★★★★★ Federal Rulemaking, www.uscourts.gov/rules/

Besides courtroom duties, the federal judiciary is responsible for establishing and maintaining the rules governing practice and procedure, and evidence, in the federal courts. This responsibility encompasses a continuing obligation to study the operation and effect of the rules. When changes in the rules seem called for, the Judicial Conference of the U.S. recommends amendments or additions. Using the site, the Judicial Conference posts the complete text of proposed amendments. Conveniently, this site allows those wishing to comment to do so using a Web comment form.

★★★★★ IndexMaster, www.indexmaster.com

IndexMaster is a one-of-a-kind service for reviewing and purchasing legal treatises over the Web. It features a unique database containing the actual indices and tables of contents for thousands of treatises from more than sixty legal publishers. Search the database by keyword, topic, title, author or publisher to find the treatise that most precisely matches your needs. You can then review the actual index or table of contents and read the publisher's notes online. If you like what you see, click "Buy" to order the treatise directly from the publisher. Try the service free for ten days, after which the annual subscription price ranges from $45 for small firms to $595 for the largest.

★★★★★ Internet Tools for Lawyers, www.netlawtools.com

Designed to help attorneys use the Internet in the practice of law, this useful site offers practical sections on legal research, Web site design, mailing lists and software. It also includes a number of articles on creating Web pages and using the Internet, as well as reviews of books and software related to lawyers' use of the Internet. The site is maintained by Netlawtools, Inc., a company founded by practicing lawyer Jerry Lawson. While you are here, check out Lawson's excellent book, *The Complete Internet Handbook for Lawyers*, published by the Law Practice Management Section of the American Bar Association.

★★★★★ National Conference of Commissioners on Uniform State Laws, www.nccusl.org/nccusl/DesktopDefault.aspx

The National Conference is single-minded in its purpose—to study and review state law to determine which areas of law should be uniform, and then, having targeted a topic, to draft and propose specific statutes. The conference can only propose, of course—no uniform law is effective until a state legislature adopts it. But it can nonetheless be controversial, as was proven in 1999 with the debate over its proposed

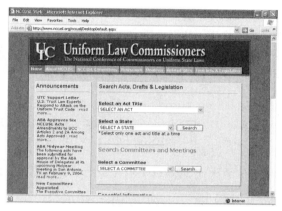

This site is a repository of uniform laws, including in-process drafts and final acts.

Uniform Commercial Code Article 2b. This site is the repository of all this lawmaking, containing all in-process drafts and final acts. Search them by act title, state or committee. They can be read online or downloaded in a choice of word processing or plain text formats. In-process laws are indexed by title and include all draft versions, from the first to the most recent. Drafts of uniform and model acts can also be seen at a companion site maintained by the University of Pennsylvania, http://www.law.upenn.edu/bll/ulc/ulc_frame.htm.

★★★★★ Network-Lawyers, http://groups.yahoo.com/group/network-lawyers

Washington, D.C. lawyer Lewis Rose started Net-Lawyers in 1994 as a discussion list for lawyers, law students, librarians, law professors and others interested in discussing how to use the Internet as a tool in connection with the practice of law, legal research and the growth and development of law and technology. After Rose stopped moderating the list in 2001, it found a home as this Yahoo group. Today, it continues to be a forum for discussing lawyers' use of the Internet, while also helping to promote that use by hosting online seminars and experimenting with Wikis,[1] Web logs ("blogs")[2] and other innovative tools for communication and collaboration. (Note: This author serves as one of the group's moderators.)

★★★★★ Project Diana, www.yale.edu/lawweb/avalon/diana/index.html

From Yale Law School comes this international archive of human rights law, featuring full-text litigation documents and links to reference sites throughout the Internet. Project Diana's archive includes legal briefs, organization charters, treaty texts, and bibliographies relating to a variety of human rights issues and ongoing cases. The entire collection can be searched by keyword and materials are also organized under a subject index. There is an extensive collection of links to human rights materials elsewhere on the Internet. The project is named for former Yale law librarian and human rights scholar Diana Vincent-Daviss.

★★★★★ Wisconsin Supreme Court, www.courts.state.wi.us

"Cool" is not a word one would normally associate with a court's Web site. But it somehow fits the site of the Wisconsin Supreme Court, where visitors can listen to recordings of all oral arguments. Using the RealPlayer software, the court offers full audio of all arguments it has heard since September 1997. New recordings are added shortly after conclusion of the argument. Search for recordings by docket number or argument date. The site is also the official location for both Supreme Court and Court of Appeals opinions. Opinions go back to 1995, and earlier years will eventually be added. Opinions are fully searchable. Included within the site are the courts' calendars, a library of forms for downloading, and general information about the state's court system.

★★★★ Animal Rights Law Project, www.animal-law.org

Rutgers University was the first law school to have animal rights law as part of its regular curriculum. The professors who teach that course and their students created this Web site, which includes course materials as well as selected documents from legal and regulatory proceedings involving animal rights. Among the topics the site covers are the right of a student to object to vivisection or dissection in the classroom; hunting and wildlife

---

[1] A wiki is a type of server software that allows visitors to a Web page to freely add and edit content.

[2] For more about blogs, see Chapter 27 *infra*.

issues; hunter "harassment"; wild horses; animal sacrifices; and animal care committees. The site also houses handbooks concerning freedom of expression and housing issues involving companion animals. In addition, the site includes various essays and journal articles on animal rights and animals and the law, and various state and federal laws and regulations.

★★★★ Lawgirl, www.lawgirl.com

The title is enough to clue you in that this is no ordinary lawyer's Web site. Take a struggling Los Angeles artist, mix in a law degree and a heaping portion of HTML, and you come up with a Web site that combines an interactive copyright tutorial with a music law forum and a Hunk o' the Month award. Jodi L. Sax is an entertainment attorney as well as a designer and Web consultant, and her Web site is one of a kind among lawyers' online.

★★★★ Law School Admission Council, www.lsac.org

The Law School Admission Test—the gateway to a legal education—is made a bit easier thanks to this site. The official LSAT Web site lets prospective law students apply for the test online and download a complete, sample exam. It also provides general information on choosing and applying to a law school and offers various tools for assisting in the process, including one that allows applicants to assess their likelihood of admission to a particular school.

★★★★ The Legal Word Processing Page, http://home.carolina.rr.com/rcbjr/index.html

Formerly known as The Legal WordPerfect page, this site has expanded to accommodate lawyers who use Word as well. The site offers both a number of articles about using WordPerfect and Word as well as more than sixty shareware macros—mostly for WordPerfect—developed by the publisher of this site, attorney/columnist/programmer Richard C. Belthoff, Jr. Among the macros: a judgment interest calculator, a target pleading due date calculator, legal timesheets, fax receipts and telephone memos.

★★★★ National Conference of Bar Examiners, www.ncbex.org

It is our rite of passage as lawyers, our common walk over hot coals. If you are taking the bar for the first time or the fiftieth, the National Conference of Bar Examiners offers a suite of information resources to smooth the way. It includes a detailed guide to the four multistate examinations—multiple choice, essay, professional responsibility, and skills performance—with test dates, study aids, and more. For recent years, the site provides detailed statistics on pass rates, bar admissions, and related information. Another page provides links to each state's bar admissions office.

★★★★ Native American Law, www.nesl.edu/research/native.cfm

Native American law is often overlooked on the Web's many indexes of legal resources. That makes this page, from the New England School of Law, a useful and needed collection. A simple, one-page index organizes links to primary materials, bibliographies, collections of resources, organizations, Indian nations and other aboriginal sites.

★★★★ Resident Agent Information, www.residentagentinfo.com

To serve process upon a company, you first must identify its resident agent—the entity it has designated as its representative in the state. Most states now have Web sites where you can search for resident agents, but finding these sites can be a chore in itself. This site, from Maryland lawyer Terry A. Berger, is a no-nonsense guide to finding this information online, covering all U.S. states, territories and possessions. If the information is not online, Berger tells you how to find it by phone or mail.

★★★★ Severe, www.severe.net

Devoted to Social Security disability benefits and law, this site is the product of Daley, DeBofsky & Bryant, Chicago. For lawyers who practice in this field, this is a soup-to-nuts site, with the text of all laws and regulations, downloadable forms, the Social Security litigation manual, a listing of impairments, and current news.

★★★ Disabled Lawyering Alliance, www.disabledlawyering.org

For his third-year Harvard Law School project in 2002, Carrie Griffin started this site as an online network for lawyers and law students with disabilities. The goal is to bring people together to foster mentoring relationships, professional networking and personal development. The primary way it does this is through online discussion forums devoted to mentoring lawyers and law students. There is also a collection of links and general information on employment and fellowships.

★★★ FindLaw Professional Development Center, http://profdev.lp.findlaw.com

Feeling dissatisfied with your job? Here is a Web site devoted to overcoming lawyer dissatisfaction by helping legal professionals find the position most consistent with their personal values and professional goals. Jointly sponsored by FindLaw and the Center for Professional Development in the Law, which provides career planning, support and guidance for lawyers, the site includes a regular column, a library of articles, and a discussion forum, all devoted to the professional development of lawyers. Ronald W. Fox, a lawyer and career counselor, and Mark L. Byers, a counseling and vocational psychologist, write many of the articles.

★★★ Judicial Clerkships.com, www.judicialclerkships.com

For law students, a judicial clerkship is the Holy Grail. Judicial Clerkships.com aims to help law students "successfully navigate the maze of courts and clerkship opportunities." Thanks to this site, I now know that the federal judiciary maintains a site exclusively for law clerks, the Federal Law Clerk Information System, https://lawclerks.ao.uscourts.gov. The site has active discussion forums, along with some useful links and bits of information. Throughout the site, there are references to the book, *Behind the Bench: The Guide to Judicial Clerkships*, written by Debra Strauss, who maintains the site.

Loosely Related to Law

★★★★★ FedStats, www.fedstats.gov

Quick, what was the median household income in 1995? What percentage of those convicted of federal crimes were sentenced to prison? Where were the ten largest oil spills this year? No matter your area of practice, you are sure to find a use for statistics, whether to bolster an argument or prove a fact. Now, the U.S. government has made finding the statistics you

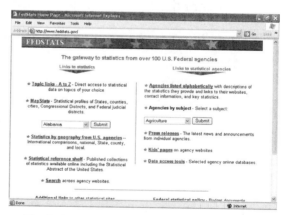

The FedStats Web site brings together statistics from more than 100 federal agencies.

need easier. The FedStats Web site brings together statistics from more than 100 federal agencies, including the Census Bureau, the Bureau of Justice Statistics, the Bureau of Labor Statistics, the Environmental Protection Agency, and many more. The site allows keyword searching of the entire statistical library or by agency. You can also browse a list of agencies and available statistics or a list of press releases relating to statistical compilations. Use the "MapStats" feature to draw statistical profiles of specific geographic regions.

★★★★ Freedom of Information Center, www.missouri.edu/~foi-www

The Freedom of Information Center is an online resource and reference library on issues relating to the free flow of information and the First Amendment. Sponsored by the University of Missouri School of Journalism, the Center specializes in information about the Freedom of Information Act. The site includes links to federal and state FOI laws and related government information and guides to using FOI laws.

★★★★ Robert's Rules of Order, www.robertsrules.com

This is, of course, the leading manual of parliamentary procedure. Whether as a corporate lawyer or a bar association officer, you are likely to come across *Robert's Rules* at some point. You will not find the full text of the rules here—although you can purchase it here. The site is nevertheless useful, with an "Ask the Authors" feature that allows visitors to search an archive of answers to questions of parliamentary procedure. A "Question and Answer Forum" allows any visitor to post a question or an answer, and it is from here that the Ask the Authors questions are selected.

★★★★ The Smoking Gun, www.thesmokinggun.com

Pleadings. Police reports. Bankruptcy petitions. Wills. For lawyers, such court and government documents are the tools of the trade. For The Smoking Gun, they are a source of news and insight, as well as an ever-present reminder that truth is, indeed, stranger than fiction. By combing court files and through Freedom of Information requests, The Smoking Gun's editors dish up a daily dose of documented dirt. Celebrities and politicians are often the subject, but so too are regular folks caught up in unusual situations. The Smoking Gun reproduces the original document, exactly as it appeared in hard copy. It was The Smoking Gun that produced the now-famous 1977 mug shot of Bill Gates, and that published the FBI's 1953 investigation into whether Groucho was a Marxist.

★★★★ Stumpers-L Archive, http://domin.dom.edu/depts/gslis/stumpers

and-

★★★★ Wonderful World of Wombats, www.regiments.org/wombats

Have a question you just cannot find the answer to, despite having consulted every resource you could lay your hands on? If you are stumped, turn

to Stumpers, an e-mail discussion group where reference librarians post questions they have been unable to answer. With more than 1,000 librarians participating worldwide and experts from other fields joining in, Stumpers has been called the world's largest and most versatile reference desk. The group has both an unofficial motto—"Stumpers does the difficult instantly, but the impossible might take a few minutes"—and an unofficial mascot—the wombat. If you wonder, "Why the wombat?" well, ask the Stumpers.

Before you pose a question to the list, you should check the archives, lest the objection, "Asked and answered." All of the list's messages back to 1993 are archived and can be searched by keyword. The archive is maintained by Dominican University in Illinois. The archive can also be explored by reading all of a single month's messages. The site includes a guide to the list and its protocol and a selection of frequently asked questions. There is also an unofficial Stumpers page, Wonderful World of Wombats. You can search the archive from here as well. In addition, you can read "the best of Stumpers" and learn all you would ever want to know about wombats.

On a more practical level, this page provides links to other question-and-answer services on the Internet, as well as "The Wombat Reference Collection," which includes an assortment of FAQs to consult before posting a question to the list.

If the archives do not have the answer, you can post your question to the list. But first you must subscribe. To do this, go to the Stumpers-L Web site and follow the instructions provided there.

One final note—be sure you really are stumped. The etiquette of the list is that, before posting your question, you must have searched diligently for the answer through the usual library and online sources. Only if you remain stumped should you turn to Stumpers. And if you are not a librarian yourself, the list's rule of thumb is: "Please ask one your question before you post to Stumpers. Your public library's reference desk is often only a phone call away."

★★★★ Television News Archive, http://tvnews.vanderbilt.edu

In preparing their cases, lawyers sometimes need to recreate what happened on a particular date. Since 1968, Vanderbilt University's Television News Archive has systematically recorded, abstracted and indexed the nightly newscasts of ABC, CBS and NBC. Its collection now holds more than 30,000 individual network evening news broadcasts and more than 9,000 hours of special news-related programming, including Nightline broadcasts since 1989. Abstracts of all those broadcasts are available at this Web site. They can either be browsed by date or searched by subject. If need be, you can order the video by e-mail.

Not Even Remotely Related to Law

★★★ Anagram Genius, www.anagramgenius.com

An anagram, in case you have forgotten, is a rearrangement of the letters of one word or phrase to form another word or phrase. Often, these rearrangements can be humorous and even telling. Rearranging the letters of "the tobacco industry," for example, yields "botchy tar seduction." "William Jefferson Clinton" gives way to "Clown joins female in flirt." Wonder what your name would produce? Visit this site, complete a short form, and anagrams of your name, or whatever phrase you provide, will be sent to you by e-mail. If you become hooked on anagrams, you can download the software to your own computer for a fee of $39.95, and generate endless sets of amusing phrases. The site's archive collects some of the gems created by others. A totally useless but absorbingly fun site.

★★★ Death Clock, www.deathclock.com

There you sit, burning the midnight oil, polishing off that pleading, your mind measuring the moments remaining before tomorrow morning's filing deadline. As lawyers, we focus so intently on the string of deadlines we face each day that we lose sight of the farther horizon, of that final deadline we all must someday meet. To regain some of this lost perspective, pay a visit to the Death Clock. Feed it your birth date and gender, and it will tell you your date of death and begin counting the seconds you have remaining. Once you know this deadline, the others might seem less ominous.

★ Bill Gates Personal Wealth Clock, http://philip.greenspun.com/WealthClock

"If you want to know what God thinks about money, just look at the people He gives it to." So says an old Irish saying that serves as the motto of this site. Its purpose, plain and simple: to track the Microsoft chairman's wealth at any given moment, as well as each U.S. citizen's personal contribution to Bill's bottom line. What does it have to do with law? Absolutely nothing, but entertaining nonetheless.

Chapter 25

Managing Knowledge Management Via the Web

Chapter Contents ---

Starting Points
Web Logs
Articles

Knowledge is information that has been processed by the human brain, the product of raw data filtered through learning and experience.

In law firms it abounds. But while firms, thanks to technology, have become pretty good at managing information, they only recently turned their attention to mining and managing the knowledge they produce so that it can be shared within the firm.

For lawyers looking for information about this burgeoning field of knowledge management, the obvious place to turn is the Web. A growing number of sites provide entrée to legal KM. Here is a sampling.

Starting Points

★★★★★ Curve Consulting, www.curveconsulting.com

Curve is a consulting firm focusing on knowledge management in the legal profession. Its chief executive, Gretta Rusanow, is a lawyer and author of the book *Knowledge Management and the Smarter Lawyer*. Curve's site presents an overview of KM in law firms and legal departments. It includes a library of articles and presentations by Rusanow and others about KM in the legal field.

★★★★★ KMWiki, www.voght. com/cgi-bin/pywiki?KmWiki

It should come as no surprise that professionals in the field of knowledge management have a compulsive urge to share knowledge. That may explain why one of the best gateways to KM resources on the Web is the KMWiki. What, you might ask, is a wiki? It is a type

The KMWiki is one of the best gateways to KM resources on the Web.

of server software that allows visitors to a Web page to freely add and edit content. "Open editing," as it is sometimes called, allows people with common interests to share information and ideas easily in a single Web location. The KMWiki, while little more than a collection of links to KM resources elsewhere on the Web, stands out because, unlike other collections of links, it is the product of not one person but of the various KM professionals who contribute to it. It is a modest looking page that accurately calls itself a "super index."

★★★★★ KMWorld, www.kmworld.com

Companion to the magazine of the same name, this site offers full-text articles from its pages dating back to 1998, along with a collection of white papers focusing on best practices in various industries and a "Knowledge Community" for online discussions of KM issues. The site's focus is broad, but it includes a number of articles on KM in the legal field. To find them most easily, search "law" and scroll through the resulting list.

★★★★★ Knowledge Management Resource Center, www.llrx. com/intranets_and_knowledge_management.html

From LLRX.com comes this broad array of articles about legal KM. This is a collection of some fifty original articles about KM, written by KM professionals, lawyers, law librarians, and other experts. The Resource Center includes a useful index of links to KM articles published elsewhere on the Web as well as to books and Web sites related to the topic.

★★★★ KMNetwork.com, www.kmnetwork.com

From the Brint Institute, New York, N.Y., this may be the most comprehensive KM portal on the Web. It provides links to books, journal articles, tools, content portals, case studies, research and more. Unfortunately, its cluttered and chaotic organization makes it difficult for a user to home in on relevant information, and its search engine proves little help.

★★★★ KnowledgeBoard, www.knowledgeboard.com

For a broad look at KM with a European bent, visit a wide-ranging collection of original editorial materials, resource libraries, discussion boards and links.

★★★★ Knowledge Management for Lawyers Resource Center, www.denniskennedy.com/kmlaw.htm

For a KM index that is focused on the legal field, start with this collection of links compiled by Dennis M. Kennedy, a lawyer and technology consultant in St. Louis, Missouri. Along with links to nearly fifty legal KM resources, Kennedy includes two useful "primers" he wrote on KM in the legal profession.

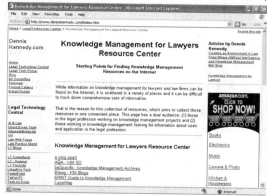

Lawyer Dennis Kennedy offers a useful collection of links to legal KM resources.

★★★ New York State Bar Association Knowledge Management Resources, www.nysba.org/Content/NavigationMenu/Attorney_Resources/Practice_Management/Knowledge_Management/Knowledge_Management1.htm

Part of the Practice Management section of the NYSBA's Web site, this page houses a small collection of articles about legal KM.

Web Logs

Web logs and knowledge managers are natural partners, with their shared focus on making knowledge and ideas widely available through easy-to-use platforms. In fact, KM professionals have their own genre of blog,[1] the K-log.

★★★★★ Blawg Links Directory, www.blawg.org

One way to find blogs that focus on KM and to track new ones is through this site, an index of law-related blogs. Follow the link for the "Research and KM" category to browse them.

★★★★★ Excited Utterances, http://excitedutterances.blogspot.com

Among the "kloggers," as KM bloggers call themselves, are some who focus on the legal field. Prominent among them is Joy London, knowledge manager at Allen & Overy, whose blog tracks KM news and developments at law firms throughout the world.

---

[1] For more about blogs, see Chapter 27 *infra*.

★★★★ How Do You Know That?, http://nycsmith.blogspot.com

Christopher Smith works in knowledge management at an unidentified "major law firm" in New York. His blog focuses on KM and legal technology, and touches along the way on topics ranging from New York to movies.

★★★★ tins, www.rklau.com/tins

KM is a frequent topic of Rick Klau's blog, where he also discusses legal technology, marketing, business strategy, and a host of related topics. Klau, a non-practicing lawyer who has focused his career on the intersection of law and technology, organizes postings to his blog by topic, making it simple to find all that pertain to KM.

Articles

Informative articles on KM in the legal profession can be found in various locations on the Web. Some worth a read are:

- "Knowledge Management in the Law Firm," www.wendytech. com/articlesknowledgemgt.htm, by legal technology writer Wendy R. Leibowitz.
- "The Power of Knowledge Management," www.law.com/jsp/ statearchive.jsp?type=Article&oldid=ZZZIKV58HLC, a collection of articles from *Corporate Counsel* magazine on KM at in-house legal departments.
- "Law in Order," www.cio.com/archive/040100_law.html, a case study from *CIO* magazine of a KM initiative at the Washington, D.C. firm Dickstein Shapiro Morin & Oshinsky.
- "Uncommon Knowledge: The KM Questions for Service Firms," www.mahlab.com.au/files/Professional_Review_Knowledge_ Management.pdf, an extract from the forthcoming book by Matthew Parsons, *Effective Knowledge Management for Law Firms*.
- "Global Law Firm Knowledge Management Survey Report," www.curveconsulting.com/pages/Presentations/Key%20Findings.p df, findings of a survey of sixteen large U.S., U.K. and Australian firms conducted by Curve Consulting, New York, N.Y.
- "A Stages of Growth Model for Knowledge Management Technology in Law Firms," http://elj.warwick.ac.uk/jilt/02-2/gottschalk.html, by Petter Gottschalk, professor at the Norwegian School of Management, published in the Journal of Information, Law & Technology.

Chapter 26

Preserving Legal History and Culture

———————————— **Chapter Contents** ————————————

Legal History
U.S. Legal History
Slavery and the Law
Law and Popular Culture

For historians, preservationists and chroniclers of popular culture, the Web is at once an archive and a showcase. It is a place where faded and crumbling historical documents can be preserved in digital format. It is a place where history can be recorded and presented for all to see.

Those who chart the history of law and the role of law through the ages are building invaluable historical archives online. From ancient Greece to the Magna Carta, from the origins of the common law to contemporary jurisprudence, Web sites document and explore the rule of law and the role of law.

This chapter looks at sites that explore the history of law from its earliest recorded beginnings, and then moves on to sites that focus on the legal history of the United States. The chapter concludes with sites that focus on the portrayal of law in popular fiction, film, drama and television.

Legal History

★★★★★ Avalon Project, www.yale.edu/lawweb/avalon/avalon.htm

Yale Law School's Avalon Project publishes on the Web historical documents from the fields of law, economics, politics, diplomacy and government. Materials span ancient Greece to contemporary times, and include such pre-Eighteenth Century documents as the Athenian Constitution by Aristotle, the Code of Hammurabi and the Magna Carta. Documents are organized by century, as well as by author, subject and title. Documents are also grouped into major thematic collections, such as "American Diplomacy: Multilateral Treaties 1864-1999," and "Nuremberg War Crimes Trial." The entire site can be searched using keywords. The project's scope is wide-ranging and ambitious. The directors of the site say they intend not merely to post these documents but also to add value by linking to supporting documents referred to in the posted documents.

★★★★★ **Bracton Online,** http://hlsl.law.harvard.edu/bracton/index.htm

Thirteenth Century English judge Henry of Bracton is credited with compiling *De Legibus et Consuetudinibus Angliae*—an attempt to describe rationally the whole of English law—five hundred years before Blackstone ever sat down to write his *Commentaries*. Although Bracton's authorship is subject to question, the work remains invaluable to legal scholars. Now, the Ames Foundation, the Harvard Law School library, and Cornell University's Legal Information Institute have published this treatise on the Web, in both its original Latin and in English translation. It can be browsed or searched in either language, and an optional framed version simultaneously shows both the Latin and English texts.

★★★★★ **Nuremberg Trials Project: A Digital Document Collection,** http://nuremberg.law.harvard.edu

The Harvard Law School Library hosts this Web site devoted to analysis and digitization of documents relating to the Nuremberg Trials. The project is devoted to preserving and expanding access to the library's 1 million pages of documents relating to the trials of Nazi Germany's military and political leaders. The documents—which include trial transcripts, briefs, document books, evidence files and other papers—became too fragile to be handled, so the library began to digitize them and will make them available on the Web in stages. The first stage provides 6,755 pages of documents relating to the Medical Case, which was the first of the trials conducted by the Nuremberg Military Tribunals (U.S.A. v. Karl Brandt et al.), as well as analysis of many documents relating to the second (U.S.A. v. Erhard Milch) and fourth (U.S.A. v. Oswald Pohl et al.) cases. The Medical Case, held in 1946-1947, involved twenty-three defendants accused of organizing and participating in war crimes and crimes against humanity in the form of harmful or fatal medical experiments and other medical procedures.

U.S. Legal History

★★★★★ **A Century of Lawmaking for a New Nation: U.S. Congressional Documents and Debates 1774-1873,** http://lcweb2. loc.gov/ammem/amlaw/lawhome.html

Beginning with the Continental Congress in 1774 and continuing through the forty-second Congress in 1873—the year in which the Government Printing Office began publishing the Congressional Record—our national lawmakers maintained records of their pro- ceedings. Together, they form a rich documentary history of the construction of the nation and the development of the federal gov- ernment. Thanks to the Library of Congress, these records are avail-

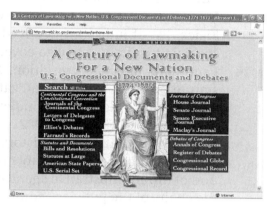

From the Library of Congress comes this collection of early U.S. legislative materials.

able online in a linked set. The collection offers the records of the Continental Congress, the Constitutional Convention and ratification debates, and the first forty-two federal congresses, 1774-1873. It includes the Journals of the Continental Congress (1774-1789), the Records of the Federal Convention of 1787, and the Debates in the Several State Conventions on the Adoption of the Federal Constitution (1787-1788); the Journals of the House of Representatives (1789-1873) and the Senate (1789-1873), including the Senate Executive Journal (1789-1873); the Journal of William Maclay (1789-1791), senator from Pennsylvania in the first Congress; the debates of Congress as published in the Annals of Congress (1789-1821), the Register of Debates (1824-1837), and The Congressional Globe (1833-1873); and the Statutes at Large (1789-1873). The collection continues to grow, and now includes the complete U.S. Serial Set.

★★★★★ **History of the Federal Judiciary,** www.fjc.gov/history/ home.nsf

Part of the larger Federal Judicial Center's Web site, History of the Federal Judiciary is a basic reference source for information about the history of the federal courts and the judges who have served on them since 1789. Of most practical use to practicing lawyers is the access it provides to the Federal Judges Biographical Database, containing entries for more than 2,800 indi- viduals who have served as federal District, Circuit, and Court of Appeals judges, as well as Supreme Court justices. The record for each judge includes information on the nomination and confirmation process and service on the federal courts. Other parts of this site are:

- Courts of the Federal Judiciary, with a legislative history of every District Court, Circuit Court and Court of Appeals as well as a chronological list of judges who served on each court. Article III courts of special jurisdiction are also covered.
- Landmark Judicial Legislation, containing the text of twenty-one statutes related to the organization and jurisdiction of the federal judiciary, ranging from the Judiciary Act of 1789 to the law establishing the Federal Circuit in 1982.
- Topics in Federal Judicial History, presenting various reference materials, including a list of notable records of judicial service, a description of the administrative agencies that have served the judiciary, and the chairs of the judiciary committees in Congress.
- Courthouse Photograph Exhibit, displaying photographs of thirty-five courthouses constructed under the direction of the Office of the Supervising Architect of the Department of the Treasury between 1852 and 1939.

★★★★★ Indian Affairs: Laws and Treaties, http://digital.library.okstate.edu/kappler

Published in 1904 by the U.S. Government Printing Office, *Indian Affairs: Laws and Treaties*, edited by Charles J. Kappler, was a seven-volume compilation of U.S. treaties, laws and executive orders pertaining to Native American tribes. The volumes cover U.S. government treaties with Native Americans from 1778-1883 (Volume II) and U.S. laws and executive orders concerning Native Americans from 1871-1970 (Volumes I, III-VII). In May 1996, the Oklahoma State University Library began a project to convert 150 pages of text from Volume II to a digital format, maintaining as much as possible the appearance of the original work while allowing for full-text indexing. These pages included all of the pre-removal treaties of the five tribes most significant to Oklahoma: Cherokee, Chickasaw, Choctaw, Creek and Seminole. In 1999, with new funding provided by the Coca-Cola Foundation, the library took up where it left off, converting the remaining text from Volume II and continuing with Volumes I and III. Volume II is available in its entirety through this site, with Volumes I and III still in process, but partially available.

★★★★★ **The Religious Liberty Archive,** www.churchstatelaw.com

Religious freedom as it has played out in courts and legislatures is the focus of this unique Web site from the Denver law firm Rothgerber Johnson & Lyons. The site is a virtual library of religious freedom law, housing the full texts of pertinent Supreme Court cases since 1815, commentary on the cases, federal and state laws, treatises and historical materials. News of recent developments and links to related materials round out the site.

★★★★ **Cases & Materials on American Federalism,** www.agh-attorneys.com/3_camo_contents.htm

Indiana lawyer Douglas G. Amber has now published the sixth edition of this online textbook he wrote for the American government classes he teaches at Purdue University Calumet. Although he wrote the text for college freshmen, Amber, a partner with Amber, Golding & Hofstetter, Munster, relies heavily on original source documents and court opinions, making it of value to anyone with an interest in federalism and its origins. The text covers such topics as American socio-political heritage, constitutional beginnings, and the consequences of federalism. Each chapter is an outline, with links to full-text cases and documents.

Slavery and the Law

★★★★★ Historical Records Project, http://stlcourtrecords.wustl.edu

In 1819, a woman slave named Winny filed a lawsuit in St. Louis Circuit Court that would establish an important judicial precedent. Winny sought freedom for herself and her children, charging one Phebe Whitesides with trespass, assault and battery and false imprisonment. On February 13, 1822, a jury agreed and the court declared Winny and her children free. Whitesides appealed to the Missouri Supreme Court, which upheld the verdict, establishing as law that slaves who had once resided in a free territory or state were to be freed.

Between 1814 and 1860, nearly 300 of these freedom suits were filed in the St. Louis court. Now, thanks to that court's Historical Records Project, the records of these freedom suits are available online. They include Winny v. Whiteside as well as the original Dred Scott case. The files displayed here show the original, tattered, handwritten papers, among them an array of petitions, affidavits, depositions, summonses, motions, jury instructions, and evidentiary papers, all documenting these petitioners' fights for freedom.

The freedom cases are a significant feature of the project's Web site, but by no means all it contains. The archive includes all the court's records from

1804 to 1875, most of which involve, as the site itself describes it, "civil suits brought by ordinary men and women pursuing justice in disputes over debts, damages and broken promises." But another collection worthy of note is devoted to Lewis and Clark. It consists of eighty-two court actions in which Meriwether Lewis, William Clark or other members of their Corps of Discovery were parties or prominent actors. Most of these cases are disputes concerning promissory notes, debts, and the payment and assignment of notes and debts.

★★★★★ Slaves and the Courts, 1740-1860 http://memory.loc. gov/ammem/sthtml

From the Library of Congress comes this collection of 105 pamphlets and books published between 1772 and 1889 illustrating the legal difficulties experienced by slaves in America. The documents, drawn mostly from the Law Library and the Rare Book and Special Collections Division of the Library of Congress, deal with cases, reports, arguments, accounts, examinations of cases and decisions, proceedings, journals, a

This Library of Congress site explores the legal difficulties experienced by slaves in America.

letter, and works of historical importance. Search the collection by keyword, or browse by subject, author or title. Documents can be viewed as images or as text.

Law and Popular Culture

★★★★ Famous Cases, www.courttv.com/trials/famous

Court TV has assembled and published on the Web materials from some of the more notorious trials it has covered. Among the trials it includes are those of the Unabomber, British nanny Louise Woodward, Timothy McVeigh, sportscaster Marv Alpert, the Menendez brothers, and Bosnia Serb Dusko Tadic. The site includes a complete history of each case, selected pleadings and rulings, selected trial transcripts, transcripts of on-air interviews, and even Marv Alpert's DNA test results.

★★★★ Law in Popular Culture, www.law.utexas.edu/lpop

Lawyers have been fodder for literature at least since the time of Shakespeare. Now, a Web site documents the depiction of lawyers in books and movies. Based on the Law in Popular Culture collection of the Tarlton Law Library at the University of Texas at Austin, the site provides an extensive bibliography, listing more than 200 works of fiction, humor, plays, pulp and comics, as well as a filmography of more than 600 feature films. The primary criterion for an item's inclusion is that it must either include a lawyer as a central character or have been authored by a lawyer. Many of the books are available through interlibrary loan programs. The site includes a gallery of movie posters and stills as well as links to related Web sites.

★★★ Picturing Justice, www.usfca.edu/pj/index.html

Do movies and television strengthen the public's understanding of law and justice? Picturing Justice is a Web site devoted to discussing that question. It does so by publishing commentaries that focus on how law, lawyers and legal issues are treated in movies, on television and even in computer programs. Commentaries are written by staff editors and outside contributors. Visitors to the site can add their own comments to the discussions of particular movies or programs. It is sponsored by the University of San Francisco School of Law.

Chapter 27

Web Logs: Practical, Political and Polemical

—————————————— Chapter Contents ——————————————

Blog Indexes
Law and Practice
Topics of Law
Legal Research and Technology
Legal and Political Punditry

The number of Web logs—called "blogs" or, in the legal field, "blawgs"—has grown dramatically. Personal Web pages, formatted to resemble online journals, they range in content from introspectively personal to pungently political.

But many bloggers see themselves as a kind of new journalist, reporting and commenting on current events in a single stroke. This is true of many of the lawyers with blogs, some of whom have built up loyal followings of readers who look to them to report current developments in a field and, at the same time, to provide perspective.

This chapter introduces three tools for locating law-related blogs, and then surveys some of the more noteworthy Web logs being written by lawyers and legal professionals. I have arranged them under four general categories:

- Law and practice. Blogs that deliver general news and commentary on law and law practice.
- Topics of law. Blogs that deliver news and commentary on topics related to particular practice areas.
- Legal research and technology. Blogs that focus on legal research and law office technology.
- Legal and political punditry. Blogs by lawyers that deliver news and commentary on broader social and political issues.

Blogs vary widely in their content, reflecting the interests and intellect of each individual blogger. Given this, this chapter forgoes the ratings applied to sites elsewhere in this book. All of the blogs listed below are at least worth a first look; after that, the reader is left to choose his or her favorites.

Blog Indexes

Blogs have established themselves as legitimate sources of legal news and information. But tracking the topics they cover remains cumbersome. Either you must follow them religiously or take your chances with a general search engine such as Google.

Three sites address this problem, helping legal professionals zero in on law-related Web logs.

Blawg.org, www.blawg.org

This useful site organizes law-related blogs into a hierarchical, topical index. Find blogs by drilling down through listings for legal subjects, legal research, state law, federal law, law students, and many others. Or search all listings by keyword.

Blawg Search, http://blawgs.detod.com

This site allows you to search across the full text of a variety of blogs. You can also use it to view all postings for a selected blog. The front page aggregates the latest blog headlines. It is operated by Detod Communications, a company that has built online communities for the Oklahoma Bar Association and the National Association of Bar Executives. Eventually, Blawg Search will be part of a larger site, which a Detod principal describes as "a legal portal like no other."

Daily Whirl, www.dailywhirl.com

For a quick review of daily headlines from law-related news and information sites, go here. It snags the headlines from a range of legal Web logs and news sources and displays them on a single page. You can customize the configuration, meaning that you can select the blogs you want displayed and your preferred font size, background color and number of columns. This comes from the same folks in St. Louis, Missouri who offer Daily Rotation, www.dailyrotation.com, a similar site with headlines from more than 190 tech sites.

Law and Practice

Many of the best blogs come from practicing lawyers who are as likely to discuss their day in court as their new baby or their favorite book. They remind us through their writing that the practice of law is only one component of a lawyer's life well lived.

Bag and Baggage, http://bgbg.blogspot.com.

A handful of lawyers seem to show up on everybody's short list of must-read bloggers. Denise M. Howell is one. A Los Angeles appellate and IP lawyer, she offers clever and insightful commentary on the news, other blogs, her practice areas, and life in general.

beSpacific, www.bespacific.com.

Sabrina I. Pacifici, founder of LLRX.com, provides daily news reports covering law and technology. This blog stands out for its consistency, accuracy and usefulness.

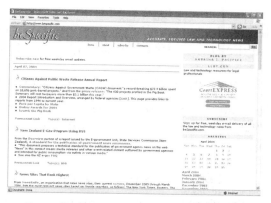

From the founder of LLRX.com, beSpecific provides daily law and technology news.

DeLawOffice.com, www.delaw office.com/news.html.

Larry D. Sullivan, a general practice lawyer in Delaware, and William Slawski, an Internet businessman and non-practicing lawyer, write about Delaware law as well as about the Web, the day's headlines, and the practice of law.

Ernie the Attorney, http://ernieattorney.typepad.com.

Maybe it's the clever name, but more likely it's the compelling content that has made Ernest E. Svenson, a partner with Gordon Arata McCollam Duplantis & Eagan, New Orleans, one of the most popular law-related bloggers. He writes generally about law, law practice, legal technology, and the Web.

New Orleans Lawyer Ernest E. Svenson is one of the most popular law-related bloggers.

EthicalEsq. & haikuEsq., http://blogs.law.harvard.edu/ethicalesq.

David Giacalone, a retired attorney in upstate New York, writes thoughtfully about legal ethics . . . and about haiku. Why lawyers and haiku? Visit his site to find out.

How Appealing, http://appellateblog.blogspot.com.

Thanks to Howard J. Bashman, chair of the Appellate Group at Philadelphia's Buchanan Ingersoll, this is one of the best resources on the Web for tracking appellate litigation throughout the U.S.

Jurist's Paper Chase, http://jurist.law.pitt.edu/paperchase.

To call this excellent site a blog is misleading—it's more like a daily newspaper for the legal profession, providing news, commentary, event listings, court dockets, and much more. It is operated by Bernard Hibbitts, professor at the University of Pittsburgh School of Law.

LawMeme, http://research.yale.edu/lawmeme.

Yale Law School's Information Society Project operates this blog, subtitled "Legal Bricolage for a Technological Age," delivering law and technology news and commentary.

LessigBlog, http://cyberlaw.stanford.edu/lessig/blog.

Stanford Law School Professor Lawrence Lessig discusses cyberlaw, intellectual property, the Internet, and whatever else he chooses.

MyShingle.com, http://myshingle.com.

Washington, D.C. lawyer Carolyn Elefant writes this site for and about solos and small firms. More than a simple blog, Elefant intends the site to be a resource for lawyers to exchange advice, seek guidance or find local counsel in other jurisdictions.

SCOTUSblog, www.goldsteinhowe.com/blog/index.cfm.

Published by the Washington, D.C. firm Goldstein & Howe, this is the only blog devoted to tracking litigation before the United States Supreme Court.

Statutory Construction Zone, www.statconblog.blogspot.com.

This innovative blog from Washington, D.C. lawyer Gary O'Connor analyzes current federal cases that involve matters of statutory construction. For each case, he sets out the statute construed, the court's conclusion, and the statutory construction tools used by the court.

TalkLeft, www.talkleft.com.

An unabashedly left-leaning look at the law and politics of crime from Denver lawyer Jeralyn Merritt.

Topics of Law

Through blogging, lawyers who practice in particular fields of law serve as significant sources of news and commentary on developments in their fields.

Blog 702, http://www.daubertontheweb.com/blog702.html.

Philadelphia lawyer Peter B. Nordberg maintains this blog to accompany his site Daubert on the Web (http://www.daubertontheweb.com/) and track developments in the field.

CopyFight: The Politics of IP, www.copyfight.org.

Donna Wentworth, an affiliate of Harvard Law School's Berkman Center for Internet Law and Society, tracks legal rulings, Capitol Hill policy-making, technical standards development and technological innovation that relate to intellectual property and the Internet.

Election Law, http://electionlawblog.org.

Richard Hasen, professor of law, and William M. Rains, fellow at Loyola Law School in Los Angeles, write this blog focused on election law, campaign finance, redistricting, and related legislation.

GrepLaw, http://grep.law.harvard.edu.

Another blog from Harvard's Berkman Center for Internet Law and Technology, it follows Internet law developments throughout the world.

HIPAA blog, http://hipaablog.blogspot.com.

Jeffery P. Drummond, a partner with Jackson Walker, Dallas, comments on the policy and politics of medical privacy and the Health Insurance Portability and Accountability Act.

icann.Blog, http://icann.blog.us.

A nationally known writer and commentator on Internet law, San Francisco lawyer Bret A. Fausett maintains this excellent blog about ICANN, the Internet domain name authority.

ICANNWatch, www.icannwatch.org.

A pioneering group of Internet law scholars collaborate to maintain this blog. They include Temple University Law Professor David Post, Wayne State Law Professor Jonathan Weinberg, University of Miami Law Professor A.

Michael Froomkin, and Milton Mueller, associate professor at the Syracuse University School of Information Studies.

Jottings By An Employer's Lawyer, http://employerslawyer.blog spot.com.

A management-side employment lawyer with the Texas firm Haynes and Boone, Michael W. Fox highlights important employment law developments and adds the perspective of a practitioner.

KinsellaLaw, www.kinsellalaw.com.

N. Stephan Kinsella, a patent attorney in Houston, Texas, reports on developments in patent law and comments on resources and findings of interest to patent lawyers.

Securities Litigation Watch, http://seclitblog.typepad.com.

Bruce Carton, executive director of Securities Class Action Services, writes about developments involving securities litigation and securities law enforcement.

Tech Law Advisor, http://techlawadvisor.com.

A blog devoted to copyright, trademark, parody, fair use and technology legal issues, from lawyer Kevin J. Heller, a lawyer in New York City.

The Manifest Border, http://manifestborder.com.

Randy Tunac publishes this blog focused on U.S. immigration law and policy.

The Trademark Blog, www.trademarkblog.com.

New York City lawyer Martin Schwimmer writes this blog providing news about trademarks and domain names.

Tillers on Evidence, http://jurist.law.pitt.edu/views/blogs/tillers/index.htm.

Cardozo Law School Professor Peter Tillers blogs the latest developments in the field of evidence.

VoteLaw, www.votelaw.com/blog.

This informative blog is part of a larger Web site devoted to the topic of voting law, from Birmingham, Alabama lawyer Edward Still. He covers elections, voting rights, campaign finance and other topics.

Legal Research and Technology

Bloggers are, by nature, technology-friendly. So it is both expected and fortunate that many of them use their blogs to share their knowledge of online research and legal technology.

DennisKennedy.blog, www.denniskennedy.com/blog.

Dennis Kennedy, a lawyer and legal technology expert in St. Louis, Missouri, offers his musings on legal technology, technology law, and whatever else strikes him.

Digital Practice of Law, http://arkfeld.blogs.com/dpl.

Michael R. Arkfeld, a lawyer and author of the book *The Digital Practice of Law*, writes this blog, which he describes as "a daily digest of cases, comments and practical references for applying technology to the practice of law."

eLawyer Blog, www.elawyerblog.org.

This group-written blog is targeted at using technology and the Internet to enhance the delivery of legal services to moderate- and low-income Americans.

ESQlawtech, www.lawyer-lounge.com/lawtech.php.

Glenn K. Garnes writes this Web log about legal technology as part of a larger site devoted to law office technology, management and marketing.

The focus of this blog is on using technology to enhance the delivery of legal services.

Excited Utterances, http://excitedutterances.blogspot.com.

Devoted to "a sociological and psychological perspective of law firm knowledge management," this blog by Joy London, knowledge manager at a large law firm, provides commentary along with a number of links to useful articles and other Web sites.

Inter Alia, www.inter-alia.net.

Tom Mighell publishes the informative electronic newsletter, "Internet Legal Research Weekly," and maintains this companion blog to provide timely updates of new Web sites and legal research tools.

Netlawblog, www.fedlawyers.org/netlawblog.

Jerry Lawson, a lawyer and legal technology expert, writes this consistently informative and insightful blog about Internet tools for lawyers.

Rory Perry's Weblog, http://radio.weblogs.com/0103705.

As Clerk of the Supreme Court of Appeals of West Virginia, Rory Perry is well situated to examine the interplay among law, technology and the courts. That is what he does here, covering electronic filing, case management, and more.

Strategic Legal Technology, www.prismlegal.com/wordpress.

Ron Friedmann, founder of Prism Legal Consulting and former chief information officer of Mintz Levin Cohn Ferris Glovsky & Popeo, writes this insightful blog about legal technology.

TVCAlert, www.virtualchase.com/tvcalert/index.html.

Genie Tyburski, a law librarian who maintains the legal research Web site The Virtual Chase, reports on law, legal research and legal technology through this daily bulletin.

Unintended Consequences, www.dougsimpson.com/blog.

Connecticut lawyer Doug Simpson writes about "the collision of law, networks and disruptive technologies."

Legal and Political Punditry

When Trent Lott resigned as Senate Republican leader, several political observers attributed his downfall to the criticism leveled at him through the "blogosphere."

Prominent among the bloggers credited with forcing Lott to resign was Glenn Reynolds, law professor at the University of Tennessee, who comments on current events through his blog, appropriately named InstaPundit, www.instapundit.com. Reynolds has written two books and contributed op-eds to national newspapers, but it is his blog, more than anything else, that has put him in the limelight.

Many lawyers, like Reynolds, publish blogs that may touch on the law, but are by no means preoccupied with it. Some are political, some are polemical, some offer parody, and some gaze at their own navels, but all are interesting in their own ways.

American Constitution Society, http://americanconstitutionsoci-ety. blogspot.com.

A blog by and for members of the American Constitution Society.

BurtLaw's Law and Everything Else, www.lawandeverythingelse.com.

After more than twenty-five years in the Minnesota Supreme Court clerk's office, Burton R. Hanson lost his campaign in 2000 to be elected the court's chief justice. Now he writes, often with humor and irony, about law and its connections to just about everything.

Cyberspaces: Words-Not-Deeds, www.cyberspaces.org/webzine.

Rod Dixon lectures about the intersection of law and technology at Rutgers University School of Law. In his blog, he comments on current developments in technology, new media and the law.

Decnavda's Dialectic, http://decnavda.blogspot.com.

California lawyer Tim Carter writes about tax law, politics and philosophy.

Dilan Esper's Blog, http://dilan.blogspot.com.

A business litigator with the Los Angeles firm Stein & Flugge, Dilan A. Esper writes intelligently about "politics, society, feminism, sex, law and anything else."

explodedlibrary.info, http://explodedlibrary.typepad.com/salonblog.

Morgan Wilson, a law librarian at Hamline University, considers the "explosion" of libraries onto the Internet and what this means for information consumers.

Howling Point, http://howlingpoint.net/life.

A former State Department counterintelligence officer, San Diego solo practitioner Charles E. Hartley is a beach-loving lawyer with the motto "No shirt, no shoes, better service." His Web log includes the shirtless photos to prove it, along with commentary on politics, technology, law practice and life.

IsThatLegal?, www.isthatlegal.org.

University of North Carolina law professor Eric L. Muller, author of *Free to Die for Their Country: The Story of the Japanese American Draft Resisters in World War II,* muses on various matters of law and politics.

Jack Bog's Blog, http://bojack.org.

Being director of the tax program at Lewis & Clark Law School, John A. Bogdanski sometimes comments on tax law and policy. But you are more likely to read about his hometown, his daughter, his musical tastes, and whatever else interests him.

Lawpsided, www.lawpsided.com.

Sean Carter, a lawyer, stand-up comedian and humor writer, follows the lighter side of legal news, culling reports of offbeat lawsuits and other legal news and compiling them here.

Lex Communis, http://peterseanesq.blogspot.com.

Peter Sean Bradley practices in the areas of business litigation and plaintiffs' employment law in Fresno, California. His blog touches on history, philosophy, religion, science and law, all from a conservative Catholic perspective.

MadKane, www.madkane.com/.

Madeleine Begun Kane has been called "one of the funniest women in the blogosphere." One thing is for sure: she is one of the funniest lawyers. Besides her Web log, check out her political parody feature, "Dubya's Dayly Diary," and her collection of legal humor columns by following the links from the front page.

NathanNewman.org, www.nathannewman.org/log.

Besides working for a union-side labor firm in New York City, Nathan Newman is national vice president of the National Lawyers Guild and a columnist for The Progressive Populist. He comments on law, politics, economics and technology.

Ninomania, http://ninomania.blogspot.com.

Regent University Law Professor David Wagner publishes this blog "to extol the wit and wisdom of Justice Antonin Scalia." He also comments on court decisions, politics and other news.

Power Line, www.powerlineblog.com.

Three lawyers conspire to offer their opinions on law and politics, all from a decidedly conservative point of view.

Sneaking Suspicions, www.sneakingsuspicions.com.

Delaware lawyer Frederick H. Schranck provides insightful commentary on a range of topics, law primary among them.

The Buck Stops Here, http://stuartbuck.blogspot.com.

Having been law clerk to Judge Stephen F. Williams of the District of Columbia Circuit Court of Appeals and Judge David A. Nelson of the Sixth. Circuit Court of Appeals and an editor of the Harvard Law Review, Stuart Buck now shares his thoughts on the courts and law.

The LitiGator, www.litig8r.net.

A Michigan trial lawyer writing under the pseudonym Franco Castalone remarks on law, litigation, technology and politics.

The Shout: Opinions on Everything, www.granick.com/blog.

Jennifer S. Granick, director of the Center for Internet and Society at Stanford Law School and former criminal defense lawyer, comments on criminal law and cyberlaw, with an emphasis on free speech, privacy and computer security.

the talking dog, www.thetalkingdog.com.

A left-leaning lawyer in New York City, Seth J. Farber opines on law, politics, current events and cultural trends.

tins, www.rklau.com/tins.

At the University of Richmond School of Law in the early 1990s, Rick Klau founded the first student-edited law journal to publish exclusively online. Now a software marketing executive, he blogs about technology, movies, politics and other topics that strike his fancy.

The Legal Reader, www.legalreader.com.

John Hoar, staff attorney for a California court, presents this guide to random legal news that he finds interesting. Hoar blogs "semi-anonymously," in that he does not promote his identity. He is more a news aggregator, he says, who adds a small amount of commentary.

WOIFM?, www.perpetualbeta.com/woifm.

The acronym stands for "What's On It For Me?," and Michael Alex Wasylik, a lawyer in McLean, Virginia, who has been at it since 1999, believes it may be the first lawyer blog.

Appendix I

Getting to Know the Supreme Court

Time was, it was a big deal to get U.S. Supreme Court opinions via the Internet. Today, opinions are only the tip of the online iceberg of Supreme Court information. Briefs, arguments, biographies, calendars and more are available at the click of a mouse.

Ironically, however, even though the court has been disseminating its opinions electronically since 1990, it was not until 2000 that it had a Web site

The Supreme Court includes its opinions and dockets, along with transcripts of arguments.

of its own, www.supremecourtus.gov. Its site publishes the Court's opinions beginning with the 1999 term. It also features the Court's automated docket, through which users may access information about cases, both pending and decided. Beginning in October 2000, the Court added transcripts of all oral arguments to the site, where they will be archived permanently. Other features include orders, an argument calendar, the Court's schedule, the Rules of the Supreme Court, bar admission forms and instructions, visitors' guides, case handling guides, special notices, press releases and general information.

One resource the Supreme Court's site does not include is briefs. Those you can find at FindLaw's Supreme Court Center, supreme.lp.findlaw.com, which has all briefs filed with the Court beginning with the October 1999 term. Provided by the legal portal FindLaw, the library includes all the briefs filed in each case the court agrees to hear—those from the parties as well as from amici curiae. Briefs are added to the library weekly. With lawyers allowed only thirty minutes to make their oral arguments, their briefs become the best source for fully understanding the arguments in a case and the Court's eventual ruling, making them an invaluable research tool for lawyers.

Besides briefs, FindLaw provides a broad array of resources. It includes all the Court's opinions since 1893; the Court's docket, including summaries of the questions presented and links to the lower court opinions; the Court's orders; its calendar; its rules; a filing guide; and biographies of all the justices. FindLaw columnists provide commentary on the Court.

If you would rather listen to the arguments than read the briefs, the Web accommodates. Jump over to the Oyez Project, www.oyez.org, where you can hear the actual, complete oral arguments. (You will need to have the free RealPlayer installed on your computer.) Created by Northwestern professor Jerry Goldman in 1996 with a few dozen recordings, the Oyez project has grown into a significant multimedia database dedicated to the Court, with more than 900 hours of audio materials, summaries of 1,000-plus Supreme Court opinions, biographical materials on all 108 justices, and a panoramic, virtual reality tour of the Supreme Court building.

Oyez—which takes its name from the phrase by which the marshal of the Court calls the courtroom to order—has added MP3 versions of selected arguments, which you can download and listen to on your computer or an MP3 player.

For one-stop shopping of Supreme Court information, Jurist: The Law Professors' Network, offers a comprehensive guide to the Court, http://jurist.law.pitt.edu/issues/issue_scotus.htm. Compiled by Bernard J. Hibbitts, professor of law at the University of Pittsburgh School of Law, the page is an index of links to Supreme Court resources. From here, you can jump to the Court's latest decision in full text, then see what the nation's major media had to say about it, surf over to a biography of the opinion author, see what other decisions he or she recently wrote, and finish up with a review of the Court's coming schedule of arguments.

For a journalist's perspective on the Supreme Court, visit On the Docket, http://journalism.medill.northwestern.edu/docket, a project of Northwestern University's Medill School of Journalism. The site lists pending and prior-term cases, with a story on each case, additional feature stories on selected cases, links to Web sites relevant to the cases, information provided by attorneys and parties in the cases, the dates for scheduled oral arguments, the questions presented to the Court, names of the attorneys in the cases, and citations for the lower court opinions. Coverage dates back to the 1998-99 term.

Another useful resource for information about the goings on at the Supreme Court is Appellate.net, www.appellate.net, the Web site of Mayer, Brown, Rowe & Maw's appellate and Supreme Court practice group. The site covers a range of appellate courts, but its Supreme Court coverage focuses on cases of interest to the business community, as well as on cases in which Mayer, Brown attorneys played a role.

You might also want to visit the Web site of The Supreme Court Historical Society, www.supremecourthistory.org. This fascinating site looks at the history of the Supreme Court through features such as "Supreme Court Decisions and Women's Rights," which explores how the court has reviewed laws that discriminate by sex, and "FDR & the Court-Packing Controversy," a Flash documentary about FDR's 1937 attempt to enlarge the court.

Opinions

Of course, there are times when you really do want the opinion itself. On the Web, there is no shortage of places to find it. In fact, the Supreme Court has been disseminating its opinions electronically for a decade.

As noted, the Supreme Court's own Web site, www.supremecourtus.gov, includes the Court's opinions beginning with the 1999 term. And for sheer breadth, FindLaw's collection is the best of the free sites, with a searchable database of all decisions issued since 1893. Cases can be browsed by year and U.S. Reports volume number or searched by citation, case title and full text.

The Court's current opinions are also available through the Legal Information Institute at Cornell Law School, http://supct.law.cornell.edu/supct/. It contains all Supreme Court decisions since 1990, posted shortly after their release. You can search for a decision by key words or topic, and decisions are indexed by party name, date and docket number. Read the decision in your choice of HTML or Adobe Acrobat format.

A more limited library of older Supreme Court cases is available at the FedWorld/FLITE Supreme Court Decisions Homepage, www.fedworld.gov/supcourt/index.htm. It provides a database of more than 7,000 Supreme Court opinions issued between 1937 and 1975.

USSCPlus, www.usscplus.com, is a commercial site, charging $39 a year for its database that includes all Supreme Court decisions since 1879 and selected cases as far back as 1793. The site offers free access to current term opinions.

If all this surfing of Supreme Court Web sites is giving your mouse motion sickness, you can opt to sit back and have the Court's news delivered directly to your computer. The Legal Information Institute provides a free service that automatically sends you via e-mail syllabi of Court decisions on the day they are issued. These are official syllabi prepared by the Court's reporter of decisions. If you wish to obtain the full text of an opinion, you e-mail back a request and it is e-mailed back to you—again, at no cost. To subscribe to this service, follow the instructions at http://liibulletin.law.cornell.edu.

Others offer similar free services. FindLaw sponsors its own e-mail service with abstracts of Supreme Court opinions as they are released. You can subscribe to this through FindLaw's Web site at http://newsletters.findlaw.com. Another is sponsored by USSCPlus, and includes a one-paragraph summary of each opinion and a link to the full text in Adobe Acrobat format. Subscribe at the company's Web site.

In May 2003, the LII began offering summaries of Supreme Court decisions delivered via an RSS feed. There are two feeds. One includes only decisions handed down that day. The other includes recent decisions, which, when the Court is in session, means the most recent thirty days. The daily RSS feed is at: http://supct.law.cornell.edu/supct/rss/0.91/supct_today.rss. The recent decisions feed is at: http://supct.law.cornell.edu/supct/rss/0.91/supct_recent.rss.

Finding Court Opinions on the Web

In July 1995, I surveyed the availability of free court opinions on the Internet. I found opinions from the Supreme Court, three U.S. circuit courts, no U.S. district or bankruptcy courts, four state supreme courts and one state intermediate appellate court.

What few courts' opinions there were came as the result of an even smaller number of pioneering legal Web sites. Cornell University's Legal Information Institute published those of the Supreme Court and the New York Court of Appeals. Emory University School of Law hosted the Sixth and Eleventh Circuits. Villanova University School of Law provided the opinions of the Third Circuit.

To the extent the opinions were out there, they were not always easy to obtain. This was a time when the Web was a nascent, still inconsequential subset of the Internet. Opinions were likely to be found on the then more popular Gopher sites or as file downloads from FTP servers.

The most comprehensive case law collection on the Internet in 1995 belonged to Law Journal EXTRA!, a subscription service operated by the *National Law Journal*. Ironically, LJX no longer exists.

We've come a long way. As the survey that follows illustrates, free access to appellate opinions over the Web is now the norm, and is quickly becoming so for trial-level courts as well. This survey begins with federal courts—U.S. circuit courts, district courts, bankruptcy courts and specialized courts— and then goes on to the states and territories.

U.S. Circuit Courts

FindLaw maintains a library of all federal circuit court opinions, which can be searched across all circuits or by any one, www.findlaw.com/casecode/courts/index.html.

Each circuit also has at least one site of its own:

- First Circuit, official site, www.ca1.uscourts.gov
- First Circuit opinions issued between November 1995 and July 2001, from Emory School of Law, www.law.emory.edu/1circuit
- Second Circuit, official site, www.ca2.uscourts.gov

- Second Circuit opinions issued between January 1995 and March 2003, from the Touro Law Center, www.tourolaw.edu/2ndCircuit
- Third Circuit, official site, www.ca3.uscourts.gov
- Third Circuit, since 1994, through Villanova University School of Law, http://vls.law.vill.edu/Locator/3/index.htm
- Fourth Circuit, official site, www.ca4.uscourts.gov
- Fourth Circuit, from Jan. 1, 1995 to July 2001, from the Hugh F. MacMillan Law Library of Emory School of Law. www.law.emory.edu/4circuit
- Fifth Circuit, official site, www.ca5.uscourts.gov
- Fifth Circuit, since 1991, from Tarlton Law Library, University of Texas School of Law, www.law.utexas.edu/us5th/us5th.html
- Sixth Circuit, official site, www.ca6.uscourts.gov
- Sixth Circuit, opinions issued between January 1995 and June 1999, from Emory School of Law, www.law.emory.edu/6circuit
- Seventh Circuit, official site, www.ca7.uscourts.gov
- Eighth Circuit, official site, www.ca8.uscourts.gov
- Ninth Circuit, official site, www.ca9.uscourts.gov
- Ninth Circuit, Office of Circuit Executive, www.ce9.uscourts.gov
- Tenth Circuit, official site (selected opinions), www.ca10.uscourts.gov
- Tenth Circuit, August 1995 to October 1997, www.law.emory.edu/10circuit
- Tenth U.S. Circuit, Oct. 1, 1997 to present, hosted by Washburn University School of Law Library, www.kscourts.org/ca10
- Eleventh Circuit, www.ca11.uscourts.gov
- Eleventh Circuit, opinions issued between November 1994 and March 2003, through Emory. www.law.emory.edu/11circuit/index.html
- Federal Circuit, opinions since 1994 , www.fedcir.gov
- Federal Circuit, since August 1995, from Georgetown University, www.ll.georgetown.edu/federal/judicial/cafed.cfm
- Federal Circuit, since August 1995, from Emory. www.law.emory.edu/fedcircuit
- District of Columbia Circuit, official Web site, opinions since September 1997, www.cadc.uscourts.gov
- District of Columbia Circuit, opinions since March 1995, www.ll.georgetown.edu/federal/judicial/cadc.cfm

U.S. District Courts

U.S. District Courts with all or some of their opinions on the Internet are:

- Alabama, Middle District, www.almd.uscourts.gov
- Alabama, Northern District, www.alnd.uscourts.gov
- Alabama, Southern District, www.als.uscourts.gov
- Alaska, www.akd.uscourts.gov
- Arizona, www.azd.uscourts.gov
- Arkansas, Eastern District, www.are.uscourts.gov
- Arkansas, Western District (via PACER), www.arwd.uscourts.gov
- California, Central District, www.cacd.uscourts.gov
- California, Eastern District, www.caed.uscourts.gov
- California, Northern District, www.cand.uscourts.gov
- Colorado, www.co.uscourts.gov/dindex.htm
- Connecticut, www.ctd.uscourts.gov
- District of Columbia, beginning in 1998, www.dcd.uscourts.gov
- Florida, Northern District, www.flnd.uscourts.gov
- Florida, Southern District, www.flsd.uscourts.gov
- Georgia, Northern District, www.gand.uscourts.gov
- Guam, www.gud.uscourts.gov
- Idaho, www.id.uscourts.gov
- Illinois, Central District, www.ilcd.uscourts.gov
- Illinois, Northern District, www.ilnd.uscourts.gov
- Illinois, Southern District, www.ilsd.uscourts.gov
- Indiana, Northern District, www.innd.uscourts.gov
- Indiana, Southern District, www.insd.uscourts.gov
- Iowa, Northern District, www.iand.uscourts.gov
- Iowa, Southern District, www.iasd.uscourts.gov
- Kansas, www.ksd.uscourts.gov
- Kentucky, Western District, www.kywd.uscourts.gov
- Louisiana, Middle District, www.lamd.uscourts.gov
- Maine, www.med.uscourts.gov
- Maryland, www.mdd.uscourts.gov
- Massachusetts, www.mad.uscourts.gov
- Michigan, Eastern District, www.mied.uscourts.gov
- Michigan, Western District, www.miwd.uscourts.gov
- Minnesota, www.mnd.uscourts.gov
- Mississippi, Northern District, www.msnd.uscourts.gov

- Mississippi, Northern District, opinions issued between August 1994 and September 2000, published by the University of Mississippi School of Law Library, http://sunset.backbone.olemiss.edu/~llib-coll/ndms
- Missouri, Eastern District, www.moed.uscourts.gov
- Missouri, Western District, www.mow.uscourts.gov
- New Hampshire, www.nhd.uscourts.gov
- New Jersey, http://pacer.njd.uscourts.gov
- New Mexico, www.nmcourt.fed.us/web/index.htm
- New York, Eastern District, www.nyed.uscourts.gov
- New York, Northern District, www.nynd.uscourts.gov
- New York, Southern District, www.nysd.uscourts.gov
- North Carolina, Middle District, www.ncmd.uscourts.gov
- North Carolina, Western District, www.ncwd.uscourts.gov
- North Dakota, www.ndd.uscourts.gov
- Northern Mariana Islands, www.nmid.uscourts.gov
- Ohio, Northern District, www.ohnd.uscourts.gov
- Ohio, Southern District, www.ohsd.uscourts.gov
- Oregon, www.ord.uscourts.gov
- Pennsylvania, Eastern District, www.paed.uscourts.gov
- Pennsylvania, Middle District, www.pamd.uscourts.gov
- Pennsylvania, Western District, www.pawd.uscourts.gov
- Rhode Island, www.rid.uscourts.gov
- South Carolina, www.scd.uscourts.gov
- South Carolina, opinions since 1994, published by the University of South Carolina Law Center. Opinions can be searched by name, date or key word. www.law.sc.edu/dsc/dsc.htm
- South Dakota, opinions since 1996 (published by the State Bar of South Dakota), www.sdbar.org/opinions/indices/DSD/dsdindex.htm
- Tennessee, Eastern District, www.tned.uscourts.gov
- Tennessee, Middle District, www.tnmd.uscourts.gov
- Tennessee, Western District, www.tnwd.uscourts.gov/index.asp
- Texas, Eastern District, www.txed.uscourts.gov
- Texas, Northern District, www.txnd.uscourts.gov
- Texas, Southern District, www.txsd.uscourts.gov
- Texas, Western District, www.txwd.uscourts.gov
- Utah, www.utd.uscourts.gov
- Vermont, www.vtd.uscourts.gov
- Virginia, Eastern District, www.vaed.uscourts.gov
- Virginia, Western District, www.vawd.uscourts.gov
- Virgin Islands, www.vid.uscourts.gov
- Washington, Eastern District, www.waed.uscourts.gov

- West Virginia, Northern District, www.wvnd.uscourts.gov
- West Virginia, Southern District, www.wvsd.uscourts.gov
- Wisconsin, Western District, www.wiwd.uscourts.gov
- Wyoming, www.ck10.uscourts.gov/wyoming/district

Other U.S. district court sites on the Web, but without opinions, include:

- California, Southern District, www.casd.uscourts.gov
- Delaware, www.ded.uscourts.gov
- Florida, Middle District, www.flmd.uscourts.gov
- Georgia, Middle District, www.gamd.uscourts.gov
- Georgia, Southern District, www.gasd.uscourts.gov
- Hawaii, www.hid.uscourts.gov
- Kentucky, Eastern District, www.kyed.uscourts.gov
- Louisiana, Eastern District, www.laed.uscourts.gov
- Louisiana, Western District, www.lawd.uscourts.gov
- Mississippi, Southern District, www.mssd.uscourts.gov
- Montana, www.mtd.uscourts.gov
- Nebraska, www.ned.uscourts.gov
- Nevada, www.nvd.uscourts.gov
- New York, Western District, www.nywd.uscourts.gov
- North Carolina, Eastern District, www.nced.uscourts.gov
- Oklahoma, Eastern District, www.oked.uscourts.gov
- Oklahoma, Northern District, www.oknd.uscourts.gov
- Oklahoma, Western District, www.okwd.uscourts.gov
- Puerto Rico, www.prd.uscourts.gov
- South Dakota, www.sdd.uscourts.gov
- Washington, Western District, www.wawd.uscourts.gov
- Wisconsin, Eastern District, www.wied.uscourts.gov

U.S. Bankruptcy Courts

Bankruptcy Appellate Panels:

- Eighth Circuit, www.ca8.uscourts.gov/bap/bapinf.htm
- Ninth Circuit, www.ce9.uscourts.gov/bap
- Tenth Circuit, www.bap10.uscourts.gov

Bankruptcy court sites with available opinions are:

- Alabama, Middle District, www.almb.uscourts.gov
- Alabama, Northern District, www.alnb.uscourts.gov

- Alabama, Southern District, www.alsb.uscourts.gov
- Alaska, www.akb.uscourts.gov
- Arkansas, www.arb.uscourts.gov
- California, Central District, www.cacb.uscourts.gov
- California, Eastern District, www.caeb.uscourts.gov
- California, Northern District, www.canb.uscourts.gov
- California, Southern District, www.casb.uscourts.gov
- Colorado, www.cob.uscourts.gov/bindex.htm
- Connecticut, www.ctb.uscourts.gov
- Delaware, www.deb.uscourts.gov
- District of Columbia, www.dcb.uscourts.gov
- Florida, Middle District, www.flmb.uscourts.gov
- Florida, Northern District, www.flnb.uscourts.gov
- Florida, Southern District, www.flsb.uscourts.gov
- Georgia, Middle District, www.gamb.uscourts.gov
- Georgia, Southern District, www.gasb.uscourts.gov
- Hawaii, www.hib.uscourts.gov
- Idaho, www.id.uscourts.gov
- Illinois, Central District, www.ilcb.uscourts.gov
- Illinois, Southern District, www.ilsb.uscourts.gov
- Indiana, Northern District, www.innb.uscourts.gov
- Indiana, Southern District, www.insb.uscourts.gov
- Iowa, Northern District, www.ianb.uscourts.gov
- Iowa, Southern District, www.iasb.uscourts.gov
- Kansas, www.ksb.uscourts.gov
- Kentucky, Eastern District, www.kyeb.uscourts.gov
- Louisiana, Western District, www.lawb.uscourts.gov
- Maine, www.meb.uscourts.gov
- Maryland, www.mdb.uscourts.gov
- Massachusetts, all opinions published since Jan. 1, 1995, courtesy of "The Massachusetts Bankruptcy Page," www.craigmacauley.com/cases/mabank.htm
- Michigan, Eastern District, www.mieb.uscourts.gov/
- Michigan, Western District, www.miwb.uscourts.gov
- Minnesota, www.mnb.uscourts.gov
- Mississippi, Northern District, www.msnb.uscourts.gov
- Missouri, Western District, www.mow.uscourts.gov
- New Hampshire, www.nhb.uscourts.gov
- New Jersey, www.njb.uscourts.gov
- New Mexico (requires account and password), www.nmcourt.fed.us/bkdocs

- New York, Northern District, www.nynb.uscourts.gov
- New York, Western District, www.nywb.uscourts.gov
- North Carolina, Middle District, www.ncmb.uscourts.gov
- North Carolina, Western District, www.ncwb.uscourts.gov
- North Dakota, www.ndb.uscourts.gov
- Ohio, Northern District, www.ohnb.uscourts.gov
- Oklahoma, Eastern District, www.okeb.uscourts.gov
- Oklahoma, Northern District, www.oknb.uscourts.gov
- Oregon, www.orb.uscourts.gov
- Pennsylvania, Eastern District, www.paeb.uscourts.gov
- Pennsylvania, Western District, www.pawb.uscourts.gov
- Rhode Island, www.rib.uscourts.gov
- South Carolina, www.scb.uscourts.gov
- South Dakota, opinions since 1987, www.sdb.uscourts.gov
- South Dakota, opinions since 1998 (published by the state bar), www.sdbar.org/opinions/default.htm
- Tennessee, Western District, www.tnwb.uscourts.gov
- Texas, Northern District, www.txnb.uscourts.gov
- Texas, Southern District, www.txsd.uscourts.gov
- Texas, Western District, www.txwb.uscourts.gov
- Utah, www.utb.uscourts.gov
- Vermont, www.vtb.uscourts.gov
- Virginia, Eastern District, www.vaeb.uscourts.gov
- Washington, Eastern District, www.waeb.uscourts.gov
- West Virginia, Northern District, www.wvnb.uscourts.gov
- West Virginia, Southern District, www.wvsd.uscourts.gov/bankruptcy/index.htm
- Wisconsin, Western District, www.wiw.uscourts.gov/bankruptcy
- Wyoming, www.wyb.uscourts.gov

U.S. Bankruptcy courts with Web sites without opinions are:

- Arizona, www.azb.uscourts.gov
- Georgia, Northern District, www.ganb.uscourts.gov
- Illinois, Northern District, www.ilnb.uscourts.gov
- Kentucky, Western District, www.kywb.uscourts.gov/fpweb/index.htm
- Louisiana, Eastern District, www.laeb.uscourts.gov
- Louisiana, Middle District, www.lamb.uscourts.gov
- Massachusetts, www.mab.uscourts.gov
- Mississippi, Southern District, www.mssb.uscourts.gov
- Missouri, Eastern District, www.moeb.uscourts.gov

- Montana, www.mtb.uscourts.gov
- Nebraska, www.neb.uscourts.gov
- Nevada, www.nvb.uscourts.gov
- New York, Eastern District, www.nyeb.uscourts.gov
- New York, Southern District, www.nysb.uscourts.gov
- North Carolina, Eastern District, www.nceb.uscourts.gov
- Ohio, Southern District, www.ohsb.uscourts.gov
- Oklahoma, Western District, www.okwb.uscourts.gov
- Pennsylvania, Middle District, www.pamb.uscourts.gov
- Puerto Rico, www.prb.uscourts.gov
- Tennessee, Eastern District, www.tneb.uscourts.gov
- Tennessee, Middle District, www.tnmb.uscourts.gov
- Texas, Eastern District, www.txeb.uscourts.gov
- Virginia, Western District, www.vawb.uscourts.gov
- Virgin Islands, www.vid.uscourts.gov
- Washington, Western District, www.wawb.uscourts.gov
- Wisconsin, Eastern District, www.wieb.uscourts.gov

The federal judiciary's PACER system (Public Access to Court Electronic Records) provides Web or dial-up access to district and bankruptcy court case information and court dockets. PACER systems charge a user fee of 7 cents per page for Web access or 60 cents per minute for dial-up access. Complete information on PACER and a complete list of PACER telephone numbers for U.S. district and bankruptcy courts can be found on the Internet at: www.uscourts.gov.

Specialized U.S. Courts

- U.S. Court of International Trade, opinions since Jan. 1, 1999, www.cit.uscourts.gov
- U.S. Court of Federal Claims, opinions since 1997 (from U.S. Dept. of Commerce), www.uscfc.uscourts.gov
- U.S. Court of Appeals for Veterans' Claims, opinions since 1989, www.vetapp.gov
- U.S. Court of Appeals for the Armed Forces, opinions since 1996, www.armfor.uscourts.gov
- U.S. Tax Court, www.ustaxcourt.gov. Opinions issued since Jan. 1, 1999.

State Courts

Alabama

- Supreme Court and Courts of Civil and Criminal Appeals opinions since 1994 are available at www.alalinc.net. You can access opinions at this site only by first purchasing a subscription, which costs $200 a year.
- A searchable database of state appellate court opinions is available from M. Lee Smith Publishers, but requires payment of monthly subscription fees, www.alalaws.com.
- An Alabama law firm, Wallace, Jordan, Ratliff & Brandt, provides free access to opinions issued by the Supreme Court of Alabama since April 1998. They are at: www.wallacejordan.com/decisions/index.html.
- Supreme Court opinions since 1998, from FindLaw, www.findlaw.com/11stategov/al/alca.html.

Alaska

- Supreme Court, opinions since 1991, www.touchngo.com/sp/sp.html.
- Supreme Court, slip opinions, www.state.ak.us/courts/sp.htm
- Supreme Court, memorandum opinions, www.state.ak.us/courts/smoj.htm
- Court of Appeals, opinions since 1991, www.touchngo.com/ap/ap.htm
- Court of Appeals, slip opinions, www.state.ak.us/courts/ap.htm
- Court of Appeals, memorandum opinions, www.state.ak.us/courts/moj.htm
- Supreme Court and Court of Appeals since 1991, from FindLaw, www.findlaw.com/11stategov/ak/akca.html
- Alaska trial court and unreported opinions, via the Alaska Bar Association, www.alaskabar.org/index.cfm?id=5145

Arizona

- Arizona Supreme Court opinions, since 1998, www.supreme.state.az.us/opin
- Court of Appeals, Division One, www.cofad1.state.az.us
- Court of Appeals, Division Two, opinions issued within the preceding six months, www.apltwo.ct.state.az.us/
- Arizona Supreme Court and Court of Appeals, since 1997, from FindLaw, www.findlaw.com/11stategov/az/azca.html

Arkansas

- Supreme Court and Court of Appeals opinions, September 1994 to present, courts.state.ar.us
- Supreme Court and Court of Appeals opinions since 1996, from FindLaw, www.findlaw.com/11stategov/ar/arca.html

California

- The Judicial Branch offers Supreme Court and Courts of Appeal slip opinions issued within the preceding sixty days, available in Word and Adobe Acrobat formats, as well as an archive of unofficial opinions dating from January 2000, www.courtinfo.ca.gov/opinions
- Supreme Court and Courts of Appeal opinions are provided by Law.com, together with a daily e-mail opinion alert, for an annual subscription of $199, www.law.com/regionals/ca/
- Supreme Court and Courts of Appeal opinions since 1934, from FindLaw, www.findlaw.com/cacases/index.html

Colorado

- Supreme Court, official site, with slip opinions, case announcements, oral argument schedules and rule changes, www.courts.state.co.us
- Colorado Court of Appeals, official court site with slip opinions, www.courts.state.co.us/coa/coaindex.htm
- Supreme Court and Court of Appeals opinions, posted by the Colorado Bar Association, www.cobar.org/ors.cfm
- Supreme Court and Court of Appeals, since 1998, from FindLaw, www.findlaw.com/11stategov/co/coca.html

Connecticut

- Supreme Court and Appellate Court, opinions remain here for one month after release, www.jud.state.ct.us/external/supapp/aro.htm

Delaware

- Supreme Court opinions, since November 1998, courts.state.de.us/supreme/opinions.htm
- Court of Chancery, courts.state.de.us/chancery, official home page, includes opinions via a link to the Delaware Corporate Law Clearinghouse, discussed below.
- Court of Chancery, opinions since 1999, published by the Delaware Corporate Law Clearinghouse, Widener University School of Law, http://corporate-law.widener.edu/ctofchan.htm

- Delaware Supreme Court, Court of Chancery, Family Court and Superior Court, www.law.widener.edu/Law-Library/library/research/de_court_opinions.shtml. (This is an index of opinions prepared by Widener University; full text can be ordered by e-mail.)
- Supreme Court and Court of Chancery, published by the Delaware Law Weekly, www.delawarelawweekly.com.
- Supreme Court since 1998, from FindLaw, www.findlaw.com/11state-gov/de/deca.html

District of Columbia

- Court of Appeals, no opinions, www.dcca.state.dc.us
- Court of Appeals, opinions since 1997, courtesy of the D.C. Bar, www.dcbar.org/for_lawyers/courts/court_of_appeals/opinions.cfm
- Court of Appeals, published by Law.com and Legal Times, www.law.com/dc

Florida

- Supreme Court, official site, opinions since September 1999, www.flcourts.org/sct/sctdocs/index.html
- Supreme Court, all opinions issued between September 1995 and 2000, maintained by the University of Florida, Levin College of Law, www.law.ufl.edu/opinions/supreme/index.shtml
- Supreme Court, since 1995, from FindLaw, www.findlaw.com/11stat-egov/fl/flca.html
- First District Court of Appeal, www.1dca.org/decisions/data/opinions.html
- Second District Court of Appeal, www.2dca.org/opinions.htm
- Third District Court of Appeal, www.3dca.flcourts.org/Opinions.htm
- Fourth District Court of Appeal, www.4dca.org/recentopfrm.html
- Fifth District Court of Appeal, www.5dca.org/Opinions/opinion.htm

Georgia

- Supreme Court opinions between 1997 and October 28, 2002, and Court of Appeals opinions between 1997 and September 6, 2002, www.ganet.org/ appellatecourt
- Supreme Court, official site, www2.state.ga.us/Courts/Supreme
- Court of Appeals (no opinions on site, but link to LexisONE free opinions), www.gaappeals.us
- Supreme Court and Court of Appeals opinions, published by Law.com and Fulton County Daily Report, www.law.com/ga. Subscriptions start at $275 a year.

Guam

- Supreme Court of Guam, opinions issued since 1996, www.guam-supremecourt.com/OPINIONS.htm
- Superior Court opinions, www.guamjustice.net/superior/superior.htm

Hawaii

- Supreme Court and Court of Appeals, opinions since January 1998, maintained by the Supreme Court Law Library, www.courts.state.hi.us
- Supreme Court and Court of Appeals, opinions since 1989, sponsored by the State Bar Association, www.hsba.org/HSBA/Legal_Research/Hawaii/cases.cfm
- Supreme Court and Court of Appeals, since 1998, from FindLaw, www.findlaw.com/11stategov/hi/hica.html

Idaho

- Supreme Court and Court of Appeals, www2.state.id.us/judicial
- Supreme Court and Court of Appeals since 1998, from FindLaw, www.findlaw.com/11stategov/id/idca.html

Illinois

- Supreme Court and Appellate Court opinions, posted by the Reporter of Decisions, since May 1996, www.state.il.us/court/Opinions
- Supreme and Appellate Court opinions since 1996, from FindLaw, www.findlaw.com/11stategov/il/ilca.html
- Illinois Court Reports publishes Supreme Court and Appellate Court opinions since 1998. Register here to receive daily e-mail notices of new cases, www.prairienet.org/law

Indiana

- Supreme Court, Court of Appeals and Tax Court opinions, current day and archives, official site, www.in.gov/judiciary/opinions

Iowa

- Supreme Court and Court of Appeals, official Judicial Branch site, www.judicial.state.ia.us
- Supreme Court, Court of Appeals, workers' compensation and attorney general opinions, courtesy of the state bar, www.iowabar.org (click on "Legal Resources").

- Supreme Court and Court of Appeals since 1998, from FindLaw, www.findlaw.com/11stategov/ia/iaca.html

Kansas

- Supreme Court and Court of Appeals, opinions since October 25, 1996, www.kscourts.org/kscases
- Supreme Court and Court of Appeals since 1996, from FindLaw, www.findlaw.com/11stategov/ks/ksca.html
- Johnson County District Court, courts.jocogov.org

Kentucky

- Court of Justice (Supreme Court and Court of Appeals opinions), www.kycourts.net/Supreme/SC_Opinions.shtm
- Supreme Court opinions since 1999, and some from 1996-1998, from FindLaw, www.findlaw.com/11stategov/ky/kyca.html

Louisiana

- Supreme Court opinions since February 28, 1996, www.lasc.org
- First Circuit Court of Appeal, opinions beginning in 2000, www.la-fcca.org
- Second Circuit Court of Appeal, opinions beginning in December 2000, www.lacoa2.org
- Third Circuit Court of Appeal, opinions since February 2003, www.la3circuit.org/
- Fourth Circuit Court of Appeal, 4thcir-app.state.la.us
- Fifth Circuit Court of Appeal, opinions since October 2001, www.fifthcircuit.org
- Civil District Court for the Parish of Orleans, www.orleanscdc.gov

Maine

- Supreme Judicial Court opinions since Jan. 1, 1997, www.courts.state.me.us
- Supreme Judicial Court, since 1997, from FindLaw, www.findlaw.com/11stategov/me/meca.html

Maryland

- Court of Appeals and Court of Special Appeals opinions since 1992, www.courts.state.md.us
- Court of Appeals, since 1995, from FindLaw, www.findlaw.com/11stategov/md/mdca.html

Massachusetts

- Supreme Judicial Court, official slip opinions, www.massreports.com
- Appeals Court, official slip opinions, www.massreports.com
- Supreme Judicial Court and Appeals Court opinions since 1997, from Massachusetts Lawyers Weekly, www.masslaw.com
- Recent Supreme Judicial Court and Appeals Court opinions available free. Databases of SJC opinions since 1930 and Appeals Court opinions since 1972 are available to paid members of Boston's Social Law Library, www.socialaw.com
- Superior Court, selected opinions via Social Law Library, www. socialaw.com/superior/superior.html
- Supreme Judicial Court and Appeals Court opinions since 1998, from FindLaw, www.findlaw.com/11stategov/ma/maca.html

Michigan

- The Michigan court system publishes a database of Supreme Court and Court of Appeals opinions, containing published opinions since January 2001 as well as Court of Appeals unpublished decisions since July 1996, courtofappeals.mijud.net/resources/opinions.htm
- Opinions of both the Supreme Court and Court of Appeals can be found at the following sites:
    - Institute of Continuing Legal Education, Supreme Court since October 1, 1995, and Court of Appeals since August 1, 1996, www.icle. org/michlaw/index.htm
    - State Bar of Michigan, Supreme Court and Court of Appeals opinions since 1998, www.michbar.org/opinions
    - Michigan Lawyers Weekly, Supreme Court and Court of Appeals opinions since 1996, www.michlaw.com
    - FindLaw, opinions since 1995, www.findlaw.com/11stategov/mi/mica.html
    - Calhoun County Courts (summaries of recent probate decisions), courts.co.calhoun.mi.us
    - Washtenaw County Trial Court, www.co.washtenaw.mi.us/depts/courts/index.htm

Minnesota

- Supreme Court and Court of Appeals, since May 1996, www.courts.state.mn.us
- Full text opinions of the Supreme Court, Court of Appeals, Tax Court, Office of Administrative Hearings, Workers' Compensation Court,

and Attorney General since February 1996 are published by Minnesota Lawyer (subscription required), www.minnlawyer.com

- Supreme Court and Court of Appeals opinions since 1996, from FindLaw, www.findlaw.com/11stategov/mn/mnca.html

Mississippi

- Mississippi Supreme Court and Court of Appeals, since 1996, www.mssc.state.ms.us
- Supreme Court opinions since February 1996 and Court of Appeals opinions since April 1996, www.mslawyer.com/mssc

Missouri

- Supreme Court and Court of Appeals opinions, www.osca.state.mo.us
- Supreme Court and Court of Appeals since 1997, from FindLaw, www.findlaw.com/11stategov/mo/moca.html

Montana

- Supreme Court opinions since January 1997, www.lawlibrary.state.mt.us/dscgi/ds.py/View/Collection-36
- Supreme Court opinions since 1997, from FindLaw, www.findlaw.com/11stategov/mt/mtca.html

Nebraska

- Supreme Court and Court of Appeals opinions, http://court.nol.org/opinions
- Supreme Court and Court of Appeals opinions since 1997, from FindLaw, www.findlaw.com/11stategov/ne/neca.html

Nevada

- Supreme Court opinions (most recent ninety days), www.leg.state.nv.us/law1.cfm
- Supreme Court opinions since 1998, from FindLaw, www.findlaw.com/11stategov/nv/nvca.html

New Hampshire

- Supreme Court opinions since November 1995, official court site, www.courts.state.nh.us/supreme/index.htm
- Superior Court, selected orders and opinions, www.courts.state.nh.us/superior/superorders/index.htm

- Supreme Court opinions since November 1995, from FindLaw, www.findlaw.com/11stategov/nh/nhca.html

New Jersey

- Supreme Court and Appellate Division, recent opinions only, www.judiciary.state.nj.us/opinions/index.htm
- Opinions of the Supreme Court (since March, 1994), Appellate Division (since September, 1995), and Tax Court, provided by the Administrative Office of Courts and Rutgers University School of Law -Camden, http://lawlibrary.rutgers.edu/search.shtml
- Supreme Court and Appellate Division opinions, published by Law.com and the *New Jersey Law Journal*, www.law.com/nj

New Mexico

- Supreme Court and Court of Appeals, www.supremecourt.nm.org
- Supreme Court and Court of Appeals opinions since 1998, from FindLaw, www.findlaw.com/11stategov/nm/nmca.html
- Second Judicial District Court (no opinions), www.cabq.gov/cjnet/dst2alb

New York

- Court of Appeals, official site, opinions since January 2000, www.courts.state.ny.us/ctapps/decision.htm
- Court of Appeals opinions since 1990, from the Legal Information Institute, www.law.cornell.edu/ny/ctap
- Court of Appeals, synopses of decisions by e-mail. To subscribe, follow the instructions here: http://liibulletin.law.cornell.edu.
- New York Slip Opinions Service, http://nyslip.westgroup.com. Current slip opinions from the Court of Appeals, the Appellate Division of the Supreme Court, the Supreme Court and miscellaneous trial-level courts, provided free by West Group pursuant to its contract with the state to publish the New York Official Reports. Opinions remain on this site for approximately a month following their release.
- New York Courts, www.nycourts.com. From Law.com and the New York Law Journal, a six-month archive of opinions from the Court of Appeals, the Appellate Division of the Supreme Court and the Supreme Court.
- Court of Appeals opinions since 1992, from FindLaw, www.findlaw.com/11stategov/ny/nyca.html

North Carolina

- Supreme Court and Court of Appeals opinions since 1996, www.aoc.state.nc.us/www/public/html/opinions.htm
- Supreme Court and Court of Appeals opinions since 1994, from FindLaw, www.findlaw.com/11stategov/nc/ncca.html
- North Carolina Business Court, selected opinions since 1996, www.ncbusinesscourt.net

North Dakota

- Supreme Court opinions since 1992, www.court.state.nd.us
- Supreme Court opinions since 1996, from FindLaw, www.findlaw.com/11stategov/nd/ndca.html

Ohio

- Supreme Court opinions since 1992, as well as decisions of Ohio's First through Twelfth District Courts of Appeals and Ohio's Court of Claims, from the Reporter of Decisions, www.sconet.state.oh.us/rod/documents/default.asp
- Supreme Court opinions since January 1997, published by Ohio Lawyers Weekly, www.ohiolawyersweekly.com
- Supreme Court opinions since 1997, from FindLaw, www.findlaw.com/11stategov/oh/ohca.html
- First District Court of Appeals, opinions since November 2000, www.hamilton-co.org/appealscourt
- Second District Court of Appeals, opinions since 2001, www.sconet.state.oh.us/District_Courts/Districts/District2.htm
- Third District Court of Appeals, opinions beginning January 2001, www.sconet.state.oh.us/District_Courts/Districts/District3.htm
- Fourth District Court of Appeals, opinions beginning January 2001, www.sconet.state.oh.us/District_Courts/Districts/District4.htm
- Fifth District Court of Appeals, recent opinions, http://fifthdist.org
- Sixth District Court of Appeals, opinions beginning 1999, www.sconet.state.oh.us/District_Courts/Districts/District6.htm
- Seventh District Court of Appeals, opinions beginning 2001, www.sconet.state.oh.us/District_Courts/Districts/District7.htm
- Eighth District Court of Appeals, opinions since 1990, www.cuya-hoga.oh.us/appeals/default.htm
- Ninth District Court of Appeals, opinions beginning January 2001, www.ninth.courts.state.oh.us
- Tenth District Court of Appeals, www.sconet.state.oh.us/District_Courts/Districts/District10.htm

- Eleventh District Court of Appeals, opinions, www.11thcourt.co. trumbull.oh.us
- Twelfth District Court of Appeals, opinions since January 2000, www.twelfth.courts.state.oh.us
- Cuyahoga County Common Pleas Court, www.cuyahoga.oh.us/common
- Delaware Municipal Court, no opinions, but live, streamed court proceedings, www.municipalcourt.org

Oklahoma

- Oklahoma Supreme Court since 1890, Court of Criminal Appeals since 1908, Court of Civil Appeals since 1968, from the Oklahoma State Courts Network, www.oscn.net
- Opinions of the Supreme Court since 1922, Court of Appeals since 1968 and Court of Criminal Appeals from June 1995, along with Attorney General opinions since 1948, provided by the Oklahoma Attorney General's Public Legal Research System, http://oklegal. onenet.net
- Supreme Court since 1945 and Court of Appeals since 1936, from FindLaw, www.findlaw.com/11stategov/ok/okca.html

Oregon

- Supreme Court, Court of Appeals and Tax Court opinions since 1998, via official Judicial Department site, www.publications.ojd.state.or.us
- Supreme Court and Court of Appeals, opinion summaries and e-mail notification, provided by Willamette University College of Law, www.willamette.edu/law/wlo/oregon/index.htm
- Supreme Court, Court of Appeals and Tax Court, from FindLaw, www.findlaw.com/11stategov/or/orca.html

Pennsylvania

- Supreme Court opinions since November 1996, Superior Court opinions since December 1997, and Commonwealth Court opinions since January 1997, published by the state's Unified Judicial System, www.courts.state.pa.us/Index/Opinions/IndexOpinions.asp
- Supreme Court opinions since 1997, from FindLaw, www.findlaw. com/11stategov/pa/paca.html
- Supreme Court, Superior Court and Commonwealth Court, published by Law.com and The Legal Intelligencer, www.law.com/pa. To access opinions, a subscription is required at a cost of $170 a year, which includes a daily e-mail alert.

- Chester County, Lancaster County, Monroe County and Westmoreland County Courts of Common Pleas opinions, published by paopinions.org, www.paopinions.org

Rhode Island

- Supreme Court, opinions since September 1997, www.courts.state.ri.us/supreme/opinions.htm
- Superior Court opinions, www.courts.state.ri.us/superior/published-decisions.htm
- Supreme Court opinions since 1997, from FindLaw, www.findlaw.com/11stategov/ri/rica.html

South Carolina

- Supreme Court opinions since 1997 and Court of Appeals opinions since 1999, official site, www.judicial.state.sc.us/opinions/index.cfm
- Supreme Court opinions since 1996, from the University of South Carolina Law Center, www.law.sc.edu/opinions/opinions.htm
- Court of Appeals, beginning in 1999, from the University of South Carolina Law Center, www.law.sc.edu/ctapp/scctapp.htm
- Supreme Court opinions since 1997 and Court of Appeals opinions since 1999, from FindLaw, www.findlaw.com/11stategov/sc/scca.html

South Dakota

- Supreme Court opinions since 1996, official site, www.sdjudicial.com
- Supreme Court opinions since 1996, courtesy of the state bar, www.sdbar.org/opinions/default.htm
- Supreme Court opinions since 1996, from FindLaw, www.findlaw.com/11stategov/sd/sdca.html

Tennessee

- Supreme Court, Court of Appeals and Court of Criminal Appeals opinions, beginning from the latter half of 1995, www.tsc.state.tn.us
- Supreme Court and Court of Appeals opinions since 1995, from FindLaw, www.findlaw.com/11stategov/tn/tnca.html

Texas

- Supreme Court of Texas, opinions since 1997, www.supreme.courts.state.tx.us
- Court of Criminal Appeals, opinions since 1998, www.cca.courts.state.tx.us

- First Court of Appeals, Houston, opinions since November 1999, www.1stcoa.courts.state.tx.us
- Second Court of Appeals, Fort Worth, since September 2000, www.2ndcoa.courts.state.tx.us
- Third Court of Appeals, Austin, www.3rdcoa.courts.state.tx.us
- Fourth Court of Appeals, San Antonio, opinions since 1998, www.4thcoa.courts.state.tx.us
- Fifth Court of Appeals, Dallas, published and unpublished decisions, http://courtstuff.com/5th
- Sixth Court of Appeals, Texarkana, www.6thcoa.courts.state.tx.us
- Seventh Court of Appeals, Amarillo, www.7thcoa.courts.state.tx.us
- Eighth Court of Appeals, El Paso, opinions beginning in 2000, www.8thcoa.courts.state.tx.us
- Ninth Court of Appeals, Beaumont, www.9thcoa.courts.state.tx.us
- Tenth Court of Appeals, Waco, www.10thcoa.courts.state.tx.us
- Eleventh Court of Appeals, Eastland, www.11thcoa.courts.state.tx.us
- Twelfth Court of Appeals, Tyler, www.12thcoa.courts.state.tx.us
- Thirteenth Court of Appeals, Corpus Christi, www.13thcoa.courts.state.tx.us
- Fourteenth Court of Appeals, Houston, opinions since 1999, www.14thcoa.courts.state.tx.us
- Supreme Court and Courts of Appeals, published by Law.com and Texas Lawyer, www.law.com/tx. Access to opinions requires a subscription, which costs $125 a year.
- Supreme Court and Court of Criminal Appeals opinions since 1997, from FindLaw, www.findlaw.com/11stategov/tx/txca.html.

Utah

- Supreme Court and Court of Appeals opinions, since 1996, www.utcourts.gov/opinions
- Supreme Court opinions since 1996 and Court of Appeals opinions since 1997, from FindLaw, www.findlaw.com/11stategov/ut/utca.html.

Vermont

- Supreme Court opinions since 1994, http://dol.state.vt.us/www_root/000000/html/decisions.html
- Supreme Court opinions since 1997, from FindLaw, www.findlaw.com/11stategov/vt/vtca.html

Virginia

- Supreme Court and Court of Appeals opinions, available in WordPerfect or plain text, www.courts.state.va.us/opin.htm
- Supreme Court and Court of Appeals, published by Virginia Lawyers Weekly, www.virginialaw.com
- Supreme Court and Court of Appeals opinions since 1995, from FindLaw, www.findlaw.com/11stategov/va/vaca.html

Washington

- Supreme Court and Appeals Court opinions issued within the last ninety days, official courts' site, www.courts.wa.gov/opinions
- Supreme Court and Appeals Court opinions since 1998, from FindLaw, www.findlaw.com/11stategov/wa/waca.html
- LegalWA.org, www.legalwa.org. This site provides Supreme Court opinions beginning from 1939 and Appeals Court opinions beginning from 1969. The site is a joint project of the Washington State Bar Association, the Washington State Office of the Code Reviser, and the Municipal Research and Service Center.

West Virginia

- Supreme Court of Appeals, opinions since 1991, www.state.wv.us/wvsca/opinions.htm
- The Supreme Court also offers RSS newsfeeds of its recent opinions. The court has four feeds: recent opinions, civil topics, criminal topics and family topics. More information is available on the court's main opinions page, above.
- Supreme Court opinions since 1991, from FindLaw, www.findlaw.com/11stategov/wv/wvca.html
- West Virginia Court of Claims, opinions since 1985, www.legis.state.wv.us/Joint/Court/main.html

Wisconsin

- The Wisconsin court system provides full-text opinions of the Supreme Court since September 1995 and the Court of Appeals since June 1995, www.courts.state.wi.us
- Supreme Court and Court of Appeals, opinions since October 1995, from the Wisconsin Bar Association, www.wisbar.org/legalres
- Supreme Court and Court of Appeals opinions since 1995, from FindLaw, www.findlaw.com/11stategov/wi/wica.html

Wyoming

- Supreme Court opinions since January 1996, official site, courts.state.wy.us
- Supreme Court opinions since 1996, from FindLaw, www.findlaw.com/11stategov/wy/wyca.html

State Laws on the Internet

That government of the people, by the people, for the people, shall not perish from the Earth.

When President Lincoln spoke these words in 1863, he could hardly have imagined the Internet. Yet were he alive today, he undoubtedly would perceive the Internet's significance in bridging the information gap between the people, their government and the law.

A mere decade ago, the written laws were all but inaccessible, compiled in dense, dusty tomes shelved in libraries' most isolated corners. But by the middle of the 1990s, a handful of states had begun to experiment with putting their statutes on the Internet, foreshadowing a sea change in public access to the law. Today, every U.S. state's statutes are published on the Web, free to whomever wants them, with search tools that make it easy for anyone to pinpoint the pertinent law.

Were Lincoln a witness to this information revolution, he might well have viewed the Internet as an important guarantor of his vision that government remain of and for the people.

Herewith, a guide to finding state laws and legislative materials on the Internet.

Alabama

- Alabama Legislative Information System, www.legislature.state.al.us/ALISHome.html.
  ALIS includes the Code of Alabama, the state constitution, all bills and resolutions introduced in the current session, and all acts of the current session.
- Alabama Law Institute, www.ali.state.al.us.
  The text and status of bills to be presented before the legislature, courtesy of the Alabama Law Institute.

Alaska

- Alaska Legislature Online, www.legis.state.ak.us.
  This is a comprehensive site that includes the full text of statutes and bills, as well as session laws, executive orders, administrative regulations, legislative journals and committee reports, and more. Everything can be searched by key words,

- Republican Legislative Caucus, www.akrepublicans.org.
- Democratic Legislative Caucus, www.akdemocrats.org.
- Alaska's Republican and Democratic legislative caucuses each have Web sites that provide extensive information on current legislation, including links to full text and background information provided by a bill's sponsor. The sites also have press releases and other official announcements.

Arizona

- Arizona State Legislature, www.azleg.state.az.us.
  The legislature's site includes the full text of the Arizona Revised Statutes, the status and full text of all bills and adopted amendments, and all session laws, as well as floor calendars and committee agendas.

Arkansas

- Arkansas General Assembly, www.arkleg.state.ar.us.
  The General Assembly provides the full text of bills, acts and resolutions. Follow the "Research Resources" link to find the complete Arkansas Code and Constitution.

California

- Official California Legislative Information, www.leginfo.ca.gov.
  California, one of the first states to make its statutes and bills available on the Internet, has a Web site that includes the Constitution, the California Codes, the full text of all bills, the history and status of all bills, analyses of all bills, schedules, votes and related matters.
- FindLaw California: Codes and Statutes, http://california.lp.findlaw.com/ca01_codes/index.html.
  The California Code and Constitution are available here from FindLaw.

Colorado

- Colorado General Assembly, www.state.co.us/gov_dir/stateleg.html.
  Colorado's legislative body has the Colorado Revised Statutes, the text and status of House and Senate bills, bill digests since 1997, and executive branch rules and regulations.
- Colorado Revised Statutes, http://crs.aescon.com.
  Access to the statutes requires a subscription of $50 annually or $20 for three months.

Connecticut

- Connecticut General Assembly, www.cga.state.ct.us.
  Search full text of current statutes, bills, resolutions, public and special acts, and more, at the General Assembly's Web site. From the main page, follow the link, "Text Search."
- Connecticut State Library, www.cslib.org/psaindex.htm.
  The library provides the Connecticut General Statutes, revised to 2003, together with special and public acts through the current legislative term.

Delaware

- Michie Publications, www.michie.com.
  Michie, a division of LexisNexis, provides the full text of the Delaware Code and the Delaware Constitution.
- Delaware General Assembly, www.legis.state.de.us.
  All bills and legislation are published here. The Delaware Code is available via a link to Lexis Publishing.

District of Columbia

- Michie Publications, www.michie.com.
  Michie, a division of LexisNexis, provides the full text of the District of Columbia Code.

Florida

- Online Sunshine, www.leg.state.fl.us.
  Florida's Web site, called "On-Line Sunshine," offers the full text of the state's constitution, statutes and bills.

Georgia

- Georgia Constitution, www.law.emory.edu/GEORGIA/gaconst.html.
  Emory Law School publishes this version of the state constitution.
- Georgia General Assembly, www.legis.state.ga.us.
  The General Assembly provides the George Code and the text and status of bills.

Guam

- Guam Code Annotated, www.guam.net/guamlaw.

Hawaii

- Hawaii State Legislature, www.capitol.hawaii.gov.
  The state legislature provides the full text of Hawaii Revised Statutes, all bills and resolutions, session hearing notices, committee reports, and other legislative documents.
- Hawaii Legislative Reference Bureau, www.state.hi.us/lrb.
  The LRB prepares reports on bills passed and resolutions adopted. The site includes the text of the state constitution.

Idaho

- Access Idaho, www.state.id.us.
  Idaho's Web site offers the full text of the state constitution, statutes, current legislation and administrative rules.

Illinois

- Illinois General Assembly, www.legis.state.il.us.
  The General Assembly provides the state constitution, the Illinois Compiled Statutes, Public Acts, House and Senate schedules, and current legislation.

Indiana

- Indiana General Assembly, www.in.gov/legislative. The Indiana General Assembly provides the full text of the state constitution, the Indiana Code, the Indiana Register, and current bills.

Iowa

- Iowa General Assembly, www.legis.state.ia.us.
  The web site includes the full text of the Iowa Constitution, the Code of Iowa, session laws, administrative regulations and all bills and amendments.

Kansas

- accessKansas, www.accesskansas.org/government/laws-legal.html.
  The Information Network of Kansas has the full text of all bills and session laws, Kansas statutes and the state constitution. For a $75 annual subscription, accessKansas offers access to premium levels of government information, including an annotated version of the statutes.

Kentucky

- Kentucky Legislature, www.lrc.state.ky.us.
  This site has the full text of the Kentucky Constitution, Revised Statutes, Administrative Regulations, and pending bills.

Louisiana

- Louisiana State Legislature, www.legis.state.la.us.
  The legislature's Web site provides the full text of the state constitution, the state's codified laws, and all bills and legislation. From the main page, follow the link, "Louisiana Laws."

Maine

- Maine Legislature, http://janus.state.me.us/legis.
  The web site has the constitution, statutes, session laws and pending bills.

Maryland

- Maryland General Assembly, http://mlis.state.md.us.
  Available here are the full texts of current statutes and bills.
- Michie, www.michie.com.
  Michie provides the complete text of the Maryland code and rules.

Massachusetts

- General Court of Massachusetts, www.state.ma.us/legis/legis.htm.
  The state legislature provides the full text of the General Laws, session laws and bills.

Michigan

- Michigan Legislature, www.michiganlegislature.org.
  The state legislature publishes the Michigan Compiled Laws and current bills and resolutions.

Minnesota

- Minnesota State Legislature, www.leg.state.mn.us.
  The legislature publishes the full text of the constitution, statutes, session laws, administrative rules, and house and senate bills.

Mississippi

- Mississippi Code, www.mscode.com.
  This commercial site provides the Mississippi Code as revised through the current legislative session. Users can browse code sections using the table of contents at no cost. Full text searching of the code and access to current bills is limited to users who purchase a subscription.
- Mississippi Legislature, www.ls.state.ms.us.
  The full text and status of current bills are available from the state legislature.
- Michie Publications, www.michie.com.
  Michie, a division of LexisNexis, provides the full text of the Mississippi Code of 1972 and the state constitution.

Missouri

- Missouri General Assembly, www.moga.state.mo.us.
  This site offers the full text of the Missouri Constitution, Revised Statutes and bills, all of which can be searched by key word.

Montana

- Montana Legislative Branch, http://leg.state.mt.us.
  The legislature's site includes the Montana Constitution, the Montana Code Annotated, bills, journals and legislative histories.

Nebraska

- Nebraska Legislature Online, www.unicam.state.ne.us.
  The full text of Nebraska statutes, the state constitution and bills are at the legislature's Web site.

Nevada

- Nevada Legislature, www.leg.state.nv.us.
  Nevada Revised Statutes and Nevada Administrative Code are available through the state legislature's home page. The site also includes the full text of all proposed bills and resolutions.

New Hampshire

- New Hampshire General Court, http://gencourt.state.nh.us.
  The General Court has the full text of the state constitution, the Revised Statutes, and current bills and resolutions.

New Jersey

- New Jersey State Legislature, www.njleg.state.nj.us.
  The state legislature's home page has the text, index and history of bills in the current session; state statutes; the state constitution; the latest legislative calendar and digest; and related publications.

New Mexico

- New Mexico Legislature, http://legis.state.nm.us.
  The legislature provides the full text of all pending legislation and modifications and a bill locator service.
- Michie Publications, www.michie.com.
  Michie, a division of LexisNexis, provides the full text of the state's statutes, constitution and administrative code.

New York

- New York State Assembly Legislative Information System, http://assembly.state.ny.us/leg.
  This provides the full text of the constitution, consolidated and unconsolidated laws, chapters and bills.
- New York Consolidated Laws, http://caselaw.lp.findlaw.com/nycodes/index.html.
  FindLaw publishes this version of the New York statutes.

North Carolina

- North Carolina General Assembly, www.ncleg.net.
  The General Assembly's Web site offers the full text of statutes, bills and session laws, as well as the state constitution.

North Dakota

- North Dakota Legislative Branch, www.state.nd.us/lr.
  The constitution, statutes, bills, resolutions, journals and session laws are available in full text at this site.

Ohio

- Anderson's Ohio, http://onlinedocs.andersonpublishing.com.
  Anderson Publishing provides the full text of Ohio's constitution, Revised Code, session laws, and administrative code. They can be searched or browsed by their tables of contents.
- Ohio General Assembly, www.legislature.state.oh.us.

The General Assembly provides access to the constitution, Revised Code, session laws, and full text of bills and legislation. Some of these resources are on this site; others are provided through links to the Anderson Publishing site, above.

- Ohio Legislative Service Commission, www.lsc.state.oh.us.
  Bill analyses and status reports, from the Legislative Service Commission.

Oklahoma

- Oklahoma State Courts Network, www.oscn.net.
  This State Courts Network provides a "citationized" version of the Oklahoma Statutes, with each section followed by citations to court opinions that interpreted the section, and hyperlinks to the actual opinion.
- Oklahoma Legislature, www.lsb.state.ok.us.
  The legislature provides the full text of the constitution, statutes and legislative measures.
- Oklahoma Public Legal Research System, http://oklegal.onenet.net.
  The statutes of Oklahoma and the state constitution are available at this site, sponsored by the Oklahoma Attorney General.

Oregon

- Oregon State Legislature, www.leg.state.or.us.
  The legislature's site makes available the full text of Oregon statutes, pending bills, the Constitution, and related materials.

Pennsylvania

- The Pennsylvania Code, published and distributed by Fry Communications Inc., in cooperation with the Legislative Reference Bureau, www.pacode.com.
- Pennsylvania Consolidated Statutes, http://members.aol.com/StatutesPA/Index.html.
  A private lawyer operates this site, which includes the statutes, the constitution, court rules, and other materials.
- Pennsylvania General Assembly, www.legis.state.pa.us.
- The General Assembly provides the full text of bills and resolutions.

Rhode Island

- Rhode Island General Assembly, www.rilin.state.ri.us/gen_assembly/genmenu.html.

This site provides the full text of the constitution, the General Laws, Public Laws and current bills.

South Carolina

- South Carolina Legislature, www.scstatehouse.net.
  This site includes the text of current bills, the full text of the Code of Laws of South Carolina, the South Carolina Constitution, the Code of Regulations and the State Register.

South Dakota

- Legislative Research Council, http://legis.state.sd.us.
  This official site provides the full text of the state constitution and Codified Laws, session laws, current bills and state administrative rules.
- Michie Publications, www.michie.com.
  Michie, a division of LexisNexis, publishes the South Dakota Constitution and Codified Laws.

Tennessee

- Michie Publications, www.michie.com.
  Michie, a division of LexisNexis, publishes the full text of the Tennessee Code and the state constitution.
- Tennessee General Assembly, www.legislature.state.tn.us.
  The General Assembly publishes the text of bills and other legislative information. It provides access to the Tennessee Code via a link to Michie Publications.

Texas

- Texas Legislature Online, www.capitol.state.tx.us.
  The Texas legislature's site features the full text of the state constitution, statutes and bills, as well as bill history and information about the legislature.

Utah

- Utah State Legislature, www.le.state.ut.us.
  Utah's legislative site has the full text of the state code and constitution, as well as bills and legislative materials for the current and past legislative sessions.
- Michie Publications, www.michie.com.
  Michie, a division of LexisNexis, provides the Utah constitution and code.

Vermont

- Vermont Legislature, www.leg.state.vt.us.
  The full texts of statutes and bills are available via the legislature's home page.
- Michie Publications, www.michie.com.
  Michie, a division of LexisNexis, provides the full text of Vermont's statutes, constitution and court rules.

Virginia

- Virginia Legislative Information System, http://leg1.state.va.us.
  This Web site includes the full text, summaries, status and history of bills and resolutions. It also has the full text of the Code of Virginia and the Virginia Administrative Code.

Virgin Islands

- Michie Publications, www.michie.com.
  Michie, a division of LexisNexis, provides the full text of the Virgin Islands Code and the Revised Organic Act of 1954.

Washington

- Washington State Legislature, www.leg.wa.gov.
  The Revised Code, session laws, pending bills and the state administrative code are available through the legislature's Web site. Both statutes and bills are offered in full text and can be searched using key words.
  LegalWA.org, www.legalwa.org.
  This site provides current versions of the Revised Code of Washington and Washington Administrative Code. The site is a joint project of the Washington State Bar Association, the Washington State Office of the Code Reviser, and the Municipal Research and Service Center.

West Virginia

- West Virginia Legislature, www.legis.state.wv.us.
  The legislature provides the full text of the West Virginia code and current bills.

Wisconsin

- Wisconsin Legislature, www.legis.state.wi.us.
  The legislature's Web site includes the full text of statutes and annotations, available in a choice of Folio or Adobe Acrobat format. It also has the constitution, acts, bills and resolutions, legislative histories, and the state administrative code.

Wyoming

- Wyoming State Legislature, http://legisweb.state.wy.us.
  This site includes the full text of the state constitution, state statutes, House and Senate bills, and related information.

Appendix IV

A Brief Summary: Free Briefs on the Web

If you do not mind paying for them, you can obtain copies of legal briefs via the Web from several sources. But where can you find briefs for free?

Among the services that offer briefs for a price are Westlaw, www.westlaw.com, and LexisNexis, www.lexis.com, both of which have Supreme Court briefs. Westlaw includes briefs beginning with the Court's October 1990 term, while Lexis has briefs in some cases beginning from January 1979.

Two other services that sell copies of briefs are Brief Reporter, www.briefreporter.com, and BriefServe.com, www.briefserve.com. Brief Reporter offers briefs from a variety of state and federal courts, contributed by the lawyers who wrote them. Briefs are arranged by topic. The price of a brief is $40, or you can subscribe for $35 a month and pay $10 per brief.

BriefServe has Supreme Court briefs beginning with the 1984 term. It also offers all U.S. circuit court briefs since 1981, and a selection of California and New York appellate briefs. Briefs cost $25 each, but there is a two brief minimum. But a number of sites offer copies of briefs at no cost. Some provide briefs from a range of courts covering a variety of topics, others are more focused.

Briefs for Free

Sites with broad collections include:

- American Law Sources On-Line, www.lawsource.com/also/usa. cgi?usb. While ALSO does not directly provide copies of briefs, it has assembled a useful collection of links to amicus curiae briefs available elsewhere on the Web. These include briefs filed in both state and federal courts.
- Appellate.net, www.appellate.net/briefs. More than 250 state and federal briefs covering a range of topics are available here. All were written by lawyers in the Supreme Court and Appellate Practice Group of Chicago-based Mayer, Brown, Rowe & Maw. Briefs are listed by case and subject matter, and include citations to the appellate decision.
- Capital Defense Weekly, http://capitaldefenseweekly.com/briefbank.html. A guide to finding briefs relating to the defense of capital cases.

- FindLaw's Supreme Court Center, http://supreme.lp.findlaw.com/supreme_court/briefs. FindLaw has Supreme Court briefs beginning with the 1999-2000 term. You can download them for free in various formats.
- Samuelson Law, Technology and Public Policy Clinic, http://brief-bank.samuelsonclinic.org/notices.cfm. This clinic at Boalt Hall Law School maintains a brief bank devoted to law, technology and public policy. Its broad-ranging collection of briefs filed in U.S. courts is organized by case name.
- Securities Class Action Clearinghouse, http://securities.stanford.edu. This Stanford Law School site maintains an archive of filings in federal class action securities fraud litigation. Its collection includes more than 2,000 litigation documents, including briefs.

Court Archives

A growing number of appellate courts are publishing on the Internet the briefs they receive. This includes two federal circuit courts:

- Seventh U.S. Circuit Court of Appeals, www.ca7.uscourts.gov/briefs.htm. Includes briefs filed with the court beginning in 2001.
- Eighth U.S. Circuit Court of Appeals, www.ca8.uscourts.gov/brfs/brFrame.html. Includes briefs filed beginning in 2000.

Briefs filed in a handful of state supreme courts are also available:

- Florida Supreme Court, www.flcourts.org/pubinfo/summaries/archives.html.
- Kentucky Supreme Court, www.nku.edu/~chase/library/kysct-briefs.htm.
- Michigan Supreme Court, http://courts.michigan.gov/supreme-court/Clerk/msc_orals.htm.
- Montana Supreme Court, http://www.lawlibrary.state.mt.us/dscgi/ds.py/View/Collection-1981.
- North Dakota Supreme Court, www.court.state.nd.us.
- Texas Supreme Court, www.supreme.courts.state.tx.us/ebriefs/CURRENT.HTM.
- Wisconsin Supreme Court, http://library.law.wisc.edu/elecresources/databases/wb.

Federal Entities

The federal government is one of the best sources of free legal briefs. Federal entities that publish their briefs on the Web include:

- Federal Labor Relations Authority, www.flra.gov/solicitor/briefs/brf_list.html. Briefs filed by the FLRA.
- Federal Trade Commission, www.ftc.gov/ogc/briefs.htm. Amicus briefs filed by the FTC.
- U.S. Department of Justice, www.usdoj.gov/05publications/05_2.html. The Justice Department's legal documents collection includes all Supreme Court briefs filed by the solicitor general since 1988 and selected briefs beginning in 1982. It also includes a wide-ranging collection of appellate briefs filed by the Antitrust Division dating back to 1993, along with selected briefs filed by the Civil Division and the Civil Rights Division.
- U.S. Department of Justice, ADA briefs, www.ada.gov/briefs/adabrief.htm. Briefs filed by the Justice Department on issues relating to the Americans With Disabilities Act.
- U.S. Department of Labor, Office of the Solicitor, www.dol.gov/sol/media/briefs/main.htm. Significant briefs filed in cases involving occupational safety, fair labor practices and benefit security.
- U.S. Equal Employment Opportunity Commission, www.eeoc.gov/litigation/appbriefs.html. Selected EEOC appellate and amicus briefs addressing significant legal issues.
- U.S. Office of Special Counsel, www.osc.gov/library.htm. Briefs filed by this independent federal investigative and prosecutorial agency.
- U.S. Securities and Exchange Commission, www.sec.gov/litigation/briefs.shtml. Selected briefs filed by the SEC and its staff.

Bar and Legal Associations

- American Bar Association, Section of Intellectual Property Law, http://www.abanet.org/intelprop/amicusarchive.html. Amicus briefs filed by the Section starting in 2003.
- American Intellectual Property Law Association, www.aipla.org/Content/NavigationMenu/IP_Issues_and_Advocacy/Amicus_Briefs/Amicus_Briefs1.htm. Amicus briefs since 1995.
- American Association of Law Libraries, www.ll.georgetown.edu/aall-wash/briefs.html. Selected amicus curiae briefs filed since 1997.
- Association of Corporate Counsel, www.acca.com. Amicus briefs dating back to 1983.

- Association of Trial Lawyers of America, http://www.atla.org/IntheCourts/Tier3/AmicusCuriaeProgram.aspx. ATLA provides copies of amicus briefs it has filed starting in 2000.
- Intellectual Property Owners Association, www.ipo.org. Follow the link "IP in the Courts" for briefs dating back to 1997.
- International Trademark Association, http://www.inta.org/policy/amicus.html. Recent amicus briefs filed by INTA.

Advocacy Groups

Advocacy organizations publish briefs filed in cases in which they appeared as parties or as amicus curiae.

- American Civil Liberties Union, www.aclu.org. Follow the link "Supreme Court" for a library of documents related to Supreme Court cases in which the ACLU played a role dating back to 1994. The library includes a number of briefs filed by the ACLU as amicus curiae. From that page, look for the link "Legal Documents" to find documents filed by the ACLU in other courts. Here, too, are a number of briefs. Search by topic or ACLU affiliate.
- American Society of Association Executives, www.asaenet.org/publicpolicy/amicus. The association's 2000 Supreme Court amicus brief on the lobby tax.
- Anti-Defamation League, www.adl.org/Civil_Rights/ab. Amicus briefs in cases involving issues that range from the separation of church and state to racial discrimination to censorship.
- Atlantic Legal Foundation, www.atlanticlegal.org/briefs.html. Amicus briefs on issues that include courtroom science, charter schools and reverse discrimination.
- Capital Defense Network, http://www.capdefnet.org./fdprc/contents/appellate_briefs/brief_frames.htm. A number of briefs on issues relating to capital defense.
- Cato Institute, www.cato.org/pubs/legalbriefs/lbriefs.html. Briefs cover a range of issues, including race-based preferences, school vouchers, drug testing and interstate commerce.
- Center for Democratic Communications, www.nlgcdc.org/briefs.html. This arm of the National Lawyers Guild has briefs related to FCC licensing of low power radio transmissions.
- Children's Rights, http://childrensrights.org/Legal/cases.htm. Briefs filed in cases involving child welfare and foster care.

- cyberSLAPP.org, http://www.cyberslapp.org/litigation/index.cfm. Briefs in cases in which people were sued for online speech.
- Electronic Frontier Foundation, www.eff.org. This San Francisco-based organization, devoted to protecting civil liberties in cyberspace, maintains extensive collections of legal documents from cases in which it has been involved, including its own briefs and those of its opponents. To find them, follow the link labeled "Cases."
- Electronic Privacy Information Center, www.epic.org. Briefs on free speech and privacy.
- Harvard University Civil Rights Project, www.civilrightsproject.harvard.edu/policy/legal_docs/legal_briefs.php. Small collection of briefs related to affirmative action and race-conscious admissions.
- Institute for Justice, www.ij.org/cases/school/facts/body.shtml. Its School Choice Information Center has briefs on both sides of the school choice issue.
- Institute for Public Affairs, www.ou.org/public/publib/briefs.htm. Briefs filed by this division of the Union of Orthodox Jewish Congregations of America.
- Jewish Law, www.jlaw.com/Briefs. A collection of briefs filed by various Jewish organizations.
- Lambda Legal, www.lambdalegal.org/cgi-bin/iowa/library?class=5. Briefs on issues of interest to lesbians and gays.
- NORML Legal Brief Bank, http://www.norml.org/index.cfm?Group_ID=3411. All briefs submitted by the National Organization to Reform Marijuana Laws.
- NOW Legal Defense and Education Fund, www.nowldef.org/html/issues/whr/briefs.shtml. Briefs related to women's human rights.
- PsycLAW.org, www.psyclaw.org/amicus.html. Amicus briefs filed by the American Psychological Association on a surprisingly diverse array of topics, from confidentiality and competency to antitrust and employment. For older cases, only summaries of the briefs are provided.
- Public Citizen, www.citizen.org/litigation/briefs. This consumer organization, founded by Ralph Nader in 1971, provides briefs on corporate accountability, union democracy, consumer rights, health and safety, and other topics.
- Public Interest Litigation Clinic, http://www.pilc.net/bref.html. Sample briefs by this Missouri legal clinic.
- Society for American Archaeology, www.saa.org/Repatriation/kennewickbriefs.html. Fascinating but esoteric briefs filed in litigation concerning ownership of the remains of the 9,000-year-old Kennewick Man.

- Trial Lawyers for Public Justice, http://www.tlpj.org/briefs_docu-ments.htm. Briefs filed in cases involving the civil justice system, civil rights, consumers' rights, environmental enforcement, and other issues.
- University of Florida, Center on Children & the Law, www.law.ufl.edu/centers/childlaw/library.shtml. Briefs relating to custody and educational services.

Index

(Note: Web sites listed in the Appendices have not been indexed unless they are also listed in a Chapter)

F

G

H

J

O

S

V

W-X

Y

Z

Southern Living

Party
Snacks
Cookbook

Jean Wickstrom
Assistant Foods Editor

Library of Congress Catalog Card Number: 74-79236

Manufactured in the United States of America

First Printing 1974

Cover Photo   By Taylor Lewis

Cover Recipes By Lee Vliet
               Kaspin Stuffed Eggs
               Marinated Broccoli
               Stuffed Cherry Tomatoes
               Mushrooms Stuffed with
                   Spinach Soufflé
               Hot Cocktail Turnovers
               Shrimp Mousse

Illustrated   By Amasa Smith, Jr.

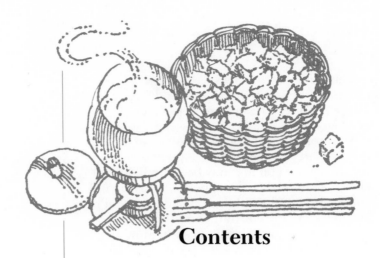

Contents

Introduction

Tempting party snacks can be the difference between the success and failure of an open house, a reception, or just a casual get-together.

Your selection of snacks will depend on the type of party you're hosting. Appetizers served before a dinner may be quite light and just enough to whet the appetite. Heavier and more substantial snacks are called for if you're hosting a lengthy cocktail party. When planning your party menu, keep in mind that party food should be planned with consideration for variety in color, texture, temperature, and contrast in flavor.

We have included all kinds of party snacks in our collection of over 400 recipes—hot appetizers, cold appetizers, spreads and dips, canapés, dainty party food, and beverages. Many of these foods can be prepared ahead of time and frozen. Spreads and dips actually improve as flavors blend in chilling. Hot appetizers can be made early and kept warm in chafing dishes or on hot trays. Advance preparation of food gives you more free time to spend with your guests.

The perfect snacks are those which are easy to serve and easy to eat. Whether you're serving an intimate group or a large crowd, concentrate on bite-size servings and pick-up foods that can be served with wooden picks or picked up with the fingers.

Hot Appetizers

Bacon-Bobs

1 (¾-pound) package wafer-thin bacon
1 cup Sauterne
¼ cup soy sauce
½ pound chicken livers, cut into halves
1 (1-pound) package frozen potato bites

Cut bacon slices in half; dip into mixture of Sauterne and soy sauce. Wrap around chicken liver pieces and potato bites. Thread on skewers or fasten each with a wooden pick. Place in a shallow dish and bake at 400° for 25 minutes or until bacon is crisp and golden. Yield: about 5 dozen.

Bacon-Chestnut Appetizers

15 slices bacon, cut lengthwise
2 (5-ounce) cans water chestnuts, drained (30 chestnuts)

Wind bacon slices around whole chestnuts; secure with wooden picks. Place on a cookie sheet and bake at 350° for about 25 minutes, until bacon is well done and crisp, turning the chestnuts when half done if necessary. Drain on paper towels and keep warm until serving time. Yield: 2½ dozen.

Hot Bacon Appetizers

½ pound bacon, cooked
¾ cup shredded pasteurized process American cheese
¼ cup butter or margarine, softened
2 teaspoons caraway seed
 Melba rounds

Crumble bacon; combine with cheese, butter, and caraway seed. Spread on melba rounds. Place on a cookie sheet and broil about 4 inches from source of heat until cheese is melted and bubbling hot. Remove from broiler and serve immediately. Yield: about 4 dozen.

Bacon Roll-Ups

¼ cup butter or margarine
½ cup water
1½ cups packaged herb-seasoned stuffing
1 egg, slightly beaten
¼ pound hot or mild bulk pork sausage
½ to ⅔ pound sliced bacon

Melt butter in water in a saucepan. Remove from heat; stir into stuffing, then add egg and sausage. Blend thoroughly. Chill for about an hour for easier handling; then shape into small oblongs about the size of pecans. Cut bacon slices into thirds, crosswise; wrap one piece around dressing mixture and fasten with a wooden pick. Place in a shallow pan and bake at 375° for 35 minutes, or until brown and crisp, turning at halfway point in cooking. Drain on paper towels and serve hot. May be made the day before baking; also freezes well before baking. Yield: about 3 dozen.

Curry-Coconut Cheese Balls

2 (8-ounce) packages cream cheese
1⅓ cups flaked coconut
1½ teaspoons curry powder

Form 64 small cream cheese balls; set aside. Toss coconut with curry powder until well mixed; spread in a thin layer in a shallow baking dish. Toast at 350° for 8 to 12 minutes or until delicately browned. Stir or shake dish often to brown coconut evenly. Cool. Roll cream cheese balls in curry-coconut. Chill until firm. Yield: 64 appetizers.

Gulfport Cheese Balls

3 egg whites
¾ pound extra sharp Cheddar cheese, shredded
⅓ cup all-purpose flour
4 dashes hot pepper sauce
   Dash salt
1 teaspoon parsley flakes
   Paprika
   Cornmeal
   Hot melted shortening or salad oil

Beat egg whites very stiff; add cheese, flour, hot pepper sauce, salt, parsley flakes, and paprika. Roll mixture into small balls and roll in cornmeal. Place balls in a skillet with about ¼-inch hot shortening or salad oil. Turn constantly with long fork. Cook until golden brown. Yield: about 25 to 30 appetizers.

Olive-Filled Cheese Balls

2 tablespoons butter or margarine, softened
1 cup shredded sharp Cheddar cheese
½ cup all-purpose flour
   Dash cayenne pepper
½ teaspoon celery seed
2 (3-ounce) jars stuffed olives

Mix butter and cheese until smooth; blend in flour, cayenne pepper, and celery seed. Shape 1 teaspoon of dough around each olive to form a ball. Place on cookie sheets; bake at 400° for 15 minutes. Serve hot or cold.

To freeze, place uncooked balls about ½ inch apart on a cookie sheet (make sure balls do not touch each other); cover with heavy-duty aluminum foil and place in the freezer. After cheese balls are thoroughly frozen, remove from cookie sheet and store in plastic bags in the freezer. To serve, place frozen balls on a cookie sheet. Bake at 400° for 18 to 20 minutes. Yield: about 3 dozen.

Olive-Cheese Snacks

1 (5-ounce) jar bacon-cheese spread
4 tablespoons butter or margarine
   Dash hot pepper sauce
   Dash Worcestershire sauce
¾ cup all-purpose flour
30 medium stuffed green olives

Blend cheese and butter together until light and fluffy. Add hot pepper sauce and Worcestershire sauce; mix well. Stir in flour; mix to form a dough. Shape around olives, using about 1 teaspoon dough for each. Place on an ungreased cookie sheet. Bake at 400° for 12 to 15 minutes or until golden brown. Yield: about 2½ dozen.

Cheese Pennies

1 (5-ounce) jar pasteurized process sharp American cheese spread
¼ cup shortening
⅔ cup all-purpose flour

Combine all ingredients; mix on medium speed of electric mixer for 20 to 30 seconds. On a lightly floured surface, mold dough into two 8-inch rolls, 1 inch in diameter. (Dough will be soft but not sticky.) Wrap in waxed paper; refrigerate for 2 hours or overnight.

Cut rolls into ⅛-inch slices; place on ungreased cookie sheets. Bake at 375° for 12 to 15 minutes or until slightly browned. Yield: about 6 dozen.

Cheese-Rice Crispy

2 cups shredded cheese
1 cup butter or margarine, softened
2 cups all-purpose flour
2 cups crisp rice cereal

Combine cheese and butter; add flour and mix well. Add crisp cereal and mix well. Shape into small balls and place on ungreased cookie sheets. Flatten each ball with a fork and bake at 375° for 10 minutes. Yield: about 5 dozen.

Olive-Cheese Tidbits

½ cup butter or margarine, softened
1 (5-ounce) jar English Cheddar cheese
1¼ cups all-purpose flour
    Dash salt
48 medium stuffed olives, drained and dried

Cut butter and cheese into flour; add salt. Form into small balls around olives and seal well. Let stand in refrigerator overnight. Bake at 400° for about 15 minutes or until brown. Yield: 4 dozen.

Caraway Biscuits

1 cup all-purpose flour
1 teaspoon dry mustard
1 teaspoon salt
½ cup shredded Swiss cheese (or Swiss and
    Parmesan cheese mixed)
½ teaspoon paprika
2 teaspoons caraway seed
⅓ cup butter or margarine
    Several drops hot pepper sauce
½ teaspoon Worcestershire sauce
    About 3 tablespoons cold water

Combine flour, mustard, and salt in a bowl. Stir in cheese, paprika, and caraway seed. Cut in butter until particles are about the size of peas. Sprinkle with hot pepper sauce, Worcestershire sauce, and cold water. Toss lightly with a fork until dough holds together. Form into a ball and roll out on a floured surface into a 13- x 9-inch rectangle. Using a pastry wheel, cut into 1-inch squares. Place on ungreased cookie sheets, sprinkle with a little paprika, and bake at 425° until brown, just about 7 minutes. Do not overbake. Will freeze. Yield: about 8 dozen.

Cheesies

1½ cups butter or margarine, softened
1½ pounds sharp Cheddar cheese, shredded
 3 cups all-purpose flour
1½ teaspoons salt
 ¾ teaspoon hot pepper sauce
4½ cups crushed corn flakes

Cream butter; add cheese, flour, and salt. Mix well. Add hot pepper sauce and corn flakes (mixture will be crumbly). Form into small balls and place on a lightly greased cookie sheet. Bake at 350° for 15 to 20 minutes or until dry and lightly browned. Yield: 7 to 8 dozen.

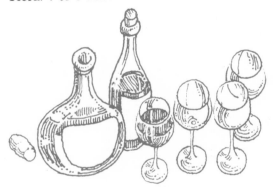

Sesame Balls

½ cup butter or margarine, softened
½ pound pasteurized process American
    cheese, shredded
1 cup all-purpose flour
    Dash salt and pepper
    Dash paprika
    Dash onion powder
    Toasted sesame seed

Combine butter and cheese. Add flour, salt, pepper, paprika, and onion powder; mix well. Form into balls; flatten and dip into toasted sesame seed. Bake on an ungreased cookie sheet at 375° for 15 to 20 minutes. Yield: about 4 dozen.

Cheese Biscuits

½ pound butter or margarine, softened
½ pound sharp Cheddar cheese, shredded
1 or 2 dashes cayenne pepper
1 egg
1 long loaf white bread, thinly sliced

Place the first 4 ingredients in small bowl of an electric mixer and beat until fluffy.

Use 1 long loaf white bread. Stack three slices; remove crusts. Cut into quarters. Spread cheese and butter mixture generously between slices; then ice top and sides very thinly. Place on a lightly greased cookie sheet and bake at 350° for 12 to 15 minutes. Serve warm. Yield: 3 dozen.

Note: Biscuits freeze beautifully and require no thawing before baking. To freeze, complete the icing, place biscuits on a flat tray and place uncovered in freezer until firm; then store in freezer container with waxed paper between layers.

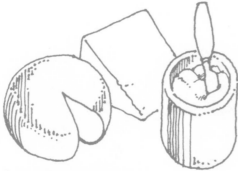

Crunchy Cheese Biscuits

½ cup butter or margarine, softened
1 cup all-purpose flour
1 cup shredded sharp Cheddar cheese, softened
½ teaspoon salt
  Hot pepper sauce and Worcestershire sauce to taste
1 cup rice cereal bits

Blend all ingredients except cereal bits by hand in a bowl until thoroughly mixed. Work in cereal bits. Pinch off into tiny balls about the size of a nickel. Place on an ungreased cookie sheet; press down with a fork and bake at 325° for 10 minutes or until faintly colored. Yield: about 4 dozen.

Sesame Cocktail Biscuits

1 (3-ounce) package cream cheese, softened
½ cup butter or margarine, softened
1¼ cups all-purpose flour
½ teaspoon seasoned salt
⅓ cup toasted sesame seed
  Coarse (kosher) salt or more seasoned salt

Cream cheese and butter together in large bowl of electric mixer until blended. Add flour, ½ teaspoon seasoned salt, and sesame seed. Mix thoroughly. Flour hands lightly and form mixture into a long roll about 1 inch in diameter. Wrap in waxed paper and chill thoroughly.

To bake, slice into ¼-inch-thick rounds; place on a greased cookie sheet and bake at 350° for about 15 minutes or until light golden. While still hot, sprinkle with a few grains of coarse salt or a little seasoned salt. Store in an airtight container; biscuits may be frozen, then thawed in same container. Yield: 7 to 8 dozen.

Note: To toast sesame seed, place in a shallow baking dish and bake at 275° for 25 minutes, shaking the dish a little from time to time.

Tiny Cheese Biscuits

4½ cups all-purpose flour
½ teaspoon salt
½ to 1 teaspoon cayenne pepper
1 pound sharp Cheddar cheese, shredded
1 pound butter or margarine, softened

Combine flour, salt, and cayenne pepper; blend in cheese and butter until smooth. Pat or roll out on a floured surface to about ⅓-inch thickness. Cut with inside of doughnut cutter or other small cutter. (To avoid dough clinging to cutter, dip cutter frequently into cold water.) Place about ⅛ inch apart on an ungreased cookie sheet and bake at 325° for about 15 minutes. Do not allow the biscuits to brown; it's easy to overbake them. Store in an airtight container, placing waxed paper between layers. Freezes beautifully; thaw in closed tin. Yield: about 10 dozen.

Parmesan Cheese Bites

1 cup all-purpose flour
1 or 2 dashes cayenne pepper
⅔ cup grated Parmesan cheese
½ cup butter or margarine, softened
    Evaporated milk or cream

Place flour in a mixing bowl; stir in pepper and cheese. Cut in butter with a pastry blender; then work dough with hands until it holds together. Roll out on a floured surface to ⅓-inch thickness and cut into 1- or 1½-inch squares. (A pastry wheel gives an attractive edge.) Transfer to an ungreased cookie sheet; brush tops with evaporated milk or cream and bake at 350° for 12 to 15 minutes. Do not overbake. Freezes well. Yield: about 2½ dozen.

Hot Cheese Logs

6 slices thinly sliced bread
3 tablespoons melted butter or margarine, divided
4 (1-ounce) wedges Gruyère cheese
1½ teaspoons anchovy paste

Trim bread crusts and cut each slice of bread in half. Brush with half the butter. Cut each cheese wedge into 3 slices. Place a slice of cheese on each piece of bread. Spread cheese with anchovy paste. Roll bread tightly around cheese. Fasten with a wooden pick. Brush with remaining melted butter. Place on a cookie sheet and broil slowly, turning to brown all sides. Yield: 1 dozen.

Cheese Nibblers

1 cup all-purpose flour
1 cup shredded pasteurized process American or Cheddar cheese
½ cup butter or margarine, softened
¼ teaspoon salt

Combine all ingredients in a bowl and blend with a pastry blender. Knead in bowl to form a dough. Shape into balls, using 1 scant teaspoonful of dough for each. Place on

ungreased cookie sheets. Bake at 350° for 12 to 15 minutes. Dough may be stored in refrigerator and baked as needed. Yield: about 5 dozen.

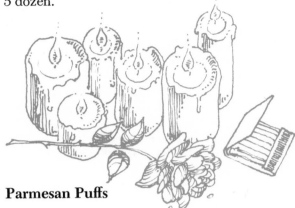

Parmesan Puffs

½ cup mayonnaise
¼ cup grated Parmesan cheese
1 teaspoon Worcestershire sauce
⅛ teaspoon onion salt
2 teaspoons sherry
48 buttery crackers

Combine mayonnaise, cheese, Worcestershire sauce, onion salt, and sherry. Blend. Spread about 1 teaspoonful of mixture on each cracker. Place on broiler pan. Place top of puffs 2 inches from source of heat; broil 2 to 3 minutes or until lightly browned. Yield: 4 dozen.

Parmesan Cheese Puffs

⅔ cup boiling water
1 cup piecrust mix
2 eggs
4 teaspoons grated Parmesan cheese
    Salad oil
    Grated Parmesan cheese

Heat water in a saucepan over medium heat; add piecrust mix and stir quickly until mixture forms a ball around spoon. Remove from heat; add eggs, one at a time, beating well after each addition. Stir in Parmesan cheese. Heat oil (enough to be 2 inches deep) in a skillet. Drop mixture by half teaspoonsful into hot oil. Fry until brown on both sides. Drain on absorbent paper. Dust with more Parmesan cheese. Yield: 3 dozen.

Cheese Puffballs

1½ cups shredded sharp Cheddar cheese
1 tablespoon all-purpose flour
½ teaspoon paprika
  Pepper
3 egg whites, stiffly beaten
  Cracker crumbs
  Salad oil

Combine cheese, flour, and seasonings. Add beaten egg whites and shape into small balls. Roll in cracker crumbs. Fry in hot oil at 375°. Drain. Serve hot. Yield: 8 servings.

Cheese Sticks

1 cup all-purpose flour
½ teaspoon salt
⅛ teaspoon cayenne pepper
1½ teaspoons baking powder
4 tablespoons butter or margarine, softened
½ cup shredded Cheddar cheese, softened
3 tablespoons commercial sour cream

Combine dry ingredients. Cut in butter and cheese with a pastry blender or 2 forks; stir in sour cream. Shape into a ball and chill for 2 hours. On a lightly floured board, roll out dough ⅛ inch thick. Cut into strips 3 x ¼ inches. Bake at 425° for 8 minutes. Yield: 2 to 3 dozen.

Cheese Straws

3½ cups all-purpose flour
¼ teaspoon salt
¾ teaspoon cayenne pepper
1½ cups butter or margarine
1 pound sharp Cheddar cheese, shredded

Combine flour, salt, and pepper in a large bowl. Cut butter into small pieces and blend into dry ingredients with fingers until mixture resembles coarse crumbs. Add cheese and continue blending until dough hangs together and is no longer crumbly.

Work with ¼ of the dough at a time. Roll out to a rectangle ⅛ inch thick; cut into strips ½ inch wide and about 4 inches long, using a pastry wheel or sharp knife. Place on ungreased cookie sheets and bake at 375° for 10 to 12 minutes, only until very lightly browned. (Do not overbake, which is easy to do.) Remove, cool, and store in an airtight container, placing waxed paper between layers. Freezes beautifully. Yield: about 10 dozen.

Favorite Cheese Straws

½ cup butter or margarine
2 cups shredded pasteurized process American cheese
½ teaspoon salt
⅛ teaspoon cayenne pepper
1½ cups all-purpose flour

Cream butter and cheese together. Add salt and cayenne pepper and work in the flour. Cover and chill for about 1 hour. Roll out about ⅛ inch thick on a lightly floured cloth or board. Cut in sticks about ½ inch wide and 4 inches long with a sharp knife or pastry wheel. Place on ungreased cookie sheets and bake at 375° for 10 to 12 minutes. Yield: about 4 dozen.

Sesame Cheese Straws

½ pound extra sharp Cheddar cheese, shredded
1 (2¼-ounce) jar sesame seed
½ cup butter or margarine, softened
1¼ cups all-purpose flour
1 teaspoon salt
⅛ teaspoon cayenne pepper

Allow shredded cheese to reach room temperature. Toast sesame seed in a heavy skillet, stirring constantly over low heat for 20 minutes or until golden brown; cool. Combine cheese, butter, flour, salt, and cayenne pepper; work dough until mixture is thoroughly blended. Add sesame seed. Roll dough to ⅛-inch thickness; cut into 4- x ½-inch strips. Bake at 400° for 12 to 15 minutes or until golden brown; cool on a wire rack. Place in an airtight container. These stay fresh for several weeks. Yield: 5 dozen.

Cheese Snappy Wafers

1 cup butter or margarine
2 cups all-purpose flour
1 (8-ounce) package sharp cheese, shredded
½ teaspoon cayenne pepper
½ teaspoon salt
2 cups crisp rice cereal

Cut butter into flour until texture resembles coarse meal. Mix in cheese, cayenne pepper, and salt. Fold in cereal. Pinch off small pieces, place on an ungreased cookie sheet, and pat flat. Bake at 350° for 15 minutes. Yield: about 5 dozen.

Magic Blue Cheese Wafers

¼ cup butter or margarine
3 ounces blue cheese, crumbled
1 cup all-purpose flour
4 teaspoons milk
  Sesame seed

Combine butter, cheese, and flour; mix with a pastry blender until mixture is crumbly. Add just enough milk to hold mixture together. Roll up in a cylinder shape, about 1¼ inches in diameter. Wrap in waxed paper or heavy-duty aluminum foil. Place in the freezer for several hours. Cut into ⅛-inch slices. Sprinkle tops of wafers with sesame seed. Bake on an ungreased cookie sheet at 400° for 5 to 6 minutes. Yield: about 4 dozen.

Welcome Cocktail Wafers

¾ cup butter or margarine
⅔ cup shredded Cheddar cheese
½ cup crumbled blue cheese
1 small clove garlic, crushed
1 teaspoon minced fresh parsley
1 teaspoon minced chives
2 cups all-purpose flour

Beat butter with Cheddar and blue cheese in large bowl of electric mixer until well blended. Add all other ingredients and beat again. Dust hands lightly with flour and shape into two rolls about 1½ inches in diameter. Chill thoroughly. Slice ⅛ inch thick and bake at 375° for 8 to 10 minutes. Yield: about 6 dozen.

Olive Whirligigs

1 cup shredded sharp pasteurized process
  American cheese
3 tablespoons butter or margarine, softened
  Dash cayenne pepper or hot pepper sauce
½ cup all-purpose flour
½ cup chopped stuffed olives

Combine cheese, butter, and cayenne pepper; stir in flour. Between sheets of waxed paper, roll to a 10- x 6-inch rectangle about ⅛ inch thick. Sprinkle pastry with chopped olives. Beginning with long side, roll up as for a jelly roll, lifting waxed paper slightly with each turn. Seal edge. Wrap roll in the waxed paper. Chill for at least 1 hour. Cut into ¼-inch slices. Place about 2 inches apart on ungreased cookie sheets; bake at 400° for 10 minutes or until edges are lightly browned. Serve hot. Yield: 3½ dozen.

Sesame Seed Sticks

¾ cup butter or margarine
2 cups all-purpose flour
1 teaspoon salt
2 dashes cayenne pepper
  Ice water
1 cup sesame seed
  Salt

Cut butter into flour mixed with salt and cayenne pepper. Sprinkle ice water over dough and toss with a fork until dough holds together, as for pastry. Roll dough out on a floured board to ⅛-inch thickness and cut into strips 1 x 3 inches. Place on an ungreased cookie sheet, sprinkle generously with sesame seed, and bake at 325° for about 15 minutes. Before removing from pan and while still hot, sprinkle with a little salt. May be frozen. Yield: about 6 dozen.

Parmesan Kisses

3 egg whites
¼ teaspoon salt
⅛ teaspoon cayenne pepper
1 (2½-ounce) jar grated Parmesan cheese
  Salad oil

Beat egg whites with salt and cayenne pepper until they hold stiff peaks. Fold in cheese. Drop by teaspoonsful into hot oil. Fry until brown on both sides. Drain on absorbent paper; serve hot. Yield: 2 dozen.

Caraway Crisps

2 cups all-purpose flour
1 teaspoon baking powder
1 teaspoon salt
½ cup butter or margarine
2 tablespoons cream cheese
1 egg, beaten
1 egg white, unbeaten, or milk
  Caraway seed
  Coarse salt or kosher salt

Combine flour, baking powder, and salt in a bowl. Cut in butter and cream cheese until granular. Add beaten egg and work with fingers until dough is smooth. Chill; then roll out between sheets of waxed paper or on pastry cloth to ¼-inch thickness. Cut into strips 1 x 3 inches. Brush with egg white or milk; sprinkle with caraway seed and salt. Twist each strip and place on an ungreased cookie sheet. Bake at 400° for about 15 minutes or just until golden. Yield: about 3 dozen.

Chicken Balls

1 pound uncooked chicken breasts
3 tablespoons chopped onions
10 water chestnuts
1 (2½-ounce) can mushrooms, drained
2 tablespoons cornstarch
½ teaspoon salt
2 tablespoons soy sauce
1 tablespoon sherry
2 egg whites, stiffly beaten
  Salad oil

Bone chicken breasts and put through food grinder with onion, water chestnuts, and mushrooms. Add cornstarch, salt, soy sauce, sherry, and stiffly beaten egg whites. Form into small balls and fry in deep hot oil. Drain and serve warm with wooden picks. Yield: about 4 dozen.

Luau Bits

10 water chestnuts, cut into halves
5 chicken livers, cut into quarters
10 slices bacon, cut into halves
¼ cup soy sauce
2 tablespoons brown sugar

Wrap water chestnuts and chicken livers in bacon slices. Secure bacon slices with wooden picks. Marinate in mixture of soy sauce and brown sugar for 4 hours. Broil about 3 inches from source of heat until bacon is crisp. Yield: about 1½ dozen.

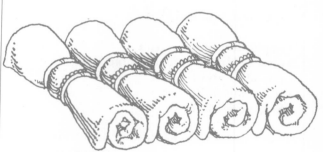

Chicken Puffs

1 (10-ounce) package frozen patty shells, thawed
1 (4¾-ounce) can chicken spread
1 tablespoon instant minced onion
1 tablespoon freshly squeezed lemon juice
2 tablespoons commercial sour cream
3 tablespoons grated Parmesan cheese

Roll each patty shell into a 3-inch square on a floured board. With a sharp knife, cut each square in half diagonally. Place triangles on a cookie sheet. Bake at 400° for 10 minutes or until golden brown. Combine chicken spread, onion, lemon juice, sour cream, and cheese. Split each triangle horizontally and fill with chicken mixture. Return to oven for 2 minutes. Serve hot. Yield: 1 dozen.

Chicken Almond Swirls

1 (8-ounce) can refrigerated crescent
    dinner rolls
1 (4¾-ounce) can chicken spread
1 tablespoon diced toasted almonds
1 tablespoon mayonnaise
½ teaspoon freshly squeezed lemon juice
    Seasoned salt

Separate dough into 4 rectangles; press along perforations to seal. Combine remaining ingredients; spread on rectangles. Roll up each rectangle, jelly roll fashion, starting with long side. Slice each roll into 8 slices. Place cut side down on a greased cookie sheet. Bake at 375° for 12 to 15 minutes or until golden brown. Serve warm. Yield: about 2½ dozen.

Polynesian Chicken Wings

1 pound chicken wings
1 (8-ounce) jar sweet-sour salad dressing

Cut chicken wings so that you have a drumstick and a wing tip. Discard the wing tip, or cook for broth and reserve for some other use.

Dip chicken portions in sweet-sour salad dressing. Arrange pieces so that they do not touch on a heavy-duty aluminum foil-lined cookie sheet. Bake at 325° for 1 hour, basting occasionally with the sauce, so that they are golden brown. Do not raise the heat or the meat will brown too quickly. Keep chicken warm in a chafing dish. Yield: 12 servings.

Cherry-Sauced Chicken Wings

3 pounds chicken wings
1 (16-ounce) can pitted dark sweet cherries
¼ cup brown sugar
2 teaspoons grated fresh gingerroot, or ½
    teaspoon ground ginger
1 small clove garlic, minced
½ cup soy sauce
¼ cup port
2 tablespoons freshly squeezed lemon juice

Cut off and discard the small wing tips of chicken wings. Cut between the main and second wing joints to make 2 pieces from each wing. Place chicken in a bowl. Place cherries with syrup in a blender and blend until smooth. Add remaining ingredients. Pour over chicken wings and marinate 2 to 3 hours, turning occasionally. Drain, reserving marinade. Place chicken wings in a single layer in baking dish. Bake at 450° for 10 minutes. Turn and bake for an additional 10 minutes. Reduce temperature to 350°. Continue to bake 20 minutes longer or until tender, brushing 2 or 3 times with reserved cherry marinade. Serve warm. Yield: about 3 dozen.

Note: Remaining marinade may be thickened with 2 tablespoons cornstarch to serve as a dipping sauce.

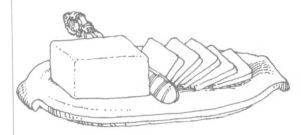

Crab Appetizers

1 pound crabmeat
1 tablespoon grated onion
¼ cup butter or margarine, melted
¼ cup all-purpose flour
1 cup milk
1 egg yolk, beaten
½ teaspoon Worcestershire sauce
¼ teaspoon salt
    Dash pepper
¾ cup dry bread crumbs
    Salad oil

Remove any shell or cartilage from crabmeat. Sauté onion in butter; blend in flour. Add milk gradually and cook until thick, stirring constantly. Combine egg yolk and seasonings. Stir a little of the hot sauce into egg yolk; add to remaining sauce, stirring constantly. Add crabmeat; blend into a paste and cool. Shape teaspoonsful of crab mixture into small balls. Roll in crumbs. Fry at 375° in a basket in deep oil for 2 minutes or until brown. Drain on absorbent paper. Serve on wooden picks. Yield: about 7 dozen.

Corned Beef Spread Puff

 1 egg white
 ¼ cup shredded sharp Cheddar cheese
 ⅛ teaspoon salt
 ⅛ teaspoon paprika
 ¼ cup mayonnaise
 24 melba rounds
 1 (4½-ounce) can corned beef spread

 Whip or beat egg white until stiff; fold in cheese, salt, paprika, and mayonnaise. Spread melba rounds with corned beef spread. Top with egg white mixture and broil until puffs are golden brown, about 5 minutes. Serve hot. Yield: 2 dozen.

Crab Dabs

 2 (6½- or 7½-ounce) cans crabmeat, drained
 ⅓ cup soft bread crumbs
 2 tablespoons dry sherry
 1 teaspoon chopped chives
 1 teaspoon dry mustard
 ¼ teaspoon salt
 10 slices bacon, cut into thirds

 Remove any remaining shell or cartilage from crabmeat; chop crabmeat. Combine all ingredients except bacon. Mix thoroughly. Chill for 30 minutes. Shape tablespoon-size portions of crabmeat into small rolls. Wrap bacon around crab rolls and secure with a wooden pick. Place crab rolls on a broiler pan. Broil about 4 inches from source of heat for 8 to 10 minutes. Turn carefully. Broil 4 to 5 minutes longer or until bacon is crisp. Yield: 2½ dozen.

Crab Newburg Appetizer

 1 pound crabmeat, fresh or canned
 4 hard-cooked eggs, grated
 1 small onion, grated
   Salt to taste
   Cayenne pepper or hot pepper sauce
 2 tablespoons butter or margarine
 2 tablespoons all-purpose flour
 2 cups milk
 ½ pound Cheddar cheese, shredded
   Miniature pastry shells or melba toast

 Combine crabmeat, eggs, onion, salt, and cayenne pepper.
 Melt butter in top of double boiler; add flour and blend until smooth. Add milk and cook until mixture thickens. Add cheese; stir and cook until cheese blends with sauce. Add crabmeat mixture and cook until hot. Serve in pastry shells or with melba toast. Yield: 20 to 25 servings.

Crab or Shrimp Puffs

 2 (6½- or 7-ounce) cans crabmeat or shrimp
 1 cup finely chopped celery
 ½ cup mayonnaise or salad dressing
 2 tablespoons chopped onion
 2 tablespoons chopped sweet pickle
   Salt to taste
   Puff Shells

 Drain crabmeat or shrimp. Combine all ingredients except Puff Shells. Mix thoroughly. Cut tops from Puff Shells. Fill each with approximately 2 teaspoonsful of salad. Yield: about 4½ dozen.

Puff Shells

 ½ cup boiling water
 ¼ cup butter or margarine
   Dash salt
 ½ cup all-purpose flour
 2 eggs

 Combine boiling water, butter, and salt in a saucepan; bring mixture to a boil. Add flour and stir vigorously until mixture forms a ball and leaves the sides of pan. Remove from heat.
 Add eggs, one at a time, beating thoroughly after each addition. Continue beating until a stiff dough is formed. Drop by level teaspoonsful onto a well-greased cookie sheet. Bake at 450° for 10 minutes. Reduce heat to 350° and bake for 10 additional minutes. Yield: about 4½ dozen.

Crabmeat Rolls

½ cup half-and-half
1 egg
2 sprigs parsley, stemmed
2 celery tops
  Salt
½ teaspoon pepper
  Dash cayenne pepper
3 slices bread, crumbled
1 (6-ounce) can crabmeat, packed in water
      or
6 ounces fresh crabmeat
10 slices bacon

Put half-and-half, egg, parsley, celery tops, salt, pepper, cayenne pepper, and half the bread in a blender. Cover and blend about 1 minute or until mixture is smooth. Empty into a bowl. Flake crabmeat and combine with blended mixture along with the rest of the crumbled bread. Shape into 10 small cakes. Wrap each in a slice of bacon. Broil on all sides until bacon is crisp. Yield: 10 appetizers.

Hot Creamed Crab

1 (8-ounce) package cream cheese, softened
½ cup mayonnaise
1 tablespoon freshly squeezed lemon juice
½ teaspoon Worcestershire sauce
1 teaspoon all-purpose flour
  Dash cayenne pepper
1 (7½-ounce) can crabmeat, drained and
  shredded
⅓ cup slivered toasted almonds
  Salt to taste
  Crackers or melba toast

Beat cheese until smooth in small bowl of electric mixer. Add mayonnaise, lemon juice, Worcestershire sauce, flour, and cayenne pepper; beat again until smooth. Fold in crabmeat, almonds, and salt to taste. Turn into a covered flameproof casserole dish and bake at 300° for 20 minutes. Place over heat (candle or other heating device), or turn into a chafing dish and keep warm until serving time. This is a very delicately flavored mixture and should be served with unsalted crackers or plain melba toast. Yield: 2½ cups.

Crabmeat Maryland

6 tablespoons butter or margarine, divided
3 tablespoons all-purpose flour
2 cups milk
1 pound crabmeat
½ cup whipping cream or half-and-half
  Salt, pepper, and paprika
¼ cup dry sherry
  Freshly squeezed lemon juice
  Toast points or melba rounds

Melt 4 tablespoons butter in top of double boiler placed over direct low heat. Blend in flour; gradually add milk, stirring constantly until thick and smooth.

Place pan over hot water, cover, and cook for about 5 minutes. Add crabmeat (which has been carefully picked over), stirring gently to avoid breaking lumps. When heated through, carefully stir in cream and remaining 2 tablespoons butter. Season to taste with salt, pepper, and paprika. Add sherry and lemon juice to taste. Keep heat low until serving time; then transfer to a chafing dish. May be served over toast points or with melba rounds for dipping. Yield: 8 servings.

Date Whirl-Ups

1 (8-ounce) package pitted dates
32 pecans
½ pound thinly sliced cooked ham
1 (8-ounce) can refrigerated crescent
  dinner rolls
¼ cup finely shredded Cheddar cheese

Stuff each date with a pecan. Cut ham slices into strips the same width as the dates and wrap a strip around each stuffed date. Roll each half of refrigerated dough (4 triangles), on a lightly floured board, into a 13- x 6-inch rectangle. Sprinkle with cheese. Cut into fourths lengthwise and crosswise. Place a stuffed date on each piece of dough and roll up. Place on an ungreased cookie sheet, seam side down. Bake at 375° for 10 to 13 minutes or until lightly browned. Serve hot. Yield: about 2½ dozen.

Caramel Fondue

2 (10-ounce) jars caramel topping
¼ cup butter or margarine
  Angel food cake cubes
  Pound cake cubes
  Marshmallows
  Pineapple chunks
  Banana chunks
  Apple wedges
  Mandarin orange sections
  Maraschino cherries
  Flaked coconut, toasted
  Chopped salted peanuts

Heat caramel topping and butter in a saucepan over low heat. Stir until butter is melted and sauce is smooth. Serve in a fondue pot or chafing dish. Spear cake cubes, marshmallows, or fruit on forks; dip in sauce, then in coconut or nuts. Yield: about 2½ cups.

Chocolate Fondue

1 (6-ounce) package semisweet chocolate
  morsels
½ cup light corn syrup
1 teaspoon vanilla extract
  Dash salt
  Marshmallows
  Assorted fruit

Combine all ingredients except marshmallows and fruit over hot (not boiling) water; stir until chocolate melts and mixture is smooth. Remove from heat; keep warm over hot water. Dip marshmallows or fruit on wooden picks into chocolate fondue. If desired, use drained canned pineapple cubes, drained mandarin oranges, canned black cherries, banana chunks, fresh apple slices, or drained canned fruits for salads, cut into chunks. Yield: about ¾ cup.

Ham Fondue

2 (4½-ounce) cans deviled ham
½ cup cream of mushroom soup
½ cup commercial sour cream
2 tablespoons sherry
  French bread cubes

Combine deviled ham and soup in the top of a double boiler; heat to boiling over direct heat, stirring occasionally. Place over boiling water; stir in sour cream and sherry. Cover and heat until warm. Serve in a fondue pot over warmer. Serve with French bread cubes. Yield: about 2 cups.

Shrimp Fondue

1 garlic clove
1 (1¾-ounce) can cream of shrimp soup
1 cup finely shredded Swiss cheese
2 tablepoons dry white wine
  Rye or French bread, unsliced

Rub chafing dish or top of double boiler with garlic; discard garlic. Add soup and cheese; heat until cheese melts. Stir in wine. Cut bread into 1½-inch squares. To serve, spear a piece of bread with a long fork and dip into hot cheese mixture. Yield: about 1¾ cups.

Swiss Fondue

1 pound Swiss cheese, shredded
¼ cup all-purpose flour
1 clove garlic, halved
2 cups Sauterne
½ teaspoon salt
½ teaspoon Worcestershire sauce
  Dash ground nutmeg
  French bread, raw vegetables, cooked ham
  cubes or cooked shrimp

Toss together cheese and flour. Rub inside of a saucepan with garlic; discard garlic. Add wine and heat until bubbles rise. Over low heat, add cheese, ½ cup at a time, stirring after each addition until cheese is melted. Add salt, Worcestershire sauce, and nutmeg. Transfer to a fondue pot. Serve with cubes of French bread, raw vegetables, cooked ham cubes, or cooked shrimp. Yield: 3½ cups.

Shrimp-Cheese Fondue

1 (10¾-ounce) can cream of shrimp soup
2 teaspoons instant minced onion
2 cups shredded Swiss cheese
1 (4½-ounce) can shrimp, drained and diced
¼ cup dry sherry
   Raw vegetables or breadsticks

Heat soup and onion in a saucepan over low heat. Add cheese and stir until cheese is melted. Add shrimp and sherry. Transfer to a fondue pot. Serve with raw vegetables or breadsticks. Yield: 2¾ cups.

Sloppy Joe Fondue

1 (15¼-ounce) can barbecue sauce and beef
   for sloppy Joes
½ teaspoon instant minced onion
½ teaspoon oregano or marjoram
1 cup (4 ounces) shredded pasteurized
   process American cheese
   French bread cubes

Combine sloppy Joe mixture, seasoning, and cheese; heat, stirring constantly, until cheese melts. Serve with bread cubes. Serve in a chafing dish, fondue pot, or casserole dish over a candle warmer. Yield: 1¾ cups.

Savory Swiss Fondue

1 clove garlic, cut in half
1 pound Swiss cheese, shredded
   Dash salt
   Dash pepper
   Dash ground nutmeg
1 cup dry white wine
¾ cup cold water, divided
¼ cup cornstarch
   Crackers
   Cooked meatballs
   Cooked ham cubes
   Cooked whole shrimp

Rub bottom and sides of a deep ovenproof dish or flameproof glass saucepan with garlic. Discard garlic. Add cheese, seasonings, wine, and ½ cup cold water. Cook over medium heat, stirring constantly, just until cheese is melted. (Cheese and liquid will not be blended.) Combine cornstarch and remaining ¼ cup cold water until smooth. Using a wire whisk, stir cornstarch mixture into melted cheese and wine. Continue cooking over medium heat for about 5 minutes or until fondue is thick and creamy. To serve, keep hot in a chafing dish or over a candle warmer. Serve with crackers, cooked meatballs, cooked ham cubes, or cooked whole shrimp. Yield: about 3 cups.

Cocktail Frankfurters

¾ cup prepared mustard
1 cup currant jelly
8 to 10 frankfurters

Combine mustard and jelly in a chafing dish or double boiler. Diagonally slice frankfurters into bite-size pieces. Add to sauce and heat through. Yield: 10 servings.

Fritosburgers

2 eggs, beaten
2 tablespoons cornstarch
1 tablespoon soy sauce
1 medium onion, finely chopped or grated
⅛ teaspoon pepper
3 cups corn chips, crumbled
1 pound lean ground beef
1 teaspoon Ac´cent

Combine eggs, cornstarch, soy sauce, onion, and pepper; mix well. Add corn chips; stir and allow to stand for 20 minutes. Crumble beef; add Ac´cent and mix well. Add beef to egg mixture. Shape into 1-inch balls; place on a heavy-duty aluminum foil-covered cookie sheet and broil until brown. Remove from heat; serve with wooden picks. Yield: about 2½ dozen.

Deviled Ham Triangles

1 (8-ounce) can refrigerated crescent
   dinner rolls
1 (4½-ounce) can deviled ham
¼ cup drained crushed pineapple

Unroll dough and separate into eight
triangles along perforated edges. Combine
deviled ham and pineapple. Place two mounds
of mixture, about ½ inch apart, in the center
of each of four triangles. Top each with a
second triangle; press dough together around
edges and in between the two mounds of
filling. Cut each in half, in between the two
mounds of filling, to form two smaller filled
triangles. Place triangles on an ungreased
cookie sheet and press edges of triangles with
a fork to seal well. Bake at 375° for 15 minutes
or until golden brown. Serve warm or cold.
Yield: 8 triangles.

Ham Pin-Ups

2 (4-ounce) packages cooked sliced ham
2 (8-ounce) cans refrigerated crescent rolls
  Barbecue sauce (optional)

Separate slices of ham. Roll strips of
crescent rolls out flat. Do not separate
triangular pieces. Place slices of ham
lengthwise on top of dough, overlapping
pieces slightly for continuity. Roll ham into
dough, jelly roll style. Cut rolled dough into
slices, ½ inch thick. Place on top rack of grill.
Cook, turning once, at medium heat until
biscuits are puffy and golden brown (about 8
to 10 minutes). If desired, sprinkle Pin-Ups
with barbecue sauce after they have been
turned on grill. Yield: 10 to 15 servings.

Fruity Bobs

1 medium banana
1 (8-ounce) can pineapple chunks, drained
1 (11-ounce) jar mandarin orange sections,
  drained
1 (8-ounce) jar maraschino cherries, drained
1 (8-ounce) jar honey
  Flaked coconut (optional)

Peel banana and cut into ½-inch slices.
Alternate fruit on skewers, topping with a
cherry. Brush with honey and place on top
rack of grill. Cook at low to medium heat until
fruit is thoroughly heated. If desired, roll
honey-coated fruit skewers in flaked
coconut before grilling. Yield: 6 to 8 servings.

Snack Kabobs

4 slices bacon, quartered
1 (7-ounce) package frozen small crab puffs,
  partially thawed
1 cooked chicken breast, boned and cut into
  chunks
1 avocado, cut into chunks
16 pineapple chunks
2 bananas, cut into thick slices
  Commercial Italian salad dressing

String meat on short skewers alternately
with fruit. Brush with salad dressing. Grill
over hot coals, turning once and basting with
dressing. Yield: 16 kabobs.

Mystery Hors d'Oeuvres

2 medium onions, finely chopped
2 tablespoons butter or margarine
  Fresh parsley, chopped
2 medium tomatoes, chopped
1 tablespoon Worcestershire sauce
  Pinch cayenne pepper
  Salt and pepper to taste
2 or 3 eggs, beaten
  Strips of buttered toast

Sauté onion in butter with chopped parsley
until faintly golden brown. Add tomatoes,
Worcestershire sauce, cayenne pepper, salt,
and pepper. Add eggs and scramble. Serve hot
on strips of buttered toast. Yield: 6 to
8 servings.

Liverwurst-Onion Cups

1 (4¾-ounce) can liverwurst spread
1 tablespoon commercial sour cream
½ teaspoon freshly squeezed lemon juice
½ cup crumbled French fried onions
1 (8-ounce) can refrigerated crescent
   dinner rolls
   Commercial sour cream

Combine liverwurst spread, sour cream, lemon juice, and onions. Unroll crescent rolls, and cut into four rectangles. Cut each rectangle into six equal pieces; roll each piece into a ball and place one in each of 24 small (1¾-inch) ungreased muffin cups. Press dough out to uniform thickness to cover bottom and sides of muffin cups, nearly to tops of cups. Fill with about 1 teaspoon liverwurst spread mixture, level with edge of dough. Top each with small dab of sour cream. Bake at 375° for 15 minutes. Serve warm. Yield: 2 dozen.

Note: Dough cups may be shaped ahead and kept covered in refrigerator an hour or so before filling and baking.

Macaroni Appetizers

2 cups small shell macaroni, uncooked
   Salad oil for frying
   Seasoned salt

Cook macaroni according to package directions, but cook only 6 minutes. Drain. Dry thoroughly on absorbent paper. Deep fry at 375° until golden brown (about 8 minutes). Drain. Turn onto absorbent paper. Sprinkle with salt to taste. Stir well with a fork. Yield: about 2½ dozen.

Lobster Boats

½ pound fresh or frozen cooked lobster meat
24 fresh mushrooms, approximately 1½ inches
   in diameter
¼ cup cream of mushroom soup
2 tablespoons soft bread crumbs
2 tablespoons mayonnaise or salad dressing
¼ teaspoon Worcestershire sauce
⅛ teaspoon hot pepper sauce
   Dash pepper
   Grated Parmesan cheese

Thaw frozen lobster meat. Drain lobster meat and remove any remaining shell or cartilage; chop meat. Rinse and dry mushrooms; remove stems. Combine soup, bread crumbs, mayonnaise, seasonings, and lobster. Stuff each mushroom cap with 1 tablespoon lobster mixture. Sprinkle with cheese. Place mushrooms on a well-greased cookie sheet. Bake at 400° for 10 to 15 minutes or until lightly browned. Yield: 2 dozen.

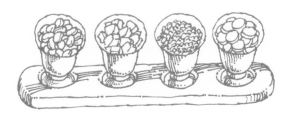

Burgundy Meatballs

1 pound ground chuck
½ cup cornflake crumbs
1 small onion, minced
¾ teaspoon cornstarch
   Dash ground allspice
1 egg, beaten
1 tablespoon Worcestershire sauce
¼ cup chili sauce
½ cup evaporated milk
1 teaspoon salt

Combine all ingredients; mix well and shape into teaspoon-size balls. Place on a cookie sheet with sides and bake at 400° for 10 to 15 minutes. (May be baked ahead; freezes well.) To serve, make Sauce and simmer in top of a chafing dish. Yield: about 3½ dozen.

Sauce

2¼ tablespoons cornstarch
1 cup water
2 beef bouillon cubes
¾ cup Burgundy
½ teaspoon salt
⅛ teaspoon pepper

Combine ingredients and cook, stirring constantly, over medium heat until mixture is thick. Yield: about 1½ cups.

Burgundy Beef Balls

⅓ cup water
1 slice white bread, toasted
1 pound ground beef
1 egg
⅛ teaspoon ground nutmeg
1 teaspoon salt
¼ cup finely chopped onion
1 tablespoon salad oil
3 tablespoons all-purpose flour
2 cups water
⅔ cup Burgundy
½ teaspoon salt
1 tablespoon light brown sugar

Pour water over toast and mix well. Add ground beef, egg, nutmeg, salt, and onion; mix until blended. Shape mixture into 45 small balls, allowing 1 rounded teaspoonful for each; brown in salad oil. Remove meatballs from pan and set aside.

Measure drippings and return 2 tablespoons to pan; add flour and stir until browned. Stir in water until smooth; add wine, salt, and brown sugar. Cook slowly, stirring constantly, for 20 minutes. Add meatballs and cook just until heated through. Yield: 45 meatballs.

Chafing Dish Meatballs

1 pound ground beef
½ cup dry bread crumbs
⅓ cup minced onion
¼ cup milk
1 egg
1 tablespoon chopped parsley
1 teaspoon salt
⅛ teaspoon pepper
½ teaspoon Worcestershire sauce
¼ cup shortening
1 (12-ounce) bottle chili sauce
1 (10-ounce) jar grape jelly

Combine ground beef, bread crumbs, onion, milk, egg, parsley, salt, pepper, and Worcestershire sauce; gently shape into 1-inch balls. Melt shortening in a large skillet; brown meatballs. Remove meatballs from skillet; drain fat. Heat chili sauce and jelly in skillet until jelly is melted, stirring constantly. Add

meatballs and stir until coated. Simmer for 30 minutes. Serve hot in a chafing dish. Yield: 5 dozen.

Gourmet Meatballs

1 (8-ounce) package liver sausage
1 egg, beaten
¼ pound ground beef
1 cup bread crumbs
¼ cup catsup
½ teaspoon salt
   All-purpose flour
¼ cup butter or margarine, melted
½ (1⅜-ounce) package dry onion soup mix
1 cup hot water

Combine liver sausage and egg; add ground beef, bread crumbs, catsup, and salt; mix just until mixture is uniform. Shape into balls the size of a walnut. Roll in flour and fry in butter until brown. Sprinkle with soup mix. Pour hot water over meatballs. Simmer for 15 minutes. Serve hot. Yield: about 4 dozen.

Lilliput Meatballs

1 pound ground beef
½ cup soft bread crumbs
1 tablespoon finely chopped onion
¼ cup milk
1 teaspoon salt
2 tablespoons butter or margarine
½ cup dry sherry or Burgundy
½ cup catsup
¼ teaspoon dried oregano

Combine beef, bread crumbs, onion, milk, and salt. Shape into little balls using 1 teaspoon meat mixture per ball. Heat butter in a large, heavy skillet; brown balls nicely on all sides. Pour off most of the fat from the skillet. Combine wine, catsup, and oregano; pour over balls; check seasonings. Cover and simmer slowly for about 30 minutes, shaking pan gently from time to time to cook balls evenly. Serve in a chafing dish or in a flameproof casserole dish set over a candle warmer. Provide wooden picks for spearing balls. Yield: about 5 dozen tiny meatballs; double the recipe for a cocktail supper for about 20.

Mini-Meatballs

1 pound ground pork sausage
¼ pound ground beef
1 egg, slightly beaten
¼ cup dry bread crumbs
1 (5-ounce) can water chestnuts
2 cups commercial barbecue sauce

Place pork sausage and ground beef in a bowl; add egg and bread crumbs; mix well. Cut each water chestnut into 4 to 6 small pieces. Shape a scant tablespoonful of meat around each piece. Roll in palms of hands to make balls. Place meatballs in an unheated skillet; cook slowly, turning carefully until browned on all sides. Transfer meatballs to a chafing dish. Add barbecue sauce and keep warm over a low flame. Serve with wooden picks. Yield: about 4 dozen.

Party Meatballs

2 tablespoons butter or margarine
½ cup finely minced onion
1½ pounds ground meat (equal parts beef, veal, and pork)
2 slices white bread
2 eggs
3 tablespoons minced fresh parsley
        or
1 tablespoon dried parsley
¼ teaspoon paprika
¼ teaspoon pepper
1 teaspoon seasoned salt
½ teaspoon grated lemon rind
1 teaspoon freshly squeezed lemon juice
1 tablespoon Worcestershire sauce
½ teaspoon anchovy paste
    About 2 tablespoons salad oil
3½ cups beef broth (bouillon cubes and hot water may be used)
    Sauce

Heat butter in a large skillet or Dutch oven. Add onion and sauté until golden. Put meat in a large bowl. Soak bread in water, squeeze dry, and add to meat. Add onions and all other ingredients except oil and broth. Mix thoroughly, using a wooden spoon or your hands. Form into 1-inch balls and brown in

heated oil. Remove to paper towels to drain. Strain drippings from skillet, reserving the brown bits that cling to the skillet if they aren't scorched.

Heat broth in the same skillet and bring to boiling point. Add meatballs, cover, and simmer for 15 minutes. Remove meatballs and prepare Sauce. Place balls in Sauce and heat gently for about 30 minutes. Transfer to a chafing dish just before serving. Yield: 6 to 8 servings.

Sauce

4 tablespoons butter or margarine
4 tablespoons all-purpose flour
2½ cups meatball liquid
1 tablespoon drained capers
1 tablespoon minced parsley
1 teaspoon freshly squeezed lemon juice

Heat butter in a large skillet. Blend in flour until smooth and barely golden. Gradually add 2½ cups of the liquid left from cooking the meatballs. Cook, stirring constantly, until smooth. Add capers and parsley, then lemon juice. May be prepared ahead and frozen. Yield: about 2½ cups.

Peanut Butter Meatballs

½ cup peanut butter (smooth or crunchy)
½ pound ground beef
¼ cup finely chopped onion, or 2 teaspoons instant minced onion
2 tablespoons chili sauce
1 teaspoon salt
⅛ teaspoon pepper
1 egg, beaten
2 tablespoons peanut oil

Combine peanut butter, beef, onion, chili sauce, salt, pepper, and egg; shape into 3 dozen small meatballs. Fry in hot peanut oil, turning to brown on all sides. Serve hot with wooden picks. Yield: 3 dozen.

Baked Creamy Stuffed Mushrooms

18 to 20 medium mushrooms
1 (4½-ounce) can deviled ham
1 (3-ounce) package cream cheese, softened
2 tablespoons commercial sour cream
1 tablespoon minced chives
1 egg yolk, lightly beaten
¼ cup fine bread crumbs

Clean mushrooms, remove stems, and chop. Place mushroom caps hollow side up on a lightly greased cookie sheet. Combine deviled ham, cream cheese, sour cream, chives, and egg yolk; add chopped mushroom stems and fill caps with mixture. Sprinkle top with bread crumbs. Bake at 450° for 8 to 10 minutes. Serve immediately. Yield: 20 appetizers.

Swedish Meatballs

3 slices white bread
2 cups water
1½ pounds ground beef
½ pound mild pork sausage
1 onion, minced
3 tablespoons butter or margarine, divided
2 medium potatoes, boiled and mashed
1 teaspoon salt
⅛ teaspoon pepper
1 teaspoon seasoned salt
2 eggs
　Gravy

Soak bread in water for a few minutes; press to drain. Combine beef and sausage with bread. Sauté onion in 1 tablespoon butter; add to meat along with mashed potatoes, seasonings, and eggs. Beat together with electric mixer until light. Shape into 1½-inch balls and brown in remaining butter, gently turning balls to brown evenly; remove carefully. When meatballs are done, prepare Gravy using the same skillet. Return meatballs to skillet. Cover and simmer for 40 minutes. Will freeze. Yield: 10 to 12 servings.

Gravy

3 tablespoons butter or margarine
3 tablespoons all-purpose flour
3 cups beef broth (bouillon cubes and water)
1 cup cream
½ teaspoon seasoned salt
1 teaspoon Kitchen Bouquet
　Pepper to taste

Heat butter in same skillet used for browning meatballs; add flour and stir until yellow. Gradually add beef broth and stir until smooth and thick. Add cream and seasoned salt, then Kitchen Bouquet and pepper.

Deviled Crab-Stuffed Mushrooms

½ cup milk
3 tablespoons butter or margarine, divided
15 cheese crackers
1 (6-ounce) package frozen crabmeat, thawed and coarsely chopped
½ teaspoon dry mustard
1 teaspoon minced onion
½ teaspoon salt
½ teaspoon horseradish
　Dash pepper
12 large fresh mushroom caps

Heat milk and 1 tablespoon butter; crumble crackers into milk. Remove from heat. Stir in remaining ingredients except mushroom caps. Spoon into mushroom caps. Melt remaining butter and brush mushroom caps. Place in a shallow baking dish. Bake at 350° for 20 to 30 minutes or until mushrooms are tender. Yield: 1 dozen.

Mushrooms Royale

1 pound medium mushrooms
4 tablespoons butter or margarine, divided
¼ cup finely chopped green pepper
¼ cup finely chopped onion
1½ cups soft bread crumbs
½ teaspoon salt
½ teaspoon ground thyme
¼ teaspoon turmeric
¼ teaspoon pepper

Wash, trim, and dry mushrooms thoroughly. Remove stems; finely chop enough stems to measure ⅓ cup. Melt 3 tablespoons butter in a skillet. Cook and stir chopped mushroom stems, green pepper, and onion in butter until tender, about 5 minutes. Remove from heat; stir in remaining ingredients except mushroom caps and remaining 1 tablespoon butter. Melt 1 tablespoon butter in a shallow baking dish. Fill mushroom caps with stuffing mixture; place mushrooms filled side up in butter in a baking dish. Bake at 350° for 15 minutes.

Broil mushrooms 3 to 4 inches from source of heat for 2 minutes. Serve hot. Yield: about 3 dozen.

Mushrooms Stuffed with Spinach Soufflé

1 (10-ounce) package frozen chopped spinach
2 tablespoons butter or margarine
2 tablespoons all-purpose flour
½ teaspoon salt
½ cup milk
½ cup grated Parmesan cheese
5 eggs, separated
2 to 3 dozen fresh mushroom caps, stems removed

Cook spinach according to package directions; drain very thoroughly and set aside. Melt butter over medium heat; add flour, stirring until well mixed. Add salt and milk; stir well. Add spinach. Cook over medium heat until mixture thickens and bubbles. Remove from heat; stir in cheese. Cool. Beat egg yolks until thick and lemon colored; stir yolks into cooled spinach mixture. Beat egg whites until stiff peaks form; carefully fold whites into spinach mixture. Fill mushroom caps with spinach soufflé. Amount of filling used will vary according to size of caps available. Bake at 350° for 15 minutes or until soufflé is puffy. Serve warm. Yield: 2 to 3 dozen.

Note: For hostesses with little time to spare, the frozen prepared spinach soufflé may be substituted for the one made from scratch. If the frozen prepared soufflé is used, it should be thawed before stuffing the mushrooms and baking.

Mushroom-Stuffed Artichoke Shells

¼ cup butter or margarine
¼ cup dry white wine
½ teaspoon salt
¼ teaspoon monosodium glutamate
   Dash pepper
30 to 40 (approximately 1 pound) small fresh mushroom caps
10 canned or freshly cooked artichoke shells, including liquid
3 tablespoons water
½ cup commercial sour cream

Melt butter; add wine, salt, monosodium glutamate, and pepper. Add mushroom caps and simmer just until tender, stirring constantly. Steam artichoke shells in their liquid. Add sour cream to mushroom mixture and heat just until sour cream and sauce are blended. Spoon 3 or 4 mushrooms and sour cream sauce into each artichoke shell. Serve hot as an appetizer. Yield: 10 servings.

Angels on Horseback

1 pint select oysters
12 slices bacon
½ teaspoon salt
⅛ teaspoon pepper
⅛ teaspoon paprika
2 tablespoons chopped parsley

Drain oysters and lay each oyster across half a slice of bacon. Sprinkle with seasonings and parsley. Roll bacon around oyster and fasten with a wooden pick. Place oysters on a rack in a shallow baking pan and bake at 450° for about 10 minutes or until bacon is crisp. Remove wooden picks and serve. Yield: 6 servings.

Oyster Beignets

1 cup all-purpose flour
½ teaspoon sugar
¼ cup butter or margarine
1 cup milk
4 eggs
1 (7½- or 8-ounce) can oysters, drained and chopped
Salad oil
Cocktail Sauce

Combine flour and sugar; set aside. Combine butter and milk in a saucepan; heat over low heat. Add flour mixture and stir vigorously until mixture forms a ball and leaves the sides of the pan; remove from heat. Add eggs, one at a time, beating thoroughly after each addition. Continue beating until a stiff batter is formed. Add oysters to the batter and mix well. Drop mixture by teaspoonsful into deep hot oil. Fry at 350° for 5 to 6 minutes or until brown. Drain on absorbent paper. Serve with Cocktail Sauce. Yield: about 5 dozen.

Cocktail Sauce

¾ cup chili sauce
¼ cup finely chopped celery
1 tablespoon freshly squeezed lemon juice
1 tablespoon horseradish
½ teaspoon salt

Combine all ingredients and chill. Yield: about 1 cup.

Appetizer Pizza

½ pound ground beef or bulk sausage
Butter or margarine
½ teaspoon salt
1 tablespoon instant minced onion
4 English muffins
Sauce
⅓ pound Mozzarella cheese, shredded
1 tablespoon oregano

Sauté meat in 1 teaspoon butter. Add salt and onion; cook until done. Split muffins; spread lightly with butter. Toast under broiler until lightly browned. Spread sauce over muffin halves. Spoon meat mixture over sauce. Sprinkle with cheese and oregano. Bake at 400° until cheese melts. Cut in quarters and serve. Yield: 8 to 10 servings.

Sauce

¼ (6-ounce) can tomato paste
¼ cup water
⅓ teaspoon salt
½ teaspoon sugar

Combine all ingredients; blend well. Yield: about ½ cup.

Pizza Sandwiches

4 English muffins, split
Softened butter or margarine
1 pound mild Italian sausage
1 (8-ounce) can tomato sauce
½ pound Cheddar cheese, cut into strips

Toast cut side of muffins; spread with softened butter. Slowly fry sausage until browned and thoroughly cooked; drain on absorbent paper towels. Place muffins on broiler pan; spread each with 1 tablespoon tomato sauce. Spread muffins with cooked sausage; top with cheese slices, crisscross fashion. Spoon 1 tablespoon tomato sauce over each. Broil until cheese is melted. Yield: 8 small pizzas.

Party Pizzas

2 (10¾-ounce) cans tomato soup, undiluted
4 teaspoons oregano
2 teaspoons garlic salt
2 tablespoons Worcestershire sauce
½ teaspoon hot pepper sauce
Saltine crackers
Pepperoni, stuffed olives, anchovies, chopped onions, or mushrooms
Sharp cheese, cut into thin slivers

Heat soup in a saucepan; add oregano, garlic salt, Worcestershire sauce, and hot pepper sauce. Cool and keep refrigerated until ready to use.

Put 1 teaspoon soup mixture on each cracker and top with pepperoni, stuffed olives, anchovies, chopped onions, or mushrooms. Place a sliver of cheese over each. Bake at 450° for 5 minutes. Yield: sauce for about 13 dozen pizzas.

Yorkshire Puffs

1 teaspoon salt
½ cup boiling water
½ cup shortening
1 cup all-purpose flour
4 eggs
1 pound ground beef
½ teaspoon onion salt
½ teaspoon Worcestershire sauce
   Salad oil

Combine salt, boiling water, and shortening; bring to a boil. Add flour all at once, stirring vigorously until ball forms in center of pan. Cool slightly. Add eggs, one at a time, beating well after each addition until mixture is smooth. Mixture should be very stiff.

Brown ground beef. Pour off fat. Add onion salt and Worcestershire sauce to ground beef; add to puff mixture. Heat oil to 365°. Drop puff mixture by teaspoonsful into hot oil. Deep fry 3 to 5 minutes or until golden brown. Yield: 7 dozen.

Beef Quiche

½ pound ground beef
½ teaspoon salt
   Pastry for a 9-inch pie shell
3 eggs
6 ounces Swiss cheese, shredded
1¼ cups half-and-half
¼ teaspoon salt
   Dash pepper
⅛ teaspoon sugar
1 teaspoon finely chopped chives

Cook ground beef in a heavy skillet until lightly browned, stirring occasionally. Drain well on absorbent paper. Put beef in a mixing bowl; add salt and mix well.

Line a 9-inch piepan with pastry; crimp edges and prick bottom and sides lightly. Beat eggs. Brush pastry with small amount of egg and bake at 450° for 10 minutes. Remove from oven and lower oven temperature to 325°.

Arrange shredded Swiss cheese in bottom of baked shell. Sprinkle ground beef evenly over cheese. To beaten eggs, add half-and-half, salt, pepper, sugar, and chives. Pour egg mixture slowly over beef and cheese. Bake at 325° for 50 minutes. Let stand 10 to 15 minutes before serving. Cut in small wedges to serve as hors d'oeuvres. Yield: 12 servings.

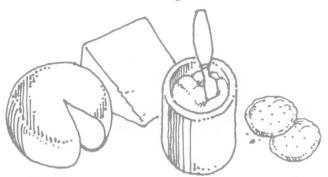

Olive Quiche

6 eggs
1 cup sliced ripe olives
1 pint commercial sour cream
1 teaspoon oregano
1½ cups shredded Swiss cheese
2 tablespoons chives
¾ teaspoon salt
   Dash cayenne pepper
   Pastry for 2 piecrusts

Beat eggs with a wooden spoon in a large mixing bowl. Add all ingredients except pastry and mix well. Prepare pastry; roll out to fit a 15- x 10- x 1-inch jelly roll pan, bringing pastry partially up sides of pan. Pour olive mixture over pastry and bake at 425° for 15 minutes. Reduce temperature to 375° and continue baking for about 25 minutes or until filling is set (when a knife inserted in center comes out clean). Cool slightly and cut into bars about 1½ x 2½ inches. Serve warm. Yield: about 4 dozen.

Cheeseapple Sausage Snacks

2 apples, cored
12 slices party rye bread, buttered
2 (5-ounce) cans Vienna sausage
1 (10-ounce) round Gouda cheese, cut into
  12 wedges
  Ground cloves

Slice each apple into 6 rings; place an apple ring on each bread slice. Cut 12 sausages in half lengthwise; place two halves cut side down on each apple ring. Broil 2 minutes or until sandwich is hot. Cut 2 remaining sausages crosswise into 6 slices each for garnish. Top sandwiches with a Gouda wedge and sausage slice. Broil 2 to 3 minutes or until cheese is melted. Sprinkle with cloves. Yield: 1 dozen.

Maxine's Pinwheels

2 cups biscuit mix
1 pound ground pork sausage
  Chopped chives (optional)

Prepare biscuit mix according to package directions. Roll dough out on a lightly floured surface into a rectangle that measures 15 x 18 inches and about ⅛ inch thick. Dot entire surface with pieces of fresh pork sausage; sprinkle with chives. Cut dough in half crosswise and roll each half, jelly roll fashion, toward the center, making 2 rolls. Chill for easy slicing (or freeze).

Cut each roll into ½-inch slices. Arrange ½ inch apart in a shallow baking dish. Bake at 450° for 15 minutes or until golden brown. Drain on absorbent paper. Serve hot. Each roll makes about 24 slices. Yield: 4 dozen.

Smoky Bobs with Pimiento and Gherkin

1 pound precooked smoked sausage
1 cup commercial Italian salad dressing
  Few drops freshly squeezed lemon juice
  Dash garlic salt
1 (4-ounce) jar whole pimientos
1 (4-ounce) jar small sweet gherkins

Cut sausage into pieces 1 inch thick. Marinate for at least 1 hour in mixture of Italian salad dressing, lemon juice, and garlic salt. Remove sausage from marinade; alternate pieces of sausage with strips of pimiento and sweet gherkins on bamboo skewers. Place on bottom rack of grill; cook at medium heat for 15 minutes. Turn kabobs once during grilling; baste on each side with marinade. Yield: 8 to 10 servings.

Note: For a different taste combination, substitute 1 (3-ounce) jar stuffed green olives and 1 (3½-ounce) jar pitted ripe olives for the pimiento and gherkins.

Sausage-Biscuit Appetizer

1 pound hot pork sausage
2⅔ cups all-purpose flour
2 tablespoons sugar
1 teaspoon baking powder
½ teaspoon soda
½ teaspoon salt
½ cup shortening
1 package dry yeast
¼ cup very warm water
1 cup buttermilk
  Melted butter or margarine

Cook sausage very slowly, stirring constantly until done (don't overcook). Drain and set aside. Combine dry ingredients; cut in shortening with a pastry blender.

Dissolve yeast in very warm water; let stand for about 5 minutes. Add to buttermilk. Stir into dry ingredients and mix well. Turn out on a pastry cloth or lightly floured board; roll or pat to about ¼ to ½ inch thick. Brush with melted butter and sprinkle sausage over half the dough. Fold other half of dough over sausage mixture and pat or roll lightly. Cut with a biscuit cutter.

Biscuits may be placed on a cookie sheet and frozen quickly. After they are frozen they may be placed in moistureproof containers and returned to freezer.

To cook, roll biscuits in melted butter, place on a greased cookie sheet, and bake at 450° for 12 minutes or until brown. Yield: 2 dozen.

Sausage-Cheese Appetizers

1 pound hot sausage, uncooked
1 pound mild Cheddar cheese, shredded
3 cups biscuit mix

Crumble sausage into a large bowl; add cheese and mix well. Blend biscuit mix into sausage and cheese mixture with a pastry blender. Shape into walnut-size balls; place on ungreased cookie sheets. Bake at 350° for 10 to 12 minutes. Yield: about 9 dozen.

Note: After baking, these can be frozen in moistureproof containers. To serve, remove from freezer and heat at 350° until warm.

Sausage Balls

1 pound hot or mild bulk pork sausage
1 egg, slightly beaten
⅓ cup seasoned bread crumbs (dry packaged herb stuffing)
¼ teaspoon ground sage
¼ cup catsup
¼ cup chili sauce
1 tablespoon soy sauce
2 tablespoons brown sugar
1 tablespoon vinegar
½ cup water

Combine first 4 ingredients and mix thoroughly. Shape into balls the size of a quarter. Brown on all sides in a dry skillet; drain on paper towels. Drain fat from skillet; combine catsup, chili sauce, soy sauce, brown sugar, vinegar, and ½ cup water in skillet. Stir well; return meatballs to skillet, cover, and simmer for 30 minutes. Refrigerate or freeze. When ready to serve, reheat, place in a chafing dish, and serve with wooden picks. Yield: about 3 dozen.

Sausage Balls in Cheese Pastry

1 pound hot or mild pork sausage
¾ cup dry bread crumbs
About ⅓ cup chicken broth
⅛ teaspoon ground nutmeg
¼ teaspoon poultry seasoning
Cheese Pastry

Combine all ingredients except Cheese Pastry. Form mixture into small teaspoon-size balls. Fry slowly in a dry skillet until done; drain on paper towels. (If you fry these at low heat, a hard crust should not form.) Make Cheese Pastry.

Cheese Pastry

1½ cups all-purpose flour
¼ teaspoon salt
1 teaspoon paprika
½ pound Cheddar cheese, shredded
½ cup softened butter or margarine

Combine flour, salt, and paprika in a large bowl. Stir in Cheddar cheese. Cut in butter; then work with hands until dough is smooth. Pinch off small pieces of dough (about 1 tablespoon) and form smoothly around sausage balls. The balls may be baked at 375° for about 15 to 20 minutes at this point, or placed unbaked in freezer until ready to use. To serve, bake unthawed balls at 400° for about 20 to 25 minutes. Yield: about 4 dozen.

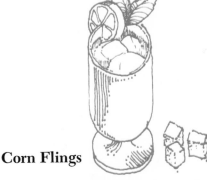

Corn Flings

1 (8-ounce) package corn muffin mix
4 frankfurters, thinly sliced
2 teaspoons oregano
1½ cups shredded Cheddar cheese

Prepare corn muffin mix according to package directions. Spread in a greased 15- x 10½-inch pan and arrange sliced frankfurters over the mix. Top with oregano and bake at 400° for 15 minutes.

Sprinkle cheese over hot bread and place under broiler until cheese bubbles, about 3 minutes. Cut into squares to serve. Yield: about 25 servings.

Snack Squares

1 (8-ounce) can refrigerated crescent
   dinner rolls
1 (4½-ounce) can corned beef spread
½ teaspoon horseradish
2 thin slices red onion, separated into rings
4 slices pasteurized process American cheese

Remove rolls from package, but do not
separate along diagonal perforations. On a
lightly floured board, roll each of the 4 pieces
into 3½- x 7-inch rectangles. Combine corned
beef spread and horseradish; spread mixture
on half of each rectangle, leaving ½ inch
border of dough uncovered. Place onion rings
on top of filling and fold rectangle in half,
pinching edges to seal in filling. Bake at 375°
for 30 minutes. Top each square with a slice
of cheese and continue baking for another 5
minutes. Quarter and serve. Yield: 16
appetizers.

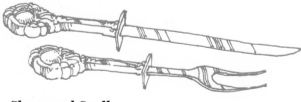

Skewered Scallops

1 pound scallops, fresh or frozen
1 pint cherry tomatoes
2 large green peppers, cut into 1-inch
   squares
⅓ cup freshly squeezed lemon juice
3 tablespoons honey
3 tablespoons prepared mustard
2 tablespoons salad oil
1½ teaspoons curry powder

Thaw frozen scallops and rinse to remove
any shell particles. Cut large scallops in half.
Alternate scallops, tomatoes, and green
peppers on 40 skewers or wooden picks
approximately 3 inches long. Place kabobs on
a well-greased broiler pan. Combine
remaining ingredients. Brush kabobs with
sauce. Broil about 4 inches from source of heat
for 5 to 7 minutes. Turn carefully and brush
with sauce. Broil 5 to 7 minutes longer,
basting once. Yield: 3½ dozen.

Scallop Kabobs

½ pound whole, fresh scallops (washed)
   Stuffed green olives
   Pitted black olives
   Maraschino cherries

Alternate scallops, green olives, and black
olives on bamboo skewers; top each skewer
with a cherry. Place on bottom rack of grill;
cook at medium heat for 8 to 10 minutes.
Yield: 10 to 12 servings.

Shrimp in Jackets

¼ cup butter or margarine
1 clove garlic, minced
½ teaspoon onion salt
1 pound shrimp, cooked, peeled, and
   deveined
   About 10 slices bacon, cut into thirds
   Chili sauce
   Cheese crackers

Melt butter; stir in garlic and onion salt.
Wrap each shrimp in a slice of bacon. Place
seam side down on a heavy-duty aluminum
foil-lined broiler rack. Broil about 2 minutes
on each side or until bacon is crisp, turning
once and brushing with butter mixture. Place
a small amount of chili sauce on crackers. Top
with shrimp. Yield: about 2½ dozen.

Shrimp Inez

¼ cup butter or margarine
1 clove garlic, minced
½ teaspoon salt
1 teaspoon monosodium glutamate
1½ pounds medium raw shrimp, peeled and
   deveined
   Dash pepper
⅓ cup chopped parsley

Melt butter in a large skillet. Add garlic,
salt, and monosodium glutamate; sauté until
garlic is brown. Add shrimp; sauté, stirring
constantly, until shrimp are pink; add pepper
and parsley; cook 1 minute longer. Serve in
a chafing dish. Yield: about 2½ dozen.

Luau Leis

1 (13¼-ounce) can pineapple chunks,
  drained and liquid reserved
2 tablespoons soy sauce
2 tablespoons freshly squeezed lemon juice
1 tablespoon salad oil
1 teaspoon dry mustard
24 shrimp, cooked, peeled, and deveined
  Macadamia nuts or peanuts, finely
  chopped
  Flaked coconut

Drain pineapple and reserve juice. Combine ¼ cup pineapple juice, soy sauce, lemon juice, oil, and mustard. Pour over shrimp; cover and let stand for 30 minutes. Soak 8 bamboo skewers in water. Alternate 3 shrimp and 4 pineapple chunks on each skewer. Brush on remaining marinade. Place on a rack or in a shallow pan. Broil 2 to 3 inches from source of heat, turning and basting until hot and lightly browned, about 3 to 5 minutes. Sprinkle 4 skewers with nuts and 4 with coconut. Yield: 8 servings.

Tuna Teasers

1 cup all-purpose flour
1½ teaspoons baking powder
1 teaspoon onion salt
½ teaspoon curry powder
  Dash cayenne pepper
¼ cup butter or margarine
½ cup milk
1 (6½-ounce) can tuna, drained and flaked
1 cup shredded pasteurized process
  American cheese
1 tablespoon minced green pepper

Combine flour, baking powder, onion salt, curry powder, and cayenne pepper; cut in butter with pastry blender or a fork until mixture resembles coarse meal. Add milk and stir until well blended. Add tuna, cheese, and green pepper; blend well.

Drop from a teaspoon onto a greased cookie sheet. Bake at 450° for 10 or 15 minutes or until golden brown. Serve warm. Yield: 3 dozen.

Hot Cocktail Turnovers

  Cream Cheese Pastry
½ small onion, minced
3 to 4 tablespoons melted butter or
  margarine
½ pound lean ground beef
1 egg, slightly beaten
  Salt and pepper to taste
2 tablespoons dillweed
1 to 2 teaspoons beef bouillon (optional)
½ cup cooked rice

Prepare Cream Cheese Pastry according to directions below. Sauté onion in butter for 1 minute. Add beef and half of the beaten egg; cook until beef is done, stirring well. Add salt, pepper, and dillweed. If mixture looks dry, add 1 to 2 teaspoons beef bouillon. Combine meat mixture with rice. Put approximately 1½ teaspoons filling in center of each pastry round. Fold round in half to make a crescent shape. Seal edges together with tines of fork. Brush each crescent with remaining half of egg. Bake at 400° for 10 minutes or until golden brown. Yield: about 2½ dozen.

Cream Cheese Pastry

1 cup all-purpose flour
½ cup butter or margarine, softened
½ (8-ounce) package cream cheese, softened

Work all ingredients together in a bowl; pat into a ball. Wrap in waxed paper and chill for several hours. Roll out pastry very thin and cut into 2-inch rounds with cutter. Yield: 2½ dozen.

Note: If you wish to freeze the turnovers, you may partially bake them and save the final browning until they are removed from the freezer for serving. Any favorite meat filling can be used with this pastry. It's a good way to use up leftover meat. If leftover meat is used, it will require less cooking time for the filling—just be sure the filling ingredients are tossed together in the pan long enough for the egg to be cooked.

Tuna Puffs

2 (6½- or 7-ounce) cans tuna
1 cup finely chopped celery
½ cup mayonnaise or salad dressing
2 tablespoons chopped onion
2 tablespoons chopped sweet pickle
Salt to taste
Puff Shells

Drain and flake tuna. Combine all ingredients except Puff Shells. Mix thoroughly. Prepare Puff Shells. Cut tops from Puff Shells and fill each shell with approximately 2 teaspoons of salad. Yield: 4½ dozen.

Puff Shells

½ cup boiling water
¼ cup butter or margarine
Dash salt
½ cup all-purpose flour
2 eggs

Combine water, butter, and salt; bring to a boil over medium heat. Add flour and stir vigorously until mixture forms a ball and leaves the sides of the pan. Remove from heat. Add eggs, one at a time, beating thoroughly after each addition. Continue beating until a stiff dough is formed. Drop by level teaspoonsful onto a well-greased cookie sheet. Bake at 450° for 10 minutes. Reduce heat to 350° and continue baking about 10 minutes longer. Yield: 4½ dozen.

Teriyaki

½ cup soy sauce
¼ cup dry white wine
1 tablespoon cider vinegar
1 tablespoon sugar
1 clove garlic, crushed
½ teaspoon ground ginger
1 pound top round, cut into thin slices about 2 inches long
Crackers

Combine soy sauce, wine, vinegar, sugar, garlic, and ginger. Pour over sliced meat.

Cover and marinate for several hours at room temperature or in the refrigerator overnight. Broil for 5 to 7 minutes, turning once. Place in a chafing dish and serve with crackers. Yield: about 18 servings.

Crescent Twists

1 (8-ounce) can refrigerated crescent dinner rolls
2 teaspoons melted butter or margarine
½ cup shredded Cheddar cheese
Garlic or onion salt

Separate dinner rolls into 4 rectangles. Press perforations to seal. Brush 2 of the rectangles with melted butter, about 1 teaspoon each; sprinkle with 1 to 2 tablespoons shredded Cheddar cheese. Sprinkle with garlic salt. Place remaining 2 rectangles on top of seasoned rectangles. Cut each crosswise into ten ½-inch strips. Twist each strip 5 to 6 times; place on an ungreased cookie sheet; secure ends by pressing onto sheet. Bake at 375° for 10 to 12 minutes or until golden brown. Serve warm. Yield: 20 appetizers.

Yule Delights

1 cup softened butter or margarine
4 cups shredded sharp cheese
2 cups all-purpose flour
2 cups finely chopped nuts
1 teaspoon cayenne pepper
2 teaspoons salt

Thoroughly cream butter and cheese together; add other ingredients and mix well. Roll into a long roll and refrigerate for several hours. Slice into thin rounds. Place on a slightly greased cookie sheet and bake at 325° for 20 minutes or until edges brown. Yule rolls may be frozen and baked months later. Yield: about 5 dozen.

Cold Appetizers

Drain artichoke hearts and cut into halves. Place in a shallow dish, cut side up. Blend dressing and mayonnaise; stir in capers. Spoon over artichoke hearts and chill for several hours. Before serving, sprinkle with paprika and, if desired, scatter a few more drained capers over all. Serve with wooden picks. Yield: 6 servings.

Marinated Broccoli

2 bunches fresh broccoli
¼ cup olive oil
1 teaspoon garlic salt
½ cup sliced stuffed green olives
¼ cup freshly squeezed lemon juice

Rinse broccoli and dry thoroughly. Cut off flowerets in bite-size pieces. Toss flowerets in olive oil to wet them until they glisten; sprinkle with garlic salt and toss again. Sprinkle olives over broccoli. Add lemon juice to mixture and toss to mix thoroughly. Cover and refrigerate for several hours, tossing occasionally. Serve chilled. Yield: 12 to 15 servings.

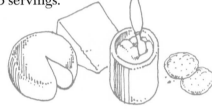

Marinated Carrot Sticks

8 small carrots
3 tablespoons vinegar
3 tablespoons salad oil
1 small clove garlic, crushed
¾ teaspoon seasoned salt
¼ teaspoon salt
  Minced fresh parsley

Peel and cut carrots into thin 3-inch sticks. Place in a shallow dish; mix other ingredients except parsley and pour over carrots, spooning marinade over the carrots so all will be coated. Cover tightly and refrigerate overnight, turning sticks occasionally if convenient. Drain off marinade; arrange carrot sticks attractively in a serving dish and sprinkle with parsley. Yield: 6 to 8 servings.

Asparagus Spears Rolled in Ham

18 canned asparagus spears
¾ cup salad oil
¼ cup wine vinegar
½ teaspoon salt
  Pepper
½ teaspoon basil
9 thin slices boiled or baked ham

Marinate asparagus in salad oil, vinegar, salt, pepper, and basil for 2 hours. Drain thoroughly. Cut ham in half crosswise and wrap around asparagus spears, securing each with a wooden pick. Yield: 6 servings.

Italian Artichoke Hearts

1 (16-ounce) can artichoke hearts, drained
3 tablespoons commercial Italian or French salad dressing
¼ cup mayonnaise
2 tablespoons capers, drained
  Paprika

Chicken-Stuffed Celery

1 (3-ounce) package cream cheese, softened
1 (4¾-ounce) can chicken spread
½ teaspoon mild curry powder
24 (1½- to 2-inch) celery slices
    Paprika

Combine cream cheese, chicken spread, and curry. Stuff celery slices. Sprinkle with paprika. Chill. Serve cold. Yield: 2 dozen.

Stuffed Celery Diable

4 to 5 stalks celery
2 ounces Roquefort or blue cheese
1 (3-ounce) package cream cheese, softened
    Big pinch cayenne pepper
¼ cup finely ground walnuts
    Paprika

Peel and cut celery into 4-inch pieces. Combine Roquefort and cream cheese until smooth in small bowl of electric mixer. Beat in cayenne pepper; then stir in walnuts. Stuff celery; sprinkle with paprika. Yield: 4 servings.

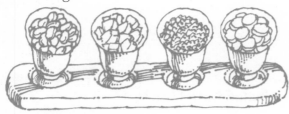

Pickled Mushrooms

1 pound fresh mushrooms, or 2 (4-ounce)
    cans button mushrooms, drained
½ cup vinegar
½ cup salad oil
1 teaspoon salt
1 clove garlic, minced
1 tablespoon chives
1 bay leaf

Wash fresh mushrooms quickly in cold water and cut off thin slice from bottom of stems. Combine remaining ingredients and pour over mushrooms. Cover and marinate at least overnight, turning several times. Yield: about 12 servings.

Lomi Lomi Cherries

1 quart cherry tomatoes
¼ pound smoked salmon, minced
1 onion, minced
1 green pepper, minced

Cut off and discard tops of cherry tomatoes. Scoop out seed and pulp with a small pointed spoon. Combine pulp with minced salmon, onion, and green pepper. Refill tomatoes with this mixture and chill before serving. Yield: 2 to 3 dozen.

Pickled Okra

Garlic (1 clove for each jar)
Hot pepper (1 for each jar)
Okra
Dillseed (1 teaspoon for each jar)
1 quart white vinegar
1 cup water
½ cup salt

Place garlic and hot pepper in the bottom of sterilized, hot pint jars. Pack firmly with clean, young okra pods from which only part of the stem has been removed. Stem end must be open. Add dillseed.

After packing jars, bring vinegar, water, and salt to a boil. Simmer about 5 minutes and pour, while boiling hot, over okra. Seal jars immediately. Yield: 5 to 7 pints.

Curried Almond-Stuffed Olives

¾ cup toasted slivered almonds, finely
    chopped
¼ teaspoon tarragon
½ teaspoon paprika
1 teaspoon curry powder
¼ teaspoon seasoned pepper
½ teaspoon salt
2 teaspoons parsley flakes
½ (8-ounce) package cream cheese, softened
2 tablespoons whipping cream
2 (7-ounce) cans pitted jumbo green or ripe
    olives, drained

Combine almonds, tarragon, paprika, curry powder, seasoned pepper, salt, and parsley. Combine cream cheese and whipping cream; blend into almond mixture. Split each olive lengthwise. Put the olive halves together with cheese stuffing. Chill for several hours. Yield: about 4 dozen.

Mexican Stuffed Olives

1 (7¼-ounce) can pitted ripe olives
4 teaspoons diced anchovy fillets
⅓ cup wine vinegar
1 tablespoon olive oil
¼ cup chopped pimiento
1 clove garlic, minced
¼ cup chopped parsley

Drain olives; stuff with anchovies. Combine vinegar, olive oil, pimiento, and garlic; pour over olives. Cover and chill for 6 hours or overnight, spooning marinade over olives occasionally. Add parsley. Yield: 2 cups.

Marinated Spanish Olives

1 (8-ounce) jar unpitted green olives
¼ cup vinegar
¼ cup olive oil
2 tablespoons minced chives
1 clove garlic, slashed
¼ teaspoon whole peppercorns

Drain olives; then add remaining ingredients to them. Fasten lid tightly on jar and let olives stand for 24 hours at room temperature, turning the jar upside down occasionally to distribute the marinade. Yield: 1 cup.

Dilled Green Olives

1 (8-ounce) jar unstuffed jumbo green olives
1 clove garlic, split
1 small whole dried red pepper*
1 teaspoon dillseed
¼ teaspoon pepper
⅔ cup salad oil
⅓ cup cider vinegar

Drain olives and put in jar with tight lid. Add all other ingredients. Prepare several days ahead of serving and keep refrigerated, turning jar upside down several times to distribute the marinade. Yield: about 1½ cups.
*Use one from your mixed pickling spices.

Spiced Ripe Olives

1 (16-ounce) jar ripe olives, drained and liquid reserved
1 small dried chili pepper*
2 cloves crushed garlic
Few sprigs fresh dill, or about ½ teaspoon dillweed
3 tablespoons olive oil

Drain olives, reserving liquid. Add other ingredients to jar; then fill jar with reserved liquid. Let olives marinate 2 days before serving. Yield: 2 cups.
*Use one from your mixed pickling spices.

Raw Vegetables with Herb Sauce

1 (8-ounce) package cream cheese, softened
1 cup commercial sour cream
1 tablespoon minced chives
1 tablespoon minced fresh parsley
2 teaspoons soy sauce
1 teaspoon tarragon
1 teaspoon dillweed
1 teaspoon curry powder
Milk
Raw vegetables

Blend sour cream into softened cheese. Add all other ingredients except vegetables, using enough milk to yield a dipping consistency. Blend thoroughly. May be prepared a day or so ahead of time. Serve with raw vegetables. Yield: about 2 cups.

Garlic Olives

2 (8-ounce) jars olives, drained and liquid
   reserved
⅓ cup olive oil
1 tablespoon minced garlic
½ teaspoon oregano

Use large green or black olives. Drain
olives, reserving ½ cup liquid. Combine liquid
with olive oil, garlic, and oregano. Pack olives
into jars; cover with marinade and refrigerate
at least 24 hours before serving. Yield: 2 cups.

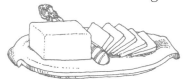

Marinated Anchovies

3 (2-ounce) cans rolled anchovies, undrained
1 clove garlic, crushed
4 tablespoons wine vinegar
1 large onion, very finely minced
6 tablespoons minced fresh parsley
   Rye bread

Arrange anchovies and some of their liquid
in a shallow serving dish. Combine garlic and
vinegar and pour over anchovies. Mix onion
and parsley; spread in a thick layer over
anchovies. Carefully spoon marinade in dish
over all to moisten; cover and refrigerate for
at least 3 hours. Serve with small rounds of
rye bread. Yield: 10 servings.

Brandy Balls

1 (12-ounce) package crushed vanilla wafers
½ cup light rum
½ cup brandy
½ cup honey
1 pound ground walnuts
   Powdered sugar

Mix wafers, rum, brandy, honey, and
walnuts. Shape into small balls and roll in
powdered sugar; store in a tightly covered
container in the refrigerator. These will keep
for 5 weeks in the refrigerator. Yield: about
4 dozen.

Zippy Cheese Ball Appetizers

2 (3-ounce) packages cream cheese, softened
1 tablespoon horseradish
1 teaspoon milk (optional)
¼ cup finely chopped dried beef
½ cup crushed potato chips
½ cup finely chopped fresh parsley

Blend cream cheese and horseradish until
smooth. (If mixture is a bit stiff, add 1
teaspoon milk.) Add dried beef and potato
chips and combine thoroughly. Chill mixture
until cream becomes stiff. Shape into 24 to 26
small balls. Roll in parsley and serve on
wooden picks. Yield: about 2 dozen.

Pecan Roquefort Hors d'Oeuvres

½ pound Roquefort cheese
¼ cup butter or margarine
1 teaspoon grated onion
⅛ cup minced celery
   Dash Worcestershire sauce
   Dash salt and pepper
48 pecan halves

Mash Roquefort cheese. Add butter, onion,
celery, and Worcestershire sauce. Beat until
smooth and well blended. Add salt and pepper
to taste. Chill.

With moistened hands, roll mixture into
small balls. Press 2 pecan halves on either side
of each cheese ball. Serve at once. Yield:
2 dozen.

Roquefort Cocktail Balls

¼ pound Roquefort cheese
1 tablespoon chopped celery
1 tablespoon chopped scallion or green
   onion
½ cup commercial sour cream
   Paprika

In a blender or with a fork, blend Roquefort
cheese, celery, scallion, and sour cream. Shape
into small balls the size of a walnut; sprinkle
with paprika. Chill. Yield: about 2 dozen.

Duo Cheese Balls

1 (3-ounce) package blue cheese
2 (3-ounce) packages cream cheese
¼ teaspoon hot pepper sauce
2 teaspoons grated onion
¼ cup finely minced parsley

Have cheese at room temperature. Combine all ingredients. Shape into small balls. Chill well. Serve on wooden picks. Yield: 3 dozen.

Anchovy-Stuffed Eggs

2 hard-cooked eggs
¼ cup butter or margarine, softened
8 anchovy fillets, mashed
1 tablespoon capers
   Pimiento strips

Cut eggs in half lengthwise and remove yolks. In small bowl, mix yolks, butter, anchovy, and capers until well blended. Stuff egg whites with mixture. Garnish each half with a pimiento strip. Yield: 2 servings.

Lobster-Stuffed Eggs

1 pound cooked lobster meat
⅔ cup mayonnaise or salad dressing
1 tablespoon chili sauce
1 teaspoon grated onion
1 teaspoon chopped green pepper
1 teaspoon chopped pimiento
1½ dozen hard-cooked eggs
   Parsley

Chop lobster meat. Add mayonnaise, chili sauce, onion, green pepper, and pimiento. Chill. Cut eggs in half lengthwise and remove yolks. Place lobster mixture in egg whites. Garnish with parsley. Yield: 3 dozen.

Deviled Eggs with Salted Almonds

12 hard-cooked eggs
4 tablespoons mayonnaise
4 tablespoons commercial sour cream
1 teaspoon salt
3 teaspoons Dijon mustard
   Dash cayenne pepper (optional)
⅓ cup chopped salted almonds

Cut eggs in half and scoop out yolks. Mash yolks with mayonnaise and sour cream; add salt and mustard and blend well. Taste and add more seasonings if mixture is too bland (you may want to add a dash of cayenne pepper). Refill egg whites and sprinkle with chopped almonds. Yield: 1 dozen.

Ham-Stuffed Eggs

2 hard-cooked eggs
1 tablespoon commercial sour cream
2 tablespoons minced green onion
2 slices boiled ham, finely chopped
½ teaspoon prepared mustard
   Salt and pepper to taste

Cut eggs in half lengthwise and remove yolks. Mix yolks and remaining ingredients except whites until well blended. Stuff whites with mixture. Yield: 2 servings.

Kaspin Stuffed Eggs

1 (10½-ounce) can beef consommé
2 dozen hard-cooked egg whites, halved
1 tablespoon curry powder
½ cup mayonnaise
1 (2-ounce) jar red caviar
   Parsley sprigs

Refrigerate consommé overnight to congeal. Put approximately 1½ teaspoons consommé in each egg white. Combine curry powder and mayonnaise. Put a dollop of curry mayonnaise on top of consommé in each egg white. Place a small amount of red caviar on top of curry mayonnaise as a garnish. Garnish serving platter with sprigs of parsley. Yield: 4 dozen.

Caper-Stuffed Eggs

4 hard-cooked eggs
3 anchovy fillets, drained and liquid
   reserved, or 2 teaspoons anchovy paste
1 tablespoon drained capers
4 ripe olives, pitted
2 tablespoons mayonnaise
½ teaspoon anchovy liquid
   Pepper to taste
   About 2 teaspoons freshly squeezed
   lemon juice
   Paprika

Cut eggs in half; put yolks through a fine sieve. Grind anchovies, capers, and olives in a food grinder or chop finely in a wooden bowl. Combine with mayonnaise and sieved yolks. Add anchovy liquid, pepper, and about 2 teaspoons lemon juice. Fill whites and sprinkle with paprika. Yield: 8 halves.

Savory Stuffed Eggs

8 hard-cooked eggs
6 tablespoons mayonnaise
¼ teaspoon curry powder
¼ cup minced celery
¼ teaspoon salt
1 (4¾-ounce) can chicken spread
   Salt and pepper
   Paprika

Halve eggs lengthwise; carefully remove yolks. Mash only 4 of the yolks and combine with remaining ingredients. Generously refill eggs. Sprinkle with salt and pepper. Cover and chill. Garnish with paprika. Yield: 16 appetizers.

Orange Chicken Fluffs

2 (4¾-ounce) cans chicken spread
2 tablespoons chopped toasted almonds
¾ cup chopped mandarin oranges
½ cup whipping cream, whipped
15 to 20 medium cream puff shells or 30 to
   40 small shells
   Mandarin orange slices

Combine chicken spread, almonds, and chopped oranges; fold in whipped cream. Chill. Fill puff shells with mixture. Garnish top of each with a mandarin orange slice. Yield: 15 to 20 servings.

Frozen Fruit Cup

1 cup fruit cocktail or fruit cut into pieces
½ cup seedless grapes
½ cup watermelon balls
1 (32-ounce) bottle ginger ale, chilled
   Mint leaves

Combine fruits; place in an ice cube tray. Pour ginger ale over fruit and freeze 1½ to 2 hours or until mixture is a mush. Serve in sherbet glasses; garnish with mint leaves. Yield: 8 servings.

Ham and Cheese Curls

1 (4½-ounce) can deviled ham
1 teaspoon freshly squeezed lemon juice
1 tablespoon minced green onion
¼ cup cracker crumbs
5 slices Mozzarella cheese
   Paprika

Combine deviled ham, lemon juice, onion, and cracker crumbs; spread on cheese slices and roll. Coat with paprika; wrap in waxed paper and chill. Slice and serve. Yield: 4 dozen.

Snappy Ham and Egg Rolls

1 (4½-ounce) can deviled ham
2 hard-cooked eggs, chopped
1 teaspoon prepared mustard
½ cup crushed potato chips
   Sour Cream Sauce

Combine deviled ham, eggs, and mustard; chill. Shape into small balls and chill well. Just before serving, roll balls in crushed potato chips. Serve on wooden picks to dunk in Sour Cream Sauce. Yield: about 2 dozen.

Sour Cream Sauce

½ cup commercial sour cream
4 tablespoons catsup
½ teaspoon seasoned salt

Combine all ingredients; chill. Yield: about ¾ cup.

Chili Almonds

2 tablespoons butter or margarine
1 tablespoon chili powder
1 large clove garlic, crushed
2 cups unblanched almonds
　Coarse salt

Put butter in a shallow pan in a 250° oven. When melted, stir in chili powder and garlic. Add almonds and stir until all are coated. Return to oven and bake for about 1½ hours, stirring every 15 minutes or so if convenient. While still hot, sprinkle generously with salt and when cool, store in an airtight container. May be made weeks ahead of time and frozen. Yield: 10 servings.

Brazil Nut Chips

1½ cups shelled Brazil nuts
2 tablespoons butter or margarine
1 teaspoon salt

Prepare nuts for shelling by placing in a saucepan and covering with cold water. Bring to a boil and cook uncovered for 3 minutes. Drain. Again cover with cold water and let stand for 1 minute. Drain. The nuts will crack with greater ease and kernels will remain whole and crunchy.

Cover shelled whole Brazil nuts with cold water. Bring slowly to a boil; then simmer 2 or 3 minutes. Drain and cut lengthwise into

thin slices about ⅛ inch thick. (A vegetable peeler or bean-cutting device is helpful.) Spread slices thinly on a shallow buttered pan. Dot with butter; sprinkle with salt. Bake at 350° for about 12 minutes. Stir two or three times. Watch carefully; they burn easily.

Stored in a well-covered container in the refrigerator, Brazil Nut Chips keep fresh for many weeks. They are best if warmed and crisped briefly before serving. Yield: 12 ounces.

Party Almonds

For each cup of almonds, use 1 teaspoon butter or salad oil. Put butter in a shallow pan in a 300° oven; when melted, stir in almonds and bake for 20 to 25 minutes, stirring frequently. Remove and toss with garlic salt and a little cayenne pepper. These keep well in an airtight container. Prepare 2 cups to serve 6.

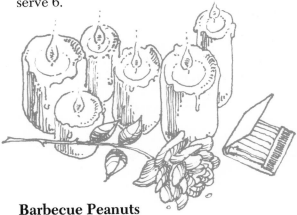

Barbecue Peanuts

1 tablespoon liquid smoke
1 teaspoon Worcestershire sauce
⅓ cup water
1½ cups salted peanuts
1 tablespoon butter or margarine, melted
¼ teaspoon garlic salt

Combine liquid smoke, Worcestershire sauce, and water in a small saucepan; bring to a boil. Add peanuts; let stand for 30 minutes. Drain off liquid; spread nuts in a shallow baking pan and bake at 250° for 1 hour. Toss nuts with butter and drain on paper towels. Sprinkle with garlic salt. Yield: 4 servings.

Curried Peanuts

1 pound salted peanuts
3 or 4 tablespoons curry powder

Put peanuts in a shallow pan. Bake at 300° for 15 to 20 minutes, stirring occasionally to prevent burning. Remove and, while still hot, stir in curry powder. Cool and place in an airtight container. Yield: 1 pound.

Parched Peanuts

Put dried peanuts in hulls in a shallow pan. Bake at 350° for 30 minutes, stirring occasionally. To test to see if they are parched, remove one from oven. Let cool; if crunchy, peanuts are ready. Different size nuts vary a little in time of cooking.

Cocktail Pecans

2 tablespoons butter or margarine
½ teaspoon seasoned salt
1 or 2 dashes hot pepper sauce
1 pound pecan halves
3 tablespoons Worcestershire sauce

Put butter, seasoned salt, and hot pepper sauce in a 12- x 8- x 2-inch baking dish. Place in a 300° oven until butter melts. Add pecans, stirring until all are butter coated. Bake for about 20 minutes, stirring occasionally. Sprinkle with Worcestershire sauce; stir again and continue baking another 15 minutes or until crisp. Will freeze. Yield: about 1 pound.

Toasted Walnuts

Drop shelled walnuts into rapidly boiling water; boil for 3 minutes. Drain well. Spread kernels evenly in a shallow pan and bake at 350°, stirring often, for 12 to 15 minutes or until kernels are a golden brown. If you like seasoned walnuts, lightly brush the hot kernels with butter and sprinkle with salt, garlic salt, onion salt, or seasoned salt. Cool. Cover tightly and store in the refrigerator.

Popcorn Crumble

2 quarts unsalted popped corn
1⅓ cups pecan halves
⅔ cup sliced almonds
1⅓ cups sugar
1 cup butter or margarine
½ cup white corn syrup
2 teaspoons vanilla extract

Mix popcorn and nuts in a large bowl and set aside. Combine sugar, butter, and corn syrup in a heavy saucepan. Bring to a boil; stir constantly and cook to 300°, using a candy thermometer.

Add vanilla and very quickly pour over popcorn and nut mixture. Stir to coat well and spread on a greased cookie sheet to harden.

When mixture has cooled, break into serving-size pieces. Yield: about 1 pound.

Party Popcorn

2 cups miniature marshmallows
⅓ to ½ cup melted butter or margarine
3 quarts unsalted popped corn
1 (3-ounce) package fruit-flavored gelatin

Combine marshmallows and butter in the top of a double boiler; cook over simmering water until marshmallows have melted. Pour over popped corn and stir to mix well. Sprinkle gelatin over popcorn and stir to coat each kernel. Yield: 3½ quarts.

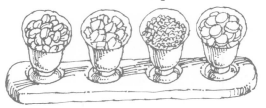

Cocktail Crunch

½ cup butter or margarine
1 (6-ounce) package blue cheese or garlic salad dressing mix
1 tablespoon Worcestershire sauce
1 teaspoon seasoned salt
4 cups bite-size shredded wheat cereal
2 cups bite-size rice cereal
2 cups unblanched whole almonds

Melt butter in a large shallow pan in a 250° oven. Stir in cheese, Worcestershire sauce, and seasoned salt. Add cereals and almonds; stir well until all are coated. Return to oven and bake for 1 hour, stirring every 15 minutes. May be prepared the day before; also freezes well. Yield: about 8½ cups.

Pretzel Pops

1 (3-ounce) package cream cheese, softened
2 ounces blue cheese, crumbled
1 (2¼-ounce) can deviled ham
¼ cup chopped pecans
⅛ teaspoon onion powder
1 cup chopped parsley
    Thin pretzel sticks

Combine first 5 ingredients. Chill. Make bite-size balls, using about 1 teaspoonful of mixture for each. Roll in parsley. Use pretzel sticks as toothpicks. Chill until ready to serve. Yield: 2 dozen.

Party Mix

½ cup butter or margarine
1 (1⅜-ounce) package dry onion soup mix
1 (7½-ounce) box cheese crackers
3 to 4 cups bite-size shredded rice cereal

Put butter in a 12- x 8- x 2-inch pan in a 250° oven. When melted, stir in dry onion soup mix and blend thoroughly. Add other ingredients; stir well to coat thoroughly and bake for about 1 hour, stirring 3 or 4 times. Will freeze. Yield: about 8 cups.

Curried Wheat Snacks

6 tablespoons butter or margarine
½ to 1 teaspoon curry powder
¼ teaspoon onion salt
⅛ teaspoon ground ginger
3 cups bite-size shredded wheat cereal

Melt butter in a large skillet. Blend in seasonings. Add shredded wheat cereal and toss to coat with butter. Heat for about 5

minutes over low heat, stirring frequently. Drain on paper towels. Serve warm or reheat in the oven just before serving. Yield: 3 cups.

Beef Sausage Stacks

2 (3-ounce) packages cream cheese, softened
2 teaspoons horseradish, drained
1 teaspoon chopped parsley
2 tablespoons grated onion
1 pound smoked beef sausage, thinly sliced

Combine cream cheese, horseradish, parsley, and onion; mix well. Spread 7 slices of beef sausage with cream cheese mixture, stacking them to form a cylinder. Top with a slice of sausage. Repeat for each cylinder. Wrap in waxed paper and chill for 3 hours or more. When ready to serve, cut each stack into 6 or 8 wedges. Yield: 42 to 56 appetizers.

Roast Pork Strips

½ cup soy sauce
¼ cup bourbon
½ teaspoon ground ginger
3 tablespoons honey
1 clove garlic, crushed
1 (3-pound) pork tenderloin
    Lettuce or parsley
    Grapefruit, apple, or pineapple, cut into pieces (optional)

Combine soy sauce, bourbon, ginger, honey, and garlic. Place pork in a shallow glass dish and pour marinade over it. Cover and refrigerate overnight, turning the meat occasionally.

Place meat in a shallow baking dish and bake at 300° for about 1½ hours, spooning marinade over meat from time to time.

To serve as an appetizer, allow meat to cool, then cut into thin slices (about ⅛ inch thick). Cut slices into strips and spear each with a wooden pick. Arrange on a bed of lettuce or parsley — or insert picks into a grapefruit or apple or pineapple.

This pork is best served at room temperature. The flavor is subtle and the pork requires no dipping sauce to enhance it. Yield: 12 servings.

Ribbon Bologna Wedges

1 (5-ounce) jar cream cheese with olives and pimiento
12 thin slices bologna
¼ cup finely chopped nuts
Parsley flakes or chopped fresh parsley

Have cheese at room temperature. Spread evenly over bologna and sprinkle each piece with chopped nuts. Divide bologna into 2 stacks of 6 slices. Garnish tops with parsley.

Cover both rolls with plastic wrap and chill. At serving time, cut each stack into 16 wedges and insert a colored wooden pick in each wedge. Yield: 32 appetizers.

Shrimp Arnaud

¼ cup vinegar
¼ cup salad oil
¼ cup chili sauce
¼ teaspoon garlic salt
1 teaspoon prepared mustard
1 pound shrimp, cooked

Combine vinegar, salad oil, chili sauce, garlic salt, and mustard. Add shrimp and toss to coat with sauce. Marinate overnight. Insert a wooden pick in each shrimp before serving. Yield: 6 servings.

Shrimp Cocktail

2 pounds boiled shrimp
½ cup olive oil
¼ cup paprika
1 tablespoon horseradish
1 tablespoon prepared mustard
¼ cup tarragon vinegar
1 teaspoon celery seed
½ teaspoon salt
⅛ teaspoon pepper
½ teaspoon onion salt
Dash hot pepper sauce

Chill shrimp and place in cocktail cups around cracked ice. Combine other ingredients and serve in a small container in middle of shrimp. Yield: 6 servings.

Marinated Shrimp Port Gibson

5 pounds raw shrimp in shell, cooked and cleaned
1 cup salad oil
½ cup vinegar
1¼ cups minced celery
2½ tablespoons minced green pepper
4 tablespoons grated onion
1 clove garlic, minced
5 tablespoons minced fresh parsley
¾ cup horseradish mustard
1½ teaspoons salt
¼ teaspoon pepper
4 tablespoons paprika

Place shrimp in a deep bowl. Mix other ingredients thoroughly and pour over shrimp. Cover and marinate in refrigerator for 24 hours before serving, stirring occasionally. This shrimp may be used as an appetizer, first course, or main dish salad. Yield: 10 to 12 servings.

Pickled Shrimp

3 to 4 pounds large raw shrimp in the shell
½ cup chopped celery tops
¼ cup mixed pickling spices
3½ teaspoons salt
2 cups sliced onion
7 or 8 bay leaves
Marinade

Put shrimp in a large saucepan; cover with boiling water. Add celery tops, pickling spices, and salt. Cover and simmer for 5 minutes. Drain. Cool by immersing in cold water; peel and devein.

In a shallow bowl, alternate shrimp with 2 cups sliced onion and 7 or 8 bay leaves. Serve shrimp with Marinade. Yield: 15 servings.

Marinade

1¼ cups salad oil
¾ cup vinegar
1½ tablespoons capers, including juice
1½ teaspoons celery seed
1½ teaspoons salt
    Dash hot pepper sauce

Combine marinade ingredients; mix well and pour over shrimp. Cover; chill at least 24 hours. Serve shrimp in bowl with marinade and provide wooden picks and small plates. Pickled shrimp will keep at least a week in the refrigerator. Yield: about 2 cups.

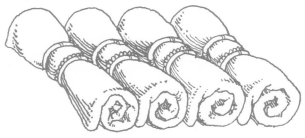

Sea Island Shrimp

2 to 3 pounds raw shrimp
2 unpeeled lemons, sliced paper-thin
1 large onion, sliced paper-thin
1⅓ cups olive oil
⅔ cup tarragon vinegar
    Juice of 2 lemons
2 teaspoons salt
    Pepper

Boil and devein shrimp; slice if desired. Place in a bowl with lemon and onion slices. Place all other ingredients in a jar with a tight-fitting cover and shake vigorously; pour over shrimp. Cover and refrigerate overnight. Serve shrimp in marinade with wooden picks for spearing. Yield: 8 to 10 servings.

Stuffed Cherry Tomatoes

1 cup pot-style cottage or cream cheese
1 tablespoon chives
2 teaspoons Worcestershire sauce
    Salt and pepper to taste
18 cherry tomatoes
    Parsley flakes

Combine cottage cheese, chives, Worcestershire sauce, salt, and pepper; blend well. Scoop out inside pulp of cherry tomatoes. Fill shell with cheese mixture. Garnish with parsley flakes. Yield: 1½ dozen.

Note: The cherry tomato shell makes a pretty "holder" for many fillings. Ideas for fillings include egg salad, crab or shrimp salad, and guacamole.

Tote'ms

Deviled Ham Tote'ms

2 (4½-ounce) cans deviled ham
1 (3-ounce) package cream cheese, softened
1 tablespoon minced onion
¼ cup finely chopped celery
4 teaspoons finely chopped pimiento
3 tablespoons pickle relish, drained
1 teaspoon prepared mustard
2 (10-inch) submarine rolls (2 inches wide)

Liverwurst Spread Tote'ms

2 (4¾-ounce) cans liverwurst spread
1 (3-ounce) package cream cheese, softened
1 tablespoon prepared mustard
⅓ cup finely chopped dill pickle
2 (10-inch) submarine rolls (2 inches wide)

Chicken Spread Tote'ms

2 (4¾-ounce) cans chicken spread
1 (3-ounce) package cream cheese, softened
2 hard-cooked eggs, finely chopped
¼ cup finely chopped celery
2 tablespoons finely chopped parsley
4 teaspoons finely chopped pimiento
½ teaspoon Worcestershire sauce
¼ to ½ teaspoon salt
2 (10-inch) submarine rolls (2 inches wide)

For each variation, combine all ingredients except rolls. Cut rolls in half vertically. Using a sharp knife and a fork, hollow out rolls almost to tip of each half, leaving a ¼-inch shell. (Save scooped-out bread for stuffings, meatloaf, etc.) Fill with meat spread mixture, pressing filling firmly to eliminate air spaces. Wrap stuffed bread halves, cut ends together, and chill well, preferably overnight. Cut into ¼-inch slices; keep chilled until served. Yield: about 4 dozen.

Dips and Spreads

Zesty Bacon Dip

4 to 6 slices bacon
½ pint commercial sour cream
1 tablespoon horseradish
1 teaspoon Worcestershire sauce
Corn chips, potato chips, or crackers

Cook bacon until crisp; drain and crumble. Combine all ingredients except chips. Serve as a dip with corn chips, potato chips, or crackers. Yield: 1 cup.

Avocado Dip

1 avocado, mashed
1 (8-ounce) package cream cheese, softened
2 tablespoons freshly squeezed lemon juice
Dash Worcestershire sauce
⅓ cup minced green onion
¾ teaspoon salt
2 green chiles, mashed
Corn chips

Blend avocado into cheese until smooth. Add other ingredients except corn chips and blend well. Cover and chill. Serve with corn chips. Yield: about 2 cups.

Note: This dip may be prepared ahead of time, even the day before serving. Spread a thin layer of mayonnaise over surface to prevent darkening; stir it in just before serving.

Avocado and Bacon Dip

1 ripe avocado, peeled and pitted
2 teaspoons freshly squeezed lemon juice
¼ cup commercial sour cream
1 teaspoon instant minced onion
¼ teaspoon garlic salt
¼ teaspoon paprika
¼ cup crumbled bacon
Crackers

Mash avocado. Add remaining ingredients except crackers. Cover tightly; refrigerate until ready to serve with crackers. Yield: about 1¼ cups.

Dilly Avocado Dip

2 avocados
1 (8-ounce) carton cottage cheese
½ teaspoon grated onion
2 tablespoons chopped dill pickle
2 tablespoons chopped parsley
1 tablespoon freshly squeezed lemon juice
¾ teaspoon salt
⅛ teaspoon dillweed

Cut avocados lengthwise into halves; remove seeds and skin. Cut into chunks; mash or sieve avocado. Stir in remaining ingredients. If dip is not to be served immediately, cover at once. Chill. Yield: about 2½ cups.

Artichoke Dip

1 (16-ounce) can artichoke hearts, drained
  About ⅓ cup mayonnaise
1 tablespoon chopped onion
  Salt, black pepper, and cayenne pepper
  to taste
3 or 4 slices bacon, cooked crisp and finely
  crumbled
  Juice of ½ lemon
  Corn chips

Chop artichoke hearts to a pulp. Add other ingredients and stir well; check seasonings and correct if necessary. Chill. Serve with corn chips for dipping. Yield: about 1½ cups.

Artichoke-Blue Cheese Dip

1 (15-ounce) can artichoke hearts, drained
¼ cup commercial sour cream
1 teaspoon crumbled blue cheese
½ teaspoon onion salt
1¼ teaspoons freshly squeezed lemon juice
¼ teaspoon paprika
1½ teaspoons sugar
  Crackers

Blend artichoke hearts, sour cream, and blue cheese in blender. Add remaining ingredients except crackers. Refrigerate until ready to serve with crackers. Yield: about 1⅓ cups.

Anchovy-Cheese Dip

2 (3-ounce) packages cream cheese, softened
2 tablespoons softened butter or margarine
⅓ cup mayonnaise
1 tablespoon anchovy paste
1 teaspoon paprika
1 teaspoon Worcestershire sauce
1 tablespoon grated onion
½ teaspoon caraway seed
  Salt, if required
1 or 2 dashes cayenne pepper

Blend cream cheese and softened butter together. Blend in mayonnaise gradually, then all other ingredients until of dipping consistency. (If you prefer a spread, reduce amount of mayonnaise.) Yield: about 1½ cups.

Note: This dip may be made a day ahead of time, but refrigeration makes the mixture stiff and buttery in consistency. It may be served that way, but it is also attractive to beat it with an electric mixer until fluffy. Serve with plain melba toast.

Cheese Dip

1 envelope (1 tablespoon) unflavored gelatin
1 cup buttermilk, divided
2 cups cottage cheese
¼ pound Roquefort cheese, crumbled
1 small onion, finely chopped
1 small clove garlic, finely chopped
¼ teaspoon salt

Soften gelatin in ¼ cup buttermilk; place over hot water and stir until gelatin is dissolved. Combine gelatin mixture with remaining ingredients in a small bowl. Beat with an electric mixer or a rotary beater until smooth and creamy. Serve with assorted vegetable dippers. If mixture stiffens while standing, whip again until smooth. Yield: about 3½ cups.

Beer Keg Dip

½ (8-ounce) package cream cheese, softened
1 (4-ounce) package blue cheese, crumbled
2 cups shredded sharp Cheddar cheese
2 tablespoons butter or margarine, softened
1 teaspoon grated onion
¼ teaspoon salt
¾ cup beer
  Dash Worcestershire sauce

Combine cheeses and butter; beat by hand or with electric mixer until smooth. Blend in onion and salt; slowly beat in beer. Add Worcestershire sauce; blend well. Pack into a jar, cover tightly, and refrigerate for at least 12 hours. Remove from refrigerator 30 minutes before serving. Yield: about 2½ cups.

Super Bean-Cheese Dip

1 (11-ounce) can black bean soup
1 teaspoon prepared mustard
½ teaspoon thyme
1 clove garlic
1 (8-ounce) package cream cheese, softened
  Corn chips, celery, carrots, and
  cauliflower

Combine soup, mustard, thyme, and garlic
in a blender. Add chunks of cream cheese,
blending until smooth. Chill for several hours.
Serve with corn chips, celery and carrot sticks,
and cauliflower buds. Yield: about 2 cups.

Caviar-Cheese Dip

1 (8-ounce) package cream cheese, softened
3 tablespoons commercial sour cream
2 tablespoons minced chives or onions
2 tablespoons freshly squeezed lemon juice
1 tablespoon Worcestershire sauce
3 tablespoons red caviar
  Paprika

Blend cheese and sour cream. Add chives,
lemon juice, and Worcestershire sauce; mix
well. Gently stir in caviar; sprinkle top with
paprika before serving. Yield: about 1 cup.

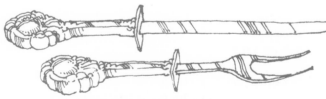

Cracker Barrel Cheese Dip

½ pound sharp pasteurized process American
  cheese, shredded
½ cup finely diced celery
¼ cup chili sauce
¼ cup finely diced onion
¼ cup finely diced green pepper
¼ cup minced green olives
  Half-and-half

Blend first 6 ingredients. Mix thoroughly
with enough half-and-half to make a smooth
and light dip. Chill. Yield: about 3 cups.

Cottage Cheese Dunk for Vegetables

2 (8-ounce) cartons cottage cheese
1 cup shredded pasteurized process
  American cheese
2 tablespoons horseradish
2 tablespoons minced onion
2 tablespoons chopped green pepper
3 tablespoons mayonnaise
¼ teaspoon salt
½ teaspoon pepper

Combine all ingredients; chill and serve
with raw vegetables. Yield: about 4 cups.

Copenhagen Dunker's Delight

½ cup commercial sour cream
¼ cup mayonnaise
2 tablespoons chopped dill pickle
¼ teaspoon onion juice
¼ teaspoon dry mustard

Combine sour cream and mayonnaise; add
dill pickle, onion juice, and mustard. Mix well.
Chill. Yield: ¾ cup.

Jalapeño Cheese Dip

2 tablespoons all-purpose flour
¾ cup half-and-half
3 tablespoons butter or margarine
2 pounds pasteurized process cheese, cut
  into pieces
1 pint cottage cheese
1 medium onion, finely chopped
1 medium green pepper, finely chopped
1 clove garlic, minced
4 jalapeño peppers

Combine flour and half-and-half in double
boiler. Add butter and cheeses; melt. Add
remaining ingredients and simmer 10 to 15
minutes or until thick, stirring occasionally. If
desired, serve warm as a dip or as a spread
for crackers and sandwiches. Yield: about 3
cups.

Clam and Cheese Dip

1 (7-ounce) can minced clams
2 (3-ounce) packages cream cheese, softened
2 teaspoons grated onion
2 teaspoons freshly squeezed lemon juice
1 teaspoon Worcestershire sauce
1 teaspoon chopped parsley
¼ teaspoon salt
3 drops hot pepper sauce

Drain clams and save liquor. Combine all ingredients except liquor; blend into a paste. Gradually add about ¼ cup clam liquor and beat until consistency of whipped cream. Chill. Serve in a bowl. Yield: about 2 cups.

Chile con Queso

2 pounds pasteurized process cheese, shredded
2 large onions, minced
1 (16-ounce) can tomatoes, drained and chopped
2 small cloves garlic, minced
2 (4-ounce) cans green chile peppers, drained and mashed
2 tablespoons Worcestershire sauce
Corn chips

Melt cheese in the top of a double boiler over hot water. Blend in other ingredients except corn chips and cook for 30 minutes, stirring occasionally. Serve in a chafing dish with corn chips for dipping. Any leftover dip may be frozen successfully. To use again, allow to thaw at room temperature; then reheat in the top of a double boiler. Yield: about 6 cups.

Clam-Cream Cheese Dip

6 (3-ounce) packages cream cheese
3 (7-ounce) cans clams, drained and liquor reserved
1 large onion, grated
Freshly squeezed lemon juice
Crackers or potato chips

Soften cream cheese thoroughly. Add clams, onion, and lemon juice (start with juice of 1 lemon, adding more to taste) or use reserved clam liquor to moisten the mixture. Turn into a chafing dish and serve hot, with crackers or sturdy potato chips for dipping. This amount will serve a crowd, the size depending on the number of other appetizers offered. Leftover mixture will freeze satisfactorily. Yield: about 5 cups.

Clamdigger Dip

1 (7½-ounce) can minced clams
1 (8-ounce) package cream cheese, softened
1 tablespoon freshly squeezed lemon juice
1 teaspoon Worcestershire sauce
1 tablespoon grated onion
1 teaspoon chopped parsley
¼ teaspoon salt
⅛ teaspoon hot pepper sauce
Assorted chips, crackers, or raw vegetables

Drain clams and reserve liquor. Combine cream cheese and lemon juice. Add seasonings and clams. Mix thoroughly. Chill for at least 1 hour to blend flavors. If it is necessary to thin the dip, add clam liquor gradually. Serve with chips, crackers, or vegetables. Yield: 1⅓ cups.

Red Dip for Crab on Ice

1 cup catsup
½ cup chili sauce
¼ teaspoon hot pepper sauce
1½ teaspoons Worcestershire sauce
1 tablespoon horseradish
1½ teaspoons prepared mustard
2 tablespoons freshly squeezed lemon juice
Chopped parsley

Combine all ingredients except parsley. Chill for at least 1 hour to blend flavors. Serve, garnished with parsley, as a dip for crab. Yield: about 1½ cups.

Curried Crabmeat Dip

1 (7-ounce) can crabmeat, drained
½ (8-ounce) package cream cheese, softened
5 tablespoons commercial sour cream
¼ teaspoon salt
Pepper to taste
¼ teaspoon curry powder
1 tablespoon minced chives
1 tablespoon capers, drained
Potato chips or melba rounds

Finely shred crabmeat. Combine cheese with other ingredients except crabmeat and capers and beat until light. Fold in crabmeat and capers; chill and serve with potato chips or melba rounds for dipping. Yield: about 2 cups.

Green Goddess Crab Dip

4 anchovy fillets, chopped
2 tablespoons finely chopped onion
2 tablespoons chopped chives
¼ cup finely chopped parsley
¼ teaspoon salt
½ teaspoon dry mustard
⅛ teaspoon pepper
¼ cup tarragon vinegar
1 cup mayonnaise
Bite-size pieces of crab

Combine all ingredients except crab in a bowl, mixing well. Cover and refrigerate for several hours or overnight to blend flavors. Serve as dip for bite-size pieces of crab on wooden picks. Yield: about ½ cup.

Deviled Crab Dip

1 (7¾-ounce) can crabmeat, drained and flaked
1 hard-cooked egg, chopped
½ cup mayonnaise
1 tablespoon freshly squeezed lemon juice
½ teaspoon dry mustard
½ teaspoon onion salt
⅛ teaspoon pepper
Assorted crackers

Combine all ingredients except crackers; mix well. Cover and chill. Serve with assorted snack crackers. Yield: 2 cups.

Cucumber Dip

2 large unpeeled cucumbers
½ cup vinegar
2 teaspoons salt
½ teaspoon garlic salt
2 (8-ounce) packages cream cheese, softened
¾ cup mayonnaise

Wash and grate unpeeled cucumbers, using grater with ½-inch holes. Add vinegar and salt; stir, cover, and allow to stand overnight in refrigerator. Next day, press out liquid. Blend garlic salt, cheese, and mayonnaise; combine with cucumbers. Yield: about 4 cups.

Fruit Sticks with Curry Dip Gregnon

Cut into finger-size pieces any firm fruit, such as melon, pineapple, apples, or pears, Chill thoroughly and place on a platter around Curry Dip Gregnon. Strawberries may be used with wooden picks inserted.

Curry Dip Gregnon

1 cup mayonnaise
2 to 4 tablespoons curry powder
3 tablespoons freshly squeezed lemon juice
1 tablespoon chutney
Dash hot pepper sauce

Mix all ingredients thoroughly in a blender. Chill well. Yield: 1½ cups.

Deluxe Dip

¼ cup commercial French dressing
¾ cup commercial sour cream
¼ teaspoon pepper (optional)
1 tablespoon chopped chives

Blend French dressing, sour cream, pepper, and chives. Serve chilled. Yield: 1 cup.

Curried Mermaid Dip

2 (3-ounce) packages cream cheese, softened
1 (8-ounce) can minced clams, drained
1 (2-ounce) jar pimientos, drained and
    chopped
¼ cup finely chopped nuts
¼ cup finely chopped celery
¼ cup commercial sour cream
½ teaspoon curry powder
½ teaspoon seasoned salt
    Chopped parsley
    Assorted crackers

Blend first 8 ingredients. Chill. Sprinkle
with parsley and serve with crackers. Yield:
1¾ cups.

Dipsy Devil

1 (5-ounce) jar cream cheese with pimiento
1 (2¼-ounce) can deviled ham
¼ cup mayonnaise or salad dressing
2 tablespoons minced parsley
1 tablespoon minced onion
4 drops hot pepper sauce
    Dash monosodium glutamate

Combine all ingredients in small mixer
bowl. Beat until creamy. Yield: 2 cups.

Guacamole Dip

1 small onion, finely chopped
1 small dried red pepper, finely chopped
    (optional)
1 medium tomato, finely chopped
6 peeled avocados, finely chopped
2½ teaspoons salt
2 teaspoons freshly squeezed lemon juice
2 tablespoons mayonnaise
1 teaspoon salad oil
4 drops hot pepper sauce

Combine all ingredients in a large chopping
bowl. Serve as a dip or dressing. Yield: 5 to
6 cups.

Dill Dip for Raw Vegetables

1 cup mayonnaise
2 cups commercial sour cream
2 tablespoons dillweed
1 tablespoon minced parsley
    Salt, if needed
    Raw vegetables
    Freshly squeezed lemon juice

Gently combine mayonnaise and other
ingredients except raw vegetables. Serve in a
bowl surrounded by crisp raw vegetables:
cauliflower flowerets, celery curls, carrot
sticks, tiny green onions, radishes, and raw
mushrooms—rinsed, dried, and rolled in lemon
juice to retain their color. Yield: about 3 cups.

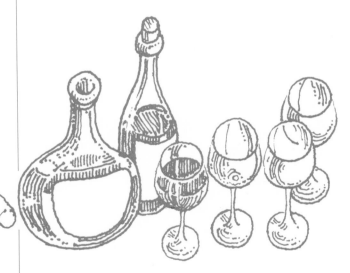

Green Goddess Dip

¾ cup commercial sour cream
¾ cup mayonnaise or salad dressing
1 (2-ounce) can anchovy fillets, drained and
    finely chopped
⅓ cup chopped parsley
3 tablespoons chopped chives
1 tablespoon vinegar
1 clove garlic, crushed
¼ teaspoon salt
⅛ teaspoon pepper

Combine all ingredients; cover and
refrigerate overnight to mellow flavors. Yield:
2 cups.

Great Lakes Dip

½ pound smoked whitefish or other
   smoked fish
1 cup commercial sour cream
2 tablespoons freshly squeezed lemon juice
1 teaspoon instant minced onion
2 teaspoons chopped chives
½ teaspoon salt
¼ teaspoon rosemary
6 peppercorns, crushed
   Dash ground cloves
   Chopped parsley
   Assorted chips, crackers, or raw vegetables

Remove skin and bones from fish. Flake fish. Combine all ingredients except parsley and crackers. Chill for at least 1 hour to blend flavors. Sprinkle dip with parsley. Serve with chips, crackers, or raw vegetables. Yield: 1¾ cups.

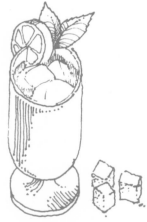

Zesty Fresh Garden Dip

1 (3-ounce) package cream cheese, softened
¼ cup mayonnaise
3 tablespoons commercial sour cream
2 tablespoons grated cucumber
2 tablespoons grated radishes
¼ teaspoon grated onion
¼ teaspoon dry mustard
   Salt and pepper to taste
   Assorted crackers

Combine cream cheese, mayonnaise, sour cream, cucumber, radishes, onion, mustard, salt, and pepper. Blend thoroughly. Cover and chill. Serve with assorted crackers. Yield: about 1 cup.

India Dip

½ cup mayonnaise
1 tablespoon peach preserves
1 teaspoon Dijon mustard

Place all ingredients in a covered blender. Whirl until smooth on medium speed. Good as a vegetable dip or a fruit salad dressing. Delightful on cold chicken, shrimp, ham, fish fingers, etc. Yield: about ½ cup.

Lemon Pepper Dip

2 (8-ounce) cartons commercial sour cream
1 tablespoon and 1 teaspoon commercial
   lemon pepper marinade
   Raw vegetables

Blend sour cream and lemon pepper marinade. Refrigerate 1 to 2 hours before serving. Serve with assorted raw vegetables such as cherry tomatoes, carrots, cauliflower, fennel, celery, and broccoli. Yield: 2 cups.

Liptauer Dip

1 (8-ounce) package cream cheese, softened
½ cup butter or margarine, softened
1½ tablespoons anchovy paste, or 1 (¾-ounce)
   can anchovies, mashed with liquid
1½ tablespoons drained capers
1 teaspoon paprika
1 teaspoon caraway seed
½ teaspoon Dijon mustard
1 cup commercial sour cream
   Juice of 1 lemon
   Raw vegetables, potato chips, or melba
   toast

Blend cream cheese and butter thoroughly. Stir in all other ingredients until smooth. The flavor of this dip improves if allowed to mellow overnight in the refrigerator. Excellent as a dip for raw vegetables, potato chips, or as a spread for melba toast. Yield: about 3 cups.

Lobster Dunk

2 tablespoons butter or margarine
2 tablespoons chopped onion
2 tablespoons chopped green pepper
½ cup half-and-half
1 tablespoon cornstarch
1 (10¾-ounce) can cream of mushroom soup
2 egg yolks, slightly beaten
2 (5½-ounce) cans lobster meat, drained and
   cut into small pieces
2 tablespoons cooking sherry
⅛ teaspoon ground nutmeg
1 cup shredded Cheddar cheese
   Crackers

Melt butter in a saucepan. Stir in onion and green pepper; sauté for 10 minutes. Blend half-and-half and cornstarch. Stir into soup and egg yolks; blend into sautéed vegetables. Stir in lobster, sherry, and nutmeg. Heat, stirring constantly, until thickened. Add cheese. Stir until cheese is melted. Serve in a chafing dish with crackers. Yield: about 3½ cups.

Western Olive Dip

1 (8-ounce) package cream cheese, softened
1 to 2 tablespoons commercial sour cream
1 teaspoon chili powder
1½ teaspoons grated onion
½ cup chopped ripe olives
   Corn chips

Beat cheese with other ingredients except olives and corn chips in small bowl of electric mixer. When smooth and light, fold in olives. Chill thoroughly and serve with corn chips. Yield: about 1½ cups.

Lobster Fondue Dip

2 tablespoons butter or margarine
2 cups (½ pound) shredded sharp pasteurized
   process American cheese
2 drops hot pepper sauce
⅓ cup dry white wine
1 (5-ounce) can lobster, drained and broken
   into small pieces

Melt butter in a small saucepan. Gradually stir in cheese over low heat until cheese melts. (Cheese and butter mixture may appear separated at this point.) Add hot pepper sauce; slowly add wine, stirring until mixture is smooth. Add lobster; stir until heated through. Serve hot in a chafing dish. Yield: about 1½ cups.

Smoked Oyster Dip

2 (8-ounce) packages cream cheese, softened
1 teaspoon Worcestershire sauce
2 teaspoons freshly squeezed lemon juice
1 cup commercial sour cream
1 (3⅔-ounce) can smoked oysters, undrained
   Corn chips

Blend cheese with Worcestershire sauce, lemon juice, and sour cream. Combine with undrained oysters. Serve with corn chips. Yield: about 3 cups.

Peanut Butter-Cheese Dip

½ cup chopped onion
1 cup chopped green pepper
1 clove garlic, chopped
2 tablespoons peanut oil
2 tomatoes, peeled and chopped
¾ cup tomato juice
¼ teaspoon thyme
¼ teaspoon oregano
½ bay leaf
½ pound Cheddar cheese, shredded
¾ cup peanut butter (smooth or crunchy)
½ teaspoon salt
⅛ teaspoon pepper
   Corn chips or potato chips

Cook onion, green pepper, and garlic in peanut oil until tender, but not browned. Add tomatoes, tomato juice, thyme, oregano, and bay leaf; cover and cook over low heat for 10 minutes. Stir once or twice. Put in top of double boiler and add cheese, peanut butter, salt, and pepper. Cook and stir over boiling water until cheese is melted and mixture is blended. Serve in a chafing dish with corn or potato chips. Yield: 4 cups.

Parisian Dip

1 (8-ounce) package cream cheese, softened
1 (3-ounce) package Roquefort cheese
3 tablespoons half-and-half
1½ teaspoons chopped chives, divided
½ teaspoon Worcestershire sauce
   Potato chips

Combine cream cheese, Roquefort cheese, half-and-half, 1 teaspoon chives, and Worcestershire sauce. Mix until well blended. Sprinkle with remaining chives. Serve with potato chips. Yield: about 1½ cups.

Dippin' Pork Barbecue

½ pound ground lean pork
2 tablespoons finely chopped onion
¼ cup chopped green pepper
1 small clove garlic, crushed
2 tablespoons butter or margarine
¼ teaspoon salt
   Pinch pepper
½ cup commercial barbecue sauce
¼ cup water
¼ cup commercial sour cream

Brown pork in a skillet until pink color disappears; drain off excess fat and reserve meat. Sauté onion, green pepper, and garlic in butter. Add pork, salt, pepper, barbecue sauce, and water. Simmer gently, stirring occasionally, for 15 minutes. Stir in sour cream; heat through, but do not boil. Transfer to a small chafing dish or fondue pot. Yield: about 1¾ cups.

Creamy Shrimp Dip

2 (8-ounce) packages cream cheese, softened
1 (3-ounce) package cream cheese with chives
1 (10¾-ounce) can cream of shrimp soup
1½ cups chopped cooked shrimp
1 teaspoon dry mustard
1 teaspoon Worcestershire sauce
¼ teaspoon garlic powder
½ to 1 teaspoon paprika
   Salt and pepper to taste
¾ to 1 cup mayonnaise
1 cup drained, cooked crabmeat (optional)

Combine ingredients in a large bowl at least 2 hours before serving. Chill. Yield: about 6½ cups.

Tallahassee Shrimp Dip

½ pound cooked, peeled shrimp, fresh or frozen
1 (1⅜-ounce) package dry onion soup mix
2 cups commercial sour cream
¼ cup catsup
1 tablespoon chopped parsley
   Assorted crackers

Thaw frozen shrimp. Chop shrimp. Combine all ingredients except crackers. Mix thoroughly. Chill. Serve with crackers. Yield: about 3¼ cups.

Zesty Shrimp Dip

½ pound fresh cooked shrimp, or 1 (5-ounce) can shrimp
1 (8-ounce) carton creamy cottage cheese
3 tablespoons chili sauce
½ teaspoon onion juice
½ teaspoon freshly squeezed lemon juice
¼ teaspoon Worcestershire sauce
4 tablespoons milk
   Potato chips, crackers, and celery

Finely chop shrimp and add to cottage cheese. Stir in chili sauce, onion juice, lemon juice, and Worcestershire sauce. Gradually beat in enough milk to give good dipping consistency. Serve with potato chips, crackers, and celery. Yield: about 2 cups.

Shrimp Chip Dip

1 (4½-ounce) can shrimp
1 cup commercial sour cream
¼ cup chili sauce
2 teaspoons freshly squeezed lemon juice
½ teaspoon salt
⅛ teaspoon pepper
1 teaspoon horseradish
    Dash hot pepper sauce

Cut shrimp into very small pieces and mix well with other ingredients. Chill. Yield: 1½ cups.

Tomato and Green Onion Dip

1 medium tomato, chopped
½ cup freshly squeezed lemon juice
½ teaspoon salt
½ teaspoon pepper
¼ cup minced green onions
2 cups commercial sour cream
¼ teaspoon Worcestershire sauce
½ teaspoon sugar
    Raw vegetables

Marinate tomato in lemon juice, salt, and pepper for 1 hour. Blend with remaining ingredients except vegetables. Serve as a dip for raw vegetables. Yield: about 3 cups.

Tuna Cream Dip

1 (6½- or 7-ounce) can tuna, drained and flaked
1 tablespoon horseradish
1½ teaspoons onion salt
1 teaspoon Worcestershire sauce
1 cup commercial sour cream
2 teaspoons chopped parsley
    Potato chips

Combine tuna, horseradish, onion salt, and Worcestershire sauce; fold in sour cream. Chill. Garnish with parsley and serve with potato chips. Yield: about 1½ cups.

"Souper" Shrimp Dip

1 (10¾-ounce) can cream of shrimp soup
1 (8-ounce) package cream cheese, softened
1 teaspoon freshly squeezed lemon juice
    Dash garlic powder
    Dash paprika

Gradually blend soup and other ingredients; beat just until smooth. (Overbeating will make dip too thin.) Chill. Serve as a dip with crackers, potato chips, corn chips, celery sticks, etc. Yield: about 2 cups.

Skinny Dip

½ cup watercress, stems and leaves included
3 tablespoons skim milk
1 cup diced green pepper
1 cup low-fat cottage cheese
12 stuffed green olives
⅛ teaspoon pepper
    Dash hot pepper sauce
    Dash salt
    Raw vegetables

Wash and dry watercress. Blend all ingredients except raw vegetables on high speed of blender until smooth. Chill. Serve with raw vegetables such as carrot sticks, celery, radishes, cauliflower, etc. Yield: about 2¼ cups.

Sour Cream Ham Dip

1 cup commercial sour cream
½ cup ground cooked ham
1¼ teaspoons dry sherry
1¼ teaspoons prepared mustard
¾ teaspoon instant minced onion

Combine all ingredients; chill until ready to serve. Yield: about 1½ cups.

Deviled Ham Dip

1 (5-ounce) jar pimiento-cheese spread
1 (2¼-ounce) can deviled ham
½ cup mayonnaise or salad dressing
1 tablespoon minced onion
Few drops hot pepper sauce

Combine all ingredients; chill. Yield: about 1⅓ cups.

Creamy Avocado Dip

2 cups mashed avocado
1 tablespoon minced onion
1 clove garlic, minced
¼ teaspoon chili powder
¼ teaspoon salt
Dash pepper
⅓ cup mayonnaise
6 slices bacon, cooked and crumbled

Combine avocado, onion, garlic, chili powder, salt, and pepper; blend well. Place in a small bowl; cover with mayonnaise, spreading over top and sides to keep avocado from turning dark. Refrigerate for several hours to blend flavors. When ready to serve, mix well and sprinkle top with crumbled bacon. Yield: 1⅓ cups.

Chili con Queso Dip

1 (10½-ounce) can tomatoes with hot peppers
1 pound pasteurized process American cheese, shredded
Crackers, corn chips, or potato chips

Combine tomatoes and cheese in top of a double boiler. Cook over simmering water until cheese has melted. Stir mixture occasionally. Serve hot or cold with crackers, corn chips, or potato chips. Yield: about 2 cups.

Dill Dip

1 (3-ounce) package cream cheese, softened
1 tablespoon finely chopped stuffed green olives
1 teaspoon grated onion
¼ teaspoon dillweed
Dash salt
1 to 2 tablespoons half-and-half
Raw zucchini, cut into sticks

Combine cream cheese, olives, onion, dillweed, and salt; stir in half-and-half to make mixture of dipping consistency. Chill. Serve with zucchini sticks as an appetizer. Yield: about ⅔ cup.

Hot Crabmeat Dip

1 (8-ounce) package cream cheese
3 tablespoons mayonnaise
1 teaspoon Dijon mustard
¼ teaspoon salt
2 tablespoons dry white wine
1 (7¾-ounce) can crabmeat, drained and flaked
Melba rounds or toast triangles

Combine cream cheese, mayonnaise, mustard, and salt in top of a double boiler over simmering water. Stir until smooth and well blended. Add wine gradually, then crabmeat; check seasonings. Transfer to a chafing dish and serve hot with melba rounds or toast triangles for dipping. Yield: about 2 cups.

Curried Cottage Cheese Dip

1 cup creamed cottage cheese
¼ cup sweet pickle relish, drained
¼ teaspoon curry powder
1 teaspoon grated onion
   Paprika

Put cottage cheese through a sieve or food mill; combine with other ingredients except paprika. Mix well. Cover and refrigerate for about 1 hour. Spoon into a serving dish and sprinkle with paprika. Yield: about 1 cup.

Shrimp Dip

1 (8-ounce) package cream cheese
⅓ cup commercial sour cream
2 teaspoons freshly squeezed lemon juice
¼ teaspoon onion juice
   Dash Worcestershire sauce
1 cup chopped cooked shrimp
   Paprika
   Potato chips

Soften cheese and blend in sour cream and seasonings. Stir in shrimp and add paprika as desired for color. Serve with sturdy potato chips or other "dippers." Yield: 2½ cups.

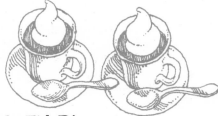

Smoky Fish Dip

¾ pound smoked fish
1 (8-ounce) package cream cheese, softened
2 tablespoons half-and-half
2 tablespoons freshly squeezed lemon juice
½ teaspoon liquid smoke
¼ teaspoon garlic salt
   Assorted crackers or chips

Remove skin and bones from fish. Chop fish very fine. Combine all ingredients except crackers; mix thoroughly. Chill. Serve with assorted crackers or chips. Yield: 2 cups.

Christmas Crab Dip

1 (8-ounce) package cream cheese, softened
1 (6½-ounce) can crab claw meat, drained
1 teaspoon mayonnaise
   Paprika
   Parsley sprigs

Blend cream cheese, crabmeat, and mayonnaise. Sprinkle with paprika and chill before serving. Garnish with parsley sprigs. Yield: 1½ cups.

Cheddar Blue Mold

8 ounces Cheddar cheese, shredded
1 (8-ounce) package cream cheese, softened
8 ounces blue cheese, crumbled
½ cup lemon soda
¼ teaspoon hot pepper sauce
¼ teaspoon Worcestershire sauce
1 teaspoon dry mustard
   Crackers

Blend all ingredients except crackers. Pack into a 3-cup mold. Chill thoroughly. Unmold; serve with assorted crackers. Yield: 3 cups.

Creamy Orange-Pecan Filling

2 (3-ounce) packages cream cheese, softened
2 tablespoons grated orange rind
4 tablespoons orange juice
1 cup chopped pecans

Combine all ingredients and mix well. Yield: about 1¼ cups.

Swiss Dip

½ pound Swiss cheese, shredded
1 (4½-ounce) can deviled ham
¼ cup catsup
¼ cup bourbon
   Assorted chips or breadsticks

Melt cheese over hot water; add deviled ham, catsup, and bourbon. Serve hot with chips or breadsticks. Yield: 2 cups.

Tapenade Dip

1 (6½-ounce) can white solid-pack tuna,
　drained
2 anchovy fillets
1 tablespoon anchovy oil
4 tablespoons chopped ripe olives
½ small onion, grated
1 clove garlic, crushed
¼ cup chopped celery
¼ cup cubed cooked potato
½ teaspoon Worcestershire sauce
　Dash hot pepper sauce
　Juice of 1 small lemon
　Pepper
½ cup mayonnaise
　Raw vegetables

Blend all ingredients except raw vegetables
in blender until smooth. Use as a dip for raw
vegetables. Yield: about 2 cups.

Note: The average home electric blender
resists blending such solid matter as the above;
you must use a rubber spatula to repeatedly
push the mixture into the path of the blades.
You might find it easier to do half the recipe
at a time. This is an excellent, different hors
d'oeuvre, well worth the trouble to prepare.
Don't omit the potatoes; they contribute to
the smooth texture.

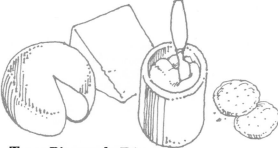

Tuna Pineapple Dip

1 (8¼-ounce) can crushed pineapple
1 (6½- or 7-ounce) can tuna, drained and
　flaked
1 (8-ounce) package cream cheese, softened
3 tablespoons pineapple juice
　Dash salt
　Dash ground nutmeg

Drain pineapple and reserve liquid.
Combine all ingredients; blend into a paste.
Chill. Yield: about 2 cups.

Tuna Party Dip

2 (6½- or 7-ounce) cans tuna in
　vegetable oil
2 cups commercial sour cream
1 (1⅜-ounce) package dry onion soup mix
1 teaspoon hot pepper sauce
　Crackers or potato chips

Combine all ingredients; chill. Serve with
crackers or potato chips. Yield: about 3½ cups.

Vegetable Chip Dip

1 tablespoon mayonnaise
1 tablespoon crumbled blue cheese
1 tablespoon chopped watercress
1½ cups cooked asparagus tips
1 hard-cooked egg, chopped
½ teaspoon salt
　Pinch pepper
　Potato chips

Combine all ingredients. Chill. Serve with
potato chips. Yield: about 2 cups.

Malley's Dip for Raw Vegetables

2 cups mayonnaise
2 cups commercial sour cream
3 tablespoons minced fresh parsley
　　　　or
1 tablespoon dried parsley
3 tablespoons grated onion
3 tablespoons dillweed
1½ tablespoons seasoned salt

Blend all ingredients together and chill
before serving. May be made several days
ahead of time. Yield: about 4½ cups.

Apricot-Almond Filling

1 cup stewed dried apricots
½ cup chopped almonds
1 tablespoon grated orange rind

Combine all ingredients and mix well.
Yield: about 1½ cups.

Anchovy Cheese

1 (16-ounce) carton cottage cheese
4 drained anchovies, finely shredded, oil
  reserved
2 tablespoons chopped fresh parsley
2 tablespoons minced chives or onion
1 teaspoon poppy seed (do not omit)
  About 1 teaspoon freshly squeezed
  lemon juice
  About ½ teaspoon oil drained from
  anchovies
  Salt to taste
  Pumpernickel, melba toast, or dark rye
  bread rounds

Combine all ingredients except salt,
pumpernickel, melba toast, and rye bread
rounds, in a bowl; taste and add salt if needed.
(The anchovies lend a good bit of salt to the
mixture.) Mound the cheese in center of a
serving dish; surround with pumpernickel,
melba toast, or dark rye bread rounds. Yield:
about 2 cups.

Corned Beef Sandwich Spread

1 cup coarsely ground or chopped canned
  corned beef
2 teaspoons prepared mustard
½ cup finely chopped celery
1 teaspoon grated onion
  Mayonnaise

Combine all ingredients, adding just enough
mayonnaise to moisten. Yield: 1½ cups.

Egg Appetizers

6 large hard-cooked eggs
½ cup finely chopped ripe olives
½ cup softened butter or margarine
2 tablespoons prepared mustard
¼ teaspoon salt
¼ teaspoon onion powder
¼ teaspoon hot pepper sauce
  Round buttery crackers

Press hard-cooked eggs through a sieve or
food mill. Add olives, butter, mustard, salt,
onion powder, and hot pepper sauce. Mix
well; cover and place in the refrigerator for
about 2 hours to allow the flavors to blend.
Spread on crackers to serve. Yield: about 3
cups.

Cheese and Egg Appetizer

2 (3-ounce) packages cream cheese, softened
4 hard-cooked eggs, grated
¼ teaspoon garlic powder
½ teaspoon salt
2 tablespoons white dry Rhine wine
⅛ teaspoon hot pepper sauce
½ teaspoon vinegar
  Yellow food coloring
  Bacon bits
  Assorted crackers

Combine first 7 ingredients and blend well.
Divide mixture. Add food coloring to ⅓ of the
mixture so it resembles an egg yolk. Shape
"yolk" and remaining ⅔ of the cheese and egg
mixture around it into the shape of an egg.
Roll in bacon bits. Chill and serve with
assorted crackers. Yield: 2 cups.

Simple Avocado Spread

2 avocados
1 tablespoon freshly squeezed lemon juice
1 teaspoon salt
¼ teaspoon Worcestershire sauce
  Cottage cheese, cream cheese, or
  mayonnaise (optional)

Cut each avocado into halves and remove
seed and skin. Force avocado through sieve or
simply mash well with fork. Blend in
remaining ingredients. (Cottage cheese, cream
cheese, or mayonnaise may be mixed with
spread to make the avocado go further.) Yield:
about 1 cup.

Black Bean Cracker Spread

1 (11-ounce) can black bean soup
1 (8-ounce) can tomato sauce
½ to 1 cup shredded sharp Cheddar cheese, divided
¼ teaspoon chili powder
   Crackers or corn chips

Combine black bean soup, tomato sauce, ½ cup cheese, and chili powder; cook over medium heat until cheese melts. Add more cheese until spread is as thick as desired. Serve warm as a spread for crackers or as a dip for chips. Yield: about 2½ cups.

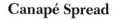

Canapé Spread

1 (8-ounce) package cream cheese, softened
¼ cup mayonnaise
1 teaspoon prepared mustard
1 teaspoon Worcestershire sauce
   Few drops hot pepper sauce
1 teaspoon horseradish
1 hard-cooked egg, minced
2 tablespoons minced stuffed olives
1 (4½-ounce) can deviled ham

Combine cream cheese, mayonnaise, mustard, Worcestershire sauce, and hot pepper sauce; whip until fluffy. Blend in other ingredients and chill. Yield: about 2 cups.

Deviled Canapé Spread

1 (8-ounce) package cream cheese, softened
¼ cup mayonnaise
1 hard-cooked egg, minced
1 teaspoon prepared mustard
   Few drops hot pepper sauce
1 teaspoon Worcestershire sauce
1 teaspoon horseradish
2 tablespoons minced stuffed olives
1 (4½-ounce) can deviled ham

Whip cheese until fluffy; blend in remaining ingredients. Chill. Yield: about 2 cups.

Seafood Canapé Spread

1 (3-ounce) package cream cheese, softened
½ cup butter or margarine, softened
½ cup cottage cheese
2 teaspoons anchovy paste
1 teaspoon caraway seed, crushed (optional)
1 teaspoon dry mustard
1 teaspoon paprika
1 teaspoon grated onion
   Sandwich bread slices
   Pimiento
   Parsley
   Anchovy, shrimp, or sardines (optional)

Beat together cream cheese, butter, cottage cheese, anchovy paste, caraway seed, mustard, paprika, and onion in small mixing bowl. Cover and chill to blend flavors. Serve at room temperature as a spread. To make canapés, remove crust from slices of sandwich bread. Cover each slice with spread. Garnish with pimiento and parsley. Cut in two. Place anchovy, shrimp, or sardine fillet on each, if desired. Yield: 1½ cups.

Aloha Cheese Spread

1 (8-ounce) package cream cheese, softened
3 ounces blue cheese, crumbled
⅓ cup crushed pineapple, drained
⅓ cup chopped pecans
½ teaspoon ground ginger
   Parsley
   Chopped pimiento

Blend cheeses. Stir in pineapple, pecans, and ginger; mix well. Chill. Garnish with parsley and pimiento. Yield: 2 cups.

Brandied Cheddar Cheese

1 pound sharp Cheddar cheese, shredded
2 tablespoons butter or margarine
1 teaspoon sugar
   Dash cayenne pepper
½ cup brandy, divided
   Crackers

Have cheese and butter at room temperature. Add sugar, cayenne pepper, and ¼ cup brandy; mix by hand or beat with electric mixer until quite smooth. Gradually add remaining ¼ cup brandy, mixing until creamy. Store in covered crock in refrigerator. Keeps indefinitely. Serve at room temperature with crackers. Yield: about 2 cups.

Molded Blue Cheese Spread

⅔ cup minced fresh parsley
2 (3-ounce) packages cream cheese, softened
1 (4-ounce) package blue cheese, crumbled
1 teaspoon Worcestershire sauce
    Dash cayenne pepper
1 tablespoon freshly squeezed lemon juice
4 tablespoons mayonnaise
    Unsalted crackers or melba rounds

Prepare small mold by generously oiling the inside. Press parsley around sides and bottom.
    Thoroughly combine cream cheese, blue cheese, Worcestershire sauce, cayenne pepper, and lemon juice in small bowl of electric mixer. Stir in mayonnaise until blended. Spoon carefully into prepared mold, cover, and chill. Unmold and serve with unsalted crackers or melba rounds. Yield: about 1¼ cups.

Clam Tempter

1 cup cottage cheese
½ cup canned minced clams, chopped
1 tablespoon clam broth
1 clove garlic, finely minced
1 teaspoon freshly squeezed lemon juice
1 teaspoon Worcestershire sauce
½ teaspoon salt
¼ teaspoon angostura bitters
    Chopped chives (optional)

Mash cottage cheese with a fork until smooth. Combine all ingredients except chives. Spoon into serving bowl. Garnish with chopped chives, if desired. Chill well before serving. Yield: 1½ cups.

Dutch Cheese Spread

1 (7-ounce) round Gouda or Edam cheese, finely shredded
½ cup commercial sour cream
¼ cup milk
½ teaspoon onion powder
¼ teaspoon caraway seed
    Chopped parsley
    Crackers

Combine cheese, sour cream, milk, onion powder, and caraway seed; blend well. Refrigerate at least ½ hour before serving. Sprinkle with parsley and serve with crackers. Yield: ⅔ cup.

Quick-as-a-Wink Cheese Spread

1 (8-ounce) jar pasteurized process cheese spread
¼ teaspoon Worcestershire sauce
1 teaspoon prepared mustard
2 tablespoons chili sauce
3 dozen crackers or toast rounds

Combine cheese spread, Worcestershire sauce, mustard, and chili sauce; blend until smooth. Spread about ½ tablespoon of the mixture on each cracker. Yield: 3 dozen.

Valley Cheese Spread

2 (3-ounce) packages cream cheese
¼ pound blue cheese
1 (5-ounce) jar garlic-flavored cheese spread
¼ cup port
½ cup chopped walnuts
¼ cup chopped parsley
2 tablespoons grated onion
½ teaspoon Worcestershire sauce

Have cheeses at room temperature. Blend the three cheeses; add remaining ingredients and mix well. Yield: 2 cups.

Walnut-Smoked Cheese Spread

¼ cup chopped walnuts
¼ cup smoked cheese spread
½ teaspoon Worcestershire sauce
¼ cup mayonnaise

Combine all ingredients and mix well.
Yield: ⅔ cup.

Sharp Gouda Spread

1 (8-ounce) round Gouda cheese
½ cup finely chopped smoked sliced beef
¼ cup commercial sour cream
2 tablespoons pickle relish
2 teaspoons horseradish

Allow cheese to come to room temperature.
Using cookie cutter, cut wax from top of
cheese. Carefully remove cheese from shell;
keep shell intact. In a small mixing bowl beat
cheese until smooth; add beef, sour cream,
pickle relish, and horseradish. Refill shell.
Yield: 1½ cups.

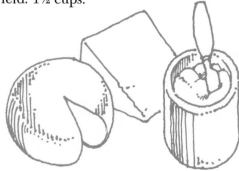

Gouda Party Scoop

1 (8-ounce) round Gouda cheese
½ teaspoon prepared mustard
½ teaspoon Worcestershire sauce
⅛ teaspoon salt
⅛ teaspoon onion salt
⅛ teaspoon garlic salt

Bring cheese to room temperature. Using
scalloped cookie cutter, cut wax from top of
cheese. Carefully remove cheese from shell;
keep shell intact. Beat cheese until smooth;
add remaining ingredients and beat until well
blended. Refill shell. Yield: about 1 cup.

Stuffed Edam Cheese

1 (8-ounce) round Edam cheese
¼ cup sherry
½ teaspoon prepared mustard
½ teaspoon Worcestershire sauce
⅛ teaspoon salt
⅛ teaspoon onion salt
⅛ teaspoon garlic salt
⅛ teaspoon cayenne pepper

Remove a 3-inch circle from top of cheese;
scoop out inside. Crumble cheese and measure
it tightly packed. (Measurements for wine and
seasonings are for 1 cup cheese. Increase
amounts for a larger Edam.) Blend wine and
seasonings into cheese. Pack mixture into
cheese shell; replace top. Chill. Bring to room
temperature to serve. Yield: 6 to 8 servings.

Chicken and Mushroom Sandwich Spread

1 cup chopped cooked chicken
⅓ cup toasted almonds (optional)
1 tablespoon minced onion
1 (3-ounce) can broiled mushrooms, chopped
½ cup diced celery
½ teaspoon salt
⅛ teaspoon pepper
½ teaspoon curry powder
½ cup mayonnaise

Put chopped chicken (preferably white
meat) through food chopper, using fine cutter.
Measure 1 cup and set aside. Put almonds
through food chopper. Combine chicken with
other ingredients; mix well. Yield: 1½ to 2
cups.

Chicken Liver Sandwich Spread

8 chicken livers (about ¼ pound)
2 tablespoons salad oil
1 very small onion, finely chopped
1 hard-cooked egg, finely chopped
¼ teaspoon coarsely ground pepper
¼ teaspoon salt
3 tablespoons mayonnaise
Pinch tarragon (optional)
Chopped parsley (optional)

Dry livers with paper towels. Heat oil in a small frying pan and sauté livers about 5 minutes on each side. Drain livers on paper towel and cool; then finely chop.

Mix chopped liver with remaining ingredients. Chill. Serve in sandwiches or on buttered toast or crackers. Yield: about 1 cup.

Egg-Peanut Spread

6 hard-cooked eggs, finely chopped
½ cup finely chopped roasted peanuts
2 tablespoons finely chopped pimiento
2 tablespoons finely chopped olives
1 tablespoon finely chopped chives
¾ teaspoon salt
¼ cup mayonnaise
¼ cup milk
¼ teaspoon Worcestershire sauce
  Crackers and potato chips

Combine all finely chopped ingredients and salt. Combine mayonnaise, milk, and Worcestershire sauce; blend with eggs and other ingredients. Stir well. Serve with crackers and potato chips. Yield: 2 cups.

Holiday Hors d'Oeuvres

1 (3-ounce) package cream cheese
1 (4½-ounce) can deviled ham
3 tablespoons crushed pineapple
  Chopped chives
  Assorted crackers

Combine first 3 ingredients. Chill. Turn mixture onto a plate; form into a large ball and cover generously with chives. Chill. Serve with assorted crackers. Yield: about 1 cup.

Pinto-Deviled Ham Spread

1 (3-ounce) can deviled ham
1 (3-ounce) package pimiento cream cheese, softened
¼ cup diced celery

Combine all ingredients and mix well. Yield: 1 cup.

Spicy Ham 'n Raisin Filling

1 (4½-ounce) can deviled ham
½ cup chopped celery
¼ cup chopped nuts
2 tablespoons mayonnaise
¼ cup chopped raisins

Combine all ingredients and mix well. Yield: 1½ cups.

Liverwurst Salad Sandwich Spread

1 (4¾-ounce) can liverwurst spread
½ cup chopped radish
⅓ cup chopped carrot
1 hard-cooked egg, chopped
1 tablespoon minced onion
  Bread

Combine all ingredients. Chill, if desired. Use as a sandwich spread on thin-sliced white, light rye, or party-size bread. Yield: about 1⅓ cups.

Olive-Cheddar Sandwich Spread

1 pound mild Cheddar cheese, shredded
¾ cup mayonnaise or salad dressing
1 (8-ounce) jar pimiento-stuffed olives, drained and chopped
  Bread or toast
  Lettuce

Combine cheese, mayonnaise, and olives; stir until well blended. Spread cheese mixture on bread or toast slices. Top with lettuce and additional slices of bread to make sandwiches. Yield: about 4 cups.

Peanut Butter-Bacon Spread

4 slices bacon
½ cup peanut butter (smooth or crunchy)
½ cup finely chopped dill pickle
2 tablespoons dill pickle juice
¼ teaspoon salt
Dash hot pepper sauce
Crackers

Cook bacon until crisp. Drain on paper towels. Crumble into small pieces. Mix with peanut butter, dill pickle, juice, and seasonings. Serve on crackers. Yield: about 1 cup.

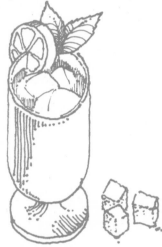

Buttered Pimiento Spread

½ cup butter or margarine, softened
¼ pound pimiento cream cheese
1 tablespoon grated onion
½ teaspoon Worcestershire sauce
1 teaspoon freshly squeezed lemon juice
1 tablespoon minced green pepper
1 teaspoon caraway seed
1 (2-ounce) can anchovies, drained
Several grinds coarse black pepper
Melba rounds

Cream butter and cheese together in large bowl of electric mixer. Add remaining ingredients except melba rounds, and blend well. Chill and serve with melba rounds. Yield: about 1 cup.

Note: If pimiento cream cheese is not available, use ¼ pound cream cheese into which a small jar of drained pimiento strips has been blended.

Deviled Peanut Spread

½ cup peanut butter (smooth or crunchy)
1 (2¼-ounce) can deviled ham
½ teaspoon celery salt
Crackers

Combine first 3 ingredients. Serve on crackers. Yield: ¾ cup.

Pineapple Sandwich Mixture

15 large marshmallows
Juice of 1 lemon
1 (8¼-ounce) can crushed pineapple
1 (8-ounce) package dates, chopped
1 cup chopped nuts
1 cup mayonnaise

Combine marshmallows, lemon juice, and pineapple in a double boiler or heavy pan; heat until marshmallows are melted. Let cool; add dates and nuts. Stir in mayonnaise. Yield: about 2 cups.

Rumaki Spread

½ pound chicken livers
Salt and pepper
Butter or margarine
1 tablespoon soy sauce
½ cup softened butter or margarine
½ teaspoon onion salt
½ teaspoon dry mustard
¼ teaspoon ground nutmeg
1 or 2 dashes cayenne pepper
1 (5-ounce) can water chestnuts, drained and minced
6 slices crisp cooked bacon, crumbled
Thinly sliced green onions for garnish (optional)
Crackers

Cook chicken livers seasoned with salt and pepper in butter. When done, place in blender with soy sauce, butter, onion salt, mustard, nutmeg, and cayenne pepper. Blend until mixture is smooth, stirring it down with rubber spatula as needed. Remove from blender; stir in chestnuts and bacon; garnish with onions. Serve with crisp crackers. Yield: 1½ cups.

Note: This spread should be prepared a day ahead of serving but should be removed from refrigerator and allowed to soften slightly at room temperature for 1 hour before serving.

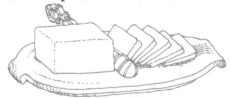

Shrimp Sandwich Filling

2 cups boiled and peeled shrimp
2 hard-cooked eggs
1 whole dill pickle
1 small onion
1 teaspoon freshly squeezed lemon juice
1 cup mayonnaise
  Salt and pepper to taste

Chop shrimp, eggs, pickle, and onion in a blender (high speed for 5 seconds) or a food chopper. Combine with other ingredients; mix well. Yield: about 2 cups.

Shrimp Mousse

1 (10¾-ounce) can tomato soup
1 (8-ounce) package cream cheese
1½ envelopes (1½ tablespoons) unflavored
  gelatin
¼ cup cold water
1 cup mayonnaise
2 (4½-ounce) cans shrimp
1 tablespoon Worcestershire sauce
3 stalks celery
6 scallions or 1 medium onion
  Salt and pepper to taste

Warm soup and cheese in a saucepan over low heat until cheese melts. Soften gelatin in cold water; add to soup and stir over heat until gelatin dissolves. Put cheese mixture and remaining ingredients in a blender and blend until smooth. Pour into a 1-quart mold and refrigerate overnight. Unmold and garnish as desired. Yield: 4 cups.

Note: Mousse may be made several days before serving. Garnish with black caviar, grated egg yolk, parsley sprigs, and pimiento strips. Serve as a spread on crackers or bread.

Tuna Sour Cream Filling

1 (7-ounce) can tuna, drained and flaked
¼ cup chopped celery
2 tablespoons minced onion
2 tablespoons pickle relish
6 tablespoons commercial sour cream

Combine ingredients and mix well. Use as a sandwich filling or a spread for crackers. Yield: 1¼ cups.

Olive and Dried Beef Spread

1 cup medium white sauce
1 cup shredded sharp Cheddar cheese
¼ teaspoon dry mustard
½ teaspoon Worcestershire sauce
½ cup sliced ripe olives
¼ cup finely shredded dried chipped beef
  Corn chips

Put white sauce in top of a double boiler over warm water; gradually add cheese, stirring until melted. Add seasonings and mix well. Stir in olives and dried beef. Transfer to a chafing dish and serve with corn chips. Yield: about 2½ cups.

Cheese Ball

6 (3-ounce) packages cream cheese, softened
½ pound sharp cheese
2 teaspoons grated onion
2 teaspoons Worcestershire sauce
2 teaspoons finely minced garlic (dried
  onion flakes and garlic powder may be
  substituted)
  Finely chopped nuts (pecan or peanut)

Put all ingredients except nuts in the large bowl of an electric mixer and blend well. Refrigerate until firm; shape into a ball. Roll in chopped nuts until well coated. Wrap in plastic or heavy-duty aluminum foil and let ripen in refrigerator for at least 24 hours. Remove from refrigerator at least 2 hours before serving. Yield: about 3 cups.

Creamy Canapé Spread

1 (3-ounce) package cream cheese, softened
1 (7-ounce) can tuna
  Mayonnaise
  Worcestershire sauce
  Hot pepper sauce
  Crackers

Stir cream cheese until smooth; add tuna and mix. Add just enough mayonnaise to make spreading consistency, and add seasonings to taste. Serve with crackers. Yield: about 1¼ cups.

Blue Cheese Whip

1 cup crumbled blue cheese
2 cups commercial sour cream, divided
  Crackers, breadsticks, or raw vegetables

Beat together cheese and ¼ cup sour cream; fold in remaining sour cream. Cover and chill. Serve as a spread for crackers, as a dip for breadsticks and raw vegetables, or as a filling for celery sticks. Yield: about 2 cups.

Christmas-Green Cheese Ball

1 (¼-pound) wedge natural blue cheese, crumbled
1 tablespoon minced celery
2 or 3 scallions or green onions, including tops, finely chopped
2 tablespoons commercial sour cream
3 (5-ounce) jars blue cheese spread
1 cup coarsely chopped parsley

Combine blue cheese, celery, scallions, sour cream, and blue cheese spread until fluffy; mix on medium speed of electric mixer. Shape into a ball, wrap in heavy-duty aluminum foil, and refrigerate overnight.

At serving time, remove foil and reshape into a ball; roll in parsley until completely coated. Yield: about 1½ cups.

Anchovy Sauce for Seafood

3 teaspoons anchovy paste
1 tablespoon paprika
  Pinch salt, if needed
2 tablespoons tarragon vinegar
1 cup mayonnaise
½ cup whipping cream, whipped

Mix anchovy paste, paprika, salt, and vinegar. Gradually blend into mayonnaise, mixing well after each addition. Fold in cream. If mixture is too thick, thin with a little cream. Yield: 2 cups.

Gourmet Cheese Ball

3 (8-ounce) packages cream cheese, softened
1 cup drained and chopped preserved ginger
¾ cup canned diced roasted buttered almonds

Combine cheese and ginger; mix until well blended. Shape into a ball, wrap in heavy-duty aluminum foil, and refrigerate overnight.

At serving time, remove foil and reshape into a ball; roll in almonds until completely coated. Yield: 3 cups.

Pecan-Cheddar Sandwich Spread

1 (16-ounce) round extra sharp natural Cheddar cheese, shredded
½ cup mayonnaise
2 teaspoons prepared mustard
1 cup finely chopped pecans

Shred cheese; add mayonnaise, mustard, and pecans; mix well. Store in refrigerator. This is a tangy spread for sandwiches or for snacks. Yield: about 4 cups.

Chicken Liver Pâté

1 pound chicken livers
4 hard-cooked eggs
2 medium onions, grated
2 teaspoons salt
¼ teaspoon pepper
2 tablespoons freshly squeezed lemon juice
½ cup butter or margarine, melted
   Crackers

Cook chicken livers for 5 minutes in a small amount of boiling water. Drain. Combine with hard-cooked eggs, grated onion, salt, pepper, and lemon juice. Finely chop or put in a blender and mix until smooth. Add melted butter and mix well. Chill at least 2 to 3 hours. Serve with crackers. Yield: about 3 cups.

Cheddar Cheese Log

1 pound Cheddar cheese
1 tablespoon grated onion
1 teaspoon Worcestershire sauce
½ teaspoon paprika
½ cup chopped nuts

Cut cheese into small pieces and allow to come to room temperature. Beat cheese until smooth and creamy; add onion, Worcestershire sauce, and paprika and continue to beat until thoroughly blended. Shape into a roll 6 inches long and 2½ inches in diameter. Roll in nuts. Yield: 2 cups.

Party Time Pâté

2 (4¾-ounce) cans liverwurst spread
½ cup butter or margarine, softened
2 tablespoons minced onion
¾ teaspoon salt
¼ teaspoon ground nutmeg
1 teaspoon dry mustard
⅛ teaspoon ground cloves
   Dash cayenne pepper
   Rye crackers

Combine all ingredients except crackers. Cover tightly and chill for at least 4 hours. Serve with rye crackers. Yield: about 1½ cups.

Christmas-Red Cheese Ball

½ pound natural Cheddar cheese, finely shredded
1 (3-ounce) package cream cheese, softened
3 tablespoons sherry
¼ cup coarsely chopped pitted ripe olives
   Dash onion salt
   Dash celery salt
   Dash garlic salt
½ teaspoon Worcestershire sauce
½ cup coarsely chopped dried beef

Combine cheeses, sherry, olives, salts, and Worcestershire sauce; mix on medium speed of electric mixer. Shape mixture into a ball; wrap in heavy-duty aluminum foil; refrigerate overnight or until needed.

About 30 minutes before serving time, remove foil; reshape into a ball; roll ball in dried beef, coating well. Yield: about 1½ cups.

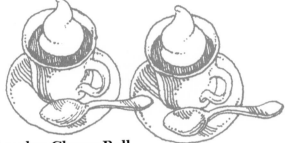

London Cheese Roll

1 (8-ounce) package cream cheese
1 (3-ounce) package cream cheese
1 (4-ounce) package blue cheese, crumbled
1 cup sliced ripe olives
2 cups coarsely chopped walnuts or pecans, divided
   Crackers or melba rounds

Have cheeses at room temperature. Blend thoroughly in large bowl of electric mixer. Stir in olives and 1 cup nuts. Spread remaining nuts on a sheet of waxed paper. Flour hands lightly and shape mixture into long roll or 2 short rolls about the size of a silver dollar. Roll back and forth in nuts until well coated; wrap in waxed paper and refrigerate overnight before using. Serve with crackers or melba rounds. This cheese freezes beautifully and may be made well in advance of serving. Yield: about 2 cups.

Zesty Cheese Ball

1 pound Cheddar cheese, softened
1 (8-ounce) package cream cheese, softened
Dash onion salt or juice
Dash garlic salt
Dash hot pepper sauce
Dash Worcestershire sauce
Dash salt
½ cup chopped nuts, toasted
Paprika

Blend softened cheeses. Add seasonings to taste; blend well. Shape cheese into a ball and roll in nuts. (Chill cheese slightly in order to roll more easily.) Sprinkle ball with paprika. Yield: 3 cups.

Easy Cheese Ball

½ pound sharp Cheddar cheese, shredded
1 (8-ounce) package cream cheese
¼ pound Roquefort or blue cheese
1 clove garlic, crushed
2 teaspoons grated onion
Cayenne pepper to taste
1 teaspoon Worcestershire sauce
1 cup finely minced parsley
1 cup chopped pecans

Thoroughly mix all ingredients except parsley and pecans. Combine parsley and pecans; blend half of parsley mixture into cheese mixture. Spread remaining parsley mixture on sheet of waxed paper. Form cheese into a ball and roll it in parsley mixture until well coated. Chill before serving. May be made long before serving. Freezes beautifully. Yield: about 2½ cups.

Blue Cheese Ball

1 (8-ounce) package cream cheese, softened
¼ cup crumbled blue cheese
1 tablespoon grated onion
½ cup chopped parsley

Beat cream cheese, blue cheese, and onion until smooth. Chill for ease in handling. Shape into a ball; wrap in waxed paper. Chill. Just before serving, roll in chopped parsley. Yield: 1¼ cups.

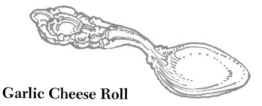

Garlic Cheese Roll

1 pound sharp Cheddar cheese, shredded
1 (8-ounce) package cream cheese
½ teaspoon salt
2 cloves garlic, crushed
3 dashes hot pepper sauce
1 tablespoon Worcestershire sauce
1 tablespoon mayonnaise
¼ teaspoon dry mustard
2 tablespoons paprika
2 tablespoons chili powder

Blend the two cheeses in the large bowl of an electric mixer. Add all other ingredients, except paprika and chili powder, mixing until smooth. Mix paprika and chili powder together and spread evenly on a piece of waxed paper placed on a flat surface. Dust hands lightly with flour and shape cheese mixture into two rolls about the diameter of a silver dollar. Roll in paprika and chili powder until completely covered. Flatten ends of roll and coat them also. Wrap in waxed paper and refrigerate 24 hours before using. This cheese freezes (and refreezes!) beautifully. Yield: 3 cups.

Party Cheese Ball

2 (8-ounce) packages cream cheese, softened
1 (8-ounce) wedge sharp natural Cheddar cheese, shredded
1 tablespoon chopped pimiento
1 tablespoon chopped green pepper
1 tablespoon finely chopped onion
2 teaspoons Worcestershire sauce
1 teaspoon freshly squeezed lemon juice
Dash cayenne pepper
Dash salt
Finely chopped pecans

Combine softened cream cheese and Cheddar cheese, mixing until well blended. Add pimiento, green pepper, onion, Worcestershire sauce, lemon juice, and seasonings; mix well. Chill. Shape into a ball and roll in chopped pecans. Yield: 3 cups.

Frosted Ham Ball

    1 pound cooked ham, ground
    ½ cup dark seedless raisins
    1 medium onion, grated
    ¾ cup mayonnaise
    ½ teaspoon curry powder
    2 (3-ounce) packages cream cheese, softened
    2 tablespoons milk
      Chopped parsley
      Assorted crackers

Combine ham, raisins, onion, mayonnaise, and curry powder. Mold mixture into a round shape on a serving plate. Chill. Blend cream cheese and milk. Frost ham mixture with cream cheese mixture. Garnish with parsley. Serve with assorted crackers. Yield: about 4½ cups.

Snowman Cheese Ball

    2 (8-ounce) packages cream cheese, softened
    2 cups crumbled Roquefort cheese
    2 tablespoons grated onion
    1½ teaspoons prepared mustard
    1 tablespoon Worcestershire sauce
    ⅛ teaspoon cayenne pepper
    3 or 4 stuffed olives
    1 strip pimiento
    1 tablespoon seedless raisins

Combine cheeses, onion, mustard, Worcestershire sauce, and cayenne pepper; mix until smooth. Cover and chill for 30 minutes or until firm enough to shape. Shape into 3 balls using 1½ cups for first, 1 cup for second, and ½ cup for third. Arrange one on top of another to form a snowman. Slice olives for eyes and nose; use pimiento strip for mouth and olive slices for buttons. Put raisins on toothpicks and insert as arms. Cut hat from cardboard and cover with foil. Yield: 3 cups.

Note: Mixture may be shaped into a single ball and dusted with paprika or rolled in ground pecans.

Versatile Cheese Ball

    2 cups shredded Cheddar cheese
    1 cup crumbled blue cheese
    ½ cup shredded Provolone cheese
    1 (3-ounce) package cream cheese, softened
    1 tablespoon milk
    1 tablespoon grated onion
    1 teaspoon Worcestershire sauce
    ½ teaspoon dry mustard
    ½ teaspoon paprika
    ¼ teaspoon garlic salt
    ¼ teaspoon celery salt
    ¼ cup toasted sesame seed

Beat Cheddar, blue, Provolone, and cream cheeses until smooth. Blend in milk, onion, Worcestershire sauce, mustard, paprika, and garlic and celery salts. Chill for ease in handling. Shape into a ball; roll in sesame seed. Wrap in waxed paper; chill. Yield: 2 cups.

Trio Cheese Ball

    1 (8-ounce) package cream cheese, softened
    ¼ pound blue cheese, crumbled
    1 cup (¼ pound) shredded sharp Cheddar cheese
    1 small onion, minced
    1 tablespoon Worcestershire sauce
    ½ cup chopped pecans
      Finely chopped parsley
      Small crisp crackers

Beat cheeses on medium speed of electric mixer until fluffy, scraping sides and bottom of bowl often. Beat in onion and Worcestershire sauce. Stir in pecans. Cover and chill for 3 to 4 hours. Mold cheese mixture into one large ball or into 30 to 36 small balls, each about 1 inch in diameter; roll in parsley. Cover and chill until firm, about 2 hours. Arrange a variety of crackers on a plate around cheese ball; serve as a spread, or insert colored wooden picks in center of small balls and serve with crackers. Yield: 2½ cups.

Walnut Cheese Ball

¼ pound natural Cheddar cheese, shredded
1 (3-ounce) package cream cheese, softened
¼ pound blue cheese, crumbled
1 tablespoon prepared mustard
3 tablespoons cooking sherry
1 teaspoon grated onion
¼ teaspoon hot pepper sauce
1 cup walnuts, chopped

Combine all ingredients except walnuts. Shape into a ball. Roll in chopped walnuts, coating surface thickly. Wrap in heavy-duty aluminum foil and chill 24 hours. Can be kept about a week if refrigerated. Yield: about 1½ cups.

Caraway Cheese Log

1 (8-ounce) package cream cheese, softened
⅓ cup white wine
1 tablespoon caraway seed
½ pound Monterey Jack cheese, shredded
½ cup grated Parmesan cheese
   Crackers

Beat cream cheese until fluffy. Blend in wine. Mix in caraway seed and Monterey Jack cheese. Sprinkle a layer of Parmesan cheese on waxed paper. Place ¼ of cheese mixture on Parmesan layer. Shape cheese, with hands, into a small log about 4 inches long and 1 inch wide, patting log with Parmesan cheese while shaping. Form 3 more logs. Chill for 1 hour or until firm enough to slice. Serve with crackers. Yield: 4 logs.

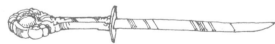

Cheese Log

1 (8-ounce) package cream cheese, softened
1 (4-ounce) roll bacon and horseradish
   cheese spread
1 (1⅜-ounce) package dry onion soup mix
1 teaspoon chili powder
¼ teaspoon garlic powder
½ cup chopped peanuts
   Rye bread

Blend all ingredients except peanuts and rye bread. Shape into a 10- x 2½-inch roll; wrap in waxed paper and chill for 4 hours. Remove paper, roll in peanuts, and serve with rye bread. Yield: 1½ cups.

Bacon Cheese Logs

1 pound bacon
1 (8-ounce) package cream cheese, softened
½ cup chopped pecans
¼ teaspoon garlic salt
¼ teaspoon Worcestershire sauce
4 drops hot pepper sauce
1 tablespoon chili powder
   Crackers

Cook bacon until crisp; drain and crumble. Blend with remaining ingredients except chili powder and crackers. Shape into 2 rolls about 1 inch in diameter. Sprinkle chili powder on waxed paper; roll logs in chili powder to coat evenly. Wrap tightly in waxed paper. Chill. Slice and serve on crackers. Yield: about 5 dozen.

Ginger Ball

3 (8-ounce) packages cream cheese, softened
2 (2-ounce) jars crystallized ginger
2 or more teaspoons ground ginger
1 cup finely chopped pecans
   Crackers or vegetables

Combine cream cheese and ginger until thoroughly blended. Shape into a ball and store in refrigerator at least 24 hours before serving. About half an hour before serving, roll ball in chopped pecans and allow to come to room temperature. Serve with crackers or with crisp vegetable wedges. Yield: about 3 cups.

Appetizer Ham Ball

2 (4½-ounce) cans deviled ham
3 tablespoons chopped stuffed olives
1 tablespoon prepared mustard
    Hot pepper sauce to taste
1 (3-ounce) package cream cheese, softened
2 teaspoons milk

Combine deviled ham, olives, mustard, hot pepper sauce, and ⅓ of the cream cheese; blend until smooth. Chill. Shape mixture into a ball. Combine remaining cream cheese and milk; frost ham ball with this mixture. Chill. Remove from refrigerator 15 minutes before serving. Yield: 1½ cups.

Appetizer Cheese Mousse

2 teaspoons unflavored gelatin
¼ cup cold water
2 cups commercial sour cream
2 teaspoons Italian salad dressing mix
¼ cup crumbled blue cheese
1 cup cream-style cottage cheese
    Parsley
    Carrot curls

Soften gelatin in cold water. Place over boiling water and stir until gelatin dissolves. Stir dissolved gelatin into sour cream. Add salad dressing mix, blue cheese, and cottage cheese; beat with electric mixer or rotary beater until well blended. Pour into a 3½-cup ring mold. Chill until firm. Unmold and garnish with parsley and carrot curls. Yield: about 3 cups.

Appetizer Cheese Roll

2 (3-ounce) packages cream cheese
2 cups shredded Cheddar cheese
⅓ cup crumbled blue cheese
    Chopped parsley

Bring cheeses to room temperature. Beat together cream, Cheddar, and blue cheeses until smooth. Chill for ease in handling. Shape into a roll 8 inches long. Roll in parsley. Chill until ready to serve. Yield: about 3 cups.

Gourmet Cheese Ring

⅔ cup chopped walnuts or pecans, divided
1 (3-ounce) package cream cheese
1½ cups finely shredded Swiss cheese
1½ cups finely shredded Cheddar cheese
1½ ounces Roquefort cheese, crumbled
2 tablespoons commercial sour cream
⅛ teaspoon cayenne pepper

Have all ingredients at room temperature. Lightly grease a 3-cup ring mold; coat with 2 tablespoons nuts. Blend the four cheeses with an electric mixer until smooth and light. Stir in sour cream, cayenne pepper, and remaining nuts. Pack into the mold. Refrigerate overnight. Unmold. Allow to stand at room temperature ½ hour before serving. Yield: 2½ cups.

Sherried Chicken Liver Pâté

1 pound chicken livers
    Flour seasoned with salt and pepper
2 tablespoons butter or margarine
1 medium onion, finely chopped
4 tablespoons dry sherry, divided
    Pinch rosemary
    Pinch thyme
6 tablespoons softened butter or margarine
2 tablespoons Cognac
    Salt, pepper, and seasoned salt to taste
    Parsley sprigs
    Melba rounds

Pat livers dry with paper towels. Sprinkle lightly with seasoned flour. Heat butter in a skillet and sauté livers over medium heat for about 5 minutes. Add onion and continue cooking and stirring until onion is barely yellow, about 3 minutes. Stir in 2 tablespoons sherry, rosemary, and thyme and simmer for a minute. Add softened butter; remove from heat and puree in electric blender, blending ⅓ of the mixture at a time and pushing down from sides into path of blades. When all has been blended until smooth, stir in remaining 2 tablespoons sherry, Cognac, salt, pepper, and seasoned salt to taste. Chill in container from which pâté is to be served. Garnish with clusters of fresh parsley and serve with melba rounds. Yield: about 2½ cups.

Velvet Chicken Liver Pâté

½ pound chicken livers
2 tablespoons butter or margarine
⅓ to ½ cup chicken broth
2 hard-cooked eggs
   Salt, pepper, and seasoned salt to taste
2 (3-ounce) packages cream cheese, softened
2 tablespoons dry sherry
   Olives and parsley sprigs (optional)

Sauté livers in butter for 10 minutes or until just tender. Stir in broth, swirl in pan a minute, then put livers, broth, and eggs through blender until smooth. (This won't be easy but the results make it worthwhile.) Blend seasonings into cheese, then combine with liver mixture. Add sherry and blend well; check seasonings, and chill before serving. Pâté may be turned into oiled mold or bowl, then turned out and garnished with olives and parsley sprigs. Yield: about 2½ cups.

Consommé Pâté Mold

1 envelope (1 tablespoon) unflavored gelatin
1 pint canned beef consommé, divided
2 (3-ounce) packages cream cheese, softened
2 tablespoons half-and-half
⅛ teaspoon garlic powder
⅛ teaspoon Beau Monde seasoning
   Sliced green olives
   Pimiento strips
½ cup mashed, fried chicken livers

Dissolve gelatin in ¼ cup consommé. Heat the remaining consommé to boiling and add dissolved gelatin. Blend cream cheese and half-and-half; add garlic powder and Beau Monde seasoning. Arrange sliced green olives and pimiento strips in bottom of round mold, and spoon ⅛ cup of the consommé mixture carefully into mold. Place in refrigerator until set, then add the remainder and return to refrigerator. Add mashed livers to cream cheese mixture and spread over congealed consommé (may be made the day before). Yield: about 3 cups.

Amsterdam Cheese Mold

1 (about 8 ounces) small round Gouda cheese
2 ounces crumbled blue cheese
½ cup commercial sour cream
4 tablespoons butter or margarine
2 tablespoons wine vinegar or cider vinegar
1 tablespoon grated onion
⅛ teaspoon cayenne pepper

Peel the rind from Gouda cheese and shred cheese into a saucepan. Add all other ingredients and heat slowly, stirring constantly with a wooden spoon until cheeses melt completely and mixture is smooth. (If you have an electric blender, use it for a more velvety texture after cheeses are completely melted.) Lightly oil a 2-cup mold and pour in cheese. Cover and chill overnight. When ready to serve, unmold by running a sharp knife around mold and shaking it onto a serving plate. This is best served at room temperature, as the flavor is delicate and serving it ice-cold tends to detract from the subtlety. Yield: about 1½ cups.

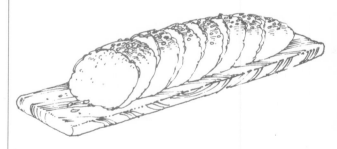

Braunschweiger Mold

½ pound braunschweiger (liver sausage), chopped
1 (3-ounce) package cream cheese, softened
4 tablespoons mayonnaise
1 to 2 tablespoons half-and-half
1 tablespoon melted butter or margarine
1 tablespoon dry sherry
½ teaspoon curry powder
¼ teaspoon salt
¼ teaspoon black pepper
   Pinch cayenne pepper
   Pinch ground nutmeg
1 tablespoon Worcestershire sauce
   Rye bread rounds

Beat sausage, cream cheese, mayonnaise, and half-and-half in small bowl of an electric mixer. When blended, beat in remaining ingredients; turn into lightly oiled mold or bowl in which spread is to be served. Chill until ready to serve. (May be made day before serving.) Surround bowl with small rounds of rye bread. Yield: about 2 cups.

Mushroom-Chive Cheese Spread

¼ cup canned mushrooms, chopped
⅓ cup chive-flavored cream cheese, softened

Combine mushrooms and cream cheese until smooth. Yield: about ½ cup.

Chopped Chicken Livers

3 tablespoons butter or margarine, divided
1 whole clove garlic
2 onions, finely minced
1 pound chicken livers
    Salt and pepper
2 hard-cooked eggs
¼ cup melted butter or margarine (or half cream and half butter)
1 tablespoon sherry (optional)

Heat 2 tablespoons butter and garlic, with a wooden pick in it, in skillet. Add onions and sauté until tender and yellow; do not brown. Discard garlic; turn onions into a bowl. Add a bit more butter to skillet and sauté livers until done: do not overcook. Stir in seasonings; put mixture and eggs through the finest blade of meat grinder. Blend in melted butter and sherry, stirring until smooth. May be made a day ahead. Leftovers freeze well. Yield: 12 servings.

Cocktail Sauce for Shrimp

2 cups catsup or chili sauce
½ cup Worcestershire sauce
½ cup minced celery
½ cup chopped fresh parsley
¼ cup horseradish
¼ cup freshly squeezed lemon juice
    Dash hot pepper sauce
    Dash sugar
    Salt to taste

Combine all ingredients the day before using. This yields enough sauce for 5 pounds raw shrimp in the shell. Yield: about 4 cups.

Curry Sauce for Raw Vegetables

½ cup mayonnaise
1 cup commercial sour cream
2 tablespoons freshly squeezed lemon juice
    Salt and pepper to taste
1 teaspoon curry powder
½ teaspoon paprika
2 tablespoons minced fresh parsley
½ teaspoon tarragon
2 tablespoons grated onion
2 teaspoons prepared mustard
1 tablespoon minced chives
    Several dashes hot pepper sauce
    Raw vegetables

Combine mayonnaise, sour cream, and lemon juice. Blend with all other ingredients except vegetables. Check seasonings and chill overnight before serving. Use as a dip for an assortment of raw vegetables (cauliflower flowerets, sliced raw yellow squash, cucumber slices, celery sticks, carrot sticks, etc.). Yield: about 2 cups.

Tangy Dip Sauce for Hot Hors d'Oeuvres

½ cup chili sauce
⅓ cup catsup
3 tablespoons horseradish
1½ teaspoons Worcestershire sauce

Combine chili sauce, catsup, horseradish, and Worcestershire sauce. Mix well. Yield: about ¾ cup.

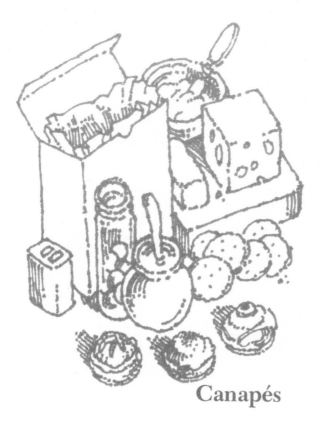

Canapés

Canapés

1 (8-ounce) package cream cheese, softened
1 egg yolk
1 teaspoon grated onion
¼ teaspoon Ac'cent
Crackers

Combine all ingredients except crackers and mix well. Spread on crackers and broil. The canapés puff up and turn golden brown. Yield: 2 dozen.

Canapé Mayonnaise

1 envelope (1 tablespoon) unflavored gelatin
¼ cup cold water
1 cup mayonnaise

Soften gelatin in cold water. Place over hot water and stir until gelatin is completely dissolved. Add to mayonnaise and blend well. Mayonnaise glaze may be stored in a tightly covered container in refrigerator. It will "moistureproof" your crisp crackers or bread and form a canapé base. Yield: 1¼ cups.

Peanut Butter-Bacon Canapés

6 slices bacon
¾ cup peanut butter
¾ cup pickle relish
2 (8-ounce) cans refrigerated biscuits

Fry bacon until crisp; drain on absorbent paper and crumble. Mix bacon, peanut butter, and pickle relish; beat until well blended. Press biscuits into 3-inch circles. Spoon 1 tablespoon of the peanut butter filling on each circle. Moisten edges of dough with water. Fold over to enclose filling and press edges together with the tines of a fork. Prick tops. Bake at 400° for 10 to 12 minutes or until lightly browned. Serve warm. Yield: 20 canapés.

Crab Canapés

1 pound crabmeat
3 tablespoons mayonnaise or salad dressing
1 tablespoon prepared mustard
¼ teaspoon salt
Dash pepper
1 tablespoon freshly squeezed lemon juice
12 slices white bread
¼ cup grated Parmesan cheese
2 tablespoons dry bread crumbs

Remove any shell or cartilage from crabmeat. Combine mayonnaise, seasonings, lemon juice, and crabmeat. Remove crusts and toast bread. Spread crab mixture on each slice of toast. Combine cheese and bread crumbs; sprinkle over top of each slice of toast. Cut each slice into 6 pieces. Broil about 3 inches from source of heat for 2 to 3 minutes or until brown. Yield: 6 dozen.

Broiled Clam Canapés

1 (3-ounce) package chive cream cheese, softened
½ teaspoon salt
1 tablespoon freshly squeezed lemon juice
3 drops hot pepper sauce
1 (7-ounce) can minced clams, drained
1 egg white, stiffly beaten
Crackers or toast
Paprika

Combine cheese, seasonings, and clams; fold into stiffly beaten egg white. Spread on crackers or toast. Sprinkle with paprika. Broil about 3 inches from source of heat for 2 to 3 minutes or until brown. Serve at once. Yield: 3 dozen.

Cheesy Crab Canapés

36 bread slices
1 cup flaked crabmeat
¼ cup mayonnaise
1 teaspoon tarragon vinegar
½ teaspoon dry mustard
¼ teaspoon salt
Dash pepper
1 tablespoon minced parsley
1 tablespoon minced chives
Grated Parmesan cheese
Paprika

Cut bread in desired shapes; toast one side. Combine crabmeat, mayonnaise, vinegar, seasonings, parsley, and chives. Spread crab mixture on untoasted sides of bread. Sprinkle with cheese and paprika. Place on a cookie sheet and, just before serving, broil 3 inches from source of heat until brown. Yield: 3 dozen.

Ham and Cheese Canapés

1 cup shredded Cheddar cheese
½ cup finely chopped cooked ham
¼ cup sweet pickle relish
¼ cup commercial sour cream
1 (1-pound) loaf unsliced sandwich bread
Butter or margarine, softened

Combine cheese, ham, relish, and sour cream. Cut crusts from bread. Slice bread lengthwise into four 3- x 7-inch strips. Place on heavy-duty aluminum foil-lined cookie sheets. Butter each strip, then spread about ⅓ cup cheese mixture on each. Broil 3 inches from source of heat until cheese melts. Cut into 1½- x 1-inch pieces for serving. Yield: 56 canapés.

Hot Crab Canapés

¾ to 1 cup crabmeat, flaked
¼ cup mayonnaise
¼ teaspoon salt
Dash pepper
4 to 6 drops hot pepper sauce
1 teaspoon freshly squeezed lemon juice
1 egg white, stiffly beaten
Bread squares or salted crackers

Combine crabmeat, mayonnaise, seasonings, and lemon juice. Fold beaten egg white into mixture. Cut crusts from bread and cut each slice into four squares. Spread mixture all over bread. Broil 4 to 5 inches from heat for 2 or 3 minutes. Leftover crab makes a good open-face sandwich the next day. Yield: about 1¼ cups spread.

Cheese-Ham Canapés

1 cup shredded Cheddar cheese
½ cup finely chopped cooked ham
¼ cup pickle relish
¼ cup commercial sour cream
1 (1-pound) loaf unsliced sandwich bread
Butter or margarine, softened
Sliced cooked ham

Combine cheese, ham, relish, and sour cream. Cut crusts from bread. Slice lengthwise into 3 or 4 strips. Butter each strip, then spread with cheese mixture. When ready to serve, place on a cookie sheet, and broil 3 inches from source of heat until cheese melts. Top with triangles or diamonds of cooked ham. Cut into 1-inch strips for serving. Yield: about 3 to 4 dozen.

Broiled Olive Canapés

Sliced white bread
2 tablespoons softened butter or margarine
1 cup shredded sharp pasteurized process
   American cheese
½ cup chopped stuffed olives
2 egg whites, stiffly beaten
3 slices bacon, finely diced
Olive slices

Cut 20 bread rounds with a 2-inch cookie cutter. Place under broiler and toast on one side. Butter untoasted side. Fold cheese and olives into egg whites; spoon on buttered side of bread rounds. Sprinkle with bacon. Top each with an olive slice. Broil 4 to 5 inches from source of heat for 5 to 8 minutes or until bacon browns and cheese melts. Yield: 20 canapés.

Olive and Crabmeat Canapés

⅓ cup pitted ripe olives, well drained,
   coarsely chopped
1 (7 ¾-ounce) can crabmeat, drained and
   flaked
1 tablespoon minced green pepper
¼ teaspoon grated lemon rind
Mayonnaise
Firm white bread
Softened butter or margarine
Minced parsley

Combine olives, crabmeat, green pepper, and lemon rind. Mix with just enough mayonnaise so mixture holds together. Cut bread into rounds with a large cookie cutter; butter and bake at 300° until lightly browned. Spread with the crab mixture and sprinkle with parsley. Yield: about 1½ dozen.

Hot Onion-Cheese Canapés

8 slices bread or 32 salted crackers
½ cup mayonnaise
½ cup grated Parmesan cheese
2 tablespoons finely chopped onion

Remove crusts from bread; cut each slice into quarters. Combine mayonnaise, cheese,

and onion. Spread on bread. Broil about 4 inches from source of heat until brown. Yield: 32 canapés.

Note: Mixture keeps several days in refrigerator.

Toasted Onion Canapés

20 (2-inch) bread rounds
¾ cup minced onion
½ cup mayonnaise or salad dressing
¼ cup grated Parmesan cheese

Place bread rounds on a cookie sheet and toast one side under broiler just until golden brown. Combine onion, mayonnaise, and cheese; spread on untoasted side of bread rounds. Broil 3 inches from source of heat for 2 to 3 minutes or until golden brown. Yield: 20 canapés.

Oyster Canapés

1 cup cracker crumbs
½ cup butter or margarine, melted
⅓ cup commercial sour cream
1 egg, slightly beaten
2 tablespoons grated onion
1 tablespoon horseradish
½ teaspoon paprika
12 to 16 toast triangles
12 to 16 oysters

Combine cracker crumbs, butter, sour cream, egg, onion, horseradish, and paprika. Spread on toast triangles. Top each with an oyster. Bake at 400° for 15 minutes. Serve hot. Yield: 12 to 16 canapés.

Scallop Canapés

2 cloves garlic, finely chopped
2 tablespoons butter or margarine, melted
½ cup shredded cheese
¼ teaspoon Worcestershire sauce
Dash salt
Dash pepper
½ pound cooked scallops, chopped
2 cups piecrust mix

Sauté garlic in butter for 2 to 3 minutes; add cheese, seasonings, and scallops. Blend well. Prepare piecrust mix according to package directions; roll very thin and cut into 90 circles, 2 inches in diameter. Place about 1 teaspoonful scallop filling in the center of 45 circles. Cover with remaining 45 circles; press edges together with a fork and put slits in tops. Place on lightly greased cookie sheets. Bake at 450° for 10 to 15 minutes or until brown. Yield: about 45 canapés.

Toasted Onion Sticks

1 (1⅜-ounce) package dry onion soup mix
½ pound butter or margarine, softened
1 loaf sliced white bread

Blend onion soup mix into butter. Let stand at room temperature until you are ready to toast the sticks.

Trim crusts from bread. Spread with onion butter; cut each slice into three strips. Place on an ungreased cookie sheet and bake at 350° for about 10 minutes or until golden. Yield: about 4½ dozen.

Crabmeat-Bacon Rounds

½ cup shredded sharp Cheddar cheese
1 (6½-ounce) can crabmeat, drained and flaked
2 egg whites, stiffly beaten
20 (2-inch) toast rounds, buttered
3 slices uncooked bacon, diced
Sliced stuffed green olives

Fold shredded cheese and crabmeat into stiffly beaten egg whites. Pile mixture on 20 buttered toast rounds (made by cutting 2-inch

circles from loaf bread, browned on both sides and lightly buttered on top). Sprinkle diced bacon on top of each; broil until cheese starts to melt and bacon is crisp. Top each with a slice of stuffed olive. Yield: 20 appetizers.

Note: To freeze ahead of time, prepare for broiler, place on a flat pan wrapped in moisture-vaporproof paper, and freeze. Remove from freezer and broil.

Hot Cheese Squares

1 loaf white bread, unsliced
½ cup butter or margarine
1 (3-ounce) package cream cheese, softened
¼ cup shredded sharp cheese
2 egg whites

Trim crusts from bread; cut into 1-inch slices, then cut each slice into quarters. Melt butter; blend in cheeses. Beat egg whites until stiff; fold into cooled cheese mixture. Spread cheese mixture on all sides of bread cubes; refrigerate at least overnight. If preferred, squares may be frozen at this point. Bake at 400° for about 15 minutes or until nicely browned; serve hot. Yield: about 5 dozen.

Toasted Garlic-Cheese Rounds

½ cup butter or margarine
2 cloves garlic, slashed
1 day-old loaf sliced white bread
    About 1 cup grated Parmesan and shredded Swiss cheese, mixed (or mixed Parmesan and Gruyère)

Combine butter and garlic in a small saucepan and heat until butter bubbles. Remove from heat, let stand for about 3 hours, then discard the garlic.

Cut crusts from bread and with a cookie cutter cut into circles about 1½ to 2 inches in diameter. Arrange on cookie sheets, brush with garlic butter, and sprinkle generously with cheese. Bake at 275° to 300° until crisp. Yield: about 3 dozen.

Shrimp Toppers with Lemon-Chili Sauce

1 cup chili sauce
1 teaspoon freshly squeezed lemon juice
  Dash hot pepper sauce
24 toast rounds
24 cooked shrimp
  Parsley sprigs

Combine chili sauce, lemon juice, and hot pepper sauce; spread on toast rounds. Top each with a cooked shrimp and a sprig of parsley. Yield: 2 dozen.

Piroshki (Russian)

Pastry

½ cup drained, small curd cottage cheese
½ cup butter or margarine
1½ cups all-purpose flour
½ teaspoon sugar
  Filling

Have cottage cheese and butter at room temperature. Blend this mixture with flour and sugar until smooth. Form into a flattish ball, wrap in waxed paper, and store in vegetable crisper (so it won't get too cold) in refrigerator overnight. (With this as a basic dough, you can make a variety of canapés and desserts.)

When ready to use, remove from refrigerator and let stand until dough is workable. For the meat filling, roll basic dough ⅛ inch thick on a floured pastry cloth. Cut into 2½-inch squares or in circles with biscuit cutter. Place teaspoon of Filling on one-half of square or circle and fold other half over until edges meet. (Make a triangle of the square.) Moisten edges; seal by pressing tines of fork firmly into edge. Now stand circle or triangle on long side on a cookie sheet with seal up; turn one corner toward you, and the other away from you, so that pastry will rest on cookie sheet with sealed edges up. Bake at 425° until pastry is golden brown, about 15 to 20 minutes. Piroshki can be served cold with hot soup or as a hot canapé. Yield: 1 dozen.

Filling

½ pound finely ground beef
½ cup minced onions
  Butter or margarine
2 hard-cooked eggs, finely chopped
1 teaspoon capers
1 teaspoon chopped chives
1 teaspoon chopped parsley
  Salt and pepper to taste
1 teaspoon commercial sour cream

Sauté meat and onions in a small amount of butter until meat turns gray. Add chopped eggs, capers, chives, parsley, salt, pepper, and sour cream. Use to fill pastry. Yield: filling for 12 piroshkis.

Shrimp-Cheese Puffs

½ cup butter or margarine, softened
2 cups shredded Cheddar cheese
1 egg yolk
1 egg white, stiffly beaten
30 bread squares
30 shrimp, cooked and cleaned

Cream butter and cheese; blend in egg yolk. Fold in stiffly beaten egg white. Arrange bread squares on ungreased cookie sheets. Top each with a shrimp and cover with a rounded teaspoonful of cheese mixture. Bake at 350° for 15 to 18 minutes or until golden brown. This may be refrigerated up to 24 hours before baking. Yield: 2½ dozen.

Avocado Fingers

1 ripe avocado
¼ teaspoon salt
⅛ teaspoon paprika
1 teaspoon freshly squeezed lemon juice
  Toast strips
  Bacon slices

Mash avocado; add salt, paprika, and lemon juice. Spread on 3- x 1-inch toast strips. Place narrow slices of bacon over avocado. Broil until bacon crisps. Yield: about 24 servings.

Chicken Tempters

8 slices soft white bread
    Softened butter or margarine
1 (4¾-ounce) can chicken spread
¼ cup minced celery
½ to ¾ teaspoon basil
    Pimiento strips

Remove crusts from bread and flatten bread with rolling pin. Lightly butter both sides of bread. Bring two diagonally opposite corners of each piece of bread together and secure with a wooden pick. Bake on an ungreased cookie sheet at 400° for 7 to 8 minutes. Remove picks and cool on a wire rack about 30 minutes. Combine chicken spread, celery, and basil; fill bread. Garnish with pimiento strips. Yield: 8 sandwiches.

Avocado-Cheese Foldovers

1 cup mashed avocado pulp
4 tablespoons Roquefort cheese
1 tablespoon freshly squeezed lemon juice
    Thinly sliced white bread
    Softened butter or margarine

Combine avocado, cheese, and lemon juice. Remove crusts from bread; roll lightly with a rolling pin. Spread butter on bread. Cut each slice into quarters. Place about 1 teaspoonful of the avocado mixture on each square. Fold two opposite corners over and secure with a wooden pick. Cover and chill for 15 minutes. Remove wooden pick before serving. Yield: about 4 dozen.

Savory Stars

1 (5-ounce) jar dried beef, chopped
1 cup commercial sour cream
¾ cup Swiss cheese, shredded
25 slices bread, cut in star shapes
    Commercial sour cream

Combine beef, sour cream, and cheese; mix well. Cover and refrigerate. Spread bread with beef spread. Serve topped with sour cream. Yield: 25 sandwiches.

Broiled Cheese Appetizers

2 (3-ounce) packages cream cheese, softened
1 cup shredded Provolone cheese
1 tablespoon chopped onion
½ teaspoon oregano
⅛ teaspoon garlic salt
1 tablespoon chopped pimiento
1 tablespoon chopped green pepper
    Toast rounds

Beat cream cheese until smooth; add Provolone cheese, onion, oregano, and garlic salt. Stir in pimiento and green pepper. Spread on toast; broil for 1 to 2 minutes or until lightly browned. Serve immediately. Yield: 1½ cups spread.

Cheese Dreams

½ cup milk
1 egg, beaten
¼ teaspoon dry mustard
½ teaspoon salt
¾ pound sharp Cheddar cheese, shredded
    Rounds of white bread
    Melted butter or margarine
    Paprika

Heat milk in top of a double boiler over hot water. When milk is scalded, add egg, mustard, salt, and cheese; cook for 15 minutes, stirring constantly. Remove from heat; cool, cover, and store in refrigerator.

When ready to use, spread cheese mixture on rounds of white bread, cover with another round in which you have cut a small hole in middle with inside of doughnut cutter. Brush with melted butter, sprinkle with paprika, and bake at 450° until nicely browned. Serve immediately. Yield: 15 servings.

Deviled Ham Nips

8 slices white bread
   Butter or margarine
1 (4½-ounce) can deviled ham
⅓ cup commercial sour cream
⅓ cup shredded Cheddar cheese

Remove crusts from bread, butter lightly, and cut each slice into four squares. Press squares buttered side down into very small muffin pans or place squares on a cookie sheet. To each add a dab of deviled ham, sour cream, and a topping of cheese. Bake at 400° for 5 minutes or until hot and bubbly. Yield: 32 canapés.

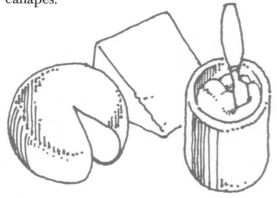

Toasted Cheese Rounds

⅓ cup grated Parmesan cheese
¾ cup mayonnaise
½ cup chopped onion
   Dash Worcestershire sauce
   Dash salt
   Dash pepper
   Rye bread rounds

Combine all ingredients except bread; mix well. Spread mixture on bread; broil until golden brown. Yield: 20 rounds.

Showtime Roll-Ups

2 cups Cheddar cheese, shredded
1 (3-ounce) package cream cheese, softened
2 tablespoons dry roasted peanuts, chopped
½ teaspoon Worcestershire sauce
   Dash salt
25 slices white sandwich bread

Combine cheese, peanuts, Worcestershire sauce, and salt; mix well. Remove crusts from bread slices; between sheets of waxed paper, flatten with rolling pin. Spread each slice with a tablespoon of cheese mixture; roll up. Place seam side down on tray; cover with sheet of waxed paper and dampened paper towel until ready to serve. Yield: 25 sandwiches.

Anchovy Roll-Ups

1 (3-ounce) package cream cheese, softened
1 tablespoon milk
1½ to 2 teaspoons anchovy paste
1 teaspoon Worcestershire sauce
   Bread
3 tablespoons melted butter or margarine

Blend cream cheese and milk until creamy (add more milk if necessary). Blend in anchovy paste and Worcestershire sauce. Trim crusts from bread. Spread on mixture and roll up. Wrap in waxed paper and store in refrigerator until ready to serve. The rolls may also be frozen. To serve, sauté rolls in melted butter. Rolls may be cut in half, if desired. Stick wooden picks in them and serve hot. Yield: 10 servings.

Onion with Peanut Butter

1 cup peanut butter
1 large onion, finely grated
⅛ teaspoon salt
   Butter or margarine
   Small rolls

Combine peanut butter, onion, and salt. Split and butter small rolls; spread with peanut butter mixture and toast under broiler until delicately browned. Yield: 1½ to 2 dozen.

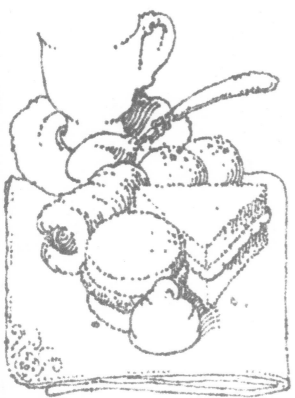

Dainty Party Food

PARTY SANDWICHES

Dainty party sandwiches are the perfect food to serve for informal daytime parties, teas, or receptions. A base of bread or other baked foods, a complementing filling, a pretty garnish, and an unusual cut: this is all that is needed to make intriguing party sandwiches.

Choosing Interesting Breads

Any bread may be used for a sandwich base, but bread and filling should be compatible. Party sandwiches are prettier on thinly sliced bread, and day-old bread holds its shape nicely while being sliced. Crusts are usually removed for dainty sandwiches. For variety, try rye, whole wheat, or cracked wheat bread, or you may bake your own raisin, date-nut, or Boston brown bread. Using two kinds of bread in one sandwich gives added color.

Selecting Complementing Fillings

Filling should be generous, but too much makes the sandwich difficult to handle. Several thin slices of meat rather than one thick slice make a more manageable sandwich. Fillings of pastel colors make eye-appealing sandwiches. Season fillings to accent and complement the flavor of the bread.

Preparing Sandwiches

Prepare all the fillings first and let them stand while you prepare the bread. Bread should be spread with softened butter or margarine so filling does not soak into bread and make it soggy. Spread filling to edge of bread.

Storing Sandwiches

Store sandwiches properly to insure freshness. Line a shallow pan with a damp towel; cover towel with waxed paper. Stack sandwiches in pan, putting waxed paper between each layer. Cover with waxed paper and a damp towel. Most party sandwiches can be made a day in advance and stored in the refrigerator.

Some sandwiches may be made ahead and frozen. Layer them in a suitable container and wrap with moistureproof and vaporproof wrapping and seal. Rolled and ribbon sandwiches may be wrapped uncut and sliced after thawing. Thaw sandwiches in original wrapping for 1 to 2 hours. Since mayonnaise, salad dressing, and jelly do not freeze well, sandwich fillings may be bound with seasoned butter or seasoned sour cream and then the sandwiches frozen. Avoid freezing sandwiches with fillings containing raw vegetables, dates, pickles, cooked egg whites, olives, or pimientos. Sandwich fillings that do freeze well include peanut butter, cooked egg yolks, and blue cheese.

Shaping Sandwiches

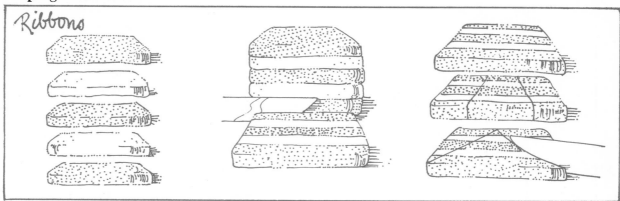

1. Stack alternately, 3 slices whole wheat and 2 slices white bread, filling with 1 or more spreads. Firmly press together each stack of slices.

2. Slice off crusts. Wrap in heavy-duty aluminum foil or plastic. Chill at least 2 hours. Cut into ½-inch-thick slices to reveal ribbons.

3. Cut each ribbon slice into thirds, halves, or into 2 or 3 triangles. If not served immediately, cover with waxed paper and a damp towel.

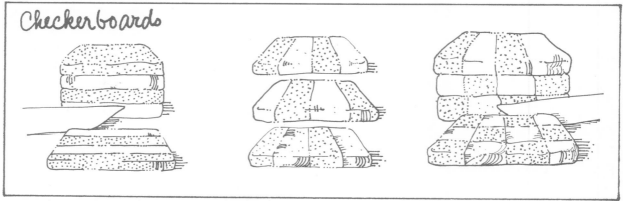

1. Stack alternately, 2 slices whole wheat and 2 slices white bread, filling with 1 or more spreads. Press each stack; trim crusts. Cut into ½-inch slices.

2. Stack 3 slices together alternating the whole wheat and white slices. Wrap and chill for several hours.

3. Using a sharp knife, cut into ½-inch slices. For miniature checkerboards, cut each slice in half.

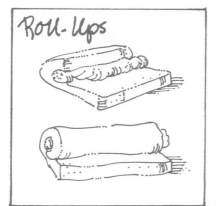

Trim crusts. Spread bread with filling. Lay an asparagus tip or stuffed celery across one end of each slice. Roll up. Roll-ups may be brushed with melted butter and toasted under broiler.

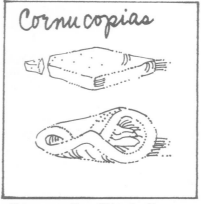

Trim crusts. Cut off ½ inch of bottom corner. Spread bread with filling. Overlap and press opposite corners; garnish.

Trim crusts from bread slices. Spread bread with filling. Fold 2 corners together and press firmly.

Almond Fingers

1 cup butter, softened (no substitute)
½ cup powdered sugar
1½ cups all-purpose flour
    Pinch salt
1 teaspoon almond extract
2 cups chopped toasted almonds
    Powdered sugar

Cream butter and sugar thoroughly in large bowl of electric mixer. Add flour mixed with salt; blend well; beat in almond extract. Stir in almonds; chill about an hour for easier handling.

To bake, pinch off about a tablespoon of mixture and roll between palms of hands into a 2-inch-long cylinder about ½ inch thick. Place on lightly greased cookie sheets and bake at 325° for 20 minutes or until very lightly browned. Remove cookies to a flat pan onto which you have sifted powdered sugar, then sift more sugar over top of cookies. Store in an airtight container with waxed paper between layers. Freezes well. Yield: about 6 dozen.

Chocolate Cherries

1 (7¼-ounce) package vanilla wafers, finely crushed
½ cup powdered sugar
½ cup chopped walnuts
¼ cup boiling water
2 tablespoons butter or margarine
1 tablespoon light corn syrup
2 teaspoons instant powdered coffee
30 maraschino cherries with stems
2 (6-ounce) packages semisweet chocolate morsels
    Flaked coconut (optional)
    Multicolored sprinkles (optional)
    Chocolate sprinkles (optional)
    Chopped nuts (optional)

Combine vanilla wafer crumbs, powdered sugar, and walnuts. Combine water, butter, corn syrup, and instant coffee; add to first mixture. Shape approximately ½ tablespoon of this mixture around each cherry. Cover and refrigerate for at least 1 hour.

Melt chocolate over warm water. Holding stem, dip coated cherries into chocolate, coating carefully and completely. Place on wire rack over waxed paper. After about 5 minutes, garnish with coconut, sprinkles, or nuts, if desired. Refrigerate until chocolate has hardened. Yield: 2½ dozen.

Walnut Balls

1 cup butter or margarine
¼ cup sugar
2 cups all-purpose flour
1 teaspoon vanilla extract
2 cups coarsely chopped walnuts
    Powdered sugar

Cream butter in large bowl of electric mixer; add sugar and beat until light and fluffy. Mix in flour, add vanilla, and beat until smooth. Stir in walnuts. Form into balls about the size of a quarter; place on greased cookie sheets. Bake at 300° for 25 to 30 minutes, watching carefully to avoid overbaking. The cookies should not be allowed to brown. When done, roll in powdered sugar and store in an airtight container. Freezes beautifully. Yield: about 5 dozen.

Ham Cornucopias

1 cup ground cooked ham
1 tablespoon finely chopped parsley
2 tablespoons mayonnaise
8 thin slices whole wheat bread
    Softened butter or margarine

Combine ham, parsley, and mayonnaise. Remove crusts from bread; roll lightly with a rolling pin. Spread with butter. Cut each slice in quarters. Place ¼ teaspoon of the ham mixture diagonally on each square of bread. Fold two opposite corners over and fasten with a wooden pick. Place on a cookie sheet, cover with waxed paper and a damp cloth, and chill for 30 minutes. Remove wooden picks before serving. Yield: 32 sandwiches.

Cornucopias

Remove crusts from bread slices; cut bread into triangles. Spread triangles with mixture of mayonnaise and mustard-with-horseradish. With longest edge of triangle on bottom, place ham strip in center with tip extending over point of triangle. Roll from left to right and tuck point under.

Strawberry Cornucopias

3 cups (1½ pints) strawberries
1 (8-ounce) package cream cheese, softened
2 tablespoons powdered sugar
¼ cup finely chopped walnuts
32 slices soft white bread (about two 1-pound loaves)

Wash strawberries and hull; mash enough to measure 2 tablespoonsful in a medium bowl; set remainder aside. Beat cream cheese and powdered sugar into mashed strawberries until smooth; stir in walnuts. Cut a round from center of each slice of bread with a 3-inch cookie cutter; roll each round thin with a rolling pin. Spread a rounded teaspoonful of cream cheese mixture over each; roll into a cornucopia shape. Halve remaining strawberries; tuck one half into end of each sandwich. Yield: 32 sandwiches.

Note: Sandwiches may be made up about an hour before serving. Place in a single layer on a cookie sheet or tray; cover tightly to prevent drying; chill. Add strawberry garnish just before serving so color doesn't run.

Orange Cream Crescents

1 cup apple jelly
1 (11-ounce) can mandarin orange sections, drained
1 (8-ounce) package cream cheese, softened
1 tablespoon grated orange rind
1 tablespoon milk
2 (8-ounce) cans orange-nut bread

Heat jelly just until melted in a small saucepan; remove from heat. Place orange sections, a few at a time, in jelly, turning to coat well. Lift out with a fork and place on a wire rack set over waxed paper; let stand until jelly sets. Blend cream cheese, orange rind, and milk in a small bowl. Slice bread into 16 rounds; halve each. Spread with cheese mixture; top each with 1 large or 2 small mandarin orange sections. Yield: 32 sandwiches.

Marzipan Cupcakes

⅓ cup butter (no substitute)
¼ cup powdered sugar
1 egg yolk
¼ teaspoon almond extract
1 cup all-purpose flour

Cream butter and sugar well in bowl of electric mixer; add egg yolk and almond extract; mix well. Blend in flour, then chill for about an hour for easier handling. Pinch off marble-size pieces and press into bottom and sides of tiny ungreased muffin tins. Bake at 375° for 7 to 8 minutes. Yield: 3 dozen.

Filling

⅓ cup butter (no substitute)
½ (8-ounce) can almond paste
½ cup sugar
2 eggs
½ teaspoon almond extract

Cream butter with almond paste until well blended; beat in ½ cup sugar thoroughly. Blend in eggs and ½ teaspoon almond extract. Spoon into each baked shell, then bake at 350° for 20 minutes. While tarts bake, prepare Frosting. Drizzle over outer edges of warm cakes. Bake cupcakes ahead of time and freeze. Yield: filling for 3 dozen cupcakes.

Frosting

¾ cup powdered sugar
Freshly squeezed orange or lemon juice to taste
¼ teaspoon almond extract

Combine all ingredients; blend well. Yield: frosting for 3 dozen cupcakes.

Diagonal Logs

Remove crusts from bread slices. Roll flat with rolling pin. Spread with mixture of mashed avocado, lemon juice, and mayonnaise. Roll bread as for a jelly roll. Cut each log diagonally into two or three parts.

Party Macaroon Muffins

  1 cup softened butter (no substitute)
½ cup sugar
  1 egg
½ teaspoon vanilla extract
½ teaspoon almond extract
  2 cups all-purpose flour
    Almond Macaroon Filling

Cream butter and sugar thoroughly in large bowl of electric mixer. Beat in egg, flavorings, and flour. Drop with teaspoon into tiny greased muffin cups, pressing dough over bottom and up around sides. Chill. Fill little cups with Almond Macaroon Filing. Bake at 325° for 25 to 30 minutes. Freezes well. Yield: 3 dozen.

Almond Macaroon Filling

  2 eggs
½ cup sugar
1¼ cups finely chopped blanched almonds
  1 teaspoon almond extract

Beat eggs until light and fluffy. Gradually beat in sugar until well blended. Fold in almonds and almond extract. Yield: filling for 3 dozen muffins.

Quick Petits Fours

Make cake using pound cake mix or bake a pound cake in two 8-inch square pans. Cut slices about ¾ inch thick. Then if desired, cut slices in fancy shapes with small cutters. Put together sandwich-fashion with jam or jelly between.

To frost and decorate, put Petits Fours on rack with tray underneath to catch drippings. Spoon Petits Fours Frosting over cakes until coated, scraping frosting up from tray to reuse. When firm, decorate, using a pastry tube, with Decorating Frosting. If you have no pastry tube, you can improvise one with a sheet of stiff white paper. Freezes beautifully. Two 8-inch square cakes will yield about 50 small squares.

Petits Fours Frosting

  1 cup sugar
    Dash cream of tartar
⅛ teaspoon salt
½ cup water
    Sifted powdered sugar
    Flavoring (½ teaspoon vanilla, almond, rum, brandy—any flavor you like)
    Food coloring (optional)

Bring sugar, cream of tartar, salt, and water to a boil; cook to 236° on a candy thermometer (soft-ball stage). Cool to lukewarm (100°). Gradually beat in enough powdered sugar until thick enough to almost hold its shape. Add flavoring. Divide into four parts. If desired, leave one part white and tint others pink, yellow, green, etc.

Decorating Frosting

Mix until smooth two parts powdered sugar to one part butter or margarine. Flavor and color as desired. Or buy tubes of colored frostings which are available with decorating tips to fit the tubes.

Cherry-Cheese Sandwich Spread

  1 (4-ounce) jar maraschino cherries (red or green)
  1 (3-ounce) package cream cheese, softened

Drain cherries and dice very fine. Add to softened cream cheese and mix well. This filling may be used for open-faced sandwiches or made into 3-layered ribbon sandwiches. Yield: about 1½ cups.

Assorted Petits Fours

Fondant

2 cups boiling water
6 cups sugar
¼ teaspoon cream of tartar

Put ingredients in a deep heavy saucepan; stir until sugar has dissolved, then cook quickly without stirring until syrup reaches 236° on a candy thermometer (or to soft-ball stage when a little is dropped into cold water). Occasionally wash off crystals that form on sides of pan, using a brush dipped in cold water.

Pour onto a buttered marble slab, large pan, or platter. Cool until lukewarm; then, using a spatula, pull sides into middle repeatedly until mixture turns white and thick. Let stand 5 minutes; then knead with buttered hands until creamy enough to form a firm ball. At first it will be crumbly, but butter hands heavily and often. Store Fondant in a tightly covered container for at least 2 days before using. Yield: 1 quart. This is too much for the recipe that follows, but it keeps well, refrigerated or frozen, and it's advisable to have enough on hand for more than one batch of cakes.

To prepare Fondant for frosting cakes, warm 1 or 2 cups slowly over hot water (do not allow water to boil or Fondant will lose its shine and become dull and unattractive). If you wish, tint desired shade with a few drops of food coloring. Stir in flavoring to taste, such as vanilla, rum, almond, or other extracts. Thin Fondant to heavy cream consistency by adding a few drops of hot water at a time.

Chocolate Fondant

Melt 2 (1-ounce) squares unsweetened chocolate; cool. Add it to 1 cup Fondant and stir mixture over low flame until it is warm to the touch. Add ½ teaspoon vanilla and thin to the right consistency with a little warm water.

Pound Cake

Pound cake is most satisfactory for Petits Fours as it cuts cleanly and does not crumble.

1 cup butter (no substitute)
1 cup sugar
6 eggs
1 teaspoon vanilla extract
2¼ cups all-purpose flour
⅛ teaspoon salt

Cream butter thoroughly in large bowl of electric mixer. Beat in sugar until mixture is light and fluffy. Add eggs one at a time, blending well after each addition. Add vanilla, then mixed dry ingredients. Butter two 8-inch square pans; line bottoms with waxed paper, butter the paper, then dust with flour. Pour equal amount of batter in each pan and spread evenly. Bake at 300° for about 40 minutes or until cakes test done. Cool in pans about 5 minutes, invert onto wire racks, and peel off paper. Let cool and if desired, wrap in heavy-duty aluminum foil and freeze until ready to use.

To complete the Petits Fours: Trim edges from cakes and cut into 1¼-inch squares or rectangles about 2 x 1¼ inches. The little cakes may now be frosted; however, the most elegant Petits Fours are filled with a butter cream before frosting. Here's the way: Cut a ⅓-inch slice from top of each cake and lay it aside. Hollow out the center of cake, fill with Butter Cream Filling, and replace top. Place cakes on a wire rack on a pan and work quickly to coat top and sides with Fondant. Decorate tops with nuts, chocolate shots, silver dragées, or candied fruit. Put in paper bonbon cups and arrange beautifully on silver tray.

Basic Butter Cream Filling

¾ cup sugar
¼ cup water
⅛ teaspoon cream of tartar
5 egg yolks
1 cup butter, softened
   Favorite extract or liqueur (optional)

Combine sugar, water, and cream of tartar in saucepan; stir until dissolved. Cook rapidly to 250° on candy thermometer or until syrup spins a thread. Meanwhile, beat egg yolks until very light. Pour syrup in a slow steady stream into yolks, beating constantly until mixture is thick and cool. Whip butter and blend thoroughly into yolk mixture; flavor with any extract or liqueur desired. Keep at room temperature to use immediately or store covered in refrigerator, or freeze, for later use. Yield: about 2 cups, enough for about 50 square Petits Fours or 30 rectangular ones cut from the two square 8-inch pound cakes.

Filling Variations: For Orange Butter Cream, blend ½ cup Basic Butter Cream with 2 teaspoons thawed frozen orange juice concentrate and ¼ teaspoon grated orange rind.

For Mocha Butter Cream, dissolve 2 teaspoons cocoa and ½ teaspoon powdered instant coffee in 1½ teaspoons hot water. Blend with ½ cup Basic Butter Cream Filling.

Finger Sandwiches

Buy large loaves of unsliced bread from your bakery and cut thin slices, crosswise, with an electric carving knife. Remove crusts; spread with butter and then with filling. Sandwiches may be cut in narrow strips or rolled and cut into finger lengths. Keep covered with a damp tea towel until time to serve.

Ginger-Cream Cheese Filling: Thoroughly mix 1 (8-ounce) package softened cream cheese, 2 tablespoons light rum, and ¼ cup finely minced candied ginger. Yield: enough filling for 25 finger sandwiches.

Chicken-Almond Filling: Grind together 2 cups chopped chicken and ½ cup blanched almonds. Stir in 2 tablespoons drained crushed pineapple and enough mayonnaise to make a spreadable mixture. Yield: filling for 25 to 30 finger sandwiches.

Roquefort-Avocado Filling: Mix together ¼ cup crumbled Roquefort, 1 cup avocado puree, and lemon juice to make a spreadable mixture. Yield: filling for 25 finger sandwiches.

Cheddar-Port Filling: Blend 1 (4-ounce) jar Cheddar cheese spread with 1 to 2 tablespoons port. Yield: filling for 15 finger sandwiches.

Seafood-Cucumber Filling

1 cup crabmeat or chopped cooked shrimp
⅓ cup grated peeled cucumber, drained (press moisture out between paper towels)
2 teaspoons minced chives
1 to 2 teaspoons freshly squeezed lemon juice
¼ teaspoon salt
⅛ teaspoon dillweed
4 tablespoons mayonnaise or commercial sour cream

Combine all ingredients and chill thoroughly. Yield: about 1½ cups.

Note: If you make up sandwiches ahead of time, be sure to spread bread lightly with soft butter before filling sandwiches; the butter will prevent the filling from seeping in and causing sogginess.

Sesame-Cheese Rolled Sandwiches

16 slices white bread, crusts removed
1 (6-ounce) jar pasteurized process cheese spread
3 tablespoons sesame seed, toasted
Melted butter or margarine

Use a rolling pin to flatten slices of bread. Spread each with cheese; sprinkle with sesame seed. Roll each slice, jelly roll fashion; brush with melted butter; cover with waxed paper or plastic wrap; chill for several hours.

Cut rolls in half crosswise and place on a cookie sheet, seam side down; bake at 425° for 10 minutes or until lightly browned. Yield: 32 sandwiches.

Mushroom Sandwich Loaf

Trim crusts from a 1-pound loaf of day-old unsliced bread. Cut into 4 lengthwise slices. Spread softened butter and Chicken Salad Filling on one slice, butter and Deviled Salad Filling on second slice, and butter and Creamy Nut Filling on third slice. Arrange slices one on top of the other and cover with fourth slice. Frost loaf with creamy cheese mixture and garnish with nuts. Wrap loaf in a damp cloth and chill for several hours. Yield: about 12 sandwich slices.

Chicken Salad Filling

½ cup cooked, diced chicken
¼ cup chopped celery
1 tablespoon minced onion
2 to 3 tablespoons mayonnaise
½ teaspoon salt
½ teaspoon curry powder
⅛ teaspoon pepper
1 (4-ounce) can sliced mushrooms, drained and chopped

Combine all ingredients; mix well. Set aside and later spread on bread slice.

Deviled Salad Filling

1 (3-ounce) can deviled ham
2 to 3 tablespoons mayonnaise
2 tablespoons pickle relish
2 hard-cooked eggs, chopped

Combine all ingredients; mix well. Set aside and later spread on bread slice.

Creamy Nut Filling

1 (3-ounce) package cream cheese, softened
4 to 6 tablespoons half-and-half
1 cup chopped nuts
Pinch salt

Combine all ingredients; mix well. Set aside and later spread on bread slice.

Frosting

3 (3-ounce) packages cream cheese, softened
½ cup light cream
1 cup chopped nuts

Combine cream cheese and cream. Reserve nuts for garnish after sandwich loaf is frosted.

Spiced Apricot Bread Dainty Sandwiches

1½ cups dried apricots, diced
1 cup sugar
½ teaspoon ground cloves
¼ teaspoon ground nutmeg
½ teaspoon ground cinnamon
½ teaspoon salt
6 tablespoons melted butter or margarine
1 cup water
1 egg, beaten
2 cups all-purpose flour
1 teaspoon soda
1 cup chopped pecans or walnuts (or mixed)
  Sandwich Fillings

Combine apricots, sugar, spices, salt, butter, and water in a saucepan. Cook for 5 minutes and cool thoroughly. Add beaten egg, then flour mixed with soda. Stir in nuts, mix well, and turn into a greased 9- x 5- x 3-inch loafpan. Bake at 350° for 1 hour. Freezes beautifully. Yield: about 3 dozen small sandwiches.

For a party, chill bread, then slice thinly and make small, dainty sandwiches. For filling use one of the following:

Sandwich Fillings

1. Softened cream cheese flavored with honey and lemon juice.
2. One cup chopped dates mixed with ¼ cup orange juice and ¼ cup finely chopped hazelnuts or walnuts.
3. Four ounces cream cheese mixed with 1 tablespoon grated orange rind, ¼ cup chopped raisins, 2 tablespoons chopped pecans, and 2 tablespoons orange juice.

Rolled Sandwiches

1 (3-ounce) package cream cheese, softened
1 teaspoon freshly squeezed lemon juice
⅓ cup commercial sour cream
⅛ teaspoon salt
1 teaspoon chopped chives
1 cup chopped watercress
18 slices white bread
2 tablespoons softened butter or margarine
    Watercress sprigs

Blend cream cheese, lemon juice, sour cream, salt, and chives. Stir in chopped watercress. Trim crusts from bread and roll slices lightly with a rolling pin to make them more pliable. Spread bread with soft butter, then with watercress mixture. Roll like a jelly roll.

Arrange close together, seam side down, in a shallow pan. Cover with plastic wrap or heavy-duty aluminum foil and chill for at least 1 hour.

To serve, slice each roll-up crosswise into two lengths (each about 1½ inches long). Stand them upright and insert sprigs of watercress in top. Yield: 3 dozen.

Gelatin Strawberries

1 (15-ounce) can sweetened condensed milk
1 pound coconut, ground (be sure the package is marked "fine"; otherwise you'll have to grind it yourself)
2 (3-ounce) packages strawberry-flavored gelatin, divided
1 cup finely ground almonds
1 tablespoon sugar
1 teaspoon vanilla extract
½ teaspoon almond extract

Combine condensed milk, coconut, 1 package dry gelatin, almonds, sugar, and flavorings. Mix well; with hands shape to form strawberries. Roll berries in the remaining package of gelatin to coat thoroughly. Allow to dry before storing.

For the leaves, use any kind of green-tinted frosting piped through a pastry tube to form leaf or stem. A piece of green candied cherry may be used, if desired.

To make small oranges, follow same directions, using orange gelatin.

These confections do not need refrigeration. They keep well for some time stored in a box or covered tin. They are delicious served as candy or to garnish fruit salads, tea trays, etc. Yield: 25 servings.

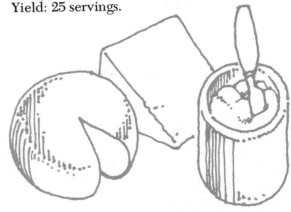

Rolled Mushroom Sandwiches

1 (3-ounce) can mushrooms
1 tablespoon freshly squeezed lemon juice
1 (3-ounce) package cream cheese, softened
1 tablespoon mayonnaise
¼ teaspoon ground nutmeg
    Salt and pepper to taste
24 slices thinly sliced fresh bread
    Small bunch of parsley

Chop mushrooms into bits and add lemon juice. Mix cream cheese, mayonnaise, nutmeg, and salt and pepper to taste. Add mushrooms and mix well.

Remove crusts from bread and spread with mushroom mixture. Roll slices and fasten with wooden pick. Place in a pan lined with a damp cloth and cover with a damp cloth. Chill well. Remove wooden picks before serving. Insert a small spray of parsley in each end of the sandwich. Yield: 2 dozen.

Tiny Party Puffs

1 cup water
½ cup butter or margarine
1 cup all-purpose flour
  Dash salt
4 eggs
  Shrimp or Salmon Salad
  Parsley or softened cream cheese

Bring water to a boil. Add butter, stirring until melted. Add flour and salt all at once. Stir well until mixture is smooth and forms a soft ball. Cool mixture slightly. Add eggs, one at a time, beating well after each addition. After last addition, continue beating until mixture is shiny. Drop batter by teaspoonful onto a lightly greased cookie sheet to make 36 small puffs. Bake at 375° for 50 minutes. Allow to cool in a warm place, away from drafts. When cool, fill with Shrimp or Salmon Salad. Decorate with parsley or cream cheese in a flower design. Yield: 3 dozen.

Shrimp Salad

1½ cups finely chopped cooked shrimp
½ cup finely chopped celery
1 teaspoon caraway seed
2 teaspoons freshly squeezed lemon juice
¾ cup mayonnaise or salad dressing

Combine all ingredients and mix well. Refrigerate for at least an hour. Yield: enough filling for 3 dozen puffs.

Salmon Salad

1½ cups flaked cooked salmon (1-pound can, drained)
½ cup chopped nuts
¼ cup finely chopped green pepper
½ cup mayonnaise or salad dressing
  Dash hot pepper sauce

Combine all ingredients and mix well. Refrigerate for at least 1 hour. Yield: enough filling for 3 dozen puffs.

Apricot-Cream Cheese Dreams

1 (3-ounce) package cream cheese, softened
  Butter or margarine, softened
8 slices sandwich bread
⅓ cup cooked dried apricots, sweetened to taste

Let cream cheese soften at room temperature. Spread softened butter on bread slices. Spread mashed cream cheese on 4 slices of bread; spread other 4 slices with mashed apricots. Put slices together and cut sandwiches in rectangles or circles. Yield: about 16 sandwiches.

Cream Wafers

1 cup butter or margarine, softened
⅓ cup whipping cream
2 cups all-purpose flour
  Sugar
  Cream Filling

Combine butter, cream, and flour thoroughly; chill. Divide dough into thirds. (Keep remainder in refrigerator until ready to roll.) Roll ⅓ of dough ⅛ inch thick on floured cloth-covered board. Cut with 1½-inch round cutter. Place rounds on waxed paper that is heavily covered with sugar. Turn each round with spatula so both sides are coated with sugar. Place on an ungreased cookie sheet; prick each about 4 times with a fork. Bake at 375° for 7 to 9 minutes. Cool; put 2 cookies together with Cream Filling. Yield: about 5 dozen double cookies.

Cream Filling

¼ cup butter or margarine, softened
¾ cup powdered sugar
1 egg yolk
1 teaspoon vanilla extract
  Food coloring (optional)

Combine butter, powdered sugar, egg yolk, and vanilla extract; mix until smooth. Tint with food coloring, if desired. Yield: about 1 cup.

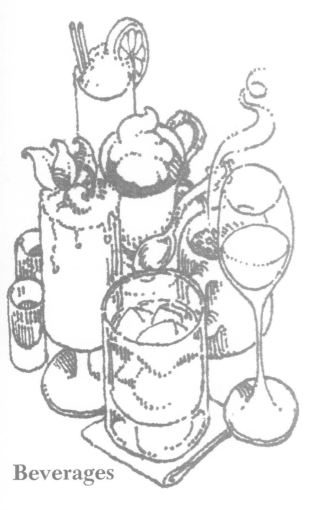

Beverages

Apple Blossom Punch

3 quarts apple juice
3 (12-ounce) cans frozen orange juice
  concentrate
3 quarts ginger ale
  Fresh orange slices
  Ice

Combine fruit juices and ginger ale. Pour over block of ice. Float orange slices on top of punch. Yield: 50 servings.

Cranberry Cooler

½ cup freshly squeezed lemon juice
1 cup orange juice
1 (16-ounce) bottle cranberry juice cocktail
1¼ cups sugar
4 cups ice water or chilled sparkling water
  Ice
  Lemon slices

Combine lemon juice, orange juice, cranberry juice, and sugar; stir until sugar is dissolved. Add ice water or chilled sparkling water. Pour in ice-filled pitcher or punch bowl; garnish with lemon slices. Yield: 16 servings.

Mock Pink Champagne

½ cup sugar
1½ cups water
2 cups cranberry juice
1 cup pineapple juice
½ cup orange juice
2 (7-ounce) bottles lemon-lime carbonated
  beverage

Boil sugar and water until sugar dissolves; cool. Stir in cranberry juice, pineapple juice, and orange juice. Chill. Just before serving, add carbonated beverage. Yield: 14 servings.

Raspberry Delight

1 (6-ounce) can frozen pink lemonade
  concentrate
  Cold water
1 pint raspberry sherbet
  Whipped topping
  Cherries

Mix lemonade with cold water as directed on can, and chill until very cold. Spoon one or two scoops raspberry sherbet in tall glasses and pour lemonade over. Just before serving, add whipped topping, and top with a cherry. (Best serve this with a straw and a parfait spoon!) Yield: 4 servings.

Cranberry Punch

4 cups cranberry juice cocktail
1½ cups sugar
4 cups pineapple-grapefruit juice
2 quarts ginger ale

Slowly add cranberry juice to sugar; stir until sugar dissolves. Add pineapple-grapefruit juice; chill. Pour into punch bowls; add chilled ginger ale. Yield: 32 servings.

Hot Spiced Orange Juice

1 pint cider or apple juice
½ cup brown sugar
½ cup sugar
2 (2-inch) cinnamon sticks
3 whole cloves
1 quart orange juice
1 cup freshly squeezed lemon juice
  Orange and lemon slices
  Cinnamon sticks

Combine first 5 ingredients; simmer for 5 minutes. Combine orange juice and lemon juice; heat to just below simmering. Add to hot cider. Serve in mugs and garnish with orange and lemon slices on a cinnamon stick. Yield: 12 servings.

Picnic Punch

2½ cups apricot nectar
2½ cups pineapple juice
1 cup freshly squeezed lemon juice
1 cup sugar syrup
  Ice cubes
2 quarts ginger ale

Combine fruit juices and sugar syrup; pour over ice in a punch bowl or a vacuum bottle, blending well. Add ginger ale when ready to serve, stirring gently to mix. Yield: about 16 servings.

Wassail Punch

1 gallon apple cider
1 quart orange juice
1 cup freshly squeezed lemon juice
1 quart pineapple juice
24 whole cloves
4 sticks cinnamon
1 cup sugar

Mix all ingredients and simmer for 10 minutes. Remove cinnamon and cloves. Serve warm in punch cups. Yield: 1½ gallons.
Note: For a festive punchbowl, float small oranges that have been precooked about 10 minutes. Stick several cloves in each orange.

Pineapple-Cranberry Punch

2 pints cranberry juice
2 cups orange juice
¼ cup freshly squeezed lemon juice
1 quart pineapple sherbet
1 quart sparkling water or ginger ale
  Ice

Combine cranberry juice, orange juice, and lemon juice; beat in pineapple sherbet; then chill. Just before serving, slowly pour in sparkling water. Pour over cracked ice and serve immediately. Yield: 14 to 16 servings.

Hospitality Tea Punch

2 quarts boiling water
15 tea bags or 5 tablespoons loose tea
2 cups freshly squeezed lemon juice
1 quart orange juice
1½ quarts grape juice
2 cups sugar
2 quarts cold water
1 quart ginger ale
  Ice cubes

Pour boiling water over tea. Steep for 3 to 5 minutes and remove tea bags, or strain tea leaves. Cool tea. Stir in remaining ingredients except ginger ale. Add ginger ale and ice cubes just before serving. Yield: 2 gallons.

Tea Wallop

2 tablespoons loose black tea
15 mint leaves
3 cups boiling water
5 tablespoons freshly squeezed lemon juice
1½ cups orange juice
1 cup grape juice
4½ cups pineapple juice
1 cup powdered sugar
  Ice

Combine tea and mint leaves and pour boiling water over them. Let steep until water is cool; strain. Combine with fruit juices and sugar; stir until sugar is dissolved. Chill. Serve over ice. Yield: 12 servings.

Spicy Iced Coffee

3 cups hot double-strength coffee
2 cinnamon sticks
4 whole cloves
4 whole allspice berries
  Ice
  Cream and sugar to taste

Pour coffee over cinnamon sticks, cloves, and allspice berries. Let stand for 1 hour. Strain and pour over ice in 4 tall glasses. Add cream and sugar to taste. Yield: 4 servings.

Instant Spiced Tea Mix

½ cup instant tea
2 cups orange-flavored instant
  breakfast drink
1 (3-ounce) package sweetened
  lemonade mix
1 teaspoon ground cloves
1 teaspoon ground cinnamon
2 cups sugar

Combine ingredients in a large bowl and mix well. Spoon into jars and seal. To serve, add 2 teaspoons to a cup of boiling water. Yield: about 40 servings.

Golden Tea Punch

3 cups boiling water
10 tea bags or 10 teaspoons tea leaves
24 whole cloves
1 (3-inch) stick cinnamon, crumbled
2¼ cups freshly squeezed lemon juice
1¼ cups orange juice
3 cups sugar
4 quarts cold water
  Ice
  Orange and lemon slices

Pour boiling water over tea bags, whole cloves, and crumbled stick cinnamon. Cover; steep for 5 minutes. Strain and cool. Add lemon juice, orange juice, and sugar, stirring until sugar is dissolved. Add cold water. Pour into ice-filled punch bowl. Garnish with orange and lemon slices. Yield: 50 servings.

Holiday Fruit Punch

2 quarts water
¼ cup loose tea
2 cups sugar
2 cups freshly squeezed lemon juice
4 cups orange juice
1½ quarts cranberry juice
1 quart water
  Ice
1 quart ginger ale
1 lemon, sliced
2 limes, sliced
  Maraschino cherries

Bring 2 quarts water to a full rolling boil. Immediately pour over the tea; brew for 5 minutes. Strain. Set aside to cool at room temperature. Combine with sugar, fruit juices, and 1 quart water. Chill. Just before serving, pour over a large piece of ice or ice cubes; then add ginger ale. Garnish with lemon and lime slices and cherries. Yield: 25 servings.

Punchmelon

1 large watermelon
2 cups orange juice
2 cups freshly squeezed lemon juice
1 (6-ounce) bottle grenadine syrup
  Ice
2 quarts bottled lemon-lime beverage,
  chilled.
1 orange, sliced
1 lemon, sliced

With melon standing on end, cut a thin slice off side so it will sit level. Remove top third of melon. Using a coffee cup as a guide, trace scallops around top outside edge. With a sharp knife, carve scalloped edge, following tracing; scoop out fruit, leaving just a trace of red showing in bowl of melon; use scraped-out melon as desired. Chill melon bowl.

Combine orange juice, lemon juice, and grenadine; chill. When ready to serve, place a small block of ice, or ice cubes, in melon bowl. Pour juices over ice; pour lemon-lime beverage down side of melon bowl into juice mixture. Float orange and lime slices on top of punch. Yield: 3½ quarts.

Spider Cider

2 quarts apple cider
12 whole cloves
4 sticks cinnamon
  Rind of 4 lemons
2 lemons, peeled and thinly sliced
¼ teaspoon ground nutmeg

Combine cider, cloves, cinnamon sticks, thinly peeled lemon rind, 2 lemons, and nutmeg. Cover and heat to boiling. Reduce heat and simmer for about 15 minutes. Allow to cool; then strain. Discard spices. Chill overnight in refrigerator to allow flavors to blend. Heat when ready to serve. Yield: 8 to 10 servings.

Vermouth Bull Shot

1 (10½-ounce) can consommé
  Dash onion juice
  Dash Worcestershire sauce
  Juice of 1 lemon
⅓ to ½ cup dry vermouth
  Ice
  Lemon peel

Combine consommé, onion juice, Worcestershire sauce, lemon juice, and vermouth. Serve over crushed ice and use strip of lemon peel for garnish. Yield: 3 servings.

Grape Punch

2 cups grape juice
1½ cups orange juice
¾ cup sugar
1 cup water
  Ice cubes
3 (7-ounce) bottles ginger ale
1 lemon, sliced

Pour fruit juices into a 2-quart pitcher. Add sugar and stir until dissolved. Add water and ice cubes. Let stand for a few minutes in refrigerator. Pour equal amounts into 16 tall glasses in which there are a couple of ice cubes. Then fill to top with ginger ale and garnish with lemon slices. Yield: 16 servings.

Red Velvet Punch

8 cups cranberry juice cocktail
1 (6-ounce) can frozen orange juice
1 (6-ounce) can frozen pineapple juice
1 (6-ounce) can frozen lemon juice
2 cups brandy
  Ice
2 (4/5-quart) bottles white Champagne

Combine juices and brandy; mix well and pour over a block of ice in a punch bowl. Add Champagne. Yield: about 30 servings.

Fruit Punch

2 (6-ounce) cans frozen orange juice
1 (6-ounce) can frozen lemonade
1 cup pineapple juice
¼ cup cherry juice (optional)
2 quarts ginger ale
  Ice

Mix fruit juices; cover and let stand for 12 hours or more in refrigerator. Add cold ginger ale to juices just before serving. Serve over crushed ice or freeze half the ginger ale in ice cube trays. Yield: 24 servings.

Minted Pineapple Tea

1 quart boiling water
15 teabags or ⅓ cup loose tea
4 tablespoons chopped fresh mint leaves
1 quart cold water
1 cup freshly squeezed lemon juice
⅔ cup sugar
1 (6-ounce) can pineapple juice
  Ice cubes
  Lemon wedges

Pour 1 quart boiling water over tea and mint leaves. Cover and let stand for 5 minutes.

Strain tea into a pitcher holding 1 quart cold water. Add lemon juice, sugar, and pineapple juice. Stir to dissolve sugar, and chill.

To serve, pour minted tea over ice cubes. Garnish with lemon wedges. Yield: about 2½ quarts.

Vegetable Juice Cooler

1 (22-ounce) can cocktail vegetable juice
2 teaspoons freshly squeezed lemon juice
½ small clove garlic, minced
　Generous dash hot pepper sauce
　Avocado slices

Combine all ingredients except avocado; chill. Garnish with avocado slices. Yield: 6 servings.

Tom and Jerry

12 egg yolks
1 cup sugar
1 cup rum
12 egg whites, stiffly beaten
　Bourbon
　Hot water
　Ground cinnamon

Beat egg yolks until light and lemon-colored. Gradually add sugar and rum alternately until the batter is thick. Fold in egg whites.

When ready to serve, ladle approximately ⅓ cup of this batter into a warm mug. Add 1 jigger of bourbon. Fill the mug with hot water. Sprinkle each cup with cinnamon. Yield: about 16 servings.

Golden Gate Punch

2½ cups sugar
1 cup water
2 (18-ounce) cans pineapple juice
2 cups strained freshly squeezed lime juice
1 quart strained orange juice
1¼ cups freshly squeezed lemon juice
2 quarts chilled ginger ale
　Colored ice cubes

Combine sugar and water; heat to boiling. Cool. Combine fruit juices. Add cooled sugar syrup. Chill. Just before serving, add ginger ale and colored ice cubes. To make colored cubes, blend food coloring with water before freezing. Yield: 5 quarts.

Holiday Punch

　Juice of 2 limes
　Juice of 1 lemon
3 (6-ounce) cans frozen orange juice
1 (6-ounce) can frozen lemon juice
1 (6-ounce) can frozen lime juice
1 (18-ounce) can pineapple juice
½ teaspoon salt
1½ quarts water
1 quart chilled ginger ale
1 pint vodka
　Red food coloring (optional)
　Ice

Several hours ahead mix together the fruit juices, salt, and water; place in a covered container in the refrigerator to chill.

At serving time, combine above mixture with ginger ale and vodka. Stir in food coloring, if desired. Serve over a block of ice in a punch bowl. Yield: 25 servings.

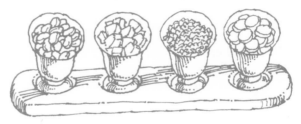

Party Perfect Eggnog

6 eggs
½ cup light corn syrup
¼ teaspoon ground ginger
¼ teaspoon ground cloves
¼ teaspoon ground cinnamon
¼ teaspoon ground nutmeg
2 quarts orange juice, chilled
½ cup freshly squeezed lemon juice, chilled
1 quart vanilla ice cream
1 quart ginger ale, chilled
　Ground nutmeg

Beat eggs well. Mix in syrup, ginger, cloves, cinnamon, and nutmeg. Stir in orange juice and lemon juice. Cut ice cream into chunks the size of small eggs; put into a large punch bowl.

Pour ginger ale over ice cream. Stir in egg mixture. Sprinkle with nutmeg. Yield: 6 quarts.

Russian Tea

1 stick cinnamon
1 tablespoon whole cloves
1 cup sugar
1 quart water
Juice of 3 lemons
Juice of 3 oranges
1 (18-ounce) can pineapple juice
2 cups strong tea

Put cinnamon stick and whole cloves in a cheesecloth bag. Place in a saucepan with sugar and water. Bring to a boil and boil for 15 minutes. Remove spices and add remaining ingredients. Heat and serve. Yield: 2 quarts.

Christmas Eggnog

1 cup sugar
1 quart half-and-half
8 eggs, separated
1 to 1½ pints bourbon, rum, or brandy
Ground nutmeg
Whipped cream

Prepare at least a day before you plan to serve. Mix sugar and half-and-half. Beat egg whites and add to the sugar and cream mixture. Fold in until egg whites cannot be seen. Add beaten egg yolks and mix well. Slowly stir in bourbon, rum, or brandy. Cover and put in refrigerator. To serve, ladle into cups, sprinkle with nutmeg, and add a spoon of whipped cream to each cup. Yield: 15 to 20 servings.

Cranberry Punch

6 pints cranberry juice cocktail
1½ quarts orange juice
1½ cups water
2½ cups freshly squeezed lemon juice
3 cups pineapple juice
3 cups sugar
Lemon slices

Combine all ingredients except lemon slices and blend well. Chill in refrigerator. Pour into a punch bowl with an ice ring and lemon slices. Yield: 50 servings.

Ruby Red Frost

1 (16-ounce) bottle cranberry juice cocktail
1½ cups freshly squeezed lemon juice
1 cup sugar
Ice
2 quarts chilled ginger ale
1 pint raspberry sherbet
Lemon slices

Combine cranberry juice cocktail, lemon juice, and sugar, blending well. Chill. To serve, pour over ice in a punch bowl. Add ginger ale and sherbet. Garnish with lemon slices. Serve at once. Yield: 24 servings.

Sea Foam Punch

½ cup sugar
1 quart cold water
1 (½-ounce) envelope unsweetened lemon-lime soft drink powder
1 pint vanilla ice cream
2 (7-ounce) bottles lemon-lime carbonated beverage, chilled

Place sugar and water in large punch bowl. Add soft drink powder and stir until powder dissolves. Add vanilla ice cream, one spoonful at a time. Pour in carbonated beverage. Serve immediately. Yield: about 16 servings.

Tangy Tomato Appetizer

1 (18-ounce) can tomato juice or vegetable juice cocktail
1 (10½-ounce) can consommé or beef broth
1 tablespoon freshly squeezed lemon juice
1 teaspoon Worcestershire sauce
Dash hot pepper sauce
Commercial sour cream (optional)
Chopped chives (optional)

Combine tomato juice, consommé, lemon juice, Worcestershire sauce, and hot pepper sauce; chill. Pour in juice glasses or mugs. Top each with a spoonful of sour cream and a sprinkling of chives, if desired. Yield: 4 to 6 servings.

Index

Index

Index

Other Helpful Books from Southern Living

Cookbooks

The Best of Our Best Recipes (0280) $1.95
Boating Cookbook (0283) $1.95
Casseroles (0357) $1.95
Cookies (0360) $1.95
Country Cooking (0284) $1.95
Fish and Shellfish (0359) $1.95
Inflation Cookbook (0275) $1.95

Gardening and Landscaping

Azaleas (0288) $1.95
Landscaping Your Home (0285) $1.95

Travel and Recreation

Bass Fishing (0361) $2.95
Missions of Texas (0350) $2.95
Quail Hunting (0362) $2.95

Hobby and Crafts

Christmas Book (0256) $3.95
Creative Crafts (0277) $1.95
Heirloom Quilts to Treasure (0186) $2.00
Needlecraft Patterns (0241) $3.95

Building, Remodeling and
Home Design

Distinctive Southern Homes (0154) $2.00
House Plans Designed for Southern Families (0242) $2.00
Practical Home Ideas (0263) $1.95

Book Division of The Progressive Farmer Company

Oxmoor House

Post Office Box 2463   Birmingham, Alabama 35202